Beginning
Writer's
Answer
Book

**Edited by
Kirk Polking
and the editors of Writer's Digest**

WRITER'S DIGEST BOOKS
Cincinnati, Ohio

ISBN 0-89879-599-0

Edited by the editors of *Writer's Digest.*

ACKNOWLEDGMENTS

Founding Editor: Kirk Polking

Fifth Edition Editors: Peter Blocksom, Tom Clark, Angela Terez, Bruce Woods

Contributing Editors: Rose Adkins, Joan Bloss, John Brady, Jane Budd, Leslie Cannon, Kay Cassill, Theodore Cheney, Jean Chimsky, Nancy Dibble, Connie Emerson, Vera Henry, Melissa Hoel, Lois Horowitz, Judson Jerome, Barb Kuroff, Michael Larsen, Victor Marton, Jack McKee, Leonard Meranus, Hugh Rawson, Ellen Roberts, David Rosenthal, Dave Schoonmaker, Evelyn Stenbock, Michael Straczynski, George Wagner, the editorial associates of Writer's Digest School and Writer's Digest Criticism Service, and the authors and friends of Writer's Digest Books.

PREFACE

Magazine writer Frank Thomas says, "I've been guided by the maxim that if you ask a question you may seem ignorant for the moment; but if you do not ask questions you may be ignorant forever." This newly revised and expanded edition of the *Beginning Writer's Answer Book* attempts to anticipate all the questions a writer has about creating and marketing his work.

Included in this completely revised edition are questions writers most often ask the editors of *Writer's Digest* arranged under subject categories for the reader's convenience. An in-depth cross index provides additional aid in locating topics.

Whether you are just starting out and need to know the specifics of manuscript preparation and submission, or you are a more seasoned writer looking for details about book proposals and contracts, you'll find the answers in these pages. You'll find explanations of how the copyright law affects writers, how to avoid suits for libel and invasion of privacy, and how to use a pen name.

You'll learn what editors mean by certain terms and the pros and cons of collaboration with another writer or a photographer. You'll learn whether the IRS considers you a "business" or a "hobby" writer and what kind of deductions you can take. Individual chapters discuss the specific problems of newspaper and magazine writers, fiction and nonfiction writers, poets and screenwriters.

Included in the appendix are sample manuscript pages and a query letter; a chart of the average lengths of short stories, novels, TV and radio scripts, speeches and children's books; and details on how to submit various types of manuscripts.

For more in-depth information on writing subjects, books and reference volumes are included in the bibliography. *Writer's Digest*, the monthly magazine containing market information and professional advice for writers, has been indexed in the *Readers' Guide to Periodical Literature* from January 1968 through December 1977; and in *Access: The Supplementary Index to Periodicals* from January 1978 to the present.

Keep in mind that information included here is meant to serve as a general guideline and is not intended to substitute for legal advice. If you have a question about a specific clause in your book contract or are unsure about current tax laws, consult an appropriate attorney or accountant.

If you have a writing-related question that is not included in this book, by all means drop the editors a note. But be sure to include an SASE. What's an SASE? A self-addressed, stamped envelope. For definitions of similar terms, see chapter five!

The Editors

Chapter 1

How Do I Know If I Have What It Takes?

Novelist Willa Cather insisted, "Most of the basic material a writer works with is acquired before the age of fifteen." And yet, the person who only starts thinking about becoming a writer at middle age has a lifetime of living and learning to bring to the task. Whether you are fifteen or fifty, here are some questions and answers that may erase some of your own self-doubts.

The "Write" Stuff

Q. *What does it take to become a writer?*
A. Curiosity, energy, persistence in learning, a willingness to research, and an awareness of human behavior all are needed in the writing field. Curiosity generates ideas and sustains interest to carry a writer through the process of writing articles, stories or books. A higher-than-average energy level helps, since a writer must sometimes work long and irregular hours to meet deadlines or to stick with, and finish, a piece of writing while the words are flowing smoothly. Persistence in learning is important. For any writer, a liberal arts education, while not absolutely necessary, is certainly an asset. There are, however, many self-taught writers who have become successful through determination, dedication to the craft, discipline, and hard work. A degree in journalism or communications might be helpful in landing a magazine or newspaper staff job, but even in this situation is not absolutely necessary. For more advice on this subject, see chapter two.

A nonfiction writer directly encounters people when conducting interviews, while a fiction writer observes people and perceives the motivations of human behavior. Research, often the key to regular sales, broadens general knowledge, sharpens the mind, and uncovers new territory for a writer.

Finally, you'll definitely need a knowledge of the markets and their needs if you hope to have your work published.

Q. *I am interested in writing, but am not sure I have the aptitude for it. Are all good writers born with writing talent?*
A. Certain writers may be born with more innate talent than others, but many

1

factors help to build a successful writing career. The chief "aptitude" a writer needs to be successful is determination to learn and to write well. Anyone with normal intelligence and the energy and willingness to develop as a writer can learn the craft and become successful at it. It is possible for a talented and gifted writer to lack the energy and persistence necessary to publish with any degree of success. A less talented writer with ambition can produce an impressive amount of publishable material.

Q. *How can I be sure I really have creative writing ability?*
A. Unless you're either extremely talented or extraordinarily lucky, you probably won't be sure for some time. The key to publication, and to eventual recognition, is believing in yourself and plugging ahead. The old cliché that claims writing success is 1 percent inspiration and 99 percent perspiration is all too true.

That said, there are some steps you can take to obtain an authoritative evaluation of your work. Take a correspondence course and have your manuscripts professionally evaluated by an instructor. Join a writers club, sign up for an evening class in creative writing, or attend a writers conference. And put your work on the market. A few acceptances will probably give you the reinforcement you need, and occasionally editors (particularly those of small or local publications) will take the time to offer positive feedback, even if they're rejecting your work.

Q. *Exactly what is a professional writer? Can this term be defined?*
A. Put simply, a professional writer is one who gets paid—regularly—to write. But he does so, in part, because he conducts himself in a professional manner. First, of course, a professional writer has a firm grasp of the skills of his craft, both in the basics of grammar and composition and the techniques required for writing successful fiction or nonfiction. In these areas, as well as in the development of his writing style, the professional constantly strives to improve. Daily writing is a work habit of the professional, as is the setting of specific writing goals. Professionals study the markets before submitting their work so that they know their audiences and the needs of specific editors, making their acceptance rate higher. When professionals receive rejection slips, they realize that their manuscripts are simply products being sold, and that there was not a need for the product in that particular market at that time. Therefore, they proceed by querying another suitable market.

Since fiction writers, poets, playwrights and filmmakers usually must deliver complete manuscripts rather than queries on their ideas, they face an even more demanding and time-consuming task of matching their manuscripts to suitable markets. Persistence, then, is another personal quality all professionals must have.

Professional writing is also defined as writing done on assignment, on the job, or on demand. This might range from beginning staff writers to freelance authors whose work brings top dollar in the marketplace. Most importantly, professional writing is an attitude. For the beginning writer, it means professional presentation of queries and manuscripts, a thorough study of the markets, and the ability to deliver assigned work on time.

Q. *I have a boxful of short stories. Since I'm only fourteen, I wonder if there's any market you could suggest for my work, or am I too young?*
A. You are never too young to submit your work to markets, but before you do, read and become familiar with magazines that publish stories similar to yours. Research the requirements of those magazines in *Writer's Market*, then prepare a typed, professionally formatted manuscript (see chapter thirteen) and send it.

Q. *I recently retired and for the first time in my life I've found the time to write. Am I too old to begin?*
A. You're never too old to start writing. Physicians, gerontologists, and other scientists agree that thinking processes, imaginative powers, and facilities for expressing oneself need not diminish with age. In fact, after sixty-five, the combination of leisure time and development of new interests tends to spark creativity. Editors never ask to see your birth certificate. Don't tell editors that you are fifteen or ninety; just write the best piece you possibly can and submit it to suitable markets.

Q. *Do writers who live in New York or Los Angeles have an advantage over those who live in other parts of the country?*
A. Not necessarily. New York writers are closer to some major publishing houses, so they may have a better chance of conducting business face to face and meeting editors socially. But no matter where you live and write, you must be able to turn out quality work, and external environment is only part of what enables you to do so. Top-quality writing attracts the attention of editors everywhere, no matter where it originates. On the other hand, while it's possible to sell a screenplay by mail, most screenwriters agree that it is a great advantage to live in Los Angeles, simply because of the increased opportunities for networking.

Q. *I have always loved to write, but I'm not sure that's what I want to do as a profession. How do I know if writing is my best career choice?*
A. Since the required skills and personal characteristics vary widely depending on the type of writing career, you'll have to learn as much about the various job opportunities as you can before making a decision. For example, can you write quickly under a tight deadline as required of a newspaper reporter? Can you generate the kind of clever copy required by some advertising clients? Do you have the educational background to be a writer for a corporation? Two government publications that provide some helpful background information are: *Toward Matching Personal and Job Characteristics* and *Occupational Outlook Handbook*, available in most libraries. The library's card catalog can also point you to vocational guidance books whose titles are frequently *Your Career in . . .* or *Your Future in . . .* publishing, or public relations, or broadcasting or advertising.

Q. *Can you point out any special advantages or disadvantages that I might face as a full-time freelance writer?*
A. You would be your own boss. You would control your working hours and, in a

sense, the amount of money you would make. You would practice as a profession the thing you enjoy most. You might have much more opportunity to be creative than if you worked as a staff writer. You could choose what you want to write about and get paid for learning something new through research. You could work at home. Therefore, you wouldn't need many business clothes and could probably save in that area of your budget. If you are a parent, you could save on childcare expenses, since you would be available when your children needed you. In addition, the research involved in writing could bring you into contact with interesting, stimulating people.

On the other hand, most writers face innumerable rejections – and no income – before making their first sale. To avoid losing faith in yourself and your career at this stage, it would help if you were thick-skinned, self-confident and persistent. Unlike a job in a company, freelance work does not bring regular paychecks in regular amounts. Further, you would be responsible for collecting your own payments. Similarly, you would receive no fringe benefits, such as insurance or retirement benefits that company employees receive. Being self-employed, you would have to spend part of your working time on administrative tasks, such as bookkeeping and filing income tax and social security forms.

Writers usually work alone, and this could be a disadvantage (depending on your personality), especially after a number of days without contact with your colleagues. If you are married it would be best to have a spouse who approves of your career and all it entails, since he or she might be affected by your irregular working hours and irregular income.

Getting Started

Q. *I am a beginner trying to sell stories and articles. Five months have passed and no sale. What can a beginner do to increase his chances of getting that first publication?*
A. The first step is to thoroughly analyze (and objectively evaluate) your work in light of the kind of material that is being published in the magazines you've targeted. Second, don't give up. Five months is not an adequate test of your writing skills. If you prepare a professional-looking manuscript (see chapter thirteen), the editors to whom you submit won't know you've never sold before.

Q. *Should I write every day? How much time should I put into developing my skills?*
A. You should be spending at least one hour a day on your freelance writing efforts if you expect to accomplish very much. A piano teacher, for example, asks her students to spend at least that much time practicing. Should a freelance writer expect less of himself?

Q. *How long must I work at writing to become a competent, professional freelancer?*
A. Writers – even established ones – are continuously developing their skills, improving their style, and learning more about their writing, their markets, and the world. In that sense, you will never stop striving to better yourself. A good test of

your competence is whether your work is being accepted by publications or book publishers that you respect. Being unpublished doesn't necessarily mean that you don't have *writing skills*, but sales will probably make you feel more like a professional writer.

At the Keyboard

Q. *How are professional writers able to write so much?*
A. Most writers are attracted almost obsessively to their work; that is, they have an inner urge to write. Professional writers find that the satisfaction their writing brings is enough to outweigh the deadlines, rejection and other problems they face. On a more practical level, self-employed writers know that if they don't write, they don't eat, so they structure their work as though they had a regular job working for an employer. For example, they begin at the same time every day (but not necessarily in the morning), produce the same number of words or pages each day, and establish a place — at home or away from home — to be used exclusively for writing. In addition, they make their working hours known to friends and family to minimize distractions. Finally, professionals get maximum mileage out of the work they do produce, such as reselling articles, using one session of research to fuel two or more related pieces, and other tactics.

Q. *I sometimes wonder if I write fast enough. Are there any standards I can measure my writing against, such as daily quotas for the fast, the average and the slow writer?*
A. It is said that Marcel Proust would spend three and four days working on a single paragraph. In contrast, Jack Kerouac is said to have written *On the Road* in a single protracted session at the typewriter. It is best for each writer to set his own goal, since writing speed seems to vary with the individual. When setting your daily quota of number of pages or number of words, you should make it a little higher than you think you might be able to reach, so that you can have something to shoot for. As a rule of thumb, try to aim for an hour of writing, or perhaps one thousand words, a day. If that's impossible, simply make sure you spend some time writing each and every day.

Q. *Would I be better off specializing, sticking to one kind of article and building a reputation in that field, or simply writing about whatever interests me?*
A. It's probably best, at least early in your career, to play the field. By doing so you'll have the opportunity to sample different types of writing to determine which brings you the most satisfaction and success. (If you're lucky, the same type of writing will do both!) Once you've learned enough to decide on a specialization, doing so can increase your work as editors come to rely on your expertise. However, many specialist writers, even after they have established themselves in one field, continue to write on other topics in which they are interested. If a specialist limits his writing to one field, he runs the risk of being without an outlet for his work should that market go sour, or of being so closely associated with it that his credibil-

ity in other fields is weakened, thereby making it difficult for him to sell to markets other than those in his special field.

Q. *After I've finished the first draft of an article or story I am never quite sure how to edit. What should I look for when revising my manuscript? Is it possible to edit too much?*

A. The process of editing is one that each writer develops on his own, with experience, trial and error. There are no definite number of drafts you should write before the piece is finished. There are, however, some techniques that will probably prove helpful. (But only if you use them; too many writers doom themselves to disappointment by submitting first drafts, with perhaps minor revisions, for publication.) First of all, if your schedule allows it, set the work aside for a few days. After the writing has had a chance to "cool," errors and awkward phrasings are often obvious. Once you do look at the work, begin by trying to cut it. Eliminate anything that doesn't provide the reader with information crucial to the story or article. (Don't worry about being too brutal. You can always put material back, but most writers have a difficult time being hard enough on themselves.)

Now let the material rest again, for at least an hour or two, then read it aloud. This is probably the best way to discover awkward phrasings. If you stumble over something, fix it. Reading aloud also can tell you where you've cut too drastically, damaging the rhythm of the piece.

You'll develop your own methods of editing as you gain experience, and these may vary from piece to piece, depending on the topic and schedule. Nevertheless, there are some things you should look for in each work you produce. First, read through the rough draft to eliminate redundancies, irrelevancies, statements that are too obvious, unnecessary words and circumlocutions. Assess the logical order of the remaining elements. Some writers use highlighting markers or felt-tip pens to color-code the work's major elements to make sure the structure best suits the point the writer is trying to make. Next, add any necessary new information, and check your word choices. Look for imprecise verbs and weak nouns that require too many modifiers. Finally, check for consistency of verb tense, verb agreement, other grammatical points, punctuation errors, and misspellings. Remember, some changes you will make in editing can be avoided by completing all your necessary research and organizing before you start the actual writing. Also, some retyping can be avoided by using scissors and tape to reorganize earlier drafts.

It is possible to over-edit. If, for example, you find yourself rewriting everything over and over, and seldom or never putting a manuscript in the mail, you might be using editing as a means of avoiding potential rejection. Most of us, though, are far more likely to be hurt by too little editing than by too much.

Q. *How important to an editor are spelling, punctuation and sentence structure? I believe I'm weak in these areas, and no matter how much I read grammar books, I just can't remember the rules. Does my writing have to contain perfect grammar, punctuation, and construction, or will an editor make corrections before publishing a* *manuscript?*

A. These elements are worth a great deal of your attention. Some famous writers have published without a perfect command of grammar or spelling (and have had their manuscripts corrected by editors), but they succeeded because they possessed genius in other areas. Unknown writers, on the other hand, *must* make a favorable impression on every editor they submit to, and knowledge of writing mechanics is part of this impression.

It might help to remember that punctuation can be learned without rules: Observing punctuation in others' work can help you become familiar with how to use punctuation, and reading your finished pieces aloud can point out errors or omissions in the punctuation you have used.

Sentence structure is flexible. For example, an editor may change the structure of one of your sentences, to change the emphasis or for some other reason, but that doesn't necessarily mean that your original structure was incorrect. A book you might find useful is Harry Shaw's *Punctuate It Right!*

Seeking Help

Q. *I am only interested in writing nonfiction, so is there any reason why I should read fiction?*
A. Nonfiction writers should be familiar with fiction techniques, as these are often incorporated into nonfiction. Dialogue, suspense, characterization, description and emotion are parts of the fiction writer's craft that the most successful nonfiction writers also use in their work. In fact, a writer should be able to learn from the study of any good writing, be it fiction, nonfiction, poetry or script.

Q. *I need some comments and advice on a manuscript that I just finished. I'd like to consult a well-known magazine writer whose work I admire. What's the best way to approach her? Should I send her a copy of the manuscript?*
A. Sending your manuscript to a writer for a critique would be an intrusion into the writer's own workday unless you know that writer provides such professional advice for a set fee. You can write and ask, but don't send the manuscript unless you've clarified this first. When writing to inquire whether an author provides critiques for a fee, specify the length of the piece to be evaluated and its subject or genre (be as specific as you can without being wordy). Ask for the writer's rates and a sample contract if she uses one. Keep the letter to one page, and enlose a SASE for reply.

Many well-known writers who speak at writers conferences set aside time for writers' individual questions and informal criticism, so it may be better to ask your questions in those situations.

Q. *What are the advantages and disadvantages of using a commercial criticism service?*
A. One advantage is that the critique is done on a one-to-one basis instead of in front of a group. A writing critic employed by a criticism service would be more

objective than a teacher, writers club member, friend or spouse. To avoid any disadvantages, check the track record of criticism services advertised in writers magazines. The professional critic should have a background in the particular field of your manuscript (novels, plays, etc.) and might, if asked, be able to provide you a sample of one of his former critiques to give you an idea of the nature, extent and content of the criticism provided. When reacting to criticism, you must remember that it is only one person's opinion. It's been said that if two writers were to comment on a specific piece of writing, they'd generate at least three opinions. Take what you can of value from a critique, but always remember that faith — in yourself and in your vision of your project — is the most important writing tool you have.

Q. *Is it a good idea to send my manuscript to those advertisers in writers magazines who offer rewriting services?*
A. Rewrite services share the advantages and disadvantages of critique services. Early in your career, you might find yourself able to learn a lot by studying a professional rewrite of your work. Still, you must check the credentials of the person doing the rewrite, and you should keep in mind that no rewrite service can guarantee that it will turn your work into publishable copy. Finally, don't let yourself turn this sort of service into a crutch; if you intend to mature as a writer, you need to learn to edit and polish your own work.

Q. *I am interested in learning more about writing. Unfortunately, I am in prison and not permitted to purchase any services. What writing opportunities are there for someone in my position?*
A. A writers organization called Poets, Playwrights, Editors, Essayists, and Novelists (PEN) American Center operates a Prison Writing Program. The center sponsors an annual writing competition for writers who are in prison and sends prisoners information on writing, ranging from answers to frequently asked questions and referrals to other programs for prisoners, to listings of magazines that will accept manuscripts from prisoners. PEN also distributes free publications, as well as books and magazines writers have donated to the prison program. (Writers wishing to donate such material to prisoners — it's tax deductible — should contact PEN for further information.)

Every year, the Center's Writing Awards for Prisoners competition presents nine awards: first-, second-, and third-place prizes in fiction, nonfiction and poetry categories. The Center accepts entries between September 1 and March 1, and presents the awards in late spring. The winning entries are published in *The Fortune News*. For contest requirements and other information, write to PEN American Center, 568 Broadway, New York NY 10012.

Good writing is bought and published regardless of where the author lives. Practice to improve your skills and your work will be judged solely on its own merits.

Chapter 2

What Education Do I Need?

Education, any kind of education, can be a valuable tool to a writer, but formal education, however valuable, is not absolutely necessary. It can be fairly said that all writers are largely self-educated, and that their training continues throughout their productive lives.

Higher Education

Q. *Which is better for a writer: a college education or a variety of experiences?*
A. As stated in the introduction to this chapter, education is always valuable to a writer. And, if your goal is to obtain a staff job at a newspaper or magazine, a journalism degree is a definite asset. Creative writing programs, too, can be extremely valuable; they force you to actually write and often include regular criticism by professors and peers. On the other hand, the habits learned while writing for a strictly academic degree may have to be broken before you can produce a salable book, magazine or newspaper copy.

Experience is valuable, as well; the more things you know the more things you can write about with authority. On the other hand, research often can be substituted for experience, and valuable experience need not be dramatic. You can find much material for your writing in what might seem a rather hum-drum existence by simply exercising your imagination. Emily Dickenson, for example, created fine, perceptive poetry though her lifestyle was, by most modern standards, frightfully dull.

As a freelance writer, you may have to modify the writing style you learned in college, because the style of newspaper and magazine articles is different (in general, it's more direct) from that used in scholarly term papers.

Q. *I'm a high school student who's interested in a career in journalism. What are some subjects I should take in high school and college to prepare for work in this field?*
A. Formal education and experience in the field can help you begin a journalism career. Most media organizations look for a college degree in job applicants, though they don't insist that it be in journalism or English. Some fields of study recommended by professionals are history, political science, psychology, and economics;

9

knowing a foreign language also can give job applicants an advantage. Of course, whatever subject you choose to study, you must have a broad knowledge of literature and a command of English grammar, usage and composition skills. If possible, work on your high school and college newspapers or literary magazines for hands-on experience. If you plan to be a freelance writer, you'll benefit from the discipline instilled by taking writing courses. Since newspaper experience and a background in printing are both valuable, look for part-time jobs in those fields.

Many college students participate in internship programs, which provide work experience before graduation. Internship opportunities in the fields of newspapers, magazine and book publishing, radio, television, advertising and public relations are outlined in the annual directory, *Internships.*

Q. *Could you tell me the rank or list of the top ten or fifteen journalism departments in our universities?*
A. There is no definitive list concerning the academic standing in journalism. However, your public library undoubtedly has the booklet, "Accredited Programs in Journalism" (Accrediting Council on Education in Journalism and Mass Communications). It lists, in alphabetical order, all the accredited schools and departments of journalism on the college level. For additional information, address your inquiry to: Secretary-Treasurer, Accrediting Council on Education in Journalism and Mass Communications, School of Journalism, P.O. Box 838, University of Missouri, Columbia MO 65205. Columbia University in New York (graduate), Northwestern University in Chicago, University of Missouri, and Stanford University in California have good journalism departments.

Q. *Can you recommend any journalism school that also has a good photography curriculum?*
A. Check your local library for the *Editor & Publisher Year Book,* which contains a list of journalism schools and describes the areas of study available in each, such as "newspapers, magazines, advertising, public relations and photography." Local community colleges may also have evening classes in photography. Local high school continuing education programs also offer courses in photography, and would be a good place for you to begin.

Q. *Where can I find a list of the best creative writing schools for would-be novelists?*
A. The best creative writing school for you would depend on what you expect from it, how much you can afford to pay, your own talents, the school faculty, and many other factors. A list of colleges throughout the U.S. and Canada with degree programs in creative writing, or at least offering some creative writing courses, can be obtained from Associated Writing Programs, % Old Dominion University, Norfolk VA 23529.

Q. *Can workshops or courses in creative writing help me become a better writer?*
A. Courses in creative writing can help by giving you motivation and discipline to

write consistently, but after the class is over you must be self-motivated enough to apply what you have learned. Community colleges, YMCA/YWCA centers and churches are good starting places when looking for creative writing classes. And, of course, many universities offer graduate degrees in creative writing.

Q. *I am a high school senior planning to enter college next fall. The field I am interested in is journalism. Where can I find information on journalism scholarships and loans?*
A. *Journalism Career and Scholarship Guide* is published by the Dow Jones Newspaper Fund, P.O. Box 300, Princeton NJ 08543. Write for a free copy. No SASE required.

Q. *Can you direct me to a list of known literary fellowships and grants connected with publishers and colleges? Also, is there a directory of foundation grants?*
A. Lists of private and government foundations of interest to writers are: *Grants and Awards Available to American Writers,* published by PEN American Center, 568 Broadway, New York NY 10012; *National Directory of Grants and Aid to Individuals in the Arts,* and the *National Directory of Arts Support by Private Foundations,* Vol. 4, published by the Washington International Arts Letter, P.O. Box 9005, Washington DC 20003; and *Study Abroad.*

Off-Campus Education

Q. *I have a college degree and have sold some articles. I still think I need to learn more about the writing craft and the writing business. What are some ways I could get more education?*
A. You could attend the national and regional workshops sponsored by professional organizations such as the American Society of Journalists and Authors, Women in Communications, Inc., and the Society of Professional Journalists, Sigma Delta Chi. The trade journals *Quill* and *Editor & Publisher* can keep you abreast of news in the newspaper field, as can *Folio* for the magazine business and *Publishers Weekly* for the book publishing industry. And, of course, *Writer's Digest* provides monthly inspiration and information on the techniques of both writing and marketing your work.

In addition, you can read books about writing. For specific titles, check *Subject Guide to Books In Print* under "Authors and Publishers," "Authorship—Handbooks, Manuals, etc.," "Authorship—Juvenile Literature," "Authorship—Study and Teaching," "Copyright," "Detective and Mystery Stories—Technique," "Fiction—Technique," "Literary Agents," "Plots," "Psychological Fiction," "Poetry—Authorship" and "Writing"; and under headings describing areas of writing, such as "Medical Writing," "Playwriting," and "Technical Writing."

You can learn about other useful books by perusing the ads in writers magazines or obtaining book catalogs directly from publishers. The two major publishers of books about writing are Writer's Digest Books and The Writer, Inc.

No matter how much formal education you have had, it's best to read as many of the literary classics as possible and keep abreast of today's popular reading, especially in the area to which you hope to contribute. *The Elements of Style*, a classic in the nonfiction field, concisely instructs and advises on usage, composition and writing style.

Q. *I'm interested in the field of technical writing. Where can I learn more about it?*
A. Southern Illinois University offers a one- to two-day seminar on technical writing. Several accomplished professionals in the field are featured each year, and give advice and instruction in the form. The fall seminar generally costs around $50, including meals. For further information contact Marie Malinauskas of the Division of Continuing Education, Southern Illinois University, Carbondale IL 62901.

If you desire to read about technical writing, *Subject Guide to Books in Print* lists many titles under that heading. Check for recent titles in your local library or ask to obtain them on interlibrary loan.

Technical writing is often learned on the job. In addition to pursuing education, consider an internship where you could work with and learn from professionals in the field.

For more information on technical writing, contact the Society of Technical Communications, 815 15th Street NW, Suite 506, Washington DC 20005. The Society produces several publications of help to a budding technical writer; you could also find the address of a local chapter of the organization through the Washington office.

Q. *What kinds of correspondence courses in writing are available, and what do they offer a writer?*
A. Correspondence courses are available through private organizations and through universities. A writer can choose the form of writing he wishes to study (for example, short stories or poetry). Some schools offer courses in special fields, such as writing for children, screenwriting, or religious writing. University courses can be taken for credit or audited. Correspondence courses provide one-to-one contact with and critique from an instructor, as well as provide a stimulus for writing. However, students generally need more self-motivation for correspondence courses than for traditional courses, since they don't actually meet with their instructors, and therefore can procrastinate more easily.

For information on which colleges offer home study courses in specific types of writing, contact the National University Continuing Education Association, One Dupont Circle, Suite 420, Washington DC 20036. For information on private organizations offering home study courses, see advertisements in writers magazines.

Q. *How can a writer evaluate correspondence courses across the nation? I would like to look into all the writing correspondence courses that are offered, and I want to be sure when I do enroll, that I've chosen a good one.*
A. There are a number of worthwhile correspondence schools available (including

the Writer's Digest School). In order to evaluate a correspondence school, you might consider seeking answers to some or all of the following questions.

- Who are the instructors and what are their qualifications?
- Are references from former students available?
- Does the school offer an 800 "help line" to answer questions beyond the scope of the correspondence lessons?
- Is there a student newsletter, and is a sample copy available?
- How long has the school been in operation?
- How much actual writing will have been critiqued at the end of each course?
- Does the school offer courses for writers of varying levels of expertise and experience?

Q. *Can I obtain college credit for a course I take from a private correspondence school?*
A. Just as some colleges will accept transfer credits from other institutions and some will not, this is an individual college decision. The private school will furnish whatever data (e.g. transcript of grades, summary of assignments completed) to the college registrar on behalf of the student, but the decision about offering credit is up to the college.

Learning by the Book

Q. *I am interested in learning how to write. But I don't have the money for a correspondence course, and most of the college texts I've seen say nothing about how to write books or magazine articles. What should I do?*
A. There are a number of books designed to take you step-by-step through the writing process, many of which are published by Writer's Digest Books and The Writer, Inc. One that gives a basic overview of writing is Evelyn Stenbock's *Teach Yourself to Write.* This is a step-by-step guide to writing for publication, with a series of assignments to complete at the end of each chapter. You can work at your own pace and master each skill before moving along to the next.

Q. *What books would you recommend for improving my grammar and punctuation?*
A. You might want to spend some time in the public library or a college bookstore to see what's available and what fits your needs. *Harbrace College Handbook* and *Random House Handbook* are examples of instructional grammar books. *The Elements of Style* is a compact refresher on composition, usage and writing style. *Make Every Word Count* is a general instructional guide to fiction and nonfiction and includes exercises in writing technique. You might also want to become a regular reader of the monthly "Grammar Grappler" column in *Writer's Digest.*

Q. *I read a lot in my spare time, for pleasure as well as for improving my writing. Some writing instructors have told me to concentrate on the classics, and others have suggested reading different magazines, especially those I hope to write for. Which kind of reading is better?*

A. You need both. If you hope to write magazine articles, you should be reading magazines, especially those you consider future markets for your work. By reading magazines, you grasp their style and editorial needs. On the other hand, if you are a fiction writer, your reading also will consist of popular novels and stories, or literary fiction, whichever you hope to publish. Reading literary classics is basic to all good writing.

Chapter 3

How Do I Get Started?

"Some writers like to think about what they are going to write, others like best holding their finished book in their hands," says Isaac Asimov, "but neither is too fond of writing itself. But for me, it's the in-between part—the writing itself—that I like best." For writers who have been doing more thinking about writing than writing, the questions and answers in this chapter may provide a pertinent prod.

Making Your Debut

Q. *What are the usual routes to a first submission?*
A. Two scenarios are quite common. The author chooses a topic—one that greatly interests him and one he feels he can write well—writes the piece, then tries to find a magazine to publish it. Or he studies a magazine he's personally interested in, to discover ideas for articles that would interest the editor of that magazine. He then queries that editor asking for an expression of interest in the article idea, or he prepares the article manuscript and submits it without querying first.

Q. *How can I decide whether to write fiction or nonfiction?*
A. One way to determine this is to look at which you most enjoy reading. Consider, too, whether you're more excited by the prospect of creating a world with your imagination (fiction) or by the idea of pursuing the treasure hunt of research, interview and investigation (nonfiction). And, of course, there are many talented writers who have made names for themselves in both fiction and nonfiction, so it's certainly not essential to limit yourself to one or the other.

Q. *How do authors usually publish their first article?*
A. First publication will usually follow a submission process similar to one of those mentioned above. In addition, first sales often result from writing about topics that the author is both very familiar with and very interested in. As the old saying goes, write what you know.

Q. *How do I get an editor to say "yes"?*

A. The best way to do so is to thoroughly research her magazine to know who her readers are, what kind of stories or articles the magazine publishes, and what it has published in the recent past. Then submit a properly prepared manuscript to the correct editor (check *Writer's Market* and *Writer's Digest* for this information), making sure that the piece of writing is appropriate to the magazine, of equal quality to the work published in the magazine, and not a repetition of a subject covered by the magazine in the recent past.

Q. *Are there shortcuts to writing success that most beginners don't know?*
A. There really are no secret shortcuts. Knowing someone on the staff of a magazine can sometimes help your work to get a fair reading, but if the publication is reputable and respected (and who'd want to be published in anything else?) only excellent work will pass the test of that reading.

Q. *How can I get up enough courage to send out a manuscript?*
A. One way is to put distance between yourself and your work. You can do this by creating a pen name for yourself (thereby separating your self-image as a writer from your self-image in other areas of life), or by pretending the manuscript belongs to a friend who asked you to submit it as a favor. Alternatively, you can impose consequences on yourself for sending out a manuscript or for neglecting to. When you send a manuscript or query, reward yourself with something you enjoy; when you fail to, deny yourself something pleasant or do some unpleasant task.

It's important to remember that the overnight successes in the writing field are exceptions: Most writers have to send out a lengthy succession of manuscripts before having one accepted.

Finally, you can adopt the insurance agent's rule of thumb: Of every twenty cold calls, expect to get two lukewarm prospects and possibly one sale.

Good Training Grounds

Q. *How does a beginner accumulate writing credits?*
A. Novice writers can often accumulate credits by donating their services to local newspapers, "penny-savers" or church, school or organizational newsletters. More projects especially suited to beginners are mentioned in chapter twenty.

Q. *What are the best markets for beginning writers?*
A. For most beginners, the best markets are those that, regardless of level of payment, offer the best opportunities for publication. These would include local or neighborhood newspapers, church, business or organization newsletters, speculative-fiction "fanzines" and (although these are more difficult to break into than the former) "enthusiast" sports or hobby magazines covering an activity in which the writer is already deeply involved.

Q. *Is newspaper reporting accepted as good training ground for creative writers in the* *short story and novel fields?*

A. Yes. Newspaper work teaches proper organization, the skill of condensing, the discipline of following a required style, and the importance of meeting deadlines. Many successful writers, such as Jimmy Breslin and Paul Gallico, have worked in the newspaper field. Though the style of news reporting is different from that of fiction, reporting offers the opportunity to observe human behavior in various situations. In reporting, writers develop the ability to generate ideas, which is necessary to any category of freelance writing, and gain experience in storytelling, since each article must have a beginning, middle and end. Many newspaper editors are seasoned journalists and are among the best writing teachers available.

Q. *How do new writers get started in the business world? I want a career in writing but I find it difficult to get started.*

A. First, read about the different fields in which writers are employed. Books published by Writer's Digest Books and the magazine *Writer's Digest* are good sources of information on all aspects of freelance writing. That magazine occasionally publishes a special guide called *Turning Your Words Into Cash*, which covers a variety of freelance writing opportunities. National Textbook Company has published the "opportunities in" series—a group of books that profile various career fields, including journalism, book publishing, magazine publishing, writing, freelance writing, advertising, broadcasting, and public relations. The U.S. Department of Labor publishes periodicals that can keep you abreast of career trends. You could consult *Occupational Outlook Handbook* and *Occupational Outlook Quarterly*. To locate pamphlets about writing and related fields, check *The Vertical File Index* in your local public or university library.

For students and newcomers to the field, an internship—a temporary job that serves to introduce the potential employee to a profession—can be a learning experience as well as a head start into the working world at job-search time. The annual directory, *Internships,* lists sixteen thousand internship opportunities.

Q. *Is it a good idea to keep a journal?*

A. A journal can be invaluable to a writer, since it records ideas, impressions and anecdotes that can be of future use. For example, describing a person you observed on a city street may have no relevance to any of your current writing projects, but you might be able to retrieve that description later to fit conveniently into a short story. The same principle applies to the nonfiction writer regarding ideas, anecdotes that are observed or overheard and recorded in a journal. Even if your journal entries never get into print, the journal-writing itself can help your career by instilling in you the habit of writing regularly. To learn more about keeping a journal, read *One to One,* by Christina Baldwin; *At a Journal Workshop,* by Ira Progoff; and *The New Diary,* by Tristine Rainer.

Getting Down to Work

Q. *Where's the best place to write?*

A. Ideally, a place that is quiet and conducive to thinking and writing. You can write at a desk in a home office, in a rented office away from home, on the kitchen table, or even in the garage. The most important thing about where you write is that you write there consistently, and that others in your household respect your writing place. Using the same place every time you write helps you establish a routine so that you will write regularly.

Q. *I have no national credits, though I have published in my local newspaper for a few years. I find interview subjects reluctant to give me their time due to my lack of credits.*
A. But you do have credits, in the form of your clippings from your newspaper experience. Tell potential interviewees that you've been writing for the paper for years. Or tell them that you've done some research on them and would like to take a little of their time to make sure your facts are accurate. If you show confidence, you'll convince most people to consent to interviews.

Q. *Are there any secrets or formulas for disciplining yourself to write regularly? Some days I just don't feel like writing.*
A. Discipline separates the would-be writer from the published writer. You should think of yourself as a professional and regard your writing as any other job. Techniques that make the writing task seem easier are finding the best time of day for your individual thinking processes and writing during those hours, and dividing a project into easily accomplished parts, so that the entire job doesn't loom above you as insurmountable. Try, too, to either pick a time when distractions are few (when the children are in bed or school, for example) or to convince your housemates that your writing time is sacred and that you're not to be interrupted during it. This is easier if you have access to a room with a door, but a desk in a temporarily unused room of the house (the bedroom in midday, for instance) will also do the job.

Q. *I've considered trying to support myself with a business writing job while I devote my free time to my "real" writing of fiction. I'm concerned, though, that writing from 9-to-5 might actually make it more difficult to work on my own time. Would it be better to look for a job completely unrelated to writing?*
A. Unfortunately, there's no simple answer to that question. Some writers find that doing any sort of writing, even if it's not related to their freelance work, sharpens their skills and is infinitely preferable to any other sort of work. Other writers do find that holding down a writing-related job makes it more difficult to devote energy to freelance work. If you're fortunate enough to find a job that pays you for writing, you should definitely give it a try and find out if it works for you.

Q. *For many years, I've had a deep-seated desire to write. I'd love to break into the field and make enough to support my family. Is there much money in freelancing?*
A. There can be, but most writers receive fairly little income while they perfect their writing and marketing abilities. On the other hand, there are hundreds of full-time freelancers who now make good livings but who started slow, freelancing

on the side while holding down a "day job." Your best bet is beginning with magazine articles, since the market is large and varied and material is literally everywhere.

Q. *As a beginner, I would like to know some ways I can make my name and services known. I write nonfiction, proofread and edit copy.*
A. You can have brochures printed that describe your services and mail them to businesses or organizations who might need editorial work done. Or you can post business cards in public places. Don't overlook university or library bulletin boards. Run classified ads in your local papers and writers magazines (where organizations look to find qualified writers). List yourself in the Yellow Pages. You could inquire to see if you qualify for a listing in a directory such as *Literary Market Place* or *Working Press of the Nation.* Although you might not be directly promoting your editorial business, you can make yourself and your name familiar to the public by becoming involved with organizations, as a volunteer, or accepting public speaking engagements for businesses and organizations. See chapter thirty-seven for more on self-promotion.

Q. *I work alone in my home office and sometimes have trouble starting to work at the beginning of the day. How can I overcome this problem?*
A. A writer can begin a day's work in various ways that are related to, but not directly connected with, the piece he is working on. One good way to begin is to edit or revise work that has already been written. Another way is to write *about* the piece, for example, as though in a letter to a friend or simply in a group of random thoughts. Some writers deliberately stop at the end of one writing session, in the middle of a thought, section, or sentence, so that they will know exactly where to resume the next day and will be less likely to procrastinate. Browsing through the *Writer's Market* or writers magazines, or reading a chapter from a how-to book on writing can also put you in the mood and is an important part of your workday. But know when to stop reading and start writing!

Chapter 4

What Equipment Do I Need?

"The ideal view for daily writing, hour on hour," said Edna Ferber, "is the blank brick wall of a cold-storage warehouse. Failing this, a stretch of sky will do, cloudless if possible." No avocation in the world has as little start-up expense as that of freelance writing. Ideas, energy, a scrap of paper and a pencil are all that a beginner requires. As skill develops, a few more tools are necessary for a professional presentation of your work. But your inventory is as inexpensive as some notebooks and a memory; and other entrepreneurs cast envious eyes on your one-man labor force.

Tools for Your Office

Q. *What equipment or supplies will I need to get started? At this stage, I'm trying to keep expenses to a minimum.*
A. All you need as a beginning writer is zeal, an idea, paper, pens and a good typewriter. Your equipment needs will expand with your success. Eventually, you'll want a sturdy table or desk on which to lay out your current project. It need not be anything elaborate; a hollow-core door across a couple of two-drawer filing cabinets is one idea. The chair and lighting for your work area are essential to your health and well-being, so make sure any bargains you find are of good quality. The chair should give your back good support and leave your feet flat on the floor. Most doctors find fluorescent lighting less desirable over long periods of time than incandescent lighting. The light you need, of course, will depend on how much natural light is available in your work area.

The telephone should also be near your work area. It is your arm to clients as well as research resources, and should be readily available. You'll save money by turning your present home phone into a business phone, rather than having a separate business line installed. If you work on a computer (see the related question in this chapter), you'll probably eventually need a separate phone line to handle modem submissions/research. The same line can service your fax machine if you feel one is necessary.

A good, sturdy office file will also become necessary. Many writers have tried to do without a file cabinet, but sooner or later have realized the need for organizing correspondence, old manuscripts, financial records, etc. You'll also need an accounting ledger to keep track of your finances.

Your final basic need is a bookcase for your reference library. This will keep your most-used books nearby for handy reference.

As you build your list of contacts, you may wish to purchase a Rolodex phone file. A telephone answering device is another possible addition as your workload increases.

Q. *What kind of typewriters are available and what kind is best for a beginning freelancer?*
A. Each writer chooses a typewriter to fit his particular needs. Typewriters are available with a variety of special options, including self-correcting features. Carbon ribbon gives sharper images when copy is to be reproduced than is possible with the less expensive cloth or nylon ribbons.

Choose a typewriter with which you feel comfortable, and that is within your budget. Most writers and editors prefer electronic models because they allow the user to type more words per minute and turn out cleaner, better-looking copy than manuals. But for those writers who work at the beach or hideaways without electricity, a manual typewriter is their choice for first drafts. Unfortunately, the last American portable machines were produced in 1983, so writers without electricity will have to depend on imports or reconditioned models (look to office supply stores for these). There are few new portables of any kind. Some companies make battery-operated, lap-top portables, but the type is often less than letter quality. Even "electric" typewriters are a thing of the past; new ones are all "electronic."

Of course, more and more writers are not looking to typewriters or even word-processors (a sort of souped-up electronic typewriter) these days, but are investing in personal computers with word-processing software. The available technology is changing too rapidly to allow us to make any kind of authoritative recommendation here. Your best bet is to seek the advice of one or more (preferably more) friends who use computers. You'll have some basic choices to make: Do you want a laptop (convenient, easy to use on the road, but usually more costly per capability) or a tabletop model (relatively inexpensive, but distinctly inconvenient to move around)? In either case, check the ads in the back of computer magazines. They often list "off brands" that have most or all of the capabilities of the big-name brands at a fraction of the price.

Yet another decision concerns the computer's operating system. As of this edition, MS-DOS, Windows and Macintosh are the systems most common to publishing, with the advantage among them going to MS-DOS (the system of IBM computers and the many IBM "clones").

You'll also have to select word-processing software. Once again, capabilities and prices are changing almost daily. Talk to several writers about their preferences in word processors and try to "test drive" several before you make your choice.

Regardless of the brand of computer or software you choose, you probably should, if your finances allow it, go for a computer rather than a typewriter. As the publishing industry becomes more and more dependent on computers, writers who are not computer-literate place themselves at a greater disadvantage.

Q. *What books should I buy first for my home reference shelf?*
A. At the top of the list is a good, desk-size dictionary, such as *Merriam-Webster's Ninth New Collegiate, American Heritage* or *Random House.* Writer and editor Art Spikol prefers the *Shorter Oxford English Dictionary* ("shorter" since the larger edition contains thirteen volumes) because of the word histories of each entry and quotes in which the word is used.

Writer's Market, published annually, tells you much that you need to know about magazines and book publishers—the markets to which you want to submit your work.

Roget's Thesaurus can be of help when you're looking for just the right word to describe something. Some writers feel the alphabetical arrangement edition is easier to use than the original subject-classified edition, and it's available in paperback.

The Elements of Style, by William Strunk and E.B. White, is a helpful aid to writing more clearly and concisely. The book covers grammatical points and principles of writing style in such a way that even the novice writer can learn to communicate well.

A good almanac can save you time you might spend looking up facts in other sources. Either *World Almanac and Book of Facts* or *Information Please Almanac* will provide you with information about events in the previous year, statistics, and other information about other years, facts about famous people and foreign countries, and much more. A one-volume reference such as *The Concise Columbia Encyclopedia* can also save you time between visits to the library to consult the multivolumed *Britannica* or *Americana* encyclopedias.

These are general references, of course, and both fiction and nonfiction writers will want to have their own basic references, depending on their interests in certain historical periods or contemporary settings, or specialties such as medicine, science, etc.

Q. *After I accumulate some basic reference books, what are other useful and enjoyable extras I can get?*
A. Once you've acquired the necessary "tools of the trade," the number of extra reference books you can obtain is limited only by your interests and your bank account. There is almost no end to the books you will find useful or interesting.

First of all, you might want to invest in a good book of quotations. *Bartlett's Familiar Quotations* has been the favorite for many years; it contains many of the memorable words of history's greatest public and literary figures. Other quotation collections worth considering are *Peter's Quotations* (more contemporary thoughts divided by subject) and *The Quotable Woman* (since the vast majority of authors quoted in *Bartlett's* are male).

For reference purposes, depending on your interests, there are a number of specialized works that can give you the information you need. Books such as the *Bantam Medical Dictionary, Harvard Brief Dictionary of Music* and H.G. Wells's *Outline of History* are good, basic works about specific topics. Other areas in which you might want to have books include science, industry, psychology and the arts.

You might also want books to help you with your writing. William Zinnser's *On Writing Well* and Gary Provost's *Make Every Word Count* can help you write more clearly, while John Brady's *The Craft of Interviewing* is a good guide for handling every type of personal contact with a source.

For help in locating additional reference sources, try *Reference Books: A Brief Guide.* This handy book will lead you to most of the references you will need in many subject areas. It's updated every few years. For other sources, check *Writer's Resource Guide,* which lists corporations, associations, museums and libraries in thirty subject areas.

Good Reading: A Guide for the Serious Reader and *Books That Changed the World* can help familiarize you with many of the great books that you may have not yet read.

Finally, some reference books don't fit into a particular category; they are simply useful and fun to read. The best known of these is perhaps the *Guinness Book of World Records,* listing the biggest, smallest, fastest, highest and other "-ests" of everything you can think of—and some you can't. *The People's Almanac* and its two sequels are billed as reference works made to be read for fun—and they live up to their billing. They feature thousands of articles on specific aspects of every topic from American history to zoology.

Q. *Is it possible to be successful as a writer without having my own writing room?*
A. It's not impossible—just a little harder. You don't need a room that is used only for writing, but most writers find they need space, a quiet spot, where they do most of their writing—a place used consistently and regularly to write. It's easier to concentrate on work when you are in the same area every day with your typewriter, books and files nearby. Kay Cassill, author of *The Complete Handbook for Freelance Writers,* says that once she set up her own work space at home, her productivity and assignments increased considerably. You don't need a plush, elaborate office—just some small place where you can go to do your work every day.

Tools for Your Writing

Q. *Is it necessary to have a tape recorder? What kind should I get?*
A. Whether or not to purchase a tape recorder is a personal decision, but many writers find recorders useful in a variety of situations. Tape recording an interview allows you to concentrate on your subject, the surroundings and other questions you want to ask. Using a recorder is a good way to verify quotes and can help establish credibility with editors. You can also use it to take down information at the library, and to record your impressions and ideas when driving home from an interview.

The ideal tape recorder should not be too large or it might intimidate the interview subject. Neither should it be too small. Some "microcorders" currently available only use certain brands of tape, and may produce poor-quality recordings. They only record thirty minutes per side. The pocket-size models that use regular cassettes are best, and the cassettes need not be expensive.

The model you choose should have a built-in microphone, since the remote mikes are too visible and might make the interview subject feel ill at ease. You should also try to get a recorder with a tape counter, so you can note points in the tape where the interviewee makes important comments. An adapter capability will allow you to run the recorder with electrical current, saving the batteries.

The recorder you buy should be reliable — a standard brand with a good guarantee. Tape recorders suitable for interviews can be bought for less than $100.

Q. *Should I consider taking my own photographs to accompany my articles? What equipment will I need?*
A. A selection of good photographs can increase the salability of an article because editors like having the complete visual and verbal package in one piece. You can either work out an arrangement with a freelance photographer, or (if you plan to use photos frequently) it will be an advantage to invest in some photographic equipment.

You don't need much to take effective pictures. You should buy a full-size, 35mm single lens reflex (SLR) camera capable of taking interchangeable lenses. It's best to select equipment from one of the major companies: Nikon, Leica, Pentax, Olympus, Canon, etc. These brands all have established reputations and service records. A bargain-basement camera could leave you high and dry when it comes to needed service and extra equipment.

You will also want to buy a flash unit, a collapsible tripod, and an equipment bag to carry it all. Depending on your taste and the equipment you choose, as well as the rate of inflation and whether you choose to buy new or used, you should plan on investing between $300 and $700 in your basic camera system. Eventually, you may wish to add wide-angle and telephoto lenses to increase the variety of your pictures.

Learning to take effective pictures is a matter of time and practice. Universities and colleges often offer courses in photography, as do continuing education programs in local school districts. The salespersons at your local camera shop can direct you to the best places to learn how to use your camera, as well as providing excellent "hands-on" advice and instruction after you've bought your equipment.

Q. *Are stationery and business cards necessary for a freelance writer? How elaborate do they have to be and how can I obtain them? What will they cost? Also, what sort of paper should I use for my manuscript submissions?*
A. Printed stationery is not necessary for a beginner, but as you develop as a freelancer, you may want to accompany your professional manuscripts with a professional-looking letterhead. It need not (indeed, *should* not) be elaborate or expen-

sively designed. Most office supply stores and "quick print" shops offer standard imprinted letterheads in a variety of typestyles, ink colors, and quality of paper. You can also order rubber stamps, invoices, and other supplies from these stores.

In 1993 the cost of a ream of five hundred imprinted letterheads on 25 percent rag bond paper averaged about $45 to $75 while matching No. 10 envelopes averaged about $60 to $100. If the imprinted letterheads ran on a twenty-pound bond without rag content, a ream would cost about $20 to $70 with $35 to $85 for envelopes.

Business cards enhance your image as a professional writer. They can be ordered at the same place that prints your stationery. A box of five hundred costs about $20 to $30. Give them to people you interview and post them on bulletin boards at locations where writers services are advertised.

More important than having stationery or business cards printed is to simply submit your work on quality paper. Look for something between fifteen- and twenty-pound bond. If you can afford it, select paper with a rag content of about 20 percent (this refers to the percentage of fabric, usually cotton, fiber in the paper). Do not use onion skin or "erasable" paper (although you can use the former for your own file copies to eliminate file overcrowding).

Q. *Will you give me the address of a supplier of carton containers for the purpose of mailing book manuscripts?*

A. Some of these firms advertise in the classified pages of *Writer's Digest.* See the latest issue for current names and addresses.

Chapter 5

What Do They Mean When They Say . . . ?

To the beginning writer it sometimes seems as though editors and established writers are from another planet, using a language she has never heard before. The jargon, a handy shortcut for the initiated, is a confusing stumbling block for the beginner struggling to enter the inner circle. Here are some down-to-earth explanations for terms you read in editorial listings, writers magazines, and books on writing. For more translations of industry jargon, see the glossary in *Writer's Market*.

Terms Involving Writing Techniques

Q. *What is reader identification and how do I achieve it in my writing?*
A. Reader identification is the process by which a reader projects himself into a work of fiction, associating himself with the adventures, conflicts, desires, feelings and responses of the characters in a story. The writer's ability to create strong, believable characters involved in a significant conflict in pursuit of a goal is a crucial element in achieving reader identification. Reader involvement is essential to commercial fiction and, surprisingly, even important in nonfiction writing. Through choice of market and treatment of subject matter, the writer attempts to address the particular interests of readers specific to his targeted market.

Q. *What does an editor mean by "objectivity"?*
A. Objectivity is the journalistic ethic requiring a reporter to present a complete, accurate and undistorted account of any news event he covers, keeping his writing as free as possible of personal opinion or prejudice. In recent years, various critics have called objectivity an unattainable ideal. Journalist Bill Moyers called it the greatest myth of journalism. Since a reporter influences each account with his personal powers of observation and consciousness and chooses the facts to include in a story, critics say that complete objectivity is an impossible goal.

Of course, impartiality is primarily a newspaper writer's code. A quick glance through most magazines and nonfiction books will serve to prove that the author's "point of view," his own opinion and stance relative to the topic discussed, often provides the driving energy behind magazine and book-length nonfiction.

Q. *What are anecdotes and how can a writer use them?*
A. An anecdote is a short narrative of a curious, amusing or insightful incident that illustrates a point or idea. An anecdote can contain dialogue, explicit detail, plays on words, and/or a humorous ending. Anecdotes can be biographical or can result from a writer's observations.

Anecdotes can be used to enliven an article and help to make it more personal, and therefore more readable. They provide a "glimpse of life" to humanize a topic. Virtually all types of articles use anecdotes in one form or another. Articles about large groups or trends use them to give specific examples or add a human-interest dimension. Profiles of public figures use anecdotes from people acquainted with the subject to show a side of him that the writer might not get from a direct interview. Even how-to articles use anecdotes, which often center on accounts of personal success or failure to enliven the article's instruction or hammer home a specific point.

In addition to being useful within the boundaries of an article, anecdotes can be sold on their own as fillers to various publications. The best-known examples of this are the various departments in *Reader's Digest* specializing in anecdotes: "Life in These United States," "All in a Day's Work," "Humor in Uniform," etc. (For more about how to write fillers, see chapter twenty.)

Terms Involving Literature

Q. *When a story is based on an actual happening, but changed to a degree, should it be called a story or an article?*
A. If a story is told only from the narrator's viewpoint and the incidents are factually accurate and based on a true personal experience, it would probably be considered an article. Fiction contains a degree of imagination, does not attempt to get in all the facts, and usually strays from the true account to add color and drama.

Q. *When editors say they want professionally written or sophisticated material, what do they mean?*
A. They mean they want the type of writing that represents a polished use of the language plus skillfully developed treatment of the subject. Flaws in grammar and word choice, lackluster style, sloppy plotting or research, poor organization, absence of a point, are all signs of the amateur rather than the professional. The demand for sophisticated material rules out anything trite or corny but suggests a desire for a certain degree of wit and subtlety that would appeal to readers who are intellectually sharp about the significance of the world around them.

Q. *What does the category "belles lettres" cover? I've seen it in several of the market listings and would like an explanation.*
A. The dictionary definition of "belles lettres" is literally "fine letters" — literature that is an end in itself and not practical or purely informative. This would seem to include all fiction, but in practice it includes only work in which the quality of the

writing transcends its subject; the literary equivalent of "art for art's sake."

Terms Involving the Industry

Q. *What is meant by the term "freelancer" and how much work and pay is involved in this classification?*
A. The term "freelancer" is used to describe an editor, writer, or other fully or part-time self-employed person who works for a variety of clients on a temporary or per-assignment basis. The term originated in medieval times when a knight or soldier who was paid for fighting and who offered his services—his lance—to any available employer, was called a "free lance."

How much work a freelancer does depends on how much time a writer wishes to devote to the job. Freelancers perform their work with varying degrees of frequency. There are the occasional freelancers, who make a few scattered sales over the course of several years. Most freelancers begin their careers part-time, writing in the evenings and on weekends while simultaneously holding down a full-time job. Many writers remain part-time freelancers, moving in and out of the field as their lives and careers change. Full-time freelancers are writers who have achieved the track record and reputation to make freelance writing a permanent career. These writers include those whose names are listed in *Publishers Weekly* as the authors of new books, or whose articles appear in issue after issue of national magazines.

Freelance writing as a full-time occupation is not easy. While it is possible to earn a living wage as a freelancer, it requires a great deal of time, skill, discipline and dedication. Art Spikol, author of *Magazine Writing: The Inside Angle,* says that considering the hours a freelancer works and the amount of money he earns, most freelancers don't even make minimum wage. "A freelance writer who miraculously sold to the top-paying dozen markets in the country in as many months—and who also managed to sell one shorter piece each month for $250—might not earn $25,000 a year," he writes. "All that work . . . and you still might end up making less than somebody in a semiskilled trade, even though your performance would make you a superstar among writers." In 1981, the Authors Guild Foundation surveyed 2,239 book authors and learned that their *average* annual income from writing was $4,775. If you wish to make writing your full-time occupation, you will have to build up experience and reputation over the course of several years. (For more information on how much a freelance writer can expect to earn, see chapter forty-one.)

Q. *How do "little" and "literary" magazines differ from general publications? Are they the same thing as literary journals?*
A. Little or literary magazines are publications with limited circulation—generally 5,000 or less—which offer writers a vehicle of expression not found in commercial magazines. They are usually literary in nature, stressing the unorthodox or experimental in approaches to poetry and prose. Little magazines aim for an audience

of writers, editors and students of literature. Their contributors are usually writers striving for literary excellence. T.S. Eliot, Flannery O'Connor and John Gardner all received their early attention by having their work published in little magazines.

Editors of the literaries do not rely on general public support; hence, they do not have to compromise the ideals of their publications with popular taste. A little magazine can be centered on a specific theme or can be "eclectic" — open to work on any idea. Pay is usually low or nonexistent; contributing authors are often paid with copies or subscriptions to the magazine. Writers submitting work to the literaries should know that some of them are not copyrighted. If submitting to a noncopyrighted journal, be sure to include the copyright notice on your work to prevent its passing into public domain. Check *Writer's Market* and *Novel & Short Story Writer's Market* for details on specific publications.

Where literary magazines rely on creative prose and poetry, literary journals rely more on criticism. These literary journals, most often connected with and financed by a foundation or university, tend to include a small proportion of imaginative literature. Unlike the little magazines, literary journals may offer some payment, but accept little work from freelance writers. Instead, they rely on academic contributors and writers sought out by the journal's editor. Publication in a literary journal carries prestige, but the competition is heavy.

Q. *What's the difference between a journal and a magazine?*
A. Although a journal and a magazine are similar in format, a magazine is intended for the general public, while a journal is usually published by and for a professional group, such as orthopedic surgeons, microbiologists or history professors. "Trade journals" are magazines published for workers in various industries; these include publications such as *American Printer and Lithographer, Broadcast Engineering* and *American Drycleaner.* Journals usually contain articles written by members of the profession that makes up their readership; manuscripts are not usually sought from writers outside the profession. Magazines, on the other hand, appeal to a general-interest audience or to consumers and businesspeople with special interests. Most magazines actively seek manuscripts from freelance writers.

Q. *What is a trade book and how does it differ from a library edition?*
A. A trade book is a hardcover or paperback title (the latter are often specified as "trade paperbacks") distributed mainly through retail bookstores. Trade books can be novels, works of nonfiction or children's books. The author's royalties, based on the retail list price, are usually escalating, for example: 10 percent of the retail price on the first five thousand copies, 12½ percent on the next five thousand and 15 percent on any additional copies sold. A library edition is a trade book with a binding stronger than that used for books to be sold to the general public. The library binding is designed to withstand the heavy use a library book will receive.

Q. *What is the difference between mass-market paperbacks and trade paperbacks?*
A. The difference can be defined in terms of size, distribution, and the amount of

royalties the author receives. Mass-market books are sold in drugstores, airports and supermarkets (that is, in the mass market), as well as in bookstores; they are published in a single size, designed to fit paperback book racks and to be conveniently carried. Trade paperbacks are larger, cost more, and are distributed mainly in bookstores and department stores (that is, distributed to "the trade"). Publishers are turning to trade paperbacks as a way of reaching the book-buying public at a lower cost than hardcover trade books. Royalties for original mass-market titles are usually based on a percentage—such as 8 percent—of the retail price on net copies sold. For example, a publisher may distribute 100,000 copies, but only 50 percent might be sold and the rest destroyed. For trade paperbacks, the author usually receives 7½ percent royalty (some contracts may call for only 5 or 6 percent) based on the retail price.

Q. *In a travel writer's newsletter I saw a reference to a "fam trip." What does this term mean?*
A. It's an abbreviation for "familiarization trip," in which the public relations agency for a country, hotel or airline invites travel agents, travel editors and travel writers to visit and become familiar with the amenities offered by the host country or firm in expectation of subsequent business and travel articles. Transportation and lodging costs might be paid for travel agents and/or offered at a considerably reduced rate for editors and writers.

Q. *What is a "potboiler"?*
A. A potboiler is a piece of writing created for the express purpose of making money quickly—in other words, to "keep the pot boiling," or to eat—while the writer works on major articles, stories or books. Depending on a writer's facility and knowledge of the marketplace, a potboiler may run anywhere from a six-line filler to a 1,500-word short story, to a 65,000-word novel. In other words, a potboiler can be any writing project designed to bring a quick paycheck with a minimum of trouble and effort on the part of the writer. Writing potboilers is a practice that can be slanted to nearly any market the writer knows well. The secret to success lies in quantity and quick production. If the project eats up more time than it's worth, it isn't practical. Because potboilers are usually written in the shortest span of time possible, they rarely are of superior literary quality. However, potboilers should appear as clean and professional as any other material. And if you find yourself thinking of a piece of work as a potboiler, it might be time for a little self-examination; because a piece is written solely to make money is no reason to allow yourself to "write down to" the reader. (That is a dangerous habit, and one that can be painfully difficult to break.)

Q. *What do editors call the small descriptive phrase or sentence that usually appears under the main title of an article?*
A. Most editors call it a "subhead," although some magazine staffs refer to it as a "deck." A subhead is usually designed to pique the reader's interest in reading the

article or story by telling just a little bit about the subject matter.

Q. *What does "mailing and remailing" or "drop-off mailing" mean in the classified ads in* Writer's Digest?
A. A mailing service agency mails an author's work from its own locality when the author travels frequently or prefers a postmark that does not reveal his place of residence.

Terms Involving Marketing

Q. *What is meant by a "market" — and what does the phrase "marketing your material" mean? I've often seen both referred to in* Writer's Digest.
A. A "market" is a magazine, publishing firm or company to which you sell what you write. "Marketing your material" means selling what you write. "Study the market" means just that — read back issues of the magazine or, in the case of a book publisher, study the company's catalog, and visit bookstores to view the books firsthand. Also study the magazine or book firm's editorial requirements in the market listings in writers publications, so you will understand what type of material the market is purchasing.

Q. *What is an unsolicited manuscript?*
A. When a writer submits a book, article, story or poem without the publisher requesting it, the manuscript is *unsolicited.* In such a case, the editor or publisher has not given any indication he will read the work; he and the writer have not communicated, either by mail or through the writer's agent. Some publishers will not read unsolicited manuscripts. Since publishers have no legal responsibility for unsolicited manuscripts, the author should always consult *Writer's Market* to make sure a specific publisher accepts them. The writer must always include a SASE when submitting unsolicited manuscripts.

Q. *What is meant by "over the transom"?*
A. "Over the transom" is a collective term for unsolicited manuscripts received by a publisher; the phrase implies that the works were not requested, but were slipped "over the transom" into the publisher's office through the small window above old office doors which were left open for air circulation.

Q. *What is meant by the term "slush pile"?*
A. "Slush pile" is a collective term for unsolicited material received by magazine editors and book publishers. This refers to any manuscripts not specifically assigned by an editor or submitted by an agent.

Q. *What does SASE mean? And why is SASE in almost every market listing in* Writer's Digest *and* Writer's Market?
A. SASE means self-addressed, stamped envelope. It should be enclosed in every

query and every manuscript submission to every editor. When requesting information from an editor or from a magazine's subscription or service departments, it's always best to enclose a SASE for the reply. Make sure the envelope is at least a No. 10 envelope — not the tiny personal-size stationery envelopes, which are useless when sending reprints of articles, flyers, publications or other literature that is requested. And when submitting a manuscript, always enclose the proper size envelope (usually the same size as the one the manuscript was mailed in), with adequate postage for return. Always *glue* the stamps to the envelope, rather than using a paper clip. If you only clip them, there's a chance that they might get separated from the manuscript. Remember: Many editors will not return material submitted without a SASE.

Q. *What are "clips" and how are they used by professionals?*
A. A clip, or clipping, is a photocopied sample of a writer's published work, usually taken from a newspaper or magazine. Editors often indicate that clips should be mailed or presented in person when sending a query letter or applying for a job. Clippings show an editor how a writer handles a variety of topics, as well as serving as proof of a writer's published credits. When sending clips, a writer should make sure they are neat and readable; a high-quality photocopy is preferable to the original, especially in the case of newspaper articles, since newspapers tend to age and deteriorate quickly. If the story is an unusual size or shape, *Writer's Digest* columnist Art Spikol recommends a reduced photocopy. Be sure you have sufficient postage on the return envelope if you want your clips returned. Some writers send photocopies of their clips to sources they have used in researching an article, to show how the piece turned out and to thank the source for his help.

Writers also use the term "clips" to refer to newspaper or magazine articles written by other writers. They file the clips for research purposes, for reference, and for possible future article ideas.

Q. *What is a "tearsheet"?*
A. "Tearsheet" is another term for "clipping," a sample of writing in its published form that has been cut — or "torn" — from the newspaper or magazine in which it appeared. Tearsheets can be a writer's own work or another writer's articles used for research purposes.

Q. *What is a synopsis?*
A. A synopsis is a brief condensation of a topic or subject. It is most frequently used to summarize the plot of a story, novel or play. A synopsis also forms part of a book proposal that an author submits to a publisher. A nonfiction book proposal generally consists of a comprehensive summary of the contents of the proposed book (the synopsis), along with two or three sample chapters and an outline detailing chapter-by-chapter highlights of the book. Some publishers require a synopsis for fiction and nonfiction works; others require a full manuscript for fiction.

Publishers of novels require a synopsis and usually want a chapter-by-chapter summary of the book, including all the characters, subplots as well as the main plot, and any other pertinent details. Such a synopsis could run from ten to thirty pages depending on the complexity and length of the novel.

Some editors use the words "synopsis" and "outline" to mean the same thing, but in general, a synopsis is a brief review of the proposed manuscript, while an outline is an organized plan.

Q. *What are "simultaneous submissions" as listed by some publishers in* Writer's Market?

A. A simultaneous, or multiple, submission is a manuscript submitted for consideration to more than one publishing company at the same time. Once taboo, multiple submission has become a moderately common practice for certain types of articles, book proposals and finished manuscripts. Some editors, however, want to be sure that their competitors are not considering the same material at the same time they are. When a major magazine pays top prices, its editors expect to get an exclusive look at the ideas writers present to them. Therefore, writers should not send multiple submissions to major magazine markets. Smaller magazines, such as religious and company publications, pay lower rates and have readerships that are not likely to overlap with other magazines in the same field; these factors make them more willing to look at simultaneous submissions. A writer may be able to sell one-time rights to the same story or article to a dozen of these publications that buy other than first rights.

It is usually acceptable for a writer to make multiple queries—especially if his article idea is timely. The outline and sample chapters of a book proposal can also be submitted simultaneously to several publishers, provided an original cover letter is included with each, addressed to the appropriate editor. Should you inform the editor in the cover letter that the manuscript is being considered by other publishers? Opinions vary. About half of the book publishers listed in *Writer's Market* indicate they will accept multiple submissions. However, many prefer that the author tell them that a multiple submission has been made. Some also require that the writer tell them the names of other publishers to whom the material has been sent.

Q. *When an editor says he will accept photocopied submissions, what does he mean?*
A. Many editors who once insisted on seeing the original, good-bond copy of a manuscript will now accept a good-quality photocopy of the original. This change in attitude is largely due to improvements in the quality of photocopies. Photocopying a manuscript is a convenience to the author; it is also a good precaution against having a manuscript lost or damaged in the mail or misplaced at an editor's office. If such a mishap should occur, the writer will still have the original copy on file, eliminating the time, expense and bother of retyping the manuscript. Also, when a well-traveled copy of a manuscript becomes dog-eared, a fresh copy can be made.

Q. *What can a writer do when a magazine or book publisher will not look at unsolicited* *manuscripts?*

A. Over the past several years, some book and magazine publishers have discontinued accepting unsolicited manuscripts and have announced in *Writer's Market* and *Novel & Short Story Writer's Market* that they only accept manuscripts submitted by an author's agent. Most writers don't have agents and some circumvent this policy by directing an advance query to a specific editor. When the idea has sufficient appeal they obtain a go-ahead to submit the manuscript to the editor's personal attention. However, most publishers accept unsolicited submissions. Check *Writer's Market* and *Novel & Short Story Writer's Market* for specific magazine and book publishers' policies.

Q. *So what are these "writer's guidelines" that editors want us to send for?*
A. Writer's guidelines are instructions from a magazine's editors on what sorts of submissions they'd like to see from writers. Guidelines often briefly describe the publication's audience, the types of articles published, and the types of material that *are not* accepted. Departments open to freelancers may be listed and described, and the editors may offer some tips on the styles of writing and article structures they favor. Writer's guidelines can be an important element of researching a market, but should not take the place of studying several recent issues of the magazine. Not all magazines make guidelines available, insisting that reading the magazine is the best guide.

A few book publishers offer guidelines, which are known as "tip sheets" among romance and some other genre publishers.

Terms Involving Contracts

Q. *What does the phrase, "payment in contributor's copies" mean?*
A. "Contributor's copies" is a term that is generally taken to mean copies of the issue in which the contributor's work appears. A magazine that "pays in copies" (as it is also phrased) offers writers no other remuneration than a copy of the magazine in exchange for the right to publish a work. This is why they are less elegantly called "non-paying markets."

Q. *What do the phrases "payment on acceptance" and "payment on publication" mean?*
A. Both refer to the time the publisher begins the check-writing process (which can take up to a month at some—notably larger—publications). "Payment on acceptance" means the check is ordered after the editor accepts the article as ready for publication (that is, after the writer completes any necessary rewrites). The article may be filed and not edited or published for a period of time, but that does not affect the writer's payment.

"Payment on publication" means the check is not ordered until the piece appears in print. At a newspaper, this is generally no more than a few days or weeks. The writer may not even notice a delay in receiving his check. At a monthly or quarterly magazine, however, publication may lag months—even *years*—after acceptance (depending on the size of the editor's manuscript inventory).

Q. *What does it mean when a publisher listed in* Writer's Market *says he will accept a writer's work "on spec"?*
A. When an editor responds to a query letter by offering to look at the proposed work "on speculation" ("on spec" for short), he means he is interested in the article idea and will consider the finished article for publication. In his response, the editor will usually indicate a deadline due date, the desired word count for the article and the terms of payment if it is accepted. However, agreeing to look at the work on spec in no way obligates an editor to buy the finished manuscript. Since an agreement on spec does not assure a sale, some leading freelancers will only write an article on assignment, with the editor giving a firm commitment to purchase the finished product, but beginning writers should celebrate an invitation to submit an article on spec. Often the editor will buy the finished manuscript, if it meets editorial specifications and is submitted within the time specified.

Q. *What is a "kill fee" and when is it used?*
A. Kill fee is a fee paid to a writer who has worked on an assignment that, for one reason or another, was not published. The writer, for example, is asked (assigned) to write a 3,000-word article, but after he does the research and writes the 3,000 words, the editor decides that the piece will not be published after all. The writer is then given a percentage (usually 20 percent of the purchase price offered for the full manuscript—or a percentage of the expected income from a discontinued project other than an article) as a kill fee. The 20 percent kill fee is flexible, depending on the publication's policy. It's rare for an editor to offer a kill fee to a writer whose work is not familiar to him or to a writer who hasn't previously worked for him. The writer is, after receiving the kill fee, permitted to submit the manuscript to other markets for possible sale. A writer should not expect to receive a kill fee unless this provision is specifically covered in the original assignment.

Q. *What is a "work-for-hire" contract?*
A. A "work-for-hire" contract is one that permanently gives all rights of a work to the person or business that assigns it, for example, to the periodical or to the publisher. A freelance writer who signs a "work-for-hire" clause gives up his copyright and also his right to any further income from that material. Unless the contract fee is particularly good, follow Kay Cassill's advice about these contracts in *The Complete Handbook for Freelance Writers*, "don't sign them."

Chapter 6

How Do I Get Ideas?

Sir William Osler, physician and medical historian, reminded us that "in science, the credit goes to the man who convinces the world, not to the man to whom the idea first occurs." The freelance writer faces the same challenge. Ideas are only as good as what you do with them. Small comfort that you're thinking salable material if you are scooped in your own backyard on an idea you, too, had for a local feature; or if a magazine carries an article you were going to query about but never got around to. Or maybe getting ideas to start with is your problem? Read on!

Founts of Inspiration

Q. *Is there some way, other than through the local newspaper, I can find out about community and corporate happenings as possible subjects for freelance articles?*
A. Most public relations departments of large organizations maintain mailing lists and notify interested persons of upcoming events on their calendars. Large companies, universities and nonprofit groups schedule a variety of events that can be grist for the freelancer's mill. Convention and Visitors Bureaus of large cities can also inform you when special-interest groups and professional organizations will be holding conventions in your area. All you have to do to start receiving information is write to the organization and ask—as a professional freelance writer—to be placed on their mailing list.

Q. *I'm having trouble coming up with fresh ideas for my fiction. What are some ways I can jog my imagination into action?*
A. The number of ways to find story ideas is almost limitless. First of all, you should read widely—not just novels and short stories, but magazines and newspapers. Something in a factual article might jog your imagination. If something makes you think, "I wonder what kind of person would do something like that," chances are you could use it as a starting point for your next story.

An interesting person you've met or something that happened to you at work, or even a daydream or nightmare can be a catalyst. Listen to what people say on the street, and jot in your notebook any interesting pieces of dialogue.

New settings might also spark your imagination. Add these descriptions to your notes. You don't have to take an expensive vacation; a trip to a neighboring town or a detour through another area of your city on your way home can show you something that could catch your imagination. Your own life experiences can also provide the foundation for a short story or novel, but you must be careful to avoid becoming entrapped by the facts. Remember that you're telling a story and that what was really said or what really happened will have to be modified, or ignored altogether, in the interest of creating readable dialogue and an entertaining plot.

History and the classics of literature can be retold in modern surroundings; Othello as chairman of a corporation or a Napoleon figure as president of the U.S. are only two of the many possible twists on old stories.

Above all, remember that inspiration doesn't always strike like a flash of lightning. Ideas generally ripen slowly, starting from a single impression or bit of information. The more opportunities you give your imagination, the greater the chance ideas will come to you.

Q. *I have in mind a story involving several character types, but I'm having trouble coming up with a strong plot. What can I do about this?*
A. Most fiction is based on what the characters do. Interesting, believable characters create the atmosphere and conflict necessary to the success of a short story or novel. And every story must have a basic conflict. By carefully examining your characters — their backgrounds, likes, dislikes, beliefs — you can gain ideas about how to set up that conflict. Ask yourself questions. What does the main character want? What obstacles might interfere with his goals? How do the characters relate to one another? Once you've set up the basic conflict, you can begin to outline the action of the story.

According to Maxine Rock's *Fiction Writer's Help Book,* there is no "right" way to outline; each writer develops a method that best suits him. But by understanding your characters, their motivations, and the conflicts they face, you lay the groundwork for your story, and make it easier to figure out "what happens next."

Q. *I know many people who have had unusual experiences or are themselves unusual in some way. I think their lives would make interesting stories or articles. But I don't want to interview all of them and write only personality sketches. Is there a way to turn these unusual experiences and people into marketable stories and articles?*
A. You are on the right track. Personality sketches give the beginning writer excellent experience in interviewing, organizing the highlights of a person's life or experience, and writing colorful, concise articles about interesting people. They also sell widely, thus providing opportunity to get your work in print. But this material can be used other ways, too. Instead of opening your focus to include the person and his or her whole life, think about using brief references as anecdotes or illustrations to strengthen an argument in another article. Quotations or clever remarks can become strong leads for both fiction and nonfiction, sometimes sparking an entire

article idea. And real people and their motivations provide the inspiration for characters in many short stories and novels.

Keep recording impressions as your path crosses the fascinating lives of strangers and acquaintances. Consider this information as money in the bank. You will draw on it for years to come.

Q. *Sometimes when I'm working on a particular story, I come across a bit of information that sparks an idea for another story. But when the current work is finished, I can never seem to recall the second story idea. How do other writers handle this?*
A. One of the most valuable tools a writer has is her notebook. The notebook is a kind of "surrogate memory," in which a writer can jot thoughts, impressions and story ideas *when they occur.* Character descriptions, bits of dialogue, facts from research—all can be recorded in the notebook for easy retrieval.

A clipping file is another valuable tool. When you find a piece of information or a newspaper article that sparks an idea, you may want to clip it (or copy it, if it's library property) and file it for later use. Your clipping file can be divided into whatever categories best suit your purposes. This method is useful because it not only preserves your idea, but also the information that triggered it.

Ideas for the Marketplace

Q. *I've written several articles for local newspapers and magazines, but I'm not sure I can write a national-interest article. How can I write something that will sell to a national publication?*
A. Many local and regional articles can be expanded in scope to fit the needs of national publications. By examining how a local story relates to a national trend, or by using it as an example of that trend, a writer can create an article that will be attractive to a national magazine. Of course, you'll have to supplement your local information with related examples from national sources, which you will have to uncover through research. You should also contact persons involved in the subject on a national level, obtain their viewpoints and comments, and add their quotes to your story.

Q. *It seems that every topic I want to write about has already been covered by a magazine currently on the newsstands. How can I use my idea without duplicating another writer's work?*
A. There are many different slants to the same subject. The creative part of marketing is the work the writer does in finding a different approach to a subject in order to interest readers of a specific magazine that has not already covered that subject. Research the specific topic that interests you in *Reader's Guide to Periodical Literature.* Read the articles you find referenced there to determine what angle of your topic they covered. Then think about alternative approaches that you might be able to target to other magazines, using the listings in *Writer's Market* as a guide. For example, an article on the postwar generation of "baby boomers" published in

Money magazine set out to answer the question, "Can they ever live as well as *their* parents?" An article for an education administration magazine might talk about the number of children this generation plans to have and how that affects the need for schools, classroom space and teachers in the coming years. By looking at the same phenomenon from different angles, you can sell articles on the same idea to a wide variety of publications.

Q. *I've come up with several ideas for articles, but I don't know enough about the topics to write the actual pieces. Do magazine editors purchase story ideas, or will writers more knowledgeable in the specific areas buy the rights to use my ideas?*
A. Magazine editors usually will only purchase completed manuscripts, not ideas. Supermarket tabloids are noteworthy exceptions to this rule. Many will consider submissions of story ideas in the form of wild or unusual news items clipped from newspapers or magazines, and will pay a small fee if the story works out. When this edition of this book was being edited, some tabloids paid as much as $25 for each idea used. Writers who specialize in specific fields of information usually have so many ideas of their own that they do not purchase from others. However, it may surprise you how little the average writer knows about a given topic before he begins to write about it. With some research and interviews with knowledgeable sources, you probably can learn enough about your subject to write the article yourself. (For more advice on finding "experts" and doing research, see chapters seven and eight.)

Chapter 7

How Can I Get in Touch With Information Sources?

It's been said that a good nonfiction writer doesn't have to know much, he just has to know people who do. Learning who such people are, how to find them, and what to ask them are among the basic tasks of a freelance nonfiction writer. Fiction writers, too, need to verify facts presented in their works, maintain historical accuracy, and sometimes even discuss the personalities of their characters with psychologists. No matter what the subject of your article, story or book (or even at times, your poem), there is probably a source available who can help you add insight and authority to your manuscript.

For tips on collecting and organizing the information these sources will lead you to, see the next chapter. For more tips on sources and research, consult *Find It Fast* by Robert Berkman (HarperCollins) and *State-of-the-Art Fact-Finding* by Trudi Jacobson and Gary McLain.

Locating Information

Q. *How can I find the addresses of authors and/or well-known persons or "experts" to request interviews by mail, by telephone or in person?*
A. Book authors can generally be reached by writing to them in care of their publishers; the publishers' addresses can be found in *Books in Print.* You might also check the directories: *Contemporary Authors*, or any one of the several *Who's Who* directories, can be used find home addresses.

Other directories contain the addresses of specialists in various fields, such as *American Men and Women of Science* and *Who's Who in American Art.* These directories can be found at most libraries.

If you cannot locate a performer's or famous person's address through the biographical directories, Celebrity Service, Inc. may be able to provide the name and telephone number of the celebrity's manager, agent or press agent for a fee of ten dollars. Contact them at 1780 Broadway, New York NY 10019.

Q. *I need information from several U.S. Government agencies for an article I am writing. Is there a central news and information bureau in Washington, and will its staff*

40

give me information by phone? How can I find the addresses of government agencies?
A. There is no central information bureau, but you can call the government operator at (202) 555-1212 for the number of a specific department or agency's Public Information Officer (P.I.O.). The P.I.O. is the person you should contact in reference to any story that deals with a government agency, since most federal officials won't give out information for publication without clearing it with their P.I.O.s. You may be able to get the answer you need by telephoning the government agency specialist the P.I.O. refers you to. Addresses of government departments, bureaus and agencies, can be found in the *United States Government Manual* available at your local library. Another valuable source is Matthew Lesko's *Information U.S.A.*

Q. *How can I contact the author of a magazine article I recently read?*
A. Write to the author in care of the magazine in which the article appeared. The magazine's editorial office address will appear somewhere on its masthead or contents page. Since some publications have their subscriptions fulfilled at a different address, be sure you write to the editorial address, not the circulation or advertising addresses. Most editors will forward mail addressed to contributing writers. However, most magazines will not give the home addresses of their contributors.

Q. *How can I obtain a copy of back issues of a magazine?*
A. Write to the magazine first; many publications operate a back-issue service. If the magazine in question is no longer being published or does not have the issue you need, check the New York City (Manhattan) Yellow Pages for advertisers under "Magazines—Back Number," or check with any used book stores in your area. A large city or college library may have back issues you could photocopy.

Q. *How can I find out which issues of a special-interest magazine contain articles on a specific topic I'm researching?*
A. Indexes to periodicals catalog information published in magazine, newspaper or journal articles by title, subject and author. Most indexes are available in large public libraries or college libraries. Indexes to publications in specialized fields include directories such as *Education Index, Business Periodicals Index, Abstracts and Indexes in Science and Technology, Film Literature Index, Abstracts on Criminology and Penology, Religion Index One: Periodicals* and *Index to Legal Periodicals.* Another good resource is *Ulrich's International Periodicals Directory,* which lists publications by subject matter and tells where each is indexed or whether it publishes its own index. If, for example, you were researching an article on interior design and *House Beautiful* was the only publication in that area with which you were familiar, finding that title in *Ulrich's* would lead you to more than 125 other periodicals on the subject and show you where each is indexed.

For general-interest magazines, indexes to consult include *Reader's Guide to Periodical Literature, The Magazine Index* and *Access: The Supplementary Index to Periodicals.*

Q. *How can I find addresses of daily and weekly newspapers to submit articles of regional interest?*
A. *Editor & Publisher* magazine produces a yearbook that contains a directory of all newspapers. The yearbook is available in most large libraries and newspaper offices. If you wish to purchase a copy, call the magazine's Manhattan office, (212) 675-4380, for the current price. Two other sources for addresses are the Newspaper Directory (volume 1) of *Working Press of the Nation* and *Gale Directory of Publications,* also available at the library. Both directories are set up geographically by state, then city, and will help you locate regional prospects.

Q. *What resources, other than books and libraries, are useful in researching an article?*
A. There are many ways of finding out what you need to know other than using the library. Professional and special interest associations exist to serve a variety of common goals and interests. An association can give you information or steer you to an expert in the topic about which you're writing. Check the key word index in the *Encyclopedia of Associations* or call the American Society of Association Executives at (202) 626-2723 and ask for the information center to find the organization that can help you.

In addition to the government experts mentioned in chapter seven, there are also many government reports on specialized topics. Check in your library for the subject indexes to material issued by the U.S. Government Printing Office. There is a *Cumulative Subject Index to the Monthly Catalog of U.S. Government Publications, 1900-1971* and annual indexes after that time. The Government Printing Office also issues a monthly bulletin of government publications.

The Library of Congress is just that—a library reference source for Congressmen, but if you can't visit the library in person, but want advice on some of the information you think it might have on your topic, write to the Library of Congress, General Reading Room, Washington DC 20540.

To find information sources on practically any subject, check *Writer's Resource Guide,* which lists many organizations, companies, libraries and museums under thirty subject headings. It might be the quickest place to find what you need.

Q. *In my novel, I'm quoting from a poem I learned years ago. How do I locate the source or author?*
A. *Granger's Index to Poetry* indexes poetry by title and first line, and by subject. *Bartlett's Familiar Quotations* also contains many well-known passages, arranged by author and indexed by the key word in the passage.

Q. *How would an author build a reference library of books about a field in which he wants to specialize? I have chosen an area of interest, but I don't know what books are available.*
A. *Subject Guide to Books in Print* lists every book currently being published in the U.S. Listings are alphabetical by subject and field of interest the books cover. For instance, a book on President Truman's Korean War policy might be listed under

Truman's name, "Korean War 1950-1953" and "Military History." Go to your library and see what marterial they have on your topic and check the *Subject Guide* to see if the books you want are still available from the publishers.

Handling Sources

Q. *What's the difference between a primary source and a secondary source?*
A. A primary source — or primary research — provides the writer with original, first-hand information. It is based on the writer's own experience and observation, direct contact with other people (usually in an interview), or information gleaned from personal papers, correspondence, diaries, or manuscripts relating to the person or subject being studied. Primary research is closer to the subject, and therefore preferable to secondary research, which is based entirely on subsequently published newspapers, books or magazines. If a writer uses only secondary sources, he runs the risk of his research being inaccurate, since his sources may contain misquotations or other errors. Secondary sources are used to gain supporting information and background material for an article.

Q. *In doing a "round-up" article in which I quote the opinions of several different people, should I obtain the consent of the individuals included when the information is not obtained by interview?*
A. While it probably isn't necessary to obtain permission to quote brief opinions from published sources (see the section on "fair use" in chapter nine), it's usually best to verify published quotes to avoid repeating another writer's error.

Q. *Many sources across the country have answered my written requests for information with long letters giving me detailed information I might not have gotten anywhere else. Is it customary to acknowledge each of these replies with a thank-you note? I owe these people a great deal for providing me with so much information, but sending individual thank-you notes can become costly and time consuming.*
A. Although notes of thanks are not obligatory in this case, they probably would be appreciated, and could help ensure that these persons will be equally helpful if you need to use their resources again. Individual notes are probably not necessary; a photocopied form letter and copy of your published article should suffice to thank them for their trouble.

Chapter 8

What's the Best Way to Do Research?

American playwright Wilson Mizner said, "When you take stuff from one writer, it's plagiarism; but when you take it from many writers, it's research." Today's writer-researcher has at his fingertips not only the traditional resources of books, magazine articles and directories of experts' names and addresses, but a host of new computer databases that can save him hours of tedious manual searching. Don't forget to ask your librarian "What's new?" in relation to your current project. A librarian may have some new resource you didn't know about.

Methods of Research

Q. *I'm writing a piece that requires a lot of research and I don't know what to do first. Where do I start?*
A. Every writer develops his own system of organization, so there is no "right way" to prepare your research. But it is important to develop *some* system to keep you from wasting time.

Kay Cassill, author of *The Complete Handbook for Freelance Writers,* recommends some general guidelines for planning your research: Think through your article outline from beginning to end and decide what *kind* of information you'll need, such as statistics, advice from experts, and illustrative anecdotes. Make a list of pertinent questions that must be answered in the course of the article, as well as secondary questions that are beneficial but not crucial. Decide what your probable sources are and list them in the order in which you should consult them. Adjust your research plans to fit your schedule (how much time can you spend on this article?), budget (is the publisher covering any of your costs?) and the scope of the topic. Cassill urges you to do your homework early and keep to a well laid-out schedule. As you gain experience, your system of research will develop and you'll gain confidence, increasing your ability to cut your research down to size.

Q. *When I'm finished researching an article, I have so much raw material that I'm overwhelmed by the sheer bulk of it and don't know where to begin. How can I distill all my research material down to a manageable size?*

A. There are probably as many ways to organize article material as there are writers who do it. Each writer has a system, ranging from complex arrangements of classified index cards to casual groupings of related notes.

The first thing to do is reduce the bulk of material you've gathered. Get rid of books you aren't going to use anymore and remove the clippings you need from the publications you've gathered, rather than keeping whole magazines and newspapers. Next, you must decide what information is essential to your article and what is only tangentially related to your topic, filing the latter for future use. One professional writer recommends that as you handle every piece of information you've gathered, you notice how the material looks—whether it's in a *green* envelope or written on *yellow* paper or in a small notebook—each will provide you with a mental trigger to help you find the material immediately when you need it.

Divide your material into subject categories. Some writers use colored pencils to code the information, others use card files and file folders to classify their material. In distilling the research into written copy, many writers cut and paste bits of information onto a single page.

It's important to have everything you need close to you as you write your article, but don't overemphasize the importance of organization. Over-organization can be used to avoid getting started with the actual writing.

Q. *I'm not sure whether to take written notes or use a tape recorder when researching an article. What are the pros and cons of each?*
A. Both methods have their good and bad points. Tape recorders allow an interviewer to concentrate on conducting the interview and observing the interviewee and the surroundings. They also provide proof of what was said should a subject later claim to be misquoted. Taping can also be useful in the library, allowing you to record lengthy bits of information quickly when a photocopy machine is not practical. A recorder can also be used to note thoughts and observations while traveling.

However, there is always the possibility that the tape recorder will go on the blink when you need it most. Also, some interview subjects are uncomfortable with tape recorders and will not talk as freely as with someone who unobtrusively takes notes. You could also mistakenly erase important material. Many serious interviewers use two tape recorders as insurance against malfunction, and stagger starting times to avoid losing material while changing tapes.

Unless you take shorthand or develop your own speedwriting system, note-taking can be difficult. Even the best set of notes may seem incomprehensible once cold and the best memories may fail. Some authors recommend using a tape recorder to be sure they have accurate information, supplementing the tape with notes. That way, not even accidental erasure can foul up a story, and written notes will provide an easy way to check the content of the interview without listening to the entire tape.

Q. *How do I go about conducting a research survey by mail?*

A. The first step in conducting your survey is to thoroughly research the topic and develop a questionnaire. The questions should be typed so as to give your respondent the opportunity and space to answer directly on your questionnaire. Be sure to include a final question such as "Any further comments you wish to make?" so that people inclined to give you more than brief answers can do so. Write a form letter to accompany the questionnaire, stating the purpose of the survey and how you intend to use the information in your article — either as general results or direct quotations from their answers. Indicate that if they don't wish to be quoted directly, you'll respect that. Your questionnaire should conclude with a place for the respondent's signature along with one of two statements the respondent can choose to check: "Permission granted to quote directly from this questionnaire (   ), or "Please do not quote me by name directly from this questionnaire (   )." Include SASEs for the respondents to return the questionnaires.

Q. *How can I get quotes from experts? Also how can I find incidents and examples to add substance to magazine articles I'm writing?*
A. After you've decided which experts you'd like to get quotes from, write them individual letters in care of their business addresses. Explain the subject matter of your article and the magazine for which you're writing and ask your appropriate questions. Be sure to enclose a SASE for the reply. As for finding incidents and examples — read a lot of other reference material on the same subject. Talk to people in your area who may have had experiences in the specific field you're writing about. Ask them and the experts you write to suggest other people in other parts of the country who may be able to help you in your research.

Q. *What are databases and how can they be useful to a writer?*
A. A database is a collection of specialized information stored in a computer. There's a wealth of information at your fingertips when you place them on the keyboard and instruct your computer to dial up electronic information services. From *Books in Print* to libraries of newspaper and magazine articles, computer databases can save a writer tremendous amounts of footwork.

To access a database, you need a modem to connect your computer to the phone lines, an unoccupied phone jack and communications software to handle dialing and transfer of information. Modems are rated according to their speed in bits per second (bps), with price following speed on an ascending curve. Because most database services charge you according to how long you're connected to their computer, a faster modem, which can transfer information more quickly, can save you money in the long run. Some such services, however, apply a surcharge to connections using faster modems, largely erasing the savings. As of 1993, few databases operate at speeds faster than 9,600 bps, and some still connect only at 2,400 bps or slower.

Pages could be filled with listings of available databases; just listing the U.S. Government computer bulletin boards would fill a couple. At this revision, some of the more popular commercial database services include:

- Dialog: 420 different databases of publications, encompassing 150 million items for business, government, science and law. (800) 334-2564, (415) 858-8079
- Dow Jones News Retrieval: company information and stock quotes, as well as full text of *The Wall Street Journal* and *Barrons*, and articles from 1,300 other publications. (609) 452-1511
- NewsNet: full-text articles from six hundred business-related newsletters and newspapers and twenty worldwide news services. (800) 345-1301, (215) 527-8030
- CompuServe: a general telecommunications service that provides numerous internal databases and access to all of the above, plus specialty databases such as Dissertation Abstracts, Medline (the library of the National Institutes of Health), PDQ (the National Cancer Institute Database), *Books in Print* and many others. If you have very specific needs and plan to do a lot of on-line research, it may be best to subscribe to the targeted service that best suits you; otherwise, CompuServe will let you avoid annual or start-up membership fees for the cost of its surcharge.

Q. I have an idea for a book that is going to require a lot of research and interviews with people from all over the country. Is there a way I can find someone who will do some of my research for pay, and are there persons in other cities I could contact for help?
A. Established book authors sometimes hire paid researchers to help them gather the raw information they need before they start to write. Newspaper editors can tell you if their policies permit any of their reporters to do extra off-hour freelance research. Editors and specialist reporters' names are listed in *Editor & Publisher Yearbook* geographically by newspaper. Most reporters are approachable—if they aren't facing a tight deadline. For persons who specialize in doing research, check ads in such publications as *Editor & Publisher, Literary Market Place* (under "Research & Information Services" and "Editorial Services"), and the classifieds in *Publishers Weekly,* and *Writer's Digest.* Rates of pay will vary according to experience, geographical area, and the nature of the work. Another possibility is to hire university students and library assistants. They can be knowledgeable in their field of specialization and will work for less money than full-time researchers. You can contact head librarians at public or college libraries either locally or in other cities where necessary, and ask if they can recommend some researchers to you. University or college financial aid offices are also likely sources of references.

Research and Writing

Q. I am currently working on a novel set in the eighteenth century. How do I go about researching it?
A. Everything in your fiction must be accurate and realistic. It isn't enough to create background details in your imagination, because a knowledgeable reader

might recognize a factual error and you'd lose credibility. Start your historical research with a relatively simple book on that period of world history or a general history of the country in which you've decided to set your novel. This will give you information about the time and the names of the period's important people.

Even if you're not writing about an actual historical figure, biographies can be a valuable source of information on the manners of the time.

To check on the customs, foods, clothing and technology of the time, novelist Roberta Gellis recommends *The Everyday Life* series. The series covers every historic period through the nineteenth century and every culture from ancient Egypt to the Vikings. More detailed books on certain areas, such as clothing and transportation, can be found at most libraries. Check the titles volume of *Books in Print* under *Everyday Life In* . . . (the specific country/time you're interested in). Also check *Subject Guide to Books in Print* under the country or historical figure around which your research is centered. Remember, however, that books might contain inaccurate information, so be sure to cross-check your research with other sources.

Q. *I'm doing some research using old, turn-of-the-century books and material from state archives, including some family papers. Can I use this material in my own manuscript? Would it be covered by copyright?*
A. Under the old (pre-1978) copyright law, copyright lasted for twenty-eight years and could be renewed for an additional twenty-eight. The new copyright law lengthened by nineteen years the renewal term of copyright on works that were in their renewed term when the law took effect. Thus, works already copyrighted and renewed as of January 1, 1978 are protected for a total of seventy-five years from the year of first publication. If that time has passed, the material would now be in the public domain and you could use it as you pleased, without first obtaining permission.

The state archives should pose no problem for you, if they aren't copyrighted. However, the family papers could possibly raise the question of invasion of privacy, if any members of the family or families survive. It would be a good idea for you to verify with any descendants whether they would object to your use of the material.

Q. *I'm researching an article and some of my sources disagree on several points. What can I do about this?*
A. One of the most difficult tasks of writing a nonfiction article or book is reconciling information received from different sources. In some cases, the writer's own prior research has given him enough knowledge about the subject or the backgrounds of his sources to judge who is right. But at other times, it becomes necessary for the writer to communicate conflicting information to the conflicting sources, letting each answer the questions raised by the other. For example, if you were writing about the effects of cigarette smoke on nonsmokers, and two researchers had given you contradictory statements, you could call or write each and say, "Dr. So-and-So of Such-and-Such University disagrees with your position (and quote the other expert). Could you comment on that?" By including such comments in

your finished piece, you allow readers to decide for themselves which source is credible. In some cases, both sources will be equally credible and readers will come to the conclusion that enough research has not yet been done on the subject to reach a firm conclusion.

Q. *Among several articles I hope to write is one of a very controversial nature. Even if an editor thinks the piece is interesting, he will likely want to be very sure of the authenticity of the source material—especially since I'm an unknown writer. How do I proceed?*
A. Most writers of controversial articles maintain a detailed list of their sources of information and have this ready for presentation to an editor who questions the author on any specific point. Send your article or query and advise the editor you'll be glad to provide verification on any points.

Q. *Is there such a thing as over-researching an article?*
A. The only way you can really over-research an article is by using further research as an excuse to avoid actually writing the piece. In other cases, the trick is not to research less, but to use your research wisely. Sometimes a writer will end up with a stack of material several inches thick and realizes she can never use it all. That's when she has to begin the long process of "weeding out" her information, choosing only the material most pertinent to her topic. Material she cannot use in the main article might shed some light on another angle of the subject or provide human interest. That material might be developed as a "sidebar"—a short feature accompanying an article to provide more depth or additional factual information that would not fit well into the body of the article. A writer could also use the material to write another article on the same subject, using a different approach and slanting it to another non-competing magazine. It's usually better to have too much information than not enough.

Q. *What are the opportunities for the would-be article writer who does not like to interview people?*
A. There are several kinds of magazine articles that do not necessarily require interviewing. Each of these can be completed with other types of research. The how-to article, for example, demonstrates or explains to the reader how to accomplish something, such as woodworking projects or sewing different types of clothing. Illustrations are often an integral part of how-to articles. The service article gives the reader information regarding the use or purchase of items, services or facilities. A guide to low-cost vacation spots or pointers on buying a used car would fit this category.

A writer can also base an article on his personal experiences. Such an article is designed to inspire, educate or entertain the reader. Writing about the experience of returning to college at age forty-five or making a career change are examples of this type of article. Your account of a personal struggle to get through a life-threatening experience or other human conflict can become a salable magazine article, for example, the "Drama in Real Life" series in *Reader's Digest*.

The think article analyzes facts, events or trends as the writer perceives them. The writer presents informed opinions, drawing conclusions intended to persuade the reader. Think articles appear in newspapers on the op-ed page and in the "quality" magazines, such as *The Atlantic* and *Harper's,* where, of course, your opinions would have to be buttressed by those of experts you had researched in periodicals, books, and perhaps through personal correspondence.

Different aspects of historical events can be covered in a light manner for popular magazines, or through in-depth research for scholarly publications. Many editors indicate their lack of interest in "routine historical pieces," but a well-written historical piece related to a magazine's content can sell almost any editor, providing the slant is right and the approach is fresh and lively.

The travel article has two objectives: to inform the reader by way of facts and to enlighten him by way of impressions. This type of article requires a certain amount of preliminary research and the writer must be perceptive enough to see the less conspicuous elements of the place he visits, such as the people, customs and atmosphere. Photos are an essential part of most travel pieces.

The humorous article, although one of the most difficult forms to write, can be one of the most financially rewarding. However, many writers of humor attain success only after years of experience.

Conducting interviews by mail is an alternative to the in-person interview, and can be used to glean enough information from an expert or celebrity to develop a salable article.

Q. *Is there any reason to keep interview notes and other research material after an article is finished?*
A. Many writers keep old research material for several reasons. They may need to answer questions from editors, readers or other writers who request information on the sources of the research. They may want to use the research for future articles. Depending on the type of research it is and how much further use the writer may have for it, most magazine writers save material for at least three to six years. Some newspaper reporters who are involved in investigative journalism have developed the practice of destroying their notes once they have served their purpose. This prevents the notes from being subpoenaed if the reporter is being questioned about his sources in an investigative piece.

In the Library

Q. *Most books now carry the legend: "No part of this book may be reproduced or utilized in any form or by any means, electronic or mechanical, including photocopying, recording, or by any information storage and retrieval system." Copying material long-hand when researching is tedious and time-consuming. Does the warning mean I can't copy material for my private research without first contacting the publisher?*
A. If the photocopy is for your research only, and you do not intend to reproduce the copied page in your article, then using the copy machine is as legal as taking

notes longhand. However, if you intend to quote much of the material verbatim in your manuscript, you will need permission. See the entry on "fair use" in chapter nine for additional guidelines.

Q. *Is there any way a library can find out if another library has a book I need?*
A. If your library has access to OCLC, yes. OCLC stands for Online Computer Library Center, a service which links the information centers of seven thousand businesses and institutions and five thousand public, private and special libraries in Australia, Belgium, Canada, China, Denmark, England, Finland, France, Iceland, Ireland, Japan, Mexico, Saudi Arabia, Sweden, Switzerland, West Germany and the U.S. It provides libraries with catalog card index files, helps them exchange information, and lends books to member libraries. OCLC's central office, in Dublin, Ohio, keeps record of more than 243 million location listings of library material. Its database contains material in 250 languages and dialects. It adds more than thirty thousand titles to its file every week.

To find a book, a librarian feeds a title into the OCLC terminal at the member library. The central computer gives the author's name, publication date, name of publisher, location of publisher, price and subject headings under which the title could be listed. The libraries having copies of the book are listed by codes. The librarian selects those libraries from which he desires borrowing privileges and makes arrangements to obtain the book for the patron. It can take a little time to get the book—four weeks or longer. If you need a book and don't mind waiting, OCLC could be beneficial to your research.

Q. *My local library doesn't have a book I need for my research. How can I get a copy of the book without buying it?*
A. Most libraries participate in a service called interlibrary loan. Through this service, a library can obtain a book from another library—a university library in the same or another city, a public library in another town or the Library of Congress. Charges for the service vary according to the requirements of the library providing the book. Ask your local librarian about this plan.

Chapter 9

How Much Can I Quote From Others' Work?

The rare occasion when one author sues another for plagiarism usually makes the headlines. The fact is, most writers — especially beginners — are scrupulous about getting permission and fairly attributing their sources when they borrow from another's copyrighted work. Here are some answers to questions about when, how much, and under what circumstances you can quote from others' work. Chapters eighteen and thirty-six cover questions on the related topics of copyright and other legal concerns.

The "Rules" of Quoting

Q. *In several articles I have written I quoted briefly from books written by doctors. In most cases I referred to the doctor by name, the title of his book and the publisher. How much can I quote without asking for special permission?*
A. There are no hard-and-fast rules on the "fair use of a copyrighted work," as the Copyright Act puts it. The act allows fair use for such purposes as criticism, teaching, scholarship or research. The law says four factors should be considered in determining if a use is "fair": the purpose and character of the use; the nature of the copyrighted work; the amount and substantiality of the portion used in relation to the entire work; and the effect of the use on the potential market for or value of the work. Court interpretations of the law provide little help in trying to state standards; most publishers (and their lawyers) have their own fair-use guidelines. Still, if you're picking up fewer than a hundred words from a full-length book, it's probably a fair use.

Q. *Is it necessary to get permission to reprint personal letters?*
A. Thoughts and ideas in personal letters are the property of the *sender*, not the receiver, so you must get permission for their publication. Personal letters may seem to belong to the person to whom they are sent, but to publish the letters, it is imperative to seek the letter-writer's permission in all cases. If you are interviewing someone by mail, this can be accomplished by enclosing a permission release form with your original letter to your subject. A statement such as "I give permission for

the publication of my letter to (So-and-So)," and an underscore with "Signature" typed under it usually will bring you a return of the letter-information and the written permission to use that information. Include this form even if your letter explains that your are writing an article or book concerning the subject of the information you're seeking.

Q. *What's the difference between a direct and an indirect quote?*
A. A direct quote is information presented in a source's exact words, enclosed in quotation marks. An indirect quote is information paraphrased by the writer. In other words, direct quotes present information verbatim, while indirect quotes present the *substance* of the information, rewritten to shorten it or make it more precise. When using indirect quotation, the writer must be careful that his paraphrase doesn't distort or misrepresent the original intent of the remarks. For example, if you were to quote a source directly, the form would be as follows: In answer to a question about U.S. monetary policy, the President said, "Well, you'd have to check with the chairman of the Federal Reserve System about that." But an indirect quote would read: In answer to a question about U.S. monetary policy, the president referred reporters to the chairman of the Federal Reserve System.

Q. *I am in the process of writing an exposé-type book. Since the materials I plan to expose are copyrighted, obviously I cannot quote from them without permission of the authors. I doubt that any author would consent to my using his material to prove a point against himself. How do I go about doing this legally?*
A. Remember that copyright protects only the exact wording of a passage. One way of accomplishing your goal without needing permission might be to paraphrase those authors' remarks, using footnotes to indicate their source.

Q. *When quoting from another source, may I omit surplus words such as "the," abbreviate or engage in other editing without using distracting dots to indicate such minor deletions?*
A. The fact that a verbatim quote has been edited should, in all fairness, be indicated primarily to show readers that this is not exactly the way the original author wrote it. The use of the ellipsis (three dots) is the accepted practice, and not usually considered distracting.

Q. *If material is paraphrased from a published source (for example, a magazine or a book), is it enough to mention the source in the bibliography or must written permission be obtained from the publisher of the original material?*
A. It depends on how extensive the material is that you are paraphrasing from the original published source. If the material is presented in only a paragraph or two, you need only to refer to the source with the standard "According to (the book *Title* by *Author*) . . ." or "in the (month, year) issue of (magazine), So-and-So states. . . ." If, however, what you are writing, in substance, deals exclusively with material quoted or taken from the original source, you must obtain written permis-

sion in addition to mentioning the source in the bibliography.

Q. *I've finished writing a novel of truth in fictional form centered around the life of a doctor, and the book includes lots of facts and quotes. Names are mentioned in actual quotes. But I cannot give proper credit for some other items because my clippings were destroyed. How should I handle the use of people's names and quotes?*
A. If you're using actual names in your novel, you'd better make sure you have permission, in case one of those persons decides to sue you for invasion of privacy, even if whatever you are quoting is not libelous. Otherwise, change the names, as well as the appearance and locale of the characters so they are not readily identifiable as real persons.

Q. *If I lift paragraphs or short quotations from published, copyrighted sources and duplicate and sell these for a profit, would that be a violation of copyright laws? I plan to start a service in the field of religion, which consists of short-length abstracts, extracts, quotations, mini-bibliographies, and how-to-do-it ideas taken from other published sources.*
A. As long as you credit the source and pick up only "short-length" copy, it probably will come under the fair-use provision of the copyright law. A rule of thumb in deciding how much copy you can use without permission from a copyrighted publication is this: "Am I impairing the fair market value of the original by the amount of copy I'm using?" Past writers in the field of religious writing were once very lenient in giving permission. Today's religious writers protect their copyrighted work and expect the same treatment as other writers.

Q. *What rules govern the use by writers of quotes and information gained from TV broadcasts? As a feature writer with an extensive clipping file, I have taken notes on some programs and speakers covering topics on which I am collecting information and leads into further research.*
A. Generally speaking, if you accurately attribute your information to the proper source, you shouldn't run into any legal difficulty. In the case of direct quotations of *any length,* it might be best to write to the network or to the speaker, requesting permission to use the particular quotes.

Seeking Permission

Q. *If I quote from a copyrighted source, should I get permission from the publisher and explain to him what material I'm using and how I'm using it?*
A. If you intend to quote at length from a copyrighted source, writing the publisher for permission is necessary, and, of course, when writing the publisher, you should specify exactly what words on which pages the permission is being requested for. If you use a *great deal* of copy from the source, then an explanation of how you plan to use the material is important. Most sources who are being quoted at length want to see the context in which their words appear, and while it probably won't

be necessary to send each person you quote a copy of your entire article, you should send them, for example, a copy of the page before and the page after the quote, and mention in your cover letter the thrust of your article. The context, length, and purpose of your material will also determine any fee that might be required.

Q. *Is it the responsibility of the author or the book publisher to obtain releases for the use of published material? How does a writer go about doing this?*
A. Although some book publishers obtain releases, most feel it's the job of the writer to do so after the final manuscript has been accepted. Releases are usually obtained from the author of a work by writing him in care of his publisher. Letters of request to reprint material are sent to the publisher, who either acts in behalf of the author or forwards the request to him for his action. The author, of course, should make copies of the letters asking for permission and forward those to his publisher, along with copies of the letters of permission received.

If permissions fees are required, the author should not pay them until the work is published—in case some items are cut in the editing process and not used.

Q. *How much do publishers usually charge for reprint permissions and to quote from their copyrighted material?*
A. If the use of the material is incidental, obtaining permission usually does not entail a fee and is sometimes unnecessary. For instance, if a novelist introduces a chapter with a few lines from another book or if a nonfiction writer quotes a paragraph from a work by an authority in the field, this would usually be considered "fair use" for which permission is not required.

If a writer is editing an anthology of fiction or a collection of articles, however, he may be required to pay permission fees to various copyright holders. These fees vary considerably. An anthology of poetry or plays could run over $15,000 in permission fees. The matter of who is to accept responsibility for paying permission fees must be settled before beginning work on a book, and is generally included in the contract. Costs may be shared with the author up to an agreed upon maximum on the publisher's part—or charged to the author completely—by deducting those costs before royalties are paid. (For further information on editing anthologies, see chapter thirty-one.)

Q. *I completed an article on assignment for a magazine. When they offered to buy it, a letter accompanying the "author contract" stated that I needed to obtain permission from the publisher of a book I quoted from. I contacted the book publisher and learned that a fee is required for using the quotes. How do I pass along this fee to the editor who is buying the article, knowing that the contract was already drawn up requesting me to obtain permission from the publisher?*
A. Phone the editor. Discuss who pays such expenses *before* you sign the contract, if possible. If the contract has been returned already, send the editor a copy of the fee request and ask if he can reimburse you on this unanticipated expense. If he says no, you can still use the material. Rephrase it completely, not using direct

quotes, and still give credit to the publisher — including title and author of the book from which the information was taken. (If, for example, the material you wish to use reads, "this colorful and delightful creature succumbs to the urge to procreate annually, when vernal rains break the back of winter." you might say, "Professor Pompous, in his *Life and Loves of the Scarlet Tanager*, notes that these birds mate each spring.") If the quotes are extensive and vital to your article, though, it's best to pay the permission fee if the editor refuses to.

Q. *Some friends and I want to publish a magazine for students. How can we obtain permission to reprint an article that previously appeared in another magazine?*
A. In order to reprint the article you will have to write to the editor of the publication in which it first appeared. Depending on whether or not that magazine purchased only first rights or all rights to the article, the editor may or may not be able to grant you permission to reprint. If he only bought first rights, he will give you the address of the author or forward your letter requesting reprint permission. In most cases, you can expect to pay the author for the use of the material you are reprinting. If the editor purchased all rights, you may have to pay a reprint fee to the magazine, but this is negotiable.

Q. *I'm writing a play in which I want to use about half a page of material from a book published several years ago. Do I have to obtain the publisher's permission for this? I can't have footnotes mixed in with the dialogue, so how should I give credit?*
A. The amount of material you are using is probably small enough that you should not need to write in advance to get the author or publisher's permission to use it. However, you should give attribution to the source. Make sure the program for any production of the play gives credit to the original source, and of course, if the play is published, credit should appear in the published version also.

Q. *In compiling a cookbook, I am taking recipes from newspapers and magazines, as well as from pamphlets put out by companies that manufacture the various ingredients. What procedure should I follow to get permission to use this material? Some of the older recipes I've saved don't show where they appeared originally.*
A. Generally, the list of ingredients in a recipe cannot be copyrighted, but the written directions can. If you take a recipe from a food company pamphlet, and it's not copyrighted, that should pose no difficulty. But if the recipe comes from a copyrighted magazine, then the material is protected by copyright law. Successful cookbooks are generally compiled by excellent cooks who have tried intriguing recipes, adapted them to their own style of cooking, and in the process developed a new recipe. Ingredients are altered and the directions completely rewritten. When original sources of recipes are unknown to you, alter the ingredients and completely rewrite the directions.

May I Use . . . ?

Q. *Is it permissible to quote directly from a document issued by the United States Government Printing Office? I have never been able to discover whether that material is copyrighted or how credit should be given. Many of the leaflets would be very useful incorporated in articles or books or as research for an article. Do our taxes, which pay for printing these items, give us the right to appropriate the words?*

A. Yes, materials published by the government are in the public domain. There are a few minor exceptions—some connected with the post office and some exceptions in which copyrighted material is inserted in an uncopyrighted public domain government publication. Such material would be accompanied by the printed copyright notice. If you have any doubts about whether a specific leaflet you want to use is copyrighted or not, the presence or absence of the copyright notice is your guideline. Even though you are legally free to use materials from government publications, you should cite the source so that both your publisher and the reader will know where your information came from.

Q. *Can I quote from the Bible without being concerned with copyright infringement?*

A. Yes, you can quote anything from the King James Version, which is in public domain. However, most modern translations such as *The Living Bible, The Holy Bible: New International Version, A Reader's Guide to The Holy Bible: Revised Standard Version, Jerusalem Bible,* and *Reader's Digest Bible* are under copyright and permission is needed. To quote from these later versions in articles you write for the general market, treat them as you would any book: Write for the original publisher's requirements, request permission to use the material, and give a proper credit line. The *New International Version* allows quotation of up to 1,000 verses without written permission. (Proper credit is required; it's on the copyright page of the *NIV*.) Many religious magazine and book publishers have standard arrangements with the Bible copyright owners, and already have permission, in which case you, as a writer, might wish to check with the editor you hope to sell to before requesting permission on your own.

Q. *I have access to a number of brochures and pamphlets about a topic I want to use as the subject of a syndicated weekly newspaper column. Is it all right to use these pamphlets as my resource material—I will use other material too—and should I write the publisher of the brochures for permission? The brochures do not carry a copyright notice.*

A. If you intend to use the pamphlets as your major resource, then a credit to the publisher—as a matter of ethics, not copyright—is certainly in order. But it usually is not necessary to request permission to use uncopyrighted material.

Q. *I'm writing an article in which I quote from a newspaper article about a university study. Is it permissible to quote or paraphrase the general findings of such a study, as well as a statement about the findings from the researcher, who was also interviewed*

in the newspaper article?
A. Quoting the general findings of the study should pose no problem; however, if you go into any detail, it would be advisable to obtain a copy of the study and quote directly from that. As far as quoting the researcher, you should check the quotes with the source. Newspaper stories produced on a tight deadline will sometimes include errors in quoting people, so it would be a good idea for you to go back to the source and make sure you quote him correctly.

Q. *For an article I'm writing, I want to use some statistics I found in a recent issue of* Reader's Digest. *If I quote from the article directly, should I write* The Digest *for permission, or can I paraphrase the material without obtaining permission?*
A. You should not need written permission to use brief statistical material from *Reader's Digest*—or any other publication—as long as you cite the source of your information in the article. Whether you quote the source verbatim or paraphrase, you should always acknowledge the original source of the material. If you intend to use *The Digest* article extensively when you write your article, then you must obtain written permission.

Q. *I have written a poem utilizing characters and themes from a novel that was published a few years ago. Do I need permission from the author or publisher of the original novel to do this?*
A. You may feel free to use the *themes* from the novel, since they are uncopyright-able. Characters, however, are a different matter. If a character—and especially a character's name—is associated with a particular work in the public mind, then the question arises of infringement of the author's right to adapt his own work to other forms. Recently, Warner Brothers, producers of the *Superman* movies, sued ABC-TV, claiming that its *The Greatest American Hero* series infringed on the Superman copyright because the series featured a flying hero with a red cape and x-ray vision who used the same arms-extended flying position as the Superman character. In a similar case, a Los Angeles woman sued *E.T.* director Steven Spielberg for $750 million of the film's profits, claiming she originated the idea in a copyrighted one-act play. Although a Manhattan federal judge rejected Warner Brothers' claims, the studio appealed the decision. The *E.T.* case was eventually dismissed. Even if you successfully fought an allegation that you had stolen a character, the legal fees could be astronomical. It's always safer to write for permission before you begin a work based on characters from already published sources.

Q. *I have been sending an article each week to a newspaper in which I use a poem (not composed by me) along with Scripture and a few words of my own. Am I allowed to use these poems?*
A. If these poems come from books, for example, whose copyright is still in effect, you will definitely need permission to quote them. You need no permission if the poems are from uncopyrighted sources.

Q. *In an original poem, I have written, "Good will upon earth, peace among men," which is based on the well-quoted phrase, "Peace on earth, good will to men." Is this legal?*

A. The line you're paraphrasing is already in public domain, so you don't have to worry on *that* score. For more current phrases that might have copyright or trademark protection, it would be advisable to completely reword the material.

Q. *Can I quote personalities whose statements are included in daily newspaper columns? Where can I obtain permission to quote? From the author? From the newspaper? Or from the columnist? I collect inspirational sayings and want to publish this material in a book.*

A. Since news cannot be copyrighted, if you are using quotations that are in *news* stories about personalities, you would not have to request permission, assuming that the quotations were accurately recorded by reporters and not of a nature that the personality would subsequently sue for inaccuracy. Many newspaper features and columns, however, are covered by copyright and you would not be able to use quotations from these without requesting permission from the newspaper or the syndicate.

Q. *Many books have statements similar to the following: All rights reserved. No part of this book may be reproduced in any form without written permission from the publisher, except for brief passages included in a review appearing in a newspaper or magazine. May brief passages be quoted by reviewers in their reviews from books that do not bear similar statements?*

A. Yes, even though books do not make this statement, reviewers may quote briefly from them under the "fair use" provision of the copyright law.

Q. *Can I quote from work that appears in an uncopyrighted magazine without obtaining the author's or the publisher's permission?*

A. Although legally this material is in the public domain and permission is not necessary, it would be a courtesy to the original author to request permission to use any sizable amount of the material.

Q. *Can an author take from one of his own published stories a sentence, a phrase, a simile — or anything for that matter — for use in another story?*

A. The use of only a sentence, a phrase, or a simile from your original story shouldn't present any ethical problems. The only prohibition would be the risk of having some alert readers tag you as belonging to that *New Yorker* category known as the "Infatuation with sound of own words" department!

Q. *Is it okay for me to take a couple hundred words from a previous book of mine and use it in a new one?*

A. No, unless the necessary permission has been obtained from the first publisher.

Also, editors generally do not like the idea of authors using old material in a new book.

Q. *In my story it would help add realism to use the titles of a few currently popular songs, and some snatches of the lyrics being played by a band or coming from the juke box. Would it be necessary to get permission or give credit for this use?*
A. If you're going to quote directly from the lyrics, you will definitely need the music publisher's permission. A list of publishers of current popular songs appears in the charts of best-selling records in music magazines such as *Billboard* and *Cashbox.*

Q. *A cartoon I have recently completed has a line from a popular song as the caption. Do I need to obtain permission for the line?*
A. Such use of a line from a popular song could be dangerous. Songwriters and poets are often fiercely protective of their copyrights, so when using their material it is always safest to query the copyright owners for permission.

Q. *If I only mention the title, do I have to have permission from the song publisher? And what about old songs I quote from memory, like ballads or nursery rhymes? Must I locate the publisher and ask permission? I plan to use quotes from some old lumberjack ballads and a few songs popular ten or fifteen years ago. I don't think a music store could help much on songs that old, could it?*
A. Since titles are not copyrightable, you may mention a song title without having to get the song publisher's permission. As for old familiar folk ballads and nursery rhymes, if they are all older than seventy-five years they are in the public domain and can be used by anyone, without obtaining permission. In the case of songs popular about fifteen years ago, however, their copyright will not have run out yet so you probably need permission. Check for the publisher of older popular songs by title in a directory called the *Variety Music Cavalcade,* available in most public libraries.

Q. *Can I use titles of television shows, books and movies in a general way? How about brand names?*
A. Yes, since titles are not copyrightable, you are free to refer to them in your writing. Brand names may also be used, as long as they are not used in a derogatory manner. Some companies, such as Coca-Cola and Xerox, object to their brand names being used generically since that jeopardizes their trademark. (An example of the usage trademark owners object to, but many writers seem to sometimes consider necessary to believable dialogue, would be to refer to a cola drink as a "Coke.")

Chapter 10

What's the Secret of a Good Interview?

When you need to learn something—be it facts for your articles or background for your short stories—the answers are probably just an interview away. Your interviews may be long, relaxed discussions or confrontational exchanges, but no two will be identical. What follows are general guidelines for planning and conducting fruitful interviews. For more detailed information, see *The Writer's Complete Guide to Conducting Interviews* by Michael Schumacher (Writer's Digest Books) and *The Craft of Interviewing* by John Brady (Vintage Books. It's out of print, but well worth the search).

Overcoming Fears

Q. *I am interested in writing magazine articles, but the thought of interviewing someone scares me. I know I have to interview to write successfully. How can I teach myself this method of gathering information?*
A. It is common for many beginning writers to feel uneasy about interviewing. One way to combat this feeling is to begin writing about topics that will permit you to interview people you already know and with whom you feel comfortable talking. For instance, an article about how parents handle their children's problems would permit you to interview a variety of friends, neighbors and relatives. If you live in a small town, talking to the local shopkeepers can give you information on how changes in economic conditions affect the small business owners. Working on these types of articles will give you the experience of interviewing and help build your confidence to handle tougher subjects.

Interviewing is a skill that grows with time and practice. Remember that your job is to *listen* to the conversation and keep it flowing without monopolizing it. Prepare your questions before you interview and try to design them so that your interviewee will do most of the talking, and you will soon begin to feel more confident in your abilities.

Q. *I'm a beginner with no credits. Why would an expert agree to be interviewed by me?*
A. An expert is only recognized as such by being visible and making his opinions

known. That means, in part, being available to be interviewed. So it is in the expert's interest to be interviewed by writers. Most people you interview will be flattered that you're interested in their opinon and will not ask about your credentials. If they do ask, explain that you are a new writer. Be confident and do not apologize for your lack of experience. (Your expert was a beginner once, too.)

You'll also encounter less resistance if you've gotten an expression of interest from a specific magazine before approaching your subject. Still, some sources may choose not to grant you an interview. But you'll be surprised at the number of "important" people who are willing to talk with you.

Before the Interview

Q. *What is the protocol for arranging an interview?*
A. For an in-person interview, phone the subject for an appointment. If the subject does not return your calls, send a short note introducing yourself, requesting an interview, and telling him you will call on a specific date to set up a meeting. In setting a date and time, be ready to be flexible. You will need to accommodate your subject's schedule.

For a phone interview, follow the same procedure — but be prepared to conduct the interview on the spot should your subject say, "How about right now?"

Q. *What are the best places to conduct an interview?*
A. You want to find a quiet setting where you can talk without frequent interruptions. Your subject's office — if he has one — can fit in the bill, but may also be full of distractions. Office conference rooms, hotel lobbies and meeting rooms, libraries, parks, and quiet cocktail lounges are all good possibilities. Restaurants may prove too distracting to maintain the conversation (also, clattering silverware and the talking of other diners may render your tape recording indecipherable).

Q. *Should I query an editor before or after I ask the interviewee for his or her permission to be interviewed? And what should I do if I can't deliver an article because my interviewee wouldn't grant me an interview?*
A. It is best to first get an editor's okay on an interview assignment before asking the subject for an interview. A subject is more willing to give you the time for an interview if he knows an editor is seeking the interview for his pages. But it can be done either way — if a subject is willing to be interviewed without a commitment from an editor, you can also work that way. If a subject refuses to give you the interview, just drop a note to the editor and say that the interview was refused. Editors understand this. If a subject refuses the interview because you *don't* have an editor interested yet, then tell the editor this, also. He may then give you a firm assignment for the interview.

Q. *How much research do I need to do for an interview?*
A. The late historian Cornelius Ryan claimed that one of the rules of writing was,

"Never interview anyone without knowing 60 percent of the answers." He said that the person being interviewed has done *his* homework, so the writer should be equally prepared. Research is the best way to discover what you need to learn in the interview and the best way to get it. Some interviewers recommend ten minutes of research for every minute of the planned interview. That may sound like a lot of work, but it's always better to be over-prepared than to run out of questions before you run out of time.

The main purpose of research is to enable yourself to talk and ask questions intelligently on any topic the interviewee raises. If you've obviously taken the time to do your research, the interviewee will expect an intelligent discussion of the subject, which is always more interesting for an interviewee than talking to someone about a topic on which he is uninformed.

To research an interview, you will use many of the same techniques discussed in chapters seven and eight. You should research the interviewee's background and any topics you think might be discussed. For a profile, interview *around* the subject, talking to friends, family and co-workers to learn more about the person before you actually meet him.

Researching for an interview takes time and you may not make use of even half the information you gather. But a thorough knowledge of the subject can help you ask good, specific questions and get the quotes that will make your article more lively and salable.

Q. *After I finish research for an interview, is it necessary to write a list of questions before the interview takes place? How many questions?*
A. By deciding on a particular list of "must-ask" questions, the interviewer makes sure he doesn't conclude the interview without obtaining all the necessary information for the article. However, the interviewer should pursue any interesting path down which his subject wanders; the list of prepared questions is a set of boundaries, rather than a hard-and-fast road map. In John Brady's *The Craft of Interviewing*, freelancer Edward Linn says, "The list of questions and the logical sequence invariably disappear very quickly. If they don't, you're in trouble."

To decide on a list of questions, first choose your angle — or let your editor tell you what he has in mind. Then look at your research and decide what you must learn from the interviewee. The number of questions you need will vary, depending on the topic of the article, the interviewee, and in some cases, the amount of time an interviewee allows. The more questions you prepare, though, the better chance of leaving the interview with the essential answers plus additional interesting information.

Structure the outline of the interview to follow a logical course. You might open with easy, mechanical questions, such as those that would establish the interviewee's relation to or view of the topic; then moving on to knottier, more thoughtful probes, such as asking what he thinks about someone else's particular criticism of his actions or point of view; then moving back to the mechanical, and ending with a query such as, "Is there anything else we've not talked about that you'd like to comment on?" This process gives the interview, and your article, a sense of direction and structure, and keeps you in charge.

In the Interview

Q. *What are some good techniques to remember when I'm conducting an interview? How can I make sure the interview is productive and interesting for both myself and the subject?*

A. First, try to build rapport with the interviewee. This serves two purposes: It not only makes your subject feel more at ease and more receptive to questions, but it can help relax *you* and keep the interview flowing smoothly. Be a little formal at the start, rather than jumping into familiarity right away. Don't take liberties you wouldn't want a guest of yours to take; this includes smoking and handling objects in the interviewee's office or home. First impressions count, so dress in such a way that you don't draw attention to yourself.

Don't talk too much at the outset. Encourage the interviewee to do as much of the talking as possible. Be flexible and follow the subject's lead. If an answer is very general, don't interrupt, but follow it up. Follow-up questions not only secure specific details and anecdotes, they reveal a lot about the interviewee's personality and bolster rapport by demonstrating your genuine interest in what he has to say. Reciting an anecdote you have previously heard about the subject will often nudge the interviewee into providing further human interest comments; this can often provide you with a good anecdote to open or close your article.

Don't overlook your article's need for specific details, anecdotes and examples. You must request these comments directly. Ask such leading questions as: "What did he look like?", "Can you tell me about the first time that happened to you?", "Do you remember a time that strategy worked for you?" Playing dumb can provide depth to your interview. When a subject rambles or is unclear, place the onus on yourself by saying, "I'm sorry, but I don't quite understand that last point. Could you explain it for me?"

Q. *Sometimes when I'm setting up interviews for an article I encounter people who are reluctant to talk about even the most innocuous of topics. The material isn't particularly controversial; they just aren't used to being interviewed and don't know what to do. How do I handle these shy interviewees?*

A. Celebrities are quite used to the questions put to them by interviewers, but business-people, scholars, doctors, and other people who are not often interviewed may be fearful of being misinterpreted. Sympathy to the subject's quandary, friendly understanding and professional performance on your part can overcome barriers. Your best response to an executive's reluctance is to point out positive effects of the article, such as complimenting the firm's managerial style and introducing its products and services to other customers. The article might also be reprinted for distribution to colleagues, stockholders and salesmen. It is sometimes helpful—if you can accomplish it—to avoid the public relations department of a large corporation and direct your request to the top. The executive may get back to you quickly or ask his PR department to do so.

Scholars and physicians can also be reluctant subjects, since many of them view publicity as unprofessional. When faced with this attitude, point out the need for public information in the subject's area of expertise. Your interest and sincere enthusiasm can be the catalysts that will spark the interviewee into sharing her knowledge.

Persistence pays off. If you become a more or less ubiquitous presence around a busy subject, you may find that he will make time for the interview in his packed schedule. John Brady tells of tracking down author Jessica Mitford at a university seminar. By "hanging around a lot," he found the right time to get the interview; although her schedule was filled each minute of the seminar, he drove her to the airport and got the interview on the way. Recommendations from friends and co-workers of reluctant interviewees can also be an aid to getting the time with them.

If none of these techniques work and the interview is necessary to the story, tell the subject that his comments are crucial to the story and he probably will appear in the article anyway, but you'd rather get his opinions firsthand.

Touchy Topics

Q. *How do I interview someone about information he might be reluctant to discuss?*
A. Making the cross into sensitive territory can be a delicate process. You know you need the information, but find it difficult to broach the subject without losing the interviewee's confidence. The tenuous path to sensitive information can only be traveled with patience and subtlety.

Each writer will find her own methods of dealing with each reluctant interviewee, but there are a few tried-and-true methods that will work in many situations. You could blame the question on someone else, such as asking an allegedly corrupt politician, "There are those who claim you do some 'creative accounting' with the budget. Since you've heard these allegations, would you like to respond to your critics?" A playful approach—"Let me play devil's advocate . . ."—can often place the question in a framework that makes it easier for your subject to answer. Prefacing a sensitive question with some praise for your interviewee can cushion the blow and make him more responsive.

Imply that you know more about a situation than you do; the interviewee may discuss the topic with you as if you know all about it and he's only filling you in on details. For example, if you wanted a government employee to admit he had awarded a contract to a company in which he owned 25 percent interest, you might ask, "When did you obtain one fourth of the Q.E.D. Corporation?" Merely asking if he actually owned the share of the business could result in his denial.

Asking a question in a straightforward, matter-of-fact way, no matter how sensitive the area, may elicit a response when all else fails. If the interviewee *still* does not respond, point out the gap in information and tell him that, in the eyes of the reader, silence can be more damaging, since it can lead to speculation on the answer.

The manner in which you cover sensitive material can influence how much information the interviewee will give you, says veteran writer Hayes Jacobs, author of *Writing and Selling Non-Fiction.* "If you manage to extract a gem that has been under lock and key, don't pounce at your notes and act as if you'd just captured the enemy's general; such lack of restraint can cause your subject to say something like, 'Oh, but—uh—maybe you'd better not print that.' Just show normal interest, not wild delight that would distract, worry or even frighten your subject."

Q. *When a subject wants to talk "off the record," should I accept or turn him down? Do anonymous sources lessen the quality of an article?*
A. Within certain limits, using "off the record" sources can be helpful to a writer, but the writer should make sure he and his source understand the ground rules for their interview. (Some writers refuse to take "off the record" information, since they may already have it from another source and it might seem they violated the ground rules.) There are two ways a source can talk off the record. He can request total anonymity, talking only to give the reporter background information; in such cases, the source is never to be quoted in the article. A source can also agree to talk "not for attribution." This means he is willing to give information for use in the article, but doesn't want his name mentioned; he can be quoted or paraphrased, but the material is attributed to "a source close to the scene," "a high-ranking official," "a veteran observer," or some other such tag.

Anonymous sources can provide the writer of an article with incisive, revealing information which he otherwise might not have been able to obtain. But there are dangers inherent in using off-the-record sources. You could conceivably hide the names of sources that should be identified to make your article complete and credible. Also, sometimes anonymity can become an excuse for a subject to grind his particular ax without fear of retribution. Check what your anonymous sources tell you, and if a source gives you information, makes charges, or provides descriptions that he cannot document, ask him to go on the record.

You can go back to him after you check out his statements, point out that another source disputed his charges and ask him to clarify his position for the record.

Q. *If I only have a few minutes of an interviewee's time, how can I get the information I need?*
A. The tightly scheduled interview makes the job more difficult in a couple of ways. Not only do you have a time limit on getting the information, you must dispense with much of the preliminary conversation that can build rapport and good will with the interviewee. Cutting the chitchat must be done carefully, however; you don't want to seem abrupt or rude, which could affect the interviewee's receptiveness to questioning.

When you're interviewing "under the gun" you should have your questions arranged in descending order of importance when the interview begins. This practice will ensure your getting as much pertinent information as you can in the time allotted. Take a gamble with your last few questions, making them more thought-provoking so that the subject is interested and permits the interview time to run longer.

To supplement your brief notes, you can, at the end of the conversation, request a more detailed interview by mail. The way to conduct a mail interview is discussed elsewhere in this chapter.

Q. *I need the opinions of average people for several articles I'm working on. Do I just walk up to people on the street and ask them? Do you have to have some sort of credentials? Do you have to name them in an article, or are you not supposed to name them?*

A. Yes, many freelance writers just walk up to people at a shopping mall or other public place and ask if they can interview them briefly for some research material they are seeking. No, you don't need any credentials, although it sometimes helps if you open the conversation by saying something like, "I'm a freelance writer researching an article on [topic] for [name of magazine]. May I ask you a few questions?" Whether you name them in the article or not depends on how you write the article. For example, if you write, "Sally Jones, a twenty-year veteran teacher in inner-city schools had this to say about merit pay increases in teacher salaries . . .," it might have more credibility than if you just referred to "One Chicago veteran teacher. . . ."

Q. *I can't afford to travel to conduct all my interviews in person. Can't I get the same information just as easily by phone? What are the advantages and disadvantages of this method?*

A. Telephone interviewing prevents the writer from observing his subject's mannerisms and surroundings; for this reason, in-person interviews are usually best. Nevertheless, interviewing someone by telephone can be useful in various situations. When you need only one key source and the subject is too far away for you to meet in person before your deadline, telephoning can get the quote you need in the least amount of time. Interviewing by phone can also be helpful when many sources are scattered far and wide. The practice even has a couple of advantages over face-to-face questioning. Many times, a subject will be willing to talk more freely if he can't watch you taking notes. Also, even the difficult subject who won't answer the door when he hears you knock will answer the telephone's insistent ring.

When interviewing by phone, always have your note-taking apparatus and your reference material nearby. If you use a tape recorder, advise the subject in advance. Remember the value of good telephone manners; be prepared to identify yourself and the publication for which you are writing, and also to answer some preliminary questions from a secretary or assistant to gain access to your subject. Keep track of differences in time zones when calling long distance, since a call made at 9 A.M. EST would rouse a Californian at 6 A.M. Remember, too, to handle names, titles and numbers with special care, to avoid errors that might result from the sound distortion inherent in talking over the telephone. Double-check this information by mail immediately.

At the end of the phone conversation, thank the subject and advise him that you might need to call again for follow-up questions, or to fill in any gaps you find after you've transcribed your notes. Be sure to give the interviewee your phone number so he can reach you with any additional information or afterthoughts about your article.

Interviews can be conducted by mail, too, as explained elsewhere in this chapter.

Q. *I've heard that some writers conduct interviews by mail. How good is this practice and how do I go about it?*

A. Although a limited substitute for the in-person interview, mail interviewing can be beneficial to the freelance writer. It can save time, especially if you need to ask many people the same questions. For example, if you were doing an article on defense spending and how it affects social programs and wanted to ask the members of the U.S. Senate for their views, mail interviewing would be one way to get a lot of their opinions in a very brief time. This would also save you money, eliminating the need for travel and long-distance telephoning.

To conduct a mail interview, query your subjects in a covering letter, rather than only sending them the questionnaire and requesting their response. Your query should be personal, explaining the nature of your project, and the name of the publication interested in your article. Your correspondence should be neatly typed. Since your letter is your only communication with your subject and serves to represent you, it could influence his willingness to answer your questions. If you are sending a number of people the same questionnaire, make good-quality photocopies and always include a personal cover letter. Make sure your questions are thoughtful and succinct and leave ample space for replies. Give your phone number and tell interviewees to feel free to call you collect if a question needs clarification or talking to you is more convenient. Tell your subjects that you have a deadline, requesting that they reply within two weeks, if possible. Always include SASEs for their replies.

Examine the replies for any possible follow-up questions that are necessary or that might provide additional, provocative answers, then write the subject(s) at once. If a subject does not return the questionnaire within two weeks, send a photocopy of the original letter and list of questions, along with a note suggesting that perhaps your original request was lost in the mail or misplaced in the shuffle of paperwork. Give a gentle prod that will not offend the interviewee, reminding him you still have a few days to meet your deadline and would appreciate any help he could give you.

Getting It on Tape

Q. *When conducting an interview, which is better—a tape recorder or written notes?*

A. Taping your interviews can allow you to ask more questions in less time and concentrate more on the replies you receive, listening for possible follow-ups. If the subject matter is at all controversial, a tape-recorded interview is your proof that an interviewee said what he said in the context being quoted. If you must interview a subject in a situation where it would be difficult for you to take notes, such as over lunch, a tape recorder can be a real lifesaver. Most reporters caution against relying *too* much on the tape recorder and suggest augmenting it with some note-taking. This can help you note where in the interview a subject says something particularly provocative or relevant. Taking highlight notes is also insurance in case the recorder or tape breaks down. Keep your interview tapes and notes in a safe place after an article has been published. An editor may need them after publication if an interviewee claims, "I've been misquoted."

(For more information on use of tape recorders, see chapter eight. Chapter four contains information on choosing a good tape recorder.)

Q. *I would like to use a tape recorder when I interview. Should I ask the interviewee beforehand if he minds, or should I simply plop it down without a word, turn it on, and proceed with the interview as if it didn't exist?*
A. It's more courteous to ask him first if he minds your using the tape recorder to make sure his statements are recorded as accurately as possible. Few interviewees will object. With experience you'll learn how to approach each interviewee with the idea. To learn how professional magazine writers have used the tape recorder in interviews, you might want to see their comments in *The Craft of Interviewing,* by John Brady.

Q. *I have a small gadget that records telephone conversations. When I conduct a phone interview, do I have to inform the person that he's being taped?*
A. Yes, that is always the safest course of action. Some states have telephone company tariffs that prohibit taping unless the party being called is notified in advance or there is a recorder connector with a beeptone every 15 seconds. Advising an interviewee that the conversation is being tape-recorded for the sake of accuracy and recording his agreement on tape at the beginning of the conversation is the best defense against later problems. Some states, such as Pennsylvania and Maryland, have laws *requiring* that both parties consent to the tape-recording of a conversation that takes place within the state. No federal law prohibits taping of telephone conversations by either party as long as the taping is not being done for an illegal purpose, but some national publications, such as *Newsweek,* have written policies prohibiting surreptitious taping of interviews.

Source Concerns

Q. *Should I ask my interview subjects to sign a realease?*
A. As a rule of thumb, no. If you identify yourself as a writer or reporter, and the subject agrees to speak with you, it is understood that he is consenting to the publication of his comments.

There are rare occasions when you might wish to have the subject sign a release in which he agrees to the publication of his comments, gives you permission to edit the manuscript and sell it to an editor, and waives any right of inspection or approval of the edited manuscript. Such occasions might be interviews regarding extremely controversial or sensitive material.

Q. *If I write a profile, must I pay the subject?*
A. Not usually. The question will rarely arise if you're interviewing a local business-man for a trade publication or a friend or neighbor for a crafts magazine. If it does, you should tell the subject that publications don't pay interviewees, other than perhaps providing complimentary copies of the article when it is published.

However, some writers and editors — including the television program *60 Minutes* — have paid for certain interviews in the past and consider the practice a good investment. When a freelancer receives a request for payment to an interview subject, he should discuss it with the editor who gave the go-ahead for the piece.

Q. *I called to set up an interview for an article on which I am currently working, but the subject told me he'd only agree to see me if he could see his quotes before the article went to press. What should I do in a situation like this?*
A. Unless the particular interviewee is essential to your article, it is best to tell him sorry, professional writers don't do that. There are a few times when it becomes necessary for a writer to allow his interviewee to see the manuscript before it is printed. When dealing with scientific, technical or medical topics, the writer may need the subject to check the facts and figures to make sure they are accurate. If the interviewee is your key source, then it may be necessary to agree to his review of the manuscript to get the interview. But the writer should make clear to any subject with whom he has such an agreement that the article is submitted for the interviewee's correction of factual material, not for his approval. It should be made clear to him that he is only proofreading the quotes and any alteration of the manuscript may be done only by the editor.

Q. *When I've interviewed thirty or forty people for an article, shouldn't I try to quote all of them, or at least as many as I can? Won't they expect to be quoted in the article?*
A. Not all the people you interview will appear in the finished manuscript. Some will be poor spokespersons, some will be misinformed and therefore useless, others will not be able to shed any new light on the subject whatsoever. Unless you are interviewing someone you *know* will be a key figure in the finished piece, you should make clear to each interviewee that you are interviewing a lot of people in order to obtain background information, as well as for quotation in the article, and that not all sources will be mentioned. If an interviewee later objects to not being quoted in the finished article, you can always say there was a problem with limited space or the article was heavily edited. If you anticipate this response from an interviewee, it's professionally polite to phone the subject in advance of the article's publication.

Q. *I recently tried to interview a celebrity, but his press agent insisted on ground rules, telling me that there were only certain topics his client would discuss. What do I do when this happens?*

A. If you need the interview, you have little recourse but to accept ground rules suggested by subjects who are "gun shy" about being interviewed. The rules are often self-serving and confine the interviewer, making it difficult to get the knowledge he needs from his subject. However, while it may be necessary to agree to ground rules in order to get someone to grant an interview, it may not limit you in the final result. Your subject may simply be wary of discussing certain topics because of the way he has been handled by writers in the past. Once you begin the conversation, he may loosen up and discuss almost anything you wish. Agree to ground rules and you may be surprised. Once your foot is in the door, the ground rules may go out the window!

Chapter 11

Should I Work With Another Writer, Artist or Photographer?

"I've always believed in writing without a collaborator," wrote Agatha Christie, "because where two people are writing the same book, each believes he gets all the worries and only half the royalties." Other writers believe that using a collaborator can divide the work and increase the income for both partners. What if your collaborator has certain skills you don't have or don't want to acquire, such as photography? The following information can help you decide the best working method for you.

Writing Partners

Q. *A friend wants to collaborate with me on a writing project. Is this a good idea?*
A. Helene Schellenberg Barnhart, author of numerous articles, novels, and *Writing Romance Fiction,* says, "Collaboration is like a marriage. It can help make a dream come true through putting two heads together. It can also turn into a nightmare when differing temperaments clash or when communication breaks down."

Collaboration has obvious advantages. Two writers can pool the resources, contacts and efforts. But two writers can also have differing opinions at any point in the development of an article, book or story. One way to help ensure the success of a collaborative arrangement is to discuss each aspect of the partnership before work begins. Two writers should agree beforehand on exactly what contribution each will make to the project and what work each will do. In the case of a book collaboration it would be a good idea to have this in writing to protect all concerned—including the heirs, should one partner die before the other.

The secrets of successful collaboration are congeniality, respect for the other writer's abilities and opinions, and a willingness to compromise. Collaboration means dividing any fees you receive, but if you've carefully considered the projects you do, and plan accordingly, you can decrease the number of hours invested by dividing the work, and possibly increase the number of sales.

Q. *I'm writing a book for which I'd like to find a writing partner—especially someone with experience in the field I've chosen. How do I find a collaborator?*

A. There is no foolproof method of choosing a writing partner, but here are a few suggestions for locating a coauthor. Talk to other writers at writers workshops and conferences, meetings of writers groups and writing classes. Review the work of newspaper and magazine freelancers and staff writers. If they've written on a topic that interests you, they might be willing to collaborate. The more writers you meet, no matter what their field, the better the chance you'll find a writer who'd like to work with you. You could also place a classified ad under "Writers Wanted," in *Writer's Digest* or other trade magazines.

Q. *I have been offered the opportunity of collaborating on some stories. A friend of mine went on safari to Africa and took some excellent photographs of his hunting trips. He wants me to write his experiences and he will furnish the photos. If the stories are sold, what percentage do I pay him? Of course, all money received for photos would be his, but I have no idea how much I should share with him of the money received for a story.*
A. If you act as the marketer and are successful in selling some articles to sport and outdoor magazines, for example, there is no set rule for collaboration fees between writers and photographers. They have to decide when the item is sold how much each person contributed to the sale (in your case, both the writing *and* the selling) and make their shares of the check reflect that. If the magazine pays the photographer and writer separately, you are relieved of making this decision yourself, since the magazine editor is deciding what proportion of the total check he feels is due each partner.

Q. *I've become friendly with a professional who would like to collaborate with me on magazine articles in his field of expertise. There is also the possibility of later doing a book. Would his contribution of expertise and the status of his title help make a sale?*
A. In certain markets, it would be a help for you to collaborate with a professional. For example, if you were writing about the problems of executive stress, a joint byline with a clinical psychologist specializing in that area could increase your chances of a sale to *Psychology Today*. Teaming with a practicing attorney for a book on avoiding lawsuits might make a book more attractive to a publisher than if a layman had written it alone. However, it isn't wise to expend a lot of time and energy on a book until you get some expression of interest from a publisher based on your ability as a writer to assemble a provocative, practical book proposal, the value of which is bolstered by your co-author's credentials as an expert in the field.

Q. *A writer I know has recently abandoned a book project (for which he had obtained a book contract) due to unforeseen circumstances. He has already amassed and organized a great deal of research material; all that remains to be done is the actual writing, which he has asked me to do. How should we handle the division of money for this project?*
A. Assuming that the first writer is not expecting you to act as a ghostwriter, the book publisher should be notified first (send samples of your writing), to find

out if he is agreeable and if the original contract can be changed to reflect your participation as co-author. As to the separate working agreement between you and the first writer, you should agree to no less than 50 percent of the advance and royalties for the work, including any subsidiary rights for film or other media. Negotiating a flat fee paid to the original author so that you can take over the entire project is another possibility. All such transactions must be in writing.

Q. *A friend has offered to relate to me the very unusual story of her life, for use in a novel. The entire writing project will be mine, as well as marketing the work. I feel she is entitled to some percentage of any profit from the novel. What is the usual percentage in such cases? Am I within my rights to request exclusive use of the material at any later date to use other than for the novel in question?*
A. In cases of this type, as well as in biographies, the subject whose life is being used is not usually given any payment except the satisfaction of seeing his life story in print. If you feel a personal obligation, why not simply offer a flat sum (whatever is agreeable to both parties) for use of this material, dependent, of course, on its sale to a publisher. If at all possible, you should secure legal help with any financial arrangement that is made. Since there are others who are probably familiar with the events of your subject's life, you cannot reasonably expect to have exclusive control over this material. Remember that "facts" themselves cannot be copyrighted, although your presentation of them in books and articles can be copyrighted.

Ghostwriting and Writing for Hire

Q. *A person with an interesting background has asked me to write his life story. Do I sign a contract with him, and what should the financial arrangements be?*
A. In any situation where a writer is working with someone else and there is no publisher lined up, the writer should not begin work on the project until there is an agreement on paper, spelling out exactly how much the writer will be earning while he's doing the writing, and how he'll be credited and paid on publication. The agreement should be as detailed as possible, covering not only the book itself, but any further money the book might earn, including subsidiary rights such as serialization, paperback and foreign reprints, dramatic, film, radio, and television adaptations. It's advisable to have a lawyer draw up the agreement, which should also cover the exact amount of work each party is to contribute.

You don't mention whether the subject intends to self-publish the book or wants you to market it as well as write it for him. If the latter, it might be wise to query a few publishers to see if there is any interest in the book idea before you — and the subject — invest time and money in the project.

In matters of money, the big question is always "how much?" Writer Hayes Jacobs recommends that you "ask for as much as you can get," but never settle for less than 50 percent of the royalties. If you are doing all the writing, 75 percent is reasonable. The money you are paid by the subject while writing the book will apply as an advance against your future percentages of royalties. This reduces your risk of putting in a lot of hard work and receiving no money if the book isn't successful in terms of sales.

Q. *If I agree to ghostwrite a book for a celebrity, do I get a cover credit? How about a percentage of the royalties? Are ghostwriters looked down on by other writers?*
A. Unless the work is specifically intended to be an "as-told-to" book, ghostwriters generally don't get a byline, and rarely receive any sort of public acknowledgment, even if they are established professionals. But because a ghostwriter must subdue his own voice, write entirely in the style of another person, and satisfy both subject and editor, he is recognized and respected in the publishing community.

While public acclaim is rare for ghostwriters, there are considerable monetary rewards. Ghostwriters usually receive a flat fee, rather than a percentage of the royalties. What that fee will be depends on the book publisher, the celebrity, the reputation of the ghostwriter and the book's salability, but it could be $25,000 or more.

Q. *I've recently been asked to collaborate on a book with a man who is interested in self-publishing his autobiography. He has already completed a first draft of the manuscript and wants me to finish the book. How much pay should I request for a job like this?*
A. It sounds as if you are being asked to do a rewrite of the man's completed manuscript. In such a case, the amount of pay you receive would depend on how much work is to be done on the book before it can be submitted to the printer. If the draft is *very* rough and needs a substantial amount of rearranging and rewriting, you probably should charge an hourly rate. If, on the other hand, you'll be doing a complete rewrite and will receive no author's credit on the finished book, ghost-writing rates might apply. These can run from $5,000 to $25,000 per book, depending on the length and difficulty of the project and the resources of the person hiring you. If the manuscript is in fairly good shape and you only have to do a little copyediting and proofreading to polish and refine it, you might charge a set fee per page. (For more information on copyediting jobs, see chapter thirty-one.)

Q. *What is an "as-told-to" book or article? What types of subjects lend themselves to this kind of writing? What financial arrangements are made between the people who collaborate on the work?*
A. An "as-told-to" work is a first-person narrative for which the actual writing is done by someone other than the person allegedly telling the story—in other words, the work is "ghostwritten." The resulting book or article may have a joint byline, giving the author credit by saying the work is written "as told to Frank Jones" or "with Joe Smith." In some works, credit is given only on the acknowledgment page.

The "as-told-to" format is most often used in three kinds of material: a story of a dramatic personal experience, an authority's opinion on a matter of public interest, and the commentary or autobiographical narrative of a celebrity. Magazine and newspaper articles can give a writer leads on prospective clients he might approach for this type of writing. The writer develops the concept for the work, "sells" the subject and the publisher on the idea, and works out the financial arrangements with both. These arrangements vary. In the case of articles, the writer usually gets the check while the subject gets the publicity; other times they split all monies fifty/fifty. If a book is being written, the author negotiates the division of advance money and royalties depending on the relative contributions of the two parties to the book's salability. Sometimes the author enlists the help of an agent or lawyer to do this. Professional writers often prefer to cover their work on a book "up front," by negotiating to receive 75 percent of the advance and a lesser percentage of the royalties, in case the book doesn't sell as well as they expected. When the manuscript is completed, the subject gives the writer permission to publish the material by signing a release form. (For advice on how to locate the home addresses of experts and celebrities, see chapter seven.)

Artistic Collaborations

Q. *How can I find a photographer to work with me on books and articles?*
A. Getting good, high-quality photographs can increase the salability of many books and articles. You could hire a professional photographer, but some charge as much as $200 per day for their services, so unless you had worked out an agreement with an editor beforehand, this could be an unwise expense for you. The American Society of Magazine Photographers (ASMP) can recommend member photographers in your area if you or your editor want to hire an experienced professional. Contact ASMP at 419 Park Ave. South, New York NY 10016.

College art departments that teach photography might be able to recommend talented students; putting notices on the department bulletin board can also help. Local camera clubs and the classified ads of your local newspaper are other good sources. Any of these methods can help you find a photographer to take the photos you need at a fraction of the top professional's fee.

When selecting a photographer, examine his portfolio, checking subject matter, quality and style, and the relation of his work to the type of writing you do. After you've found your collaborator, the two of you will have to work together to find ways to enhance your writing with his pictures. Prints chosen for publication should be accompanied by a brief, signed statement in which the photographer grants permission for his work to be used in conjunction with your manuscript.

(For more information on how photography and illustration can be used with your writing, see chapter twenty-three.)

Q. *What arrangements should I make to pay a photographer for any of his pictures I use to illustrate my article?*
A. There are a number of ways to pay photographers. The writer and photographer can agree beforehand on a flat fee to cover the photographer's labor and the cost of prints. The writer can pay the photographer a percentage of the total article

price. If the photographer belongs to a professional organization, the writer may have to agree to a fixed price. In all of these cases, the actual amount of payment will depend on several factors, including the nature of the work, the amount of the photographer's time involved, and the quality of the photographs. The price should always be negotiated before work begins. In some cases a writer can recommend a qualified photographer to the magazine editor who assigned the article, or an editor might accept responsibility for selecting a photographer.

Q. *I'm collaborating with an artist on a picture book for children. When we study the markets and make our selection, do we send color transparencies of the artwork?*
A. When marketing a picture book, send the text and good photocopies of some of the artwork you have available, but in a cover note accompanying the text, advise the editor that you can provide full-color illustrations upon request. (For further discussions of picture book submissions, see chapter twenty-eight.)

Q. *What are the opportunities for writer/artist collaboration on magazine articles or stories?*
A. There are very few opportunities for this type of collaboration. Acceptability of a manuscript with accompanying artwork is limited because an editor has to like both the writing and the artwork. Most editors prefer to assign illustrations to artists whose work they know. Illustrations have to fit the format of the magazine and the style of the article.

Chapter 12

What Is a Query? How Should I Write It?

Nonfiction writers have one great advantage over fiction writers: the query letter. Before completing research for a manuscript, the article writer or nonfiction book writer can elicit, through a query letter, the interest of an editor and sometimes even the particular slant an editor prefers. Since the editor has participated in this dialogue before seeing the finished manuscript he has a greater investment in its success. The questions and answers in this chapter will fully explain the query letter and its advantages. For more information, see *How to Write Irresistible Query Letters* by Lisa Collier Cool and *How to Write a Book Proposal* by Michael Larson (both published by Writer's Digest Books).

Magazine Queries

Q. *What information should a query letter contain?*
A. The information in a query letter serves two purposes. It should convince the editor that your idea is a good one for his publication's readership, and it should sell you as the best writer to turn out a good article on the subject. The query letter should contain an alluring, but concise, summary of the article's central idea and the angle or point of view from which you intend to approach it. Outline the structure of the article, giving facts, observations, and anecdotes that support the premise of the article. Don't give *too many* facts; the idea is to leave the editor wanting more. The letter should tell the editor why the article would be important and timely and give a convincing argument of why it would fit into this particular magazine.

You should also give the editor some indication of why you think *you* could write a good article on this particular subject. Share some sources of information and describe any special qualifications you may have for developing the idea. For example, if you were proposing an article on a topic in which you have some professional expertise or of which you have been an interested observer for some time, you should mention that. Samples of your published work will also help the editor see what you can do. The close of the query can be a straightforward request to write the article. You might also specify an estimated length and delivery date. If photographs are available, mention that, too. Don't discuss fees or request advice.

These are guidelines, of course, not a hard-and-fast pattern for a query letter. Good query letters are as individual as the writers who send them and as unique as the ideas that are proposed.

Q. *How long should a query letter be?*
A. Most successful query letters run only one page. Two or three pages of single-spaced typewritten copy facing a busy editor is more than he wants to read. If that much copy is needed to give an editor the gist of the article, you probably have failed to focus on a specific angle. If the subject warrants it, you can accompany a one-page query with a synopsis. The letter tantalizes the editor and helps him decide whether the article is right for his readers. The synopsis — double-spaced — shows the treatment of the subject.

Q. *I have very little writing experience, but I don't want to hurt my chances of having my article accepted by admitting that to an editor. How much must my query letter tell about my background?*
A. If you've never been published before, it's best to ignore the subject of past credits and discuss instead your qualifications to write the article at hand. Discuss only those aspects of your background that relate to your subject. If you're proposing an article about how small businesses use computers, for example, mentioning your computer knowledge through education or employment would be a plus. What's important to an editor is not how many articles you've had published, but how much promise is shown by your query letter. Even if you've never published anything, a thorough and professional approach to the query letter will allow you the same chance to sell an article as someone who has a few articles in print.

Q. *Should I include two or three samples of my work when sending a query letter?*
A. It's always a good idea to include a few tearsheets of your previously published articles. If an editor is not familiar with your work, looking at other pieces you've written is one way he can familiarize himself with your abilities and the quality of your work. The articles you send with your query ideally should be of the same category as the article you are proposing; if you wanted to profile Liza Minelli, for example, a copy of a previously published article on Burt Reynolds would show the editor your skills in this field. A suggestion for an article on making house painting easier could be bolstered by your published article on how to reupholster furniture. Even if the tearsheets you send differ from the type of article you're proposing, send only your best published articles. Showing the editor of a major publication insignificant tearsheets could defeat your purpose. If you are dissatisfied with something you wrote, chances are the editor will not be too impressed with it either.

Q. *Do I always have to query before sending a manuscript or are there times when it isn't necessary?*
A. For certain types of articles, editors prefer to see the finished manuscript rather than a query. For example, personal experience articles, humor, nostalgia and edi-

torial opinion pieces rely so much on the writer's personal style that reading the finished product is the best way an editor can assess their acceptability for his publication. Articles requiring extensive research, however, are best attempted after an editor has responded favorably to a query. That saves the writer time since the editor may prefer a different approach to the subject than the one the writer originally had. If you have any doubts, check *Writer's Market* for the specific magazine's policy on various types of articles.

Q. *It seems so presumptuous for a beginning and unpublished writer to query first. How much attention would be paid to a beginner?*
A. A busy editor would much rather read a query to decide whether he's interested in a certain property than plow through a lengthy manuscript for the same purpose. From the writer's standpoint, think of the savings in postage and wear and tear on the manuscript. What *is* presumptuous is the writer who disregards an editor's stated request to "query first" and deluges him with completed manuscripts. Editors pay as much attention to beginners as they do to professionals, as long as the query letters are professionally written and the ideas are suitable to the magazine's readership and the editor's needs.

Q. *Should I send a query for my short stories?*
A. Because of the nature of fiction, editors rarely expect to be queried about it. Good fiction usually defies the type of summarization or highlighting used in query letters because so many of the integral elements, for example, style, mood, and characterization, would be lost. Therefore, most editors prefer to receive the complete manuscript. A few magazines that are short-staffed may ask for queries, in which case you'll want to give a brief statement of the main theme and story line, including the conflict within the story and the resolution. (For more information on short stories, see chapter twenty-five.)

Book Queries

Q. *What are sample chapters, outlines and synopses?*
A. Many book publishers request sample chapters, outlines and synopses for non-fiction book proposals. The outline gives a brief summary of the entire content of the proposed book, followed by a chapter-by-chapter synopsis showing the organization of the book and what angle of the subject each chapter will contain; the sample chapters show the writer's style and writing ability. It is a good idea to include the first chapter, a chapter from the center of the book showing some highlight or climax, and the concluding chapter, unless the publisher's listing in *Writer's Market* indicates he wishes to see consecutive chapters. Authors who send only the first chapter or two (since the latter chapters have not been written) are sometimes disappointed by rejection, since they had not planned the book sufficiently to bring it to a well-rounded conclusion.

Although contracts may be issued on a book proposal, sometimes called "selling the partial," some publishers accepting general books from freelance writers who are unknown to them issue the contract only after the completed manuscript has been read and accepted.

Q. *I have written chapters for two nonfiction books. I have sent the sample chapters and a query letter to publishers for consideration. As you well know, it can take three to four months for a publisher to analyze the market and reply to the query. Both these potential books, however, are topical. If each publisher takes that long to reply, the material I have researched and collected will become outdated. In such a case, can I send sample chapters and queries for a book to more than one editor for consideration? If not, do you have any suggestions to speed up the process?*
A. In some cases, and especially when the topic of the book is timely, it is necessary to query several firms at one time. When sending multiple queries, some writers feel each editor should know that others are considering the idea. Other writers feel it is best not to inform the editors of multiple queries, but to work out the best deal if more than one editor expresses an interest.

One matter to consider, however, is whether such dated material is suited to books. Except in rare instances, book publishers work on a schedule involving two or more years. Topical material is better suited to magazines, while books on extremely timely subjects cannot usually withstand the normal delays at various levels of scheduling.

Q. *Is it permissible to write a book publisher regarding the status of my book manuscript? I sent the manuscript a month ago, and so far have heard nothing.*
A. It's permissible, but it sometimes takes over three months for a publisher to report on a book-length manuscript. Unless the *Writer's Market* listing for a specific publisher specifies sending the entire manuscript, you'd get faster service on a synopsis, two or three sample chapters, and a short cover letter asking if the publisher is interested in seeing more.

Query Etiquette

Q. *Is there any situation in which I can query by telephone?*
A. Most established writers query by mail. A written query allows the editor to examine the proposal at his convenience, and to show it to his associates for their opinions. An editor is better able to judge the merits of an idea if it's in tangible, written form than if it's related to him over the telephone.

To the writer, time and energy required to develop a carefully written proposal without an editor's interest seems a large investment, when a telephone call might sell the editor on an idea, with far less effort. However, a phone call interrupts the editor's workday and he is forced to answer without proper time to think the matter through. Except in rare instances (for example, when the writer may only have access to a subject for a limited time and needs a fast answer), an unexpected phone query usually receives either a no (which allows you to eliminate his publication and gives you a sense of what other similar markets might think), or a response which puts you back in square one: "We're willing to look at it if you send a detailed query by mail." If you receive a negative response by phone, you have closed the door to a query that might have been considered, had it come by mail. A few writers consider sending a query by fax as a hybrid solution—a written query sent over phone lines. This is preferable to a phone call for a time-sensitive proposal, but is frowned on for routine queries. Once you have sold an editor several articles, he may be more receptive to faxed or phoned queries.

Q. *How soon can I follow up a query letter if I don't get a response? Should I phone?*
A. If you've not heard from the editor in three to four weeks (unless the market listing in *Writer's Market* specifies a longer report time), don't hesitate to write the editor a *brief* follow-up. The note should describe the query fully so the editor can readily identify it, and should simply ask whether he's had time to consider your proposal. Be sure to include the date of the original query, since some magazine offices file unsolicited queries and manuscripts by date of arrival. In case the original query never reached the editor, you may want to enclose a photocopy of the original query to save time and correspondence searching for it. Some writers include a self-addressed postcard for a quick reply. This usually elicits a response; if not, you may then want to try a phone call. A follow-up letter, however, rarely fails to get a reply.

Q. *Is it permissible to submit a query covering the same article to two different editors at the same time? Sometimes the time element is important and if one editor delays answering, it could be too late to query another.*
A. It is permissible, but not always practical, to submit the same article idea to several magazines simultaneously. Most writers abhor the long delay it takes to get an answer from a magazine editor, but realize that if they do make simultaneous submissions to editors they are going to face the possible situation of more than one editor asking to see the article and having to be told that someone else is considering it. An editor who is told that he will have to wait in line is not going to look very kindly on the next query from that particular writer. In the case of timely article ideas, many freelance writers use this technique: They either point out in the letter to the editor that it is an extremely timely query and request a reply in a certain number of days, or tell the editor the idea is being sent to several editors. Most editors respect this, and in fact, some editors listed in *Writer's Market* indicate that they are open to multiple submissions.

Q. *What do you suggest for mailing queries: a ten-inch envelope with a six-incher for the return, or an eleven-inch envelope with a ten-incher for the return?*
A. The eleven-inch envelope with a ten-incher return would probably have a neater appearance, especially since the editor may return other material such as writers guidelines along with his answer.

Q. *After receiving a favorable reply to a query, how soon will the editor expect the manuscript?*

A. When an editor gives you a favorable response on an article idea and doesn't specify a deadline, it's up to you to decide how quickly you can get it finished. Acknowledge his letter with a note telling when you will deliver the article. If the editor has a specific issue in mind for your article, it's up to him to suggest a deadline for you.

Chapter 13

How Should the Manuscript Look?

The first impression an editor has of your manuscript is how it *looks*. The quality of your writing can change that impression for better or worse, of course, but why make your good writing work harder to overcome an unprofessional presentation of your manuscript? Here are some guidelines to help properly submit manuscripts that say, "professional." For more information on preparing manuscripts, see *The Writer's Digest Guide to Manuscript Formats*, by Dian Dincin Buchman and Seli Groves (Writer's Digest Books).

Preparing Your Manuscript

Q. *I have often read the term "manuscript mechanics." Would you please tell me what this means?*
A. "Manuscript mechanics" refers to the business of making a manuscript as attractive as possible from the standpoint of overall appearance, which includes neatness of typing, punctuation, width of margins, and centering of titles.

Q. *Okay then, what are standard manuscript mechanics?*
A. The most important criterion is to produce a manuscript page that is readable. All manuscripts must be typed on one side of 8½″ × 11″ white bond paper. Your typewriter or computer ribbon should be new enough to produce crisp, dark black letters. The text should be double-spaced (that is, there should be a line of white space between each line of text), and margins of between one and one and one-half inch should surround the text.

Q. *I don't have a typewriter, but my longhand is very legible. Does my manuscript have to be typed?*
A. All manuscripts must be typed. However, that does not mean the writer must do the typing. Some writers pay to have their final drafts typed by professional typists. You can find available typists and current fees in the classified ads in *Writer's Digest;* you can also place your own classifieds in local newspapers. College campuses often have advertisements for typing services posted on various department

bulletin boards. When using a typing service, make sure you and the typist agree on the payment, type of paper to be used, format, typestyle and any other considerations. If you are sending your manuscript to the typist via the U.S. Postal Service, you should enclose a SASE with three times the amount of postage you needed to send the copy to the typist; this covers the amount needed to mail you the original, the final typed copy and a carbon copy. Remember to keep itemized bills and receipts for all transactions with the typist, because typing costs are tax-deductible expenses for a writer.

Q. *I've heard that editors don't like dot-matrix printers? Why, and are there other reasonably priced options?*
A. The prejudice against dot-matrix printers is a legacy from the early dot-matrix technology that delivered nearly illegible manuscripts to editors' desks. Dot-matrix printers have a printhead from which tiny wires push out to strike a ribbon, transferring ink or carbon to the paper behind it. The quality of a dot-matrix printer depends on the number of wires in its head; the base models have nine pins, while top-of-the-line feature twenty-four. More pins means better-formed characters — which will be easier for editors to read. If you're using an eighteen- or twenty-four pin printer, and you're printing in letter-quality mode, your manuscripts will be welcomed by editors. (Just make sure the ribbon is fresh.)

There are alternatives to dot-matrix printers. All are more expensive, but technological developments continue to close the price gap. Ink jet printers are quieter and only slightly more expensive than twenty-four pin dot-matrix models. Operating cost is much higher, however, and compatibility with many word-processing programs can be difficult. Laser printers provide the best-quality output for both text and graphics, but they also sport price tags that may be double or triple the cost of the others. (The original daisy-wheel printers — which were, for the most part, converted typewriters — are either obsolete or soon will be.)

Q. *With the new photocopy machines accepting and reproducing copies on two sides of paper (page), is it acceptable to print on both sides of paper, then submit my book manuscript to a publisher? Such a practice could certainly save tons of paper and postage, especially when submitting lengthy manuscripts.*
A. Manuscripts copied on both sides of a page are not acceptable because they are not *workable* in that format. Editors often photocopy and cut up a page of the manuscript, rearrange paragraphs or pages, and send sections of the manuscript to another editor for input. Yes, it would save paper and postage costs for writers, but the standard manuscript format developed to what it is today because it is efficient and extremely workable for editors.

Q. *My typewriter only produces elite type. I know when manuscripts are submitted that pica is preferred. But does it make that much difference?*
A. Both pica and elite are acceptable. The more "exotic" types, such as fancy script or all capitals, are what editors find objectionable.

Q. *My computer printer has the capability to print text in italics, boldface, headline, and a variety of typefaces. Is this acceptable?*
A. No. Your manuscript should, as much as possible, duplicate the appearance of a page produced on a typewriter. Set your printer to output a 10-12 point, easily readable typeface—and then leave it alone. Use underlining to show what text should be set in italic, and avoid boldface unless there's a specific reason (magazine style, for instance). If you're submitting on disk, you'll probably need to remove from the file the special typesetting codes needed to produce these special effects before you send in the disk. And if the editor will be editing on paper, he'll still need to mark up the manuscript for typesetting regardless of your fancy fontwork.

Q. *What kind of paper should I use to type the final manuscript?*
A. Editors are immovable on two points: the manuscript must be on white paper, and it must measure 8½″ × 11″. Colored typewriter paper does not photocopy easily and is difficult for an editor to read or edit. Cheaper paper is all wood content, but is absorbent, giving a fuzzy texture and causing the type to blur. This paper also tears easily; sometimes the typewriter keys will punch right through it. Also do not use airmail stationery which is difficult for editing. The more expensive types of paper are 100 percent rag content, nice, but astronomically priced. For best results at lowest cost, use a good 25 percent cotton fiber content paper, no less than sixteen-pound bond—twenty-pound is preferred. This paper holds up well when erasing mistakes, shows type neatly, and is excellent for editing.

Q. *Please set me straight once and for all. Half the time I read that manuscripts should be prepared on non-Corrasable paper because it smudges less, and the other half of the time they say that liquid erase should be avoided, and that a good eraser is best. This leads me to believe that neither is a steadfast rule. I would, however, appreciate knowing what the general consensus is.*
A. It's general knowledge that Corrasable bond is an editing nuisance. Most editors prefer good quality bond paper, and the use of either liquid erase, or strike-over erase. If you have more than three corrections on a manuscript page, it's best to retype that page to avoid the first-draft look that editors dislike.

   If you have a book manuscript ready for final typing—a horrendous job for most writers—and plan to type it yourself, consider owning or renting a self-correcting typewriter to do a professional job in much less time.

Q. *Should I use a cover page, even on a short manuscript?*
A. Cover pages aren't usually necessary. All relevant information is included on the first page of the manuscript. Your name, street address, city, state, zip code and daytime phone number should be typed on four single-spaced lines in the upper left corner. Type the approximate number of words in the upper right corner; single-spaced beneath that, type the rights you are offering to sell the publisher. The title of the story or article and your byline should appear in two double-spaced, centered lines above the beginning of the copy, which starts halfway down the page.

Q. *A writer friend of mine recently advised me that when submitting a manuscript I should include my social security number. Is this necessary? What's the reason for such a requirement?*
A. Book publishers and major magazine publishers require social security numbers on all manuscripts since publishers who pay at least $600 to nonemployees must report such payments to the Internal Revenue Service.

While you may include your social security number on a book manuscript, such matters are usually handled by the business offices of publishers who will request the number when the contract is signed or when they ask you for other personal and promotional details.

Unless a magazine publisher is one of the few specifying this request in *Writer's Market,* it isn't required. Social security numbers are optional information; you may include yours if you wish in the upper left corner of page one, underneath your name, address and phone number.

Q. *Does it make a difference in what I'm paid if I don't include the word count on a manuscript when I submit it? Might I get paid more if I add it?*
A. Most editors prefer to have the approximate word count noted on the upper right corner of page one of the manuscript. If the magazine pays by the word, they'll pay for the number of words in the final accepted version of your manuscript.

Q. *Do the rest of a manuscript's pages differ from the first in format and appearance?*
A. Yes. For all subsequent pages, type your name and the page number at the upper left (Jones, pg. 2 or Jones−2) and the title single-spaced beneath it, with nothing at the center or right. If the title is too long, use a keyword to serve as "shorthand" for the full title. A keyword for this chapter, for instance, might be "Manuscript." See the sample manuscript page in the appendix.

Q. *Are there different manuscript formats for short stories, magazine articles, and book-length projects?*
A. No. There is only one standard manuscript submission format: double-spaced on 8½″ × 11″ white paper.

Q. *How do you type a sidebar in manuscript form?*
A. Sidebars should be typed in the standard manuscript format. Begin the sidebar on a separate sheet of paper and clearly mark it "Sidebar." Type in an identifying caption after the word "Sidebar" to indicate what main article it accompanies. Place the sidebar at the end of the feature or main article manuscript. When the sidebar is typed separately from the featured manuscript, it's easier for the editor to mark it for the typesetter, since most sidebars are printed in widths that differ from the widths used for feature material. (For a discussion of sidebars, see chapter twenty-two.)

Stylistic Concerns

Q. *How should I indicate on my manuscript that I am writing under a pseudonym?*
A. Type your real name, followed by your pen name in parentheses, then your address in the upper left corner of the first page of your manuscript; type your pen name as the byline under the title of your manuscript. Type your real name, followed by your pen name in parentheses, then a dash and the page number in the upper left corner of each page after page one; e.g., Jones (Smith)—page 2. Of course, if you don't want even your editor or publisher to know your real name, then you'll have to be a little trickier and use the pseudonym in the byline, in the upper left corner, *and* on the return envelope. If this is your wish, you'll have to notify your local post office and bank that you are using a pen name in your work. (For further information on using a pen name, see chapter sixteen.)

Q. *How should I handle quoted material in the final typed manuscript?*
A. Use quotation marks to open and close all use of quoted material. When quoting within a quotation, use single marks. If the quoted material runs eight lines or more, it generally is set off from the text, double-spaced and indented. No quotation marks are used in block quotations of this type. These are, of course, general guidelines. If you're submitting to a specific magazine or book publisher, follow their format. For other specific questions, you should consult *The Chicago Manual of Style*, a comprehensive style and editing manual. It contains detailed information on the use of quotation marks in many situations, as well as other mechanical questions about putting your manuscript into its final, typewritten form.

Q. *When using foreign words or phrases in my writing, what are the typing guidelines?*
A. When a foreign word or phrase with which the English-speaking reader would be unfamiliar appears for the first time in the text, it should be underlined, which tells the typesetter that you want it italicized. Some publishers have a style in which, after the first use, such repeated words remain in roman type, and therefore would not be underlined. For help with specific problems involving the use of foreign words and phrases, consult an unabridged dictionary or *The Chicago Manual of Style*. Most libraries have copies.

Q. *I have been told that thoughts should not be enclosed in quotation marks. This works very well in some cases, but there are instances in which I do not know how to handle the punctuation, as in the following: Jim said, "Walter is a wonderful fellow." Alice agreed and thought, "You are wonderful too." Should quotation marks be used in this case, and if not, should "You" begin with a capital letter?*
A. Quotation marks need not be used here, but the capital letter for "You" should be retained. Or, if the use of a capital in the middle of a sentence disturbs you, you might handle it this way: Alice agreed. You are wonderful too, she thought. If you like, you may underline her thought to indicate italics, which would differentiate it nicely from the direct quotations.

Q. *What is the fundamental rule, if there is one, about hyphenated words?*
A. If you consult the introductory pages of most standard unabridged dictionaries, you will find rules pertaining to the use of hyphens. Rules *can* be rather complicated. But a few simple ones to bear in mind are that the hyphen can be used (1) to clarify meaning, e.g., honey-child . . . not a child made of honey; (2) to avoid having a double vowel or a triple consonant, e.g. wall-like is preferable to walllike; (3) to aid proper pronunciation, e.g., all-embracing is less likely to be mispronounced than allembracing. In general, just remember that if the hyphen helps to make your meaning clearer, use it. Take note of compound words as you read top magazines and newspapers, since they are the trendsetters in the spelling of new words entering the printed language.

Q. *Is there any current guide with editorial sanction for the use of the three dots (. . .) and the dash (—)? If so I would appreciate knowing about it.*
A. There is no strict editorial policy governing the use of the three dots (. . .) and the dash (—). In popular magazines, the dash seems to be more prevalent than the dots. The dots are used mainly to indicate that the speaker's voice trails off . . . ; the dash is used sometimes in place of parentheses or sometimes to indicate an abrupt interruption in speech or thought or to suggest a pause longer than a comma but not as final as a period. The dots are also used to show omission of words from a quote (in which case they are called an ellipsis); e.g., *Senator John L. McGee said, "We must examine closely . . . the effect of postal rate increases on the magazine industry."* This statement could have appeared in a magazine industry newsletter where the omitted words, *"agriculture grants, education proposals, and,"* would have been of little interest to the readers of the newsletter. It's a good idea to follow the format of the particular magazine or book publisher to which you're submitting.

Q. *In many magazine articles there are subheads placed between paragraphs to attract the reader's attention to a change in thought. Should a writer put these in the manuscript or is this an editorial procedure?*
A. This is usually an editorial procedure. The editor may want them placed in certain locations for editorial emphasis and/or to help a layout paste-up problem. Writers need not include subheads (also called subtitles) in the original manuscript submitted; however, some articles lend themselves to this treatment, and appropriate subheads could enhance the possibility of a sale.

Q. *I have a question pertaining to novels and short stories. On the last page of the manuscript should I type "The End"? I've seen "30" in some places, indicating the ending of the manuscript (both for fiction and nonfiction). Which is correct?*
A. You can type "The End" at the end of a short story or novel, although you don't have to. The number 30 is usually written at the end of the copy for nonfiction, most often used in newspaper stories and reports. It is a legacy from old newspaper telegraphers who used the Roman numeral XXX as a symbol to indicate the end

of the message. Some writers also use the symbol # to indicate the end.

Q. *Where should quotation credits be given in a manuscript—at the bottom of the page where the quotation appears or at the end of the manuscript?*
A. Credits may be given in a short manuscript by placing an asterisk next to the quote and a corresponding asterisk and notation of the source at the bottom of the page. Long articles and book manuscripts should follow the style suggested by *A Manual of Style:* number each quotation within the text, and on a separate sheet write the corresponding number, followed by a period and the credit line. Footnotes or end notes (at the end of the chapter or the end of the book) are set in a different size type. The publisher decides on the basis of his own style preference whether to put the notes at the bottom of the page or elsewhere.

Q. *In my writing, I often need to refer to the days and months of the year, omitting the year. Is it correct to use ordinal numerals to designate the days (for example, January 12th, May 1st, March 5th)?*
A. The accepted practice is as follows: January 12, May 1, March 5.

Q. *I am working on a short story in which short paragraphs in italics are interspersed throughout the narrative, and I would like to know whether there is any way to indicate italics without underlining. This amounts to quite extensive underlining, which in my opinion, is not only bothersome and time-consuming but is distracting to the reader. I don't want to distract an editor who reads the manuscript.*
A. Underlining *is* the standard way to denote italics; editors would not be anymore distracted by it than readers would be by the actual italics.

Q. *Do I have to use a lot of footnotes, or is a comprehensive bibliography at the end of my book manuscript sufficient?*
A. It will depend on the individual preference of the publisher or editor. General-interest trade book publishers usually prefer a bibliography, while textbooks and scholarly efforts usually include footnotes as a way of identifying source material. It would be a good idea to use a bibliography with your sample chapter but ask in your covering letter about the publisher's preference. Many publishers produce style guides covering such details for their authors.

Q. *Is it essential that a manuscript be typed perfectly? I have a 480-page manuscript that I've retyped three times and it's still a mess. Every time I retype it, I reread it, which is disastrous because my pen flies with revisions (usually of words, not sentences). If I retype it again, I'll be wasting weeks that could be used in creating. Or should I send it out with the word substitutes neatly penned?*
A. Since you can't resist revising every time you retype, you would probably find a professional manuscript typist the answer to your problem. The cost of this service would be worth the considerable saving in time and effort. Under no circumstances should you send out a manuscript that has more than three corrections per page

marked on it. Also to save wear and tear on the finished product, send the publisher a query letter first instead of submitting the complete manuscript. A *clean* photocopy can cover "a multitude of sins." Certain pages or the entire manuscript can be corrected and photocopied to appear professionally typed.

Q. *I have never learned how writers arrive at the total number of words in a manuscript. Can you tell me?*
A. Count every word on five representative pages; divide by five to get an average number of words per page, then multiply that average by the total number of pages in the manuscript. When counting words, abbreviated words count as one word as do the words "a," "the," etc. Type approximate number of words in round figures, such as 2,700 words (not 2,693) in the upper right corner of page one.

There is a faster method that will estimate your manuscript's word count. Many production editors at book and magazine publishing companies consider the "average" word length to be six typed characters, when taking into account the number of short words, such as articles and prepositions, balanced against the longer words present, even in children's books. To estimate the number of words in your manuscript, count the number of characters in a full line of type; multiply by the number of lines on the page; multiply again by the number of pages in the manuscript; and divide by the magic number, six. The result will be a fairly accurate count of the words in your story or article.

Q. *I've seen quotes from well-known people on the jackets of books, commenting on the book's excellence. I'm sure comments like these improve sales. Would you advise me to type extra copies of the book I'm writing and send them to various people to solicit similar letters for my book?*
A. The garnering of letters of praise (testimonials) from famous people is usually the job of the publisher's publicity department. Remember that you haven't yet obtained a contract for the book you're working on, so wait until the publisher accepts your manuscript before discussing testimonials with him. After acceptance, if you have in mind people you think would respond favorably to your book, suggest them to the publisher.

Q. *When submitting a book manuscript, should I include the dedication page?*
A. No. Including the dedication page on the manuscript could seem presumptuous. It is best to wait until publication is assured before sending the dedication.

Q. *Is it necessary to include a cover letter with my manuscript?*
A. If you have already queried an editor and received an affirmative response, a brief cover note would be a good idea. All it need say is something like, "Here is the article you asked to see in your letter of July 17. I have also included a selection of photographs that I mentioned are available." If you are sending an unsolicited manuscript, no cover letter is necessary, unless it buttresses your sales effort by describing some credentials you have relating to the topic of your manuscript.

Submitting Your Manuscript

Q. *Is it acceptable to submit a photocopy of my manuscript, or must it be the original?*
A. Photocopy technology has advanced so far that it's generally impossible to distinguish between a photocopy and the original manuscript. Still, if you keep the original in your files and submit a *good-quality* photocopy, you won't have to worry about an editor or mail clerk losing or damaging your manuscript. The discussion is moot for computer users; it's generally more covenient to run off a second copy than to make a photocopy.

Q. *Must I submit my manuscripts on computer disk? And if I do, should I still send a paper copy?*
A. As more magazine and book publishers adopt computer technologies, more editors will expect the writers they work with to supply their articles, stories and books on disk. At the moment, few editors *require* it, but it is certainly a trend that new writers should consider when choosing between buying a typewriter or a computer.

The mechanics of submitting your work on disk depends on your publisher's system. Some publishers' disk requirements are listed in *Writer's Market*, or you can ask the editor you're working with for specifics. And yes, you should still submit a paper copy of the manuscript in case the disk is unreadable. A final note: Unless otherwise noted in *Writer's Market*, you should never include a disk with an unsolicited submission.

Q. *Is it acceptable to submit manuscripts via fax or electronic mail?*
A. The mail remains the standard industry practice for sending your work to editors—unless the editor specifically states some other method in his writer's guidelines or in *Writer's Market*. Many editors ask their regular contributors or writers with assignments to use these alternate delivery methods, but they generally still prefer new writers to approach them by old-fashioned mail. If you can deliver your work by fax, disk, modem or E-mail, mention it in your query or proposal.

Q. *I have a manuscript ready to send. Now what?*
A. It's not much more difficult than putting the pages in an envelope and sending it. For very short pieces, a No. 10 (business-size) envelope is fine; longer works should be sent in a 9″ × 12″ envelope. Book-length manuscripts can be shipped in a padded envelope or a typing-paper box. Always include a self-addressed envelope with your submission; affix enough postage to get your work home. If you don't need the manuscript returned, attach a note to that effect on the manuscript and send just a self-addressed, stamped No. 10 envelope for the editor's reply.

Address your submission to a specific editor at the magazine or publisher—never send off material addressed simply to "The Editor." You can verify your contact name with a brief phone call to the editorial office.

Use first-class mail for all submissions except book manuscripts, which may weigh enough to be sent either "priority" mail or by fourth-class mail. The latter option costs less. Ask your local postal clerk for more information.

Q. *Can you send more than one story at a time in the same envelope?*
A. There's no reason why you can't send more than one story in the same envelope. However, it might be a good idea to include individual SASEs for *each* story in case they are reviewed by different editors. Providing a SASE for each story will make it easier for editors to reply to you.

Chapter 14

Have I Broken the Unwritten Rules?

A writer's challenge is to send an editor what he wants. But it's also to avoid sending him manuscripts he doesn't want, or engage in practices that cause him extra work. A thorough study of market listings, editorial guidelines, sample issues and publishers' products will help you hit your target more precisely.

Marketing Concerns

Q. *What subjects are taboo in magazines?*
A. Some magazines have no taboos, and state this in their editorial requirements in *Writer's Market*. Others state what their particular taboos are. For instance, you wouldn't submit an article about a plane wreck to an airlines magazine. Car magazines sometimes specify no accidents. Many men's magazines use sexy stories; others are not markets for this type. The confession magazines are now accepting stories about racial and religious conflicts that were formerly taboo. Religious magazines have taboos which vary from magazine to magazine. Church school papers use stories that follow the precepts of their particular religion. Some state flatly, "No smoking, drinking, dancing, etc." Some police trade journals object to the use of the word "cops." When writing for the youngest of the juvenile set, keep the ending happy. You should write for sample copies of the magazines you plan to submit to and study them to see just what they use.

Q. *I've got an article that I've submitted to several different magazines, all without success.* McCall's, Vogue, Cosmopolitan, Woman's Day — *it's made the rounds of all the women's magazines. I've researched and written my article carefully, and I think I ended up with a good manuscript. Why isn't it selling?*
A. Although it's true that all the magazines you've mentioned come under the general category of "women's" publications, each one has a slightly different audience from the others; each magazine's readers have interests and characteristics that attract them to that particular publication, instead of to the others. The fact that you have submitted the same article to four very different publications might reveal that you have not *slanted* the article to one specific publication. Each maga-

94

zine has different needs to satisfy its readership. *Cosmopolitan,* for example, caters to the sophisticated single woman; *Woman's Day* concentrates on family oriented topics. It's clear that an article written for the needs of one would clearly not meet the needs of the other. *Woman's Day* would be the place to market an article on problems of child-rearing; *Cosmopolitan* would not be interested. Check *Writer's Market* for the needs of any publication, and read several issues of the magazine to learn the kinds of material it publishes.

Q. *I sent an article to a magazine and it came back without a rejection slip. Somebody had just crossed out the editor's name in my covering letter and just scrawled "Read the magazine!" across the letter. Isn't this a rather insulting reply?*
A. Apparently not, if you hadn't looked at a recent issue and learned that the editor you were addressing the submission to no longer worked there. By the same token, the editorial slant of the magazine may have changed and the type of article you were submitting was no longer appropriate. It's very important to also look at recent sample issues of a magazine in addition to reading the *latest* market requirements for a magazine. Don't depend on an old edition of *Writer's Market* for your information.

Q. *I submitted a book proposal about a year ago that was rejected. I've now come up with a better title that I think is a natural for one of the houses that rejected it. Should I resubmit it?*
A. As long as the same editor is at that publishing house, changing the title isn't likely to make the book *idea* any more appealing to this particular publisher than it was the first time. As one editor put it, "Think up new ideas, not just new strategies to sell your old one." That doesn't prevent you from submitting your new title/book idea to another publisher.

Q. *I'm going to New York with my husband to a convention just about the time I'll have my short story finished. Would it be to my advantage to hand deliver the manuscript?*
A. No, it would be a disservice to the editor who can't really tell you anything about your manuscript until he reads it, which he can't do right on the spot, and it will interrupt his day.

Q. *I have a cousin who is in sales with a leading book publisher and I sent him my manuscript asking him to pass it along to the right editor. After weeks of waiting, I sent a follow-up note inquiring. Shortly after that I got a form rejection letter from the editorial department. Am I wrong to have expected a more personal response?*
A. If the manuscript had interested the editorial department for possible publication, you would have gotten the personal response. Some beginning writers think that "knowing someone at the publishing company" will be an advantage. It isn't. Your manuscript has to sell itself.

Writer/Editor Relations

Q. *I have two minor changes I'd like to make in an article I mailed to a publisher last week. Would it be all right to send the editor a note specifying the changes I'd like made in my manuscript?*
A. No. For better or worse, the manuscript you mailed is the one the editor now has. Any changes will have to be made after the article is accepted. To send in the corrections now would only serve to exasperate the editor. If your manuscript is accepted, you will probably have an opportunity later to suggest the changes.

(For further tips on dealing with editors, see chapter thirty-five.)

Q. *I have several questions for various departments of a magazine, dealing with a query, my subscription, and other facets of their business. Is it okay to write just one letter?*
A. Such a practice can save you postage, but can also try an editor's patience. *The Basics of Selling Your Writing* includes an article by Meg Hill—"How to Drive an Editor Nuts (And Assure That Your Words Never See Print)"—in which she describes a letter to a women's magazine which contains a query, points out that last issue's recipe for banana fritters didn't work, proposes a cookbook idea, informs the publisher of an address change (to be routed to the subscription department), and encloses a letter to be forwarded to the author of an article. Honoring all those requests takes a lot of time (making photocopies, routing to various departments). It's best to send separate letters. Not only will it ensure that your requests get to the right people, it will make the editor look more kindly on you in the future.

Q. *I submitted a manuscript to a publisher a few weeks ago, and have heard nothing since. Is it okay to phone the editor to ask about the status of my manuscript?*
A. No. Most publishers and magazines receive so many manuscripts that it is impossible for the average staff member to know the status of a particular article at any given time. Most publishers have a reporting time listed in *Writer's Market*, so don't expect to hear anything from them for at least that long. If that time passes and you still have heard nothing, don't call—*write* a note requesting a report on your manuscript. Editors don't like phone calls from writers requesting immediate reports.

Q. *Why is it so important to buy expensive paper and new typewriter ribbons? Isn't the quality of the article what will make the sale?*
A. Look at the physical appearance of a manuscript as being similar to your first meeting with a prospective employer. Since *you* wouldn't show up looking less than your best, why should your manuscript? The small and careless factors in your manuscript can aggravate the most tolerant editors. A faded typewriter ribbon makes a manuscript hard to read and harder to photocopy. Heavily edited manuscripts leave no room for the editor to do *her* editing. Cut-and-paste, or cellophane

tape, also annoy an editor. The ancient, dog-eared manuscript that has obviously been seen by too many other editors makes an editor think there must be a reason no one has bought it before him. If you want a manuscript to sell, make sure it has no counts against it *before* it's even read by an editor. Neatness counts when making a positive impression with your manuscript.

Chapter 15

What Is Style?

The headmaster of an English elementary school commented, "I see four kinds of writing: 1) Just plain bad. 2) Correct but dead. 3) Incorrect but good. 4) Correct and good." The beginner's search for that last ideal is often a struggle. Editor and writer Theodore Bernstein reminds us: "Everyone who has made it at least through high school uses two languages—both of them English. They are not vastly different, yet they are distinct. One is spoken English, often colorful, clear in its intended emphasis and assisted by facial expression, tone and gestures. The other is written English."

This chapter answers a few of the most common style questions. For more detailed discussions, we recommend two classic books: *The Elements of Style* by William Strunk Jr. and E.B. White (Macmillan) and *On Writing Well* by William Zinsser (HarperPerennial). For questions regarding specific words, see *Webster's Dictionary of English Usage* (Merriam-Webster) and *Harper Dictionary of Contemporary Usage* by William and Mary Morris (HarperPerennial).

The Concept of Style

Q. *When an editor or teacher talks about my style, what does he mean?*
A. Style refers to the way an author expresses his ideas. It's *how* he says something in his work, rather than *what* he says; style is form rather than content. Each writer's work has an individual style as unique as a fingerprint; this is true whether he writes novels, magazine articles, poetry or plays. Good style need not be characterized by complex constructions and polysyllabic words; it *is* marked by a clear presentation and apt expression of ideas. A writer's personal style doesn't appear overnight. It takes time and practice to develop your own method of putting thoughts into words.

Q. *Would you explain the term "depth" in the field of writing?*
A. "Depth" means many things to many editors. But perhaps the one interpretation they would all agree on is that a piece of writing that has depth has something important to say to readers. It avoids frivolity or top-of-the-head superficiality about the ideas presented; it requires thought on the part of the writer *and* the reader.

Nonfiction of depth would be based on well-researched data. Fiction of depth would arise from thoughtful sensitivity to and perception of human behavior.

Q. *How can I improve my style?*
A. Each writer has her own personal style, her own way of expressing her ideas, so there are no set rules or guidelines for improving style. Style should be natural for the writer, acceptable to the reader, and appropriate to the content of the piece. Good style can only evolve and be refined through the practice of writing and the study of good writing.

To improve style, the writer should read widely and determine what is good about a particular piece of writing. He should not parrot the style of another writer; rather, he should evaluate his own writing by comparing flaws and strong points in what others have written. Evaluation by either a writing teacher or a professional criticism service is also helpful.

Q. *Several times I have come across literary criticism using the phrase "pedestrian writing." The phrase has been used in discussing published material without stating whether it is considered good writing. Exactly what is "pedestrian writing?"*
A. The term "pedestrian," when applied to writing, is definitely unflattering. It means the work is prosaic or dull. The Latin root "ped-" refers to the foot, and the usual definition of the noun "pedestrian" is one who travels on foot . . . such as the common man (who presumably doesn't have a better way to travel). In connection with writing, the adjective means common or ordinary.

Q. *What does my writing teacher mean when he suggests that I "loosen up" my writing style?*
A. The statement implies that you should try to lessen the formality of your writing and strive for a style that is more casual and easier to comprehend. Conventional idioms, slang, contractions ("he's" instead of "he is"), common words and shorter sentences can achieve an informal style. "Loosening up" your style gives your manuscript a more conversational tone and makes it easier to read.

Q. *I recently read an article by a well-known fiction writer who said it isn't good to read other fiction writers. He stated it confuses a writer's style and makes his work seem inferior. Is this true?*
A. The narrow view of that particular writer is not generally shared by most writers who have one love in common — the love of reading. If reading the work of others confuses a writer's style, then such a style was probably not individual enough or rooted deeply enough to begin with. The novice writer may go through several phases of stylistic expression before he establishes the one that is his own. Remember that a writer who reads only his own work may find that he is writing only for himself.

Q. *At the bottom of a form rejection slip I received for an article, an editor had written,*

"Write more naturally." What does that mean?
A. It could mean that instead of using words and phrases that an average person would, you use the longer rather than the simpler word, the convoluted rather than the straightforward sentence. "Write as you talk" is a good guideline when writing for popular magazines.

Q. *How can I make my writing more vigorous—something a writing teacher said my writing lacked?*
A. Make good use of the active voice (not, "the car was stolen by Bob," but "Bob stole the car."). Write with strong, specific nouns and verbs instead of depending on adjectives and adverbs. ("The Volkswagen skidded through the blockade.") Avoid too many qualifiers like the words "very," "little" and "rather." Read aloud what you've written to check for rhythm, pace and clarity.

Specific Points of Style

Q. *I seem to spend so much time on style that it takes forever to finish a manuscript. Is there such a thing as worrying too much about style?*
A. If you spend all your time worrying about *how* to say something, you may never get it said. While it is important to write clearly and with appealing style, too much concentration on the technique of writing can create a roadblock that prevents you from finishing a piece. It's more important and helpful to get finished pieces out into the marketplace for the perusal of professional editors than it is to spend endless time refining the same manuscript over and over again. If the content is good, an editor will probably iron out stylistic problems.

If a particular section of your article or story bothers you, it's best to leave it alone for a couple of days. If you look at one piece for an extended period of time, you can lose all perspective and find fault with even your best work.

Q. *I want to write books and stories for children, but I don't want my style to be too involved or mature for them to read. How can I make sure I'm writing for the proper age group?*
A. One way is to spend time with children and their relatives, teachers, librarians, and other people who are familiar with the way children think. Family members who have children can be a good resource. Read literature aimed at the age group for whom you intend to write. One helpful reference is *Best Books for Children*, which lists thirteen thousand books for children preschool through the sixth grade, and the age group for which each is written. The titles are arranged by subject, so you can easily find what has been written on your chosen topic.

Q. *Has grammar been updated to compensate for the use of the generic pronoun "he?"*
A. Although the phrase "Everyone does what *he* likes" would once have been read without second thought, it now raises the question of whether automatic use of the masculine pronoun in generic situations is an acceptable practice. As Casey Miller

and Kate Swift write in *The Handbook of Nonsexist Writing for Writers, Editors and Speakers,* "Like 'generic' *man,* 'generic' *he* fosters the misconception that the standard human being is male."

There are several alternatives for the writer who wishes to avoid "he" as a generic pronoun. The word *they* is often used, although—technically—the construction is grammatically incorrect. For instance, in the above sentence, "Everybody does what they like." A double pronoun construction could be used: "Everybody does what he or she likes." Used extensively, however, this technique can become awkward. It has been shortened with the use of the slash, resulting in an equally distracting "he/she" or "s/he."

Rewriting the sentence can eliminate the need for the pronoun in many cases.

Publishers in general are sticking to the masculine pronoun, understood as including everyone, but study individual publisher's guidelines and read the publication to learn the preferences of editors you're aiming toward.

Q. *Is a short title considered a virtue for a magazine article or short story?*
A. A good, short title can help catch the attention of the editor. Connie Emerson, author of *The Writer's Guide to Conquering the Magazine Market,* says that most magazine article titles have no more than six words. Always study previous issues of the magazine to which you are submitting your work to learn the kind of titles it uses. Short stories also benefit from short titles designed to pique the curiosity of readers and editors. The title should be succinct and closely related to the characters and the action. While the length of title an author chooses is part of his style, he's also subject to the editor's preferences, which are sometimes determined by the short story's placement within the magazine.

Q. *How can a humorous book written in the first person (such as those by Erma Bombeck) be thought of as fiction, even allowing for exaggerated anecdotes?*
A. Essentially these books are more imagination than reality, even though they are probably inspired by factual bits and pieces in the writer's life. Writing in first person doesn't necessarily guarantee that the material is true.

Q. *I've often seen* The Chicago Manual of Style *referred to by editors. Just what is it and where can I find a copy?*
A. *A Manual of Style* is a book which refers to the manner of preparing a manuscript according to the style guidelines developed by the University of Chicago, published in an extensive volume by The University of Chicago Press. It gives guidelines for capitalization, punctuation, italicization, and much, much more. It is not designed to help you develop your own "writing style." Style in this case refers to the way a manuscript is set up for typesetting. You can probably see a copy at the reference department in your local library, or order a copy directly from The University of Chicago Press, 5801 Ellis Ave., Chicago IL 60637. It is also available in most bookstores.

Q. *Can you please tell me why all the articles and stories in some magazines appear to have been written by the same author? The articles are the same style as the fiction. Can any of these magazines that seem to be written by one person be considered freelance markets?*

A. The stories and articles in certain magazines may seem to be the product of one prolific writer, but usually they're not. Individual magazines have specific formats and preferred styles, and in the hope of selling to them, many writers are careful to slant to their known preferences. Editors do some rewriting where material warrants it, and this tends to give an additional familiar touch to the work. So these magazines may be freelance markets, just with strong style preferences.

Chapter 16

What Do I Need to Do to Use a Pen Name?

Writers use pen names for a variety of reasons — anonymity from their families and friends, to foil sexist editors, to establish audiences for different types of work. How do you select a pen name and let your mailman and banker in on the secret so you can receive mail and cash checks? The following information will smooth the way for you.

What's in a Name?

Q. *Can a writer use a pen name, become successful or famous, and still remain anonymous? Suppose a writer dislikes publicity, and is very shy with persons outside her family and friends' circle. What in your opinion would be the advantages and disadvantages of anonymity in such a case?*
A. With the publisher's help, a writer could achieve both success and anonymity. The chief advantage of this would be the fulfillment of the author's desire to remain unidentified. The disadvantages would include lack of public acclaim and the thrill of seeing one's own name on successful books. Other disadvantages would include the necessity to reject all interviews, and worst of all, the burden of having to keep a secret.

Q. *What is the real value of using a pen name? Are pen names customarily used by professional writers today?*
A. A pen name is used to protect the identity of the writer employing it. There are any number of reasons why a writer wouldn't want his name associated with the material he writes.

Sometimes an author will use a pen name if he writes a different kind of book than he has written before, such as when mainstream novelist Evan Hunter writes mysteries under the pseudonym "Ed McBain." This practice keeps an Evan Hunter fan from picking up a book that is radically different from what he expects from the author.

Prolific writers often have to adopt pen names, since most hardcover publishers will frequently ask for exclusive rights to the name of a successful author. In the words of novelist Dean Koontz, "He [the publisher] doesn't want *his* new Sam Hepplefinger novel to be in competition with some other publisher's new Sam Hepplefinger novel." Writer Victoria Holt published under two other names because of this.

There might be a college professor of mathematics who secretly authors who-done-its and doesn't want the word to get around to his students and colleagues. Or a writer's family might object to her career and, to disassociate herself from them, she changes her name. Or a writer might simply dislike her real name — it may be hard to pronounce or look unwieldy in print — so she adopts a more suitable one. For most writers, though, there is sufficient satisfaction in seeing one's real name in a byline.

Q. *What is in a name? Would an editor be more likely to accept an article by an author with a more distinctive sounding name than a plain name? My name is very ordinary, but I don't want to use a pen name. What would you suggest?*
A. Use your real name. Editors don't care a John Doe about a name for the byline. It's always the quality of writing and the interest of subject matter that sell a manuscript. Names are incidental.

Q. *Although I am a woman writer, I am chiefly interested in the type of material that would sell to those magazines traditionally classified as "men's publications," such as* Outdoor Life *or* Field & Stream. *Can I use a male pseudonym or my initials, rather than a feminine name, and will it increase my chances of sales?*
A. In general, your writing will be judged on the basis of your authority on the subject, not your sex. It's possible that some editors might have second thoughts about running a men's article written by a woman. Although discrimination against women has decreased, it still exists; a male editor *might* assume that a woman could not write a traditionally "male" article. If using a male pen name will help make a sale, use one.

On the other hand, since women writers outnumber men in religious and small circulation periodicals, a male pen name could appear to an editor as possibly having a new slant to well-worn subjects, thus enhancing chances of a sale.

The pen name situation would apply also when men are writing female-oriented material. A number of authors of romance novels, for example, are men using female pseudonyms.

Q. *Are there any disadvantages in using a pen name?*
A. When an editor notices the same byline several times in other publications, he's more apt to buy the work of that writer who has a track record of delivering publishable material. The use of pen names dilutes the impact of your repeated sales for the editor and for the reader who looks for more material by a writer he likes.

Selecting a Pen Name

Q. *How do I go about choosing a pen name?*
A. There are no guidelines for deciding on a pen name. It can be a combination of first and last names the writer finds attractive. A baby-name book is a good source of first names; last names can be names the writer has heard or imagined, or names taken from the newspaper or phone book. Choosing a pen name is similar to naming a fictional character. The writer might wish to consider the name's appropriateness to the material carrying the byline. "Letitia Beauregarde," for example, would be more likely to write the saga of a southern family than a first-person account of a hunting trip in the Amazon jungles.

Q. *I want to use as a pen name a lovely name which happens to belong to a little girl in England, an occasional pen pal of my daughter. Must I ask permission? What if I were to pick a name out of a telephone directory?*
A. Yes, it would be best to ask permission of the little girl in England (or her parents) if you plan to use her name as a pen name in America. It's not a good idea to pick a complete name out of a telephone directory. The person with that real name may sue you for libel or invasion of privacy—depending on what you wrote and how well it sold. A better idea is to choose a combination of two different names. The spelling of a nice-sounding name can also be changed.

Q. *I would like to use a pen name, but how can I be sure the name I select isn't one that is already being used by someone else?*
A. Except in cases where extremely well-known names, such as Ann Landers, might be registered as a trademark, most writers simply go the Library of Congress Catalog card directories in their public library, look up the last name they want to use, and see if anybody else has already copyrighted books in that name. Your librarian can assist you in locating the directories of Library of Congress Catalog authors.

Q. *Because I hope to begin my political writing where George Orwell (Eric Blair) concluded his career, I would like to adopt the pen name, George Orwell II. Will I need permission from his heirs?*
A. Yes, you will need permission, but I doubt that Mr. Orwell's heirs would allow you to cash in on his reputation. Try to make it on your own!

Doing Business as . . .

Q. *Sometimes an author writes under a pen name because he doesn't want his real name known. How does the writer cash a check made out to his pen name—especially if he's well known in a small town?*
A. When the manuscript is submitted under a pen name, the author usually includes his real name and address on the title page, so that the check will be made out to him and he can cash it without letting anyone know what the check is for.

If the check is made out to the pen name, the author can simply endorse it with the pen name, then endorse it over to his real name and cash it that way. In any case, it's always best to notify both your bank and the local postmaster that you'll be using a pen name. Letting them know that you're "d.b.a. (doing business as)" your pseudonym will ensure that your mail will be delivered and that you'll be able to cash checks, should they be made out to your pen name. In some communities, a writer must register that he is doing business under another name.

Q. *If an article or book is written under a pseudonym must I copyright it under my pen name, or can I use my real name in the copyright form to protect my rights to the work?*
A. On the copyright registration form, you can list your pseudonym under "Name of Author" and your real name under "Copyright Claimant," with a brief explanation of the name difference. This guarantees proof of your authorship of the work in the event your heirs need to establish that the work is yours.

Q. *Please tell me how I can write an article under a pen name and yet be able to prove in event of a court case that I wrote it. I know that I can register it in the copyright office under my real name and the pen name, but I prefer to copyright it and register it under my pen name. The article is not going to be published by a magazine — it's a private effort — but I don't want to lose my rights when it's printed and circulated. This leaves me with the problem of having to prove that the pen name is really me. Could I mail a copy of the article to myself with both names on it and keep it unopened in a safe place — as proof? Could I send a copy to a banker or lawyer or someone? What would you suggest?*
A. Writing an article under a pen name and mailing one copy of it to yourself with both your pen name and real name included might work. Or you could get the copy notarized with both names on it. Most writers who are going to use pen names usually notify their postmaster and banker that they will be receiving mail and checks in that business name. Keep in mind that in the United States, if you privately print an article and distribute it, you must be sure to print the copyright notice on it before distribution. Otherwise you are placing your article in the public domain.

Chapter 17

How Can I Protect My Work?

Beginning writers seem to be divided into two large groups: paranoids who are afraid someone will steal all their ideas, and innocents who don't take the time to learn that they should hold on to as many rights to their work as they can. The questions and answers in this chapter and in chapter eighteen (which considers copyright in depth) will alert you to what's at stake—and help you protect your writing. For more information, see *Every Writer's Guide to Copyright and Publishing Law* by Ellen Kozak (Henry Holt) and *The Law (in Plain English) for Writers* by Leonard D. DuBoff (John Wiley & Sons).

The Matter of "Rights"

Q. *What is meant by "rights?" What rights are you supposed to sell?*
A. A writer owns all rights to his literary creation. He is entitled to decide who shall own the right to print his story for the first time or reprint it or make it into a movie or adapt it to any other print or electronic format. Such rights are his protection against those who would come along and freely use his work for their own purposes. The rights most commonly offered for sale to publications are first North American serial rights, which mean the writer is selling the right to be first to print this particular work the first time in a magazine or newspaper. All other rights still belong to the writer. On the manuscript, in the upper right corner of the title page, indicate the rights you are offering for sale. And make sure that any check you cash for an accepted work does not carry an endorsement for rights other than those you want to sell.

Q. *What is the difference between first North American rights and first serial rights when submitting to a major magazine?*
A. Both phrases mean almost the same thing, the right to publish the material once for the first time. The word "serial" refers to newspapers, magazines and publications that are published on a continuing basis. First North American serial rights covers first publication rights in both the United States and Canada (American magazines that distribute in Canada usually want this extra protection); first

serial covers first publication rights anywhere in the world.

Q. *What does "buys all rights" mean? Does it mean they buy first and subsequent rights? Or that they buy any rights offered?*
A. "Buys all rights" means they buy the rights to *all* possible avenues of sale on that manuscript—such as book, movie, TV, syndication, reprint and other rights. Some publications that buy all rights will reassign rights to the author after publication. Check this point with the editor.

Q. *Are second and reprint rights the same? Can they be sold more than once?*
A. Second serial rights is the term used by publishers to refer to the right to publish a book excerpt in a magazine or newspaper *after* book publication. But some magazine editors use the term to also mean rights granted by a work's copyright owner or author to a magazine, giving permission to reprint an article, poem or story after it has already appeared in another publication. These reprint rights may be sold as many times as the author or copyright owner wishes, to any number of publications.

Q. *What are usually the best rights and/or most profitable rights offered by writers of short stories and books?*
A. The "most profitable" or "best" rights can't be predicted in advance. Some short stories may turn out to be optioned by movie companies; others may only appear in a magazine. The main thing for the writer to do is to hold as many rights to his work as he can, selling the rights individually, never granting "all rights" to his work to any buyer. For example, a short story writer should only sell "first serial rights" or "one-time rights" to his story to a magazine.

A book contract spells out in detail what rights the author is granting to the publisher and which rights the author retains. For recommendations in this area see chapter thirty-eight on book publishing.

Q. *A local copyrighted newspaper is interested in my column. Does the paper have all rights to my column until the rights are reassigned to me; and do I put the copyright symbol on copies submitted to other publications as copyrighted by me or by the paper?*
A. Most newspapers are *not* copyrighted, but your column will be protected initially by your newspaper because it is copyrighted. Under the current copyright law it is assumed you are only selling one-time rights to this newspaper unless you both agree to something else in writing. Verify this with your newspaper editor and get a letter in reply from him that spells out exactly what rights his paper is using. Hold the letter on file. Tell the editor that you plan to resubmit some of the column material to other publications. Sell one-time rights and hold the copyright for yourself.

Q. *Some periodicals indicate "Buys all rights. Publication not copyrighted." If a periodical is not copyrighted, it seems the only rights it can claim are the rights to first publication. Am I correct?*

A. The publisher of an uncopyrighted publication may say "all rights" on his check, but the lack of copyright will permit anyone to make whatever further use of the material he wishes. So the original publisher could reprint it if he wanted to — and so could anyone else.

The Buying and Selling of Rights?

Q. *While most how to books about freelancing advocate specifying rights for sale on manuscripts, others claim this is a mark of amateurs and that editors who buy rights other than what are offered might reject the manuscript rather than dicker over rights. What is the accepted practice?*
A. It is customary and businesslike to offer first serial rights unless the magazine's editorial listing in *Writer's Market* states it buys all rights. Then the writer has to decide whether he wants to sell under those terms.

Q. *Can rights be reassigned to me from a magazine that is now defunct?*
A. If the magazine was owned and published by a still-operating corporation or association, the author's material would still be its property. You might contact the rights and permissions department of the organization that published the now-defunct magazine. If you can't locate any present owners, then indicate that fact to the editor to whom you're trying to sell reprint rights.

Q. *I sold first and reprint rights for an article to a magazine. Can I sell reprint rights to another publication, or must I wait until the first magazine has used its reprint rights?*
A. It is permissible to sell reprint rights to the second publication. The only exception would be if you sold the first magazine exclusive reprint rights for a certain period of time. Then you would have to wait until the article was reprinted before reselling.

Q. *If I sell a novelette to a publisher, and some movie producer reads it in the magazine and wants to buy the movie rights, does he buy from me or the publisher? Must I reserve some kind of rights? Will the publisher be entitled to part of the money paid for the movie rights?*
A. Reserving movie rights to a novelette depends on what rights you sell to the magazine in which it initially appears. Most magazines buy only "first serial rights." Some magazines, however, buy "all rights," which would give them complete return of money on any subsidiary sale of the story to movies, TV, etc. If you want to reserve these other rights to yourself, when you submit your novelette to a magazine publisher, you must type in the upper right corner "First North American Serial Rights Only." The magazine editor will know these are the only rights you want to sell. You should also notice carefully the check from the magazine publisher, since sometimes the endorsement on the check indicates the magazine is buying all rights. Often the accounting department of a magazine does not know what rights your manuscript indicated and if their normal procedure would be to buy all rights, the

check will so indicate. By endorsing the check, you would be giving away all rights, even though your manuscript had indicated you were interested in selling first rights only. If you receive such a check, return it to the editor requesting a check without the "all rights" endorsement.

Stolen Ideas and Other Concerns

Q. *I had an idea for an article, which was rejected by an editor, and a similar article appeared in that magazine a few months later. This has also happened when an entire manuscript was rejected. How can I protect myself from editors who steal my ideas?*
A. A writer will often suspect piracy when he sees his idea published in a magazine shortly after his query or manuscript was rejected by the same publication, but this assumption is usually false. Freelancer Gary Provost has coined what he calls his first law of plagiarism: "The better your understanding of the market, the greater the chance of your thinking you were plagiarized." In other words, similarities between your idea or manuscript and the published article are the result of both you and the author of the published piece knowing what the magazine is looking for. Since a magazine often has between three months and one year "lead time" between an issue's creation and its publication, the published piece was probably written or assigned before you even wrote your query letter.

Unless the published article uses word-for-word the same paragraphs and sentences as the rejected work, there is no proof of editorial piracy.

There are, however, steps you can take to ensure that your completed manuscript will not be stolen. First of all, be sure that your manuscript carries your copyright notice. Also, you should *always* keep a photocopy of your manuscript. If you ever have reason to believe an editor has stolen from you, consult an attorney.

Q. *An article recently appeared in a magazine, strikingly similar to one I have been trying to sell to the same magazine for some time. Because of this I am now forced to forget about selling my article, since the subject's already been covered. What can I do about this?*
A. One frustrating fact of a freelance writer's life is to find that an idea he has, someone else also has had and beaten him to publication with it—sometimes even using the same words. You're not forced to forget about submitting your manuscript elsewhere, because many articles are published on the same subject in a variety of publications within a two- or three-year period. If your article is well written, and hits the right magazine at the right time, publication of the other article will not be a deterrent to publication of yours.

Q. *A writer friend of mine recently sold an article about a topic on which I've been working for some time. I believe he stole my idea. Is there any way I can keep this from happening?*
A. Sometimes, when fellow writers gather and "talk shop," a writer will casually mention a piece he's working on. Months or years may go by and another writer

may end up doing an article on the same idea. Once your idea is discussed, you've put it out where others can get at it—consciously or unconsciously. A good rule is this: Don't discuss a work in progress with other writers. They don't intentionally steal, and may not remember that you were working on the same idea, since most writers get ideas from many different sources—newspapers, magazines, books, television, films, neighbors and fellow workers.

Q. *An article I recently sold was heavily edited, distorting the meaning of some of the opinions and quotes contained in it. Can I ask for the right of article approval on any future sales?*
A. It might not be a good idea to propose such a request in your query letter, since such preconditions might turn off the editor. The question can be raised after correspondence has passed between author and editor, and after the article has been finished and submitted. Include a paragraph in your cover letter asking that if the article is changed from your original manuscript—in terms of content, not just copyediting revisions—you would like the opportunity to see the final edited copy before publication.

Q. *Nine years ago I sent a manuscript to a publishing firm. They rejected it (as did others) after keeping it so long it was necessary to write them about it. Now I read they are publishing a book by that exact title. The title is extremely important to my book. Do they have all the rights in this case?*
A. A title cannot be copyrighted, so there's nothing stopping you from using your title. As long as your story is completely different from the published one with the same title, that publisher can't claim unfair competition by the publisher who accepts your book.

Q. *How can I protect myself from losing my manuscripts and writing equipment in a house fire or burglary?*
A. One way is to make sure your writing operation is covered by your homeowner's or personal property insurance policy. Since freelancing is a business, it's possible that your files, reference books, typewriter, word processor, or other equipment may not be covered by your current policy, and you may need a rider to add to your present coverage. You may even need a separate policy for your business. If you live in an apartment, or don't have such an insurance policy for some other reason, the Federal Crime Insurance program can insure your equipment against burglary or theft. For a premium (in 1993) of $126 per year, you receive $10,000 protection. Contact the program at Box 6301, Rockville MD 20850; telephone number is (800) 638-8780. To protect against loss by fire, fireproof strongboxes are available for your papers.

Case Histories: Who Owns What?

Q. *About five years ago, I sold a children's story to a magazine that greatly altered and shortened it. It was published with a credit line that said, "adapted from a story by*

Joseph P. Ritz." There is no question the magazine owns the publication rights to the story as it was published. But does it also own the rights to the original manuscript, to date unpublished?
A. It depends on what rights you sold to the original story that the magazine paid for and revised. If it bought only first rights, then you can resubmit your unpublished original elsewhere.

Q. *Suppose Smith wrote a manuscript, in first draft, and gave it to Jones to read. Jones, a professional writer, keeps the manuscript, and in due time writes a book based on Smith's manuscript. If the book sells, and/or a movie is made from it, or paperbacks are published, or any other form of benefit derives from the sale of this book, does Smith have any rights in this book or the benefits from it?*
A. Much would depend on the agreement Smith made with Jones when he gave him his manuscript. Why, for instance, did Smith allow Jones to keep the manuscript? Smith might be able to take this matter to court as an infringement of his copyright, which protected his unpublished manuscript. In doing so, though, he'd have to prove that Jones actually copied his exact language or the development, treatment, arrangement or sequence of ideas in the work. And he would have to take legal action within the period of the applicable statute of limitations. It would, of course, be more desirable if Smith and Jones could work out some financial arrangement agreeable to both, rather than go to the expense of court action.

Q. *Some years ago, I wrote a children's book about the whaling era. It included several stories of foreign lands, each having a special song. The book was published in 1956 and copyrighted in my name. The book is now out of print. As the stories and songs are my own material, I would like to know if I have the right to make tape recordings of them for sale to a publisher who produces visual aids and programs for school use. If there are restrictions to such usage, will you please tell me how I can meet them?*
A. Unless the book contract you signed with the original publisher of your children's book about the whaling era reserved to the publisher the right to make tape recordings of your book, you have the right to use the book in that way. These special rights for the use of material contained in books are usually the subject of a special clause in the contract and you should review the contract to see whether you, or the publisher, or both, share in these rights.

Q. *A recently published book contains verbatim, unattributed quotes from an article I wrote on the same subject for a magazine some time ago. What action, if any, should I take? Do I have the right of monetary compensation from the book's publisher for this unauthorized use of my work?*
A. How much material from your article was used? Would it be allowable under the fair use provision of the copyright act? (See details on that in chapter eighteen of this book.) If there is substantial quoting from your piece, the next question is what rights did you sell to the magazine publisher? If you sold more than first serial rights to the piece, she could have given permission to the book's author to use

portions of your work. If that is the case, then it's just a question of non-attribution.

If you sold only first rights, you may have been the victim of copyright infringement, and you should have an attorney write to the book's publisher, attach to the letter a copy of your article, and inform the publisher that you may sue for copyright infringement.

Whether you were able to collect monetary compensation from the book publisher would depend on whether you could prove you sustained actual damages as a result and/or whether the publisher was aware he was infringing your copyright.

Q. *The book on which I'm working relies heavily on information from articles I've written over the years. Only a handful of editors have given me permission; others have not replied. None of the checks I received in payment for the works indicated I signed away all rights. Can I use the material without infringing on the copyrights of the various publications involved?*
A. Since you never signed a check with a statement that you were selling all rights to your articles, and assuming the editors had not publicized in writers' magazines or *Writer's Market* a policy of buying all rights, you should be able to use material from them without being sued for copyright infringement.

Q. *A magazine to which I had sold articles recently stopped publishing. I have an opportunity to resell some of these published pieces elsewhere. Can I do this without infringing on the copyright of the defunct magazine?*
A. That would depend on what rights you sold to the first publisher. If you sold first rights only, then you can resubmit an article without any trouble. If you sold more than first rights, then you must try to locate the publisher and obtain his permission. Although the magazine is defunct, the publisher still owns the additional rights. Keep a record of all correspondence in this effort; that way, if you're unsuccessful in finding the publisher, and you don't know what rights you sold, you can resell the piece, and if he raises any objections you will have proof that you tried to contact him. Then, it's up to the judge.

Chapter 18

What Do I Need to Know About Copyright?

The most important fact a writer should know about copyright is that copyright is effective as soon as a writer creates a work. The current law puts the burden on the publisher to notify the author in writing if he wants to acquire other than one-time rights (that is, the right to publish it one time) to the author's work. The law also contains termination provisions that allow an author to regain rights he assigned to others, after a specific period. For questions and answers related to the selling various rights to your work, see chapter seventeen. For more information on copyright, see *Every Writer's Guide to Copyright and Publishing Law* by Ellen Kozak (Henry Holt).

Copyright Basics

Q. *When writers talk about the "new" copyright law, what do they mean?*
A. They mean the major revision of the copyright law that took effect on January 1, 1978. The most dramatic change in the revision concerned the sale of material by a publisher. Under the old law, the assumption was that the author sold all rights to his material, unless an agreement between him and the editor stipulated otherwise. The new law assumes the writer is selling one-time rights only. Copyrights obtained under the previous law must still operate under *its* regulations. Contact the U.S. Copyright Office (Library of Congress, Washington, D.C. 20559) for information on pre-1978 copyright law.

Q. *Once my work is copyrighted, how long is it protected?*
A. For works copyrighted on or after January 1, 1978, copyright protection lasts for the rest of the author's life and for fifty years after his death. If the work is collaborative, the death of the last surviving collaborator determines the starting point for the fifty years. If the work was produced under a pen name or anonymously, or if it is a work made for hire, copyright expires seventy-five years after first publication, or one hundred years after its first creation, whichever is earlier.

Q. *What is public domain?*

A. Any published or distributed material without a copyright notice or on which a copyright has expired is considered to be in the public domain—that is, available for use by any member of the general public without payment to, or permission from, the original author.

Q. *When I sell various rights to my work, doesn't that affect my ownership of the copyright?*
A. No. Various rights are all part of your copyright, but selling them in no way diminishes your ownership of the actual work. William Strong, in *The Copyright Book,* likens copyright to ownership of land. "If you own a parcel of land, you can sell mineral rights to *A,* water rights to *B,* and a right-of-way to *C,* and still be considered the owner of the underlying property," he writes. In the case of written work, you may sell paperback reprint rights to one company, film and television rights to another, and book club rights to still another without impairing your ownership of the original work.

Q. *When submitting a manuscript, should the writer place the symbol © "copyright by . . . author's name and the year" on the manuscript copy? Or is this unnecessary? What is the procedure regarding copyright when submitting a manuscript?*
A. It's always a good idea to show your copyright notice on the first page of your manuscript. A copyrighted magazine's copyright notice covers your individual contribution to that magazine; if you should happen to be submitting to an uncopyrighted publication it would be important to make sure your copyright notice appeared on the first page of your article, story or poem.

Q. *When an editor tightens up my article, correcting a weak ending and other flaws, is the resultant article still under my copyright?*
A. Yes. Usually, an editor's changes in your manuscript will not be extensive enough to qualify as a new work derived from your own. However, if your work is going to be heavily revised, you should clarify with the editor that the article is still yours, not his.

Q. *If I transfer certain rights to my manuscript to another party, are those rights relinquished forever, or can I get them back at some point in the future?*
A. If an otherwise specific time period is not written into the rights you grant someone—for example, such as an option on your book by a motion picture producer for a period of one year—then you still have the right to terminate the grant of those rights. This can be done thirty-five years after you granted the right. Or, if the grant covered the right of publication, the period begins at the end of thirty-five years from the date of publication or forty years from when you made the grant, whichever term ends earlier. But you must execute this right of termination within a period of five years at the end of the thirty-five years or forty-year period.

Applying for Copyright Protection

Q. *How do I copyright my articles and stories?*
A. Under the copyright law that became effective January 1978, your work is protected by statutory copyright as soon as it is created in tangible form. All you need to do is display the copyright symbol (©), the year and your name on the first page of your manuscript. It need not be published to be protected.

Only if you think you might have to go to court and fight to prove your ownership of the work, is it necessary to register the material with the U.S. Copyright Office. For the proper forms and more information, write to U.S. Copyright Office, Library of Congress, Washington DC 20559.

The fee for registering a copyright claim is twenty dollars. Make your check or money order payable to the Register of Copyrights, Copyright Office, Library of Congress, Washington, DC 20559. Send the fee and the completed appropriate application form (previously obtained from the copyright office) with one copy of the unpublished manuscript or two copies of the published book carrying the copyright notice.

Q. *How necessary is the effort and expense of having a work registered at the copyright office?*
A. Since your work is copyrighted from the moment you create it, the existence or validity of your copyright will not be affected if you don't register the work. But registration can be important to the protection of your work. It can offer proof of copyright if, for any reason, notice is omitted from distributed copies of your work. Registration is also a requirement if you want to bring a lawsuit to enforce your copyright. And if registration was made before, or within five years after first publication, the courts consider it undeniable evidence of a valid copyright.

Nevertheless, there are some writers who feel that copyright registration isn't worth the bother. "It's an awful lot of trouble, a bit of an expense, and for my money, a waste of time," writes freelancer Brian Vachon. He adds that he has never registered his work, "and in twenty years as a professional writer, never worried about that oversight." The necessity of registration is something the individual writer must decide for himself. It may be bothersome, but it is the most foolproof method of protecting your work.

Q. *How important is it for a writer to secure a copyright for his book manuscript before submitting it to trade houses? Isn't it safe to entrust this detail to the publisher if and when the book is published?*
A. The publisher who buys the manuscript usually copyrights the book in the author's name. The publisher's contract usually discusses the copyright procedure.

Q. *Who handles obtaining the copyright for a published book — the publisher or the writer?*
A. A clause in most contracts between publishers and authors sets up an agreement

whereby the publisher takes out the copyright in the name of the author. The publisher merely handles the paperwork on behalf of the author and the copyright is the author's property. If you glance through a sampling of current bestsellers, you'll find that it is the author's name that usually follows the copyright symbol.

Q. *A publisher for whom I am writing an article offers the option of either giving the writer copyright for the piece or keeping it himself. Is it possible that the publisher could do a better job of handling copyright and legal matters stemming from an article? In other words, wouldn't it be a great load off my back if the copyright was in the publisher's name?*
A. No. A writer should never give up his copyright to another party when it is possible to keep it in his name. To give up copyright means that you give up all legal rights to the work. Therefore, you could not benefit from any use of the article after the initial publication.

Q. *I made an agreement with a fellow writer for him to revise the first draft of my short novel. He's done some good work on the book, but a lot remains to be done. However, he went ahead and had the version he finished copyrighted in both our names. Can I still use my original draft? To what extent am I bound by the existing copyright?*
A. You certainly may use your original draft and apply for registration of your own copyright. Although the Copyright Office accepted the other version in good faith, that would not affect the validity of your own version being copyrighted separately.

Copyright Dangers

Q. *Under the new copyright law, how does one lose copyright protection?*
A. Since under the new law your copyright exists as soon as you create a work, for your life plus fifty years, the primary ways to lose your copyright would be: 1) By publishing your work in an uncopyrighted publication and failing to have your own copyright credit line appear with your contribution—whether it's a story, article or poem. 2) By publishing a book without your copyright notice. 3) By distributing unpublished or unproduced copies of other forms of your work—play, movie script, teleplay—that do not carry your copyright credit line.

Q. *If a publisher inadvertently omits the writer's copyright notice is the work then placed in the public domain?*
A. Not if the writer had given express direction in writing to the editor that his copyright notice was to appear. Two other circumstances under which the omission of the notice would not invalidate the copyright would be: 1) if the notice had been omitted from only a relatively small number of copies or 2) if registration for the work had been made before or within five years after the publication without notice, and a reasonable effort is made to add notice to all copies distributed after the omission was discovered.

Q. *If a copyrighted story is reprinted in an uncopyrighted publication, does this in any way affect the copyright?*
A. If the publication prints your personal copyright notice with the story, your protection will remain the same. If the copyright notice is eliminated, through the editor's error—not yours—there could be problems. They won't be as severe as losing your copyright, which was what would have happened under the old law. A copyright registered with the Library of Congress will remain in effect if the piece is published without copyright notice. If the work had not been registered, it will be protected by copyright as long as it is registered within five years of publication. In both cases, the law specifies that the writer must make a "reasonable effort" to add his copyright notice to any copies distributed after the omission is discovered.

Q. *How does a writer know which magazines are not copyrighted? Is there a way I can state on my poems, fillers, and manuscripts that I want my work copyrighted? How can an author obtain a separate copyright?*
A. Before you submit a manuscript to a magazine, you should ascertain whether that magazine is copyrighted. Look for the copyright notice, which usually appears at the bottom of the table of contents page or on the masthead page listing the staff. To copyright your material that may appear in an uncopyrighted publication, on your manuscript's first page, type your own copyright notice: © Your Name, Year. When submitting to an uncopyrighted publication, ask the editor to be sure to show your copyright credit line with your poem. Since your copyright exists from the moment you create a work, it's not necessary to formally register it unless you wish to. In that case, as soon as the work is published with your copyright notice and made available to the public, register your claim by mailing to the Copyright Office the application form plus two complete copies of the publication containing your work, and the registration fee of twenty dollars.

Using Other Writers' Work

Q. *How much can I quote from copyrighted materials without infringing on copyright?*
A. There aren't any set number of lines you can quote without getting permission. In determining whether an author has made "fair use" of, or infringed, another's copyrighted work, the copyright law says the factors to be considered shall include: 1) the purpose and character of the use, including whether such use is of a commercial nature or is for nonprofit educational purposes; 2) the nature of the copyrighted work; 3) the amount and substantiality of the portion used in relation to the copyrighted work as a whole; and 4) the effect of the use upon the potential market for or value of the copyrighted work. As current and future legal cases illustrate these points, writers will have a better idea of how these guidelines will be interpreted.

Q. *I would like to quote passages from several books in a manuscript I'm writing. Must I get permission from the author or the publisher or both, and how do I go about getting it?*

A. Who can grant you permission depends on who controls the copyright to the original work. In the case of material originally published in a book, the publisher may be able to grant you permission. Write to the publisher's Rights and Permissions Department; explain exactly what material you'd like to quote and how you intend to use the passage. If the material comes from a magazine, write the editor with the same information. If the publisher or editor isn't able to grant the permission, he should forward the request to the author (or whoever owns the copyright). Depending on the use, you may be charged a reprint fee. The author or publisher also has the right to refuse your request.

Q. *I would like to reprint a passage from a book that is no longer in print. In fact, even though the copyright is as recent as 1975, the publisher is no longer in business and the author is deceased. The publisher held the copyright to the book. How do I go about getting permission to use the material?*
A. Even though the publisher is not currently in business, it still owns the copyright, which must run its course of twenty-eight years under the old copyright law. You need the publisher's permission to use the material. Contact the local chamber of commerce of the city in which the publisher was located for the most recent address on its records for the publishing house's owners. If that search fails, then keep your correspondence showing your attempt to locate the publisher, and acknowledge your source either in the text or on an acknowledgments page.

Q. *I want to write a story in which I would use three verses from* The Rubaiyat of Omar Khayyam. *Are his verses, rendered into English by Edward Fitzgerald, in the public domain?*
A. Whether the English translation of *The Rubaiyat* that you have, which was copyrighted originally in 1938, has been renewed should be investigated before using that particular English version. A letter to the Register of Copyrights, Library of Congress, Washington DC 20559 could probably determine whether that copyright is still in effect.

Q. *Does it cost anything to have the copyright office check to see if a certain old book is still copyrighted or is now in the public domain?*
A. The Library of Congress has a search fee of ten dollars per hour to search for copyright. Most searches take at least an hour or two. For further information on the book in question, you might write the Register of Copyrights, Library of Congress, Washington DC 20559.

Q. *Although news cannot be copyrighted, can bylined newspaper articles and feature stories be?*
A. What is not copyrightable is an actual news *event* — the facts of a news happening. For example, one newspaper could not copyright the facts about a fatal airplane crash and thereby prevent other publications from writing about the story. However, the newspaper's *presentation* of the facts, the style and manner in which the

facts are given to the reader, is copyrightable. One criterion for the copyrightability of newspaper articles is the concept of "authorship"—editorial comment, conjecture, deductions, or descriptions separate from the specific facts of a story. If any of these factors is present in an article, then it may be copyrighted. For this reason, many newspaper features and analytical articles can be copyrighted.

Q. *A few months ago, while in Vienna, I read in an Austrian magazine a short article that I found impressive. I asked the doctor-author for the translation rights into English, which he gladly gave me. Under whose name should one ask for the copyright—in the name of the author or translator?*
A. You had best make sure the doctor *had* the rights to give you. Query the Austrian magazine to verify that he had the translation rights. Then, yes, you would get a U.S. copyright in your name as the author of the translation. The original author's name, of course, would appear with any published version of your translation.

Q. *I am a teacher and would like advice about photocopying articles from magazines for class distribution and use. Do I need to request permission to do this copying?*
A. The copyright law sets out certain criteria for "fair use" of copyrighted materials and states that "reproduction in copies . . . for purposes such as . . . teaching (including multiple copies for classroom use) . . . is not an infringement of copyright." Obviously, the amount of copying is a consideration when judging fair use. One copyright infringement suit, for example, established some guidelines that state: "Not more than one short poem, article, story, essay, or two excerpts may be copied from the same author; nor more than three from the same collective work or periodical volume during one class term." The Copyright Office publishes a free circular R21 "Reproduction of Copyrighted Works by Educators and Librarians" that you can obtain by writing the Copyright Office, Library of Congress, Washington DC 20559.

Q. *While cleaning out an old writing desk, I happened across several examples of a very funny old newspaper column from about fifty years ago. The columns would make amusing reading for the modern reader, and I'd like to submit them for sale. Can I do this?*
A. If the columns were not copyrighted, you would be free to use the material. But if the columns were copyrighted, as many syndicated and local columns are today, then you wouldn't be free to use the material. Since under old copyright laws, the copyright was good for twenty-eight years and could be renewed for another twenty-eight, you would have to take that fifty-six-year total into consideration. If the work had been renewed at the time the new copyright law took effect in 1978, the law extended the term forty-seven years for a seventy-five-year total rather than fifty-six-year total.

Q. *I have a book of poems that have no copyright and therefore are in the public*

domain. Can I include some of these in an anthology and publish it under my copyright?
A. If the anthology contained only the public domain poems, you could not. It isn't possible to copyright anything that's already in the public domain. If you added other poems that were copyrighted, or wrote a commentary or other original material, then you could publish the anthology with your copyright.

Q. *I've based my book on extensive research of government information from government publications and files. Can I copyright my book since most of the information is in the public domain?*
A. While government material is in itself uncopyrightable, your particular rewritten presentation of it is. However, any work that consists in any large part of verbatim government material must carry in the copyright notice a statement which identifies those parts of the work which are yours and those parts which are government-produced. For specific guidelines on your work, it would be best to check with the Information and Publications Section, LM-455, Copyright Office, Library of Congress, Washington DC 20559.

Q. *Since ideas can't be copyrighted, would it be necessary to obtain permission from the author of a short story before expanding the material to book length?*
A. You are not at liberty to base a book on another author's short story without the consent of that author, since he has the exclusive right of adaptation of his own work. If you're only using the theme (the point the author makes in the story, such as perseverance pays off or crime does not) and not the actual characters and other aspects of the story, then you're only using the idea and you can proceed without permission.

Q. *Are "facts," such as those found in medical journals and reports, in the public domain? Scientific literature, the way I understand it, is in the public domain and can be used by other writers. Is this true?*
A. Most medical journals are copyrighted, so material in them would not be in the public domain. "Facts" as such cannot be copyrighted, however, so if there are well-established findings quoted in a number of medical journals that could therefore be called "facts," you could work them into your articles without the original writers' or researchers' consent. You can't lift written copy verbatim but the information — the "facts" — can be included in your writing.

Q. *In researching a magazine article I came across a feature in a magazine that I would like to use. The magazine was not copyrighted. Can I use this material?*
A. If the item you found is in an uncopyrighted publication and the author's personal copyright notice did not appear with the article, it is in the public domain. This means that no one has placed a copyright on it to protect it. Public domain material may be used by anyone. It cannot, however, be copyrighted by someone else once it has been placed in public domain, unless you considerably revise it and add to it.

Q. *I've obtained a book of photographs taken and copyrighted in 1905. Can I use them as illustrations in my book without infringing on copyright?*
A. Under the new copyright law, any work registered for renewal or already in the renewal term before January 1, 1978, had its copyright duration extended to a total of seventy-five years from the date of original copyright. Copyright protection for your photographs would have expired December 1980. They are now in the public domain and you are free to use them.

Case Histories

Q. *Each year our writers club holds contests in several divisions: short story, article, and various types of poetry. First-, second- and third-place winners, as well as honorable mentions, are announced in the published and unpublished divisions. As the procedure now stands, no method exists for exposing the winners' entries to the view of the league membership. We would like to start a creative magazine with subscription limited to club members, or a yearbook with the same type of limited subscription. Objections concern copyright. Some members fear that such exposure of material would place the material in the public domain; or that a first rights sale to a paying magazine would be jeopardized.*
A. To make your contest entries available to members, all you need to do is copyright the magazine in which they appear. Whether circulation only to league members would jeopardize the sale to a paying magazine would have to be checked with some magazine editors. However, unless you *do* show a copyright on this material, printing it even by mimeograph or multilith with a subscription method of distribution could put it in the public domain.

Q. *I have written an original play that has been produced only once. I would like to protect it from being videotaped. Can I copyright it?*
A. Yes. "Performance" is not the same as "publication," so the production of your play did not place it in the public domain. The procedure for registration of copyright is the same for dramatic scripts as it is for books and other printed matter, except you use application form PA (performing arts) rather than form TX which is for nondramatic literary works.

Q. *I've set some poems to the tunes of old-fashioned songs. Where do I get permission to such old airs as "Flow Gently Sweet Afton" and "Jingle Bells"?*
A. Anyone may use old airs without getting permission because these songs are in the public domain. Well-known and more recent songs, however, might still be under copyright. You can check the copyright dates on older popular songs in a directory—*Variety Music Cavalcade*—available at the library.

Q. *For the last fifteen years I have been collecting jokes, riddles, funny sign slogans, and humorous writings. I've gathered these from friends, acquaintances, and therapists. I don't have a clue as to their origins, and I don't know if they are copyrighted or in*

the public domain. My problem is this: I am attempting to write a book (probably paperback length) incorporating the idea that a little humor in one's life will make the rough road of rehabilitation a little easier. Since I can't identify the author of some of these masterpieces of humor, how can I protect myself against possible plagiarism suits?
A. Short gags and jokes cannot be copyrighted, so you wouldn't have any difficulty in assembling those in a book. Two hundred- to three hundred-word short prose humor pieces, however, might present a problem. If they did appear originally in copyrighted publications, you would have to rewrite them substantially to avoid plagiarism.

Q. *Does the copyright law give copyright protection to titles? Is it legal for me to use an article title that is already the title of a published book?*
A. It is not possible to copyright titles, so you can use the title of a book for an article title. It may quickly capture an editor's attention, even if the magazine decides to change it before publication in case there is a concern about a challenge of unfair competition.

Q. *I have made up several word and other games. Should I copyright them before I try to sell them? If so, how do I go about it, and how long would they be protected?*
A. Sorry, but game ideas, titles, and methods for play cannot be copyrighted. You cannot protect your game *ideas* from public use, but you can obtain a copyright for the actual printed game board and the rules of instruction. To register the copyright for an unpublished game, you should include a photograph of your game board and the set of rules, rather than the actual game board itself, to see if that would satisfy the "deposit" rules. If accepted for copyright, the term of copyright would be the same as for any other literary property—life of the author plus fifty years. If the game is published, the Copyright Office wants a complete copy of the game if it is not larger than $12'' \times 24'' \times 6''$. For more information, write the Copyright Office, Library of Congress, Washington DC 20559 for a free copy of Circular R40b "Deposit Requirements for Registration of Claims to Copyright in Visual Arts Material."

Foreign Copyrights

Q. *How well does my U.S. copyright protect my work if it's distributed or published in a foreign country?*
A. It depends on which country. If it is one of the seventy nations belonging to the Universal Copyright Convention, the work will be protected in the same way that nation would protect the writings of any of its own citizens. But, unlike U.S. copyright requirements, the U.C.C. requires the use of the © symbol to designate copyright; the phrase "Copyright 1989 by Jon Edwards" is not adequate notice. The international notice would be printed "© 1989 Jon Edwards."

The U.S. also belongs to the Buenos Aires Convention, which includes Latin American nations and in March 1989 joined the Berne Convention. Protection in these countries is extended to the holder of a copyright in any member country.

Q. *If my work is published in Canada, will I need to register it there, too? How does Canadian copyright differ from U.S. copyright?*
A. Since Canada and the United States both belong to the Universal Copyright Convention, your Canadian-published work is protected just as if it were published in the United States. Registration, as in the U.S., is optional, but advisable to prove ownership in the event of legal action. The fee for Canadian copyright registration is $35. In general, U.S. and Canadian copyright laws are similar; the author having specific questions should contact the Copyright and Industrial Design Branch, 50 Victoria Street, Place due Portage, Tower One, Hull, Quebec.

Q. *Is a word-for-word translation of any foreign language book without the publisher's consent considered plagiarism?*
A. If the foreign language book is copyrighted and copyright has not expired, it may *not* be translated without the consent of the copyright owner.

Chapter 19

How Can I Find an Agent?

"If I only had an agent, then my manuscripts would sell!" While that's a common lament—in fact, you've probably said it yourself—it's not a particularly valid one. Finding an agent can be as long and frustrating a process as finding a publisher—most agents prefer to work with published authors—and securing an agent's representation doesn't guarantee you'll find a publisher. These questions and answers deal with how to search for an agent and how to conduct this business relationship. For more information, see *Guide to Literary Agents & Art/Photo Reps* (Writer's Digest Books) and *How to Be Your Own Literary Agent* by Richard Curtis (Houghton Mifflin).

Getting an Agent

Q. *How can I find an agent?*
A. There are several ways to locate an agent. *Guide to Literary Agents & Art/Photo Reps* is a directory similar to *Writer's Market*. It lists agents, their specialties, recent books they've represented, submission requirements, and willingness to work with beginning writers. Similar information can be found in Jeff Herman's *Insider's Guide to Book Editors, Publishers, and Literary Agents* (Prima Publishing). *Literary Market Place* lists agents and indicates whether they represent authors of books, scripts, etc. and have foreign representation. Poets & Writers, Inc., (72 Spring St., New York, NY 10012) publishes *Literary Agents: A Complete Guide,* a booklet on how to deal with agents.

Submitting your own book to publishers can sometimes lead to finding an agent. When the publisher makes an offer, ask him to recommend an agent; sometimes editors like a manuscript, but for some reason cannot buy it and will recommend an agent to the author. If you contribute regularly to a magazine, or have some rapport with an editor, he may be able to recommend an agent. Writers conferences sometimes have agents as guest speakers, and you can at least meet them before sending a query letter. Check with other writers and writers groups to see if they can guide you to an agent.

No organization regulates literary agencies, although some 250 agencies belong to the Association of Authors' Representatives (Third Floor, 10 Astor Place, New York NY 10003). To be a member of AAR, agencies must agree to adhere to a written code of professional practices. This "Canon of Ethics" is reprinted in *Insider's Guide to Book Editors, Publishers, and Literary Agents*.

Q. *How will I know whether an agent is reputable or not? Is there a list I can obtain of recommended agents? I am uncertain about the qualifications of the company representing my interests and I would like to check on them. The comparative group I have in mind is the Better Business Bureau for companies. Would they also handle literary agents?*
A. Yes, the Better Business Bureau in the city in which your prospective literary agent is located could let you know whether it has had any complaints about that agency's business operation. The Association of Authors' Representatives (Third Floor, 10 Astor Place, New York NY 10003) will send a list of its member agencies for a self-addressed envelope with two first-class stamps. Other ways you could check on the reputation of an agent are to contact publishers with whom he has dealt, or to ask the agent for the names of some of his clients whom you could write to in care of their publishers, to ask about his work with them.

Q. *Are there different types of literary agents?*
A. Yes. There are two ways in which agents differ. First, some agents charge a reading fee when considering submissions from unagented writers; others consider material without charging. (For more information on this, see the next question.) The second way to categorize agents is in terms of the material they handle. There are agents who deal only in trade books—fiction and nonfiction—and others who deal in scripts. Dramatic agents who handle plays are usually located in New York, whereas those handling scripts for films and television are on the West Coast.

Q. *Most movie producers state that they look at original scripts only if submitted by an accredited agent. They list no agent's name, so how do I go about finding their agents? Also, I have several children's stories, two of which would make excellent cartoon movies. Would the same agent handle both types of stories? What is his fee?*
A. A list of agents who deal with movie producers is available from the Writers Guild of America West, 8955 Beverly Blvd., Los Angeles CA 90048. The price is $1. The agent tries to market your work and handles the business arrangement. You have to provide him with scripts, however, not stories, he can sell. Many script agents handle both regular scripts and scripts for animated films. The agent's fee is a commission on sales—usually 10 percent or 15 percent.

Q. *Once I locate a prospective agent, how do I get him to represent me?*
A. Write the agent a query letter, describing your book and your reasons for writing it; a brief outline is also helpful. Never send an entire manuscript. Include a SASE, of course, for the reply. Sometimes the agent will ask to see the first few chapters of your manuscript.

"It's easier to get some agents to take on your book properties than others," writes veteran agent Bill Adler in *Inside Publishing*. "Obviously, some of the super-agents are difficult to get to. But most of the young agents and even some of the better-known and established agents will be willing to look at your material. Whether they will take it on depends, of course, on the material."

Standard Practices

Q. *What is the standard percentage an agent receives as his commission?*
A. Generally, agents receive 15 percent of the writer's income on manuscripts as their fee although a few charge 10 percent.

Q. *Is it routine for agents to charge a fee for reading a manuscript? What does this fee entail?*
A. Some don't; others do—claiming that the fee is compensation for time spent reading unsalable new material which might otherwise be time used in selling books. Some agents also give extensive criticism as compensation for the fee.

When dealing with an agent who charges a reading fee, you should always check his background—what books he has sold recently, who he represents, and if his clients are satisfied. Find out if the agent offers criticism on manuscripts. Find out if the agent will refund the fee if he agrees to represent you and sells your book. Make sure you know what you're getting for the fee you pay. And try to determine if reading fees or sales commissions make up the agent's *primary* source of income. Obviously, you'd prefer to be represented by an agent who is most successful at selling—not reading.

If an agent is interested, either from your letter of inquiry or sample chapters, he will read, and often comment on, your manuscript free of charge.

Q. *Do agents sign contracts with clients?*
A. Some agents require a contract before they'll do business with a writer. They feel that written agreements offer the agent protection, since the author doesn't pay him any money until a contract is drawn up by the publisher containing a clause that provides for payment to the agent. The agreement should cover several areas to benefit both author and agent. The scope of representation should be spelled out; will the agent be handling all your work or just this particular book? Also, specify if you wish to be informed of every offer the agent gets for your work. Money matters, the length of the agreement (one or two years seems to be the average), and a clause spelling out how the agreement may be terminated if there is no specific time limit mentioned, should be included in any agreement.

There are, however, agents who prefer not to have a written agreement with authors. Bill Adler, a veteran agent and author, put it this way: "If the author doesn't want to do any more business with us (or if we don't want to do any more business with the author), then we would rather sever the relationship. Life is too short to try to make bad relationships work."

Q. *Is there a way to dissolve your relationship with one agent and go with another?*
A. Sometimes a writer believes that his agent is not spending enough time on his projects and is no longer the person he wants representing his interests. But the agent will have remaining ties to the author, in terms of any works the agent sold for him, so the relationship should be kept as friendly as possible. If a writer has a problem with an agent, the writer should call the agent, discuss it, and try to settle it. When the time comes to sever ties with an agent, send a simple letter suggesting that parting company would be better for both of you.

Q. *My agent has had my novel for three months and I've heard nothing. Doesn't he at least owe me a report on which publishers he's shown the manuscript to?*
A. Just because you've heard nothing doesn't mean the agent isn't trying to sell your book. Remember, if he doesn't sell the book, he won't get his commission; a book sale would be to his benefit as well as yours. It takes time for the agent to find the right publisher for your book, and the agent represents other authors, so there isn't always time to report every move of a manuscript. Also, the agent can serve as a buffer between you and the rejecting publishers.

Nevertheless, it is your manuscript and you want to know how it's doing. If you haven't heard anything in another month or so, call or drop the agent a short letter of inquiry, and he should get back to you.

A writer can avoid this problem by establishing at the outset when he can expect to hear from the agent.

Q. *I have many manuscripts and they all need to be revised, but I'm on a pension and don't have money to pay for professional revision. Is there an agent who will revise and sell, take out his share of the money, and send me the rest?*
A. No agent is willing or financially able to do revisions on speculation in the hope that he will be paid eventually out of the sale of the work. Perhaps by studying *Writer's Digest* and the magazines to which you would like to submit, you will be able to learn to revise your own manuscripts and resubmit them for sale. *Writer's Digest* and several other advertisers in writers magazines offer professional criticism services.

By joining an organization such as The National Writers Club (1450 S. Havana, Suite 620, Aurora CO 80012) you can obtain low-cost manuscript evaluations from volunteers or from staff personnel. You might want to write them about membership and manuscript evaluation fees. Then you can do your own revisions based on suggestions from these professional writers and editors.

Author-Agent Relations

Q. *If a writer authorizes an agent to sell one or more of his works, is the author committed to pay a fee to the agent for other work he subsequently sells himself?*
A. Normally, if an author acquires an agent, he is committed to pay the agent a fee for any of his work that is sold after that date, unless there is an agreement

between them specifically exempting from commission certain work sold by the author himself—such as poetry.

Q. *If an agent decides he isn't going to handle a particular manuscript of mine, is it okay for me to start submitting it to publishers on my own?*
A. Yes. The agent has decided he no longer has any prospects for your work, or cannot sell it for some other reason. Therefore, it would be perfectly acceptable for you to submit it yourself to any publisher you think might buy it, or to contact another agent who might handle it.

Q. *Can you tell me whether it is ethical to have two agents, in this case one in Los Angeles and one in New York? Each handles the same type of material, but in his own locale. Do agents frown on this procedure even though the material submitted to each is not the same?*
A. The first agent will expect to handle all of a writer's work. If the agent rejects a project, the writer should be free to go elsewhere with it. Literary agents often use co-agents to sell film rights, foreign rights and other rights they don't sell themselves.

Q. *If a book or story is in the hands of an agent, is it possible to make such arrangements that a copy may be submitted to another agent or to a publisher?*
A. Once a manuscript has been turned over to one agent, it is not ethical to submit copies either to another agent or to a publisher. If you feel the agent is not handling your work to your satisfaction, terminate your arrangement with him, ask for the return of your manuscript and you will then be free to try marketing it yourself or to place it with another agent.

Q. *I paid a literary agency for criticism-analysis of two children's stories. They notified me of the opinions of various publishers; but when I asked to whom they showed these stories, they didn't answer my letter. Did I have a right to ask the names of the publishers?*
A. You did indeed. Any reputable agency would not hesitate to reveal the publishers to whom they had submitted material.

Q. *When an agency ignores a request to return a book manuscript sent for possible representation, what recourse does a writer have other than continuing to write letters? Is there some organization set up for the protection of writers to whom a writer might appeal?*
A. The best procedure is to write a registered letter to the agency stating that you are withdrawing the manuscript from their consideration and resubmitting it elsewhere. You should always keep a copy of the manuscript in your files; that way, in the event something like this occurs, you are free to begin resubmitting the manuscript immediately. By keeping a copy you will save time and frustration.

If the agency is a member of the Association of Authors' Representatives, you can contact that organization.

Q. *If you discontinue your relationship with an agent, do you still pay him his royalties on works he sold, including royalties for subsequent years after the break?*
A. Yes. Your former agent remains the agent of record in contracts for all works he sold before you left his representation. Therefore, the publisher will continue to send your royalties in care of that agent whether or not he continues to represent you. He sold it, so he gets the royalty checks from which he deducts his commission. If the book goes out of print and your new agent negotiates a reprint edition or you do so yourself, whether your former agent would receive any royalties would depend on the terms of the initial sale.

Do I Need an Agent?

Q. *Is it a good idea for a beginning writer to get an agent?*
A. An agent is not necessary for a beginner, and in many cases it isn't even possible for a beginner to get one. Generally, agents are only interested in representing writers who have written salable books, and unless you have a book in manuscript, finding an agent will be tough.

It is possible for a beginner to sell a book himself. "My first three novels were sold without benefit of an agent," says novelist Dean Koontz. "I believe I gained valuable marketing experience by handling my own books in those early days."

Research suitable publishers for your book through *Guide to Literary Agents & Art/Photo Reps*, and check in bookstores and libraries to see which publishers are publishing books similar to yours. Then send your manuscript to a likely publisher, including a SASE for its return. If the first publisher rejects the work, contact the next prospect. Remember, some very successful books were marketed by their authors, and rejected by several publishers before they saw print. Dr. Seuss's first book was rejected by twenty-eight publishers before the twenty-ninth bought it!

Q. *Can I get an agent to sell my short stories or magazine articles?*
A. Probably not. Unless the agent is also making a lot of money on an author's book sales, he won't handle magazine pieces or short stories because such sales aren't economically feasible for the agent. Editors of magazines and journals buy shorter pieces directly from writers on a regular basis, so an agent isn't needed on these sales. "Literary agents cannot make enough profit on 15 percent of a $500 or $1,000 magazine article sale to expend the effort," says agent Diane Cleaver. However, if you've done a series of articles on a specific topic that might be made into a book proposal, an agent might be interested in that.

Q. *I am a poet who needs a literary agent. I wonder if you could help me find a reputable one who would work with me on agreeable terms.*
A. There is such a small market for poetry that almost no agent will handle someone whose sole output is poetry. Most poets attempt to sell their poems individually to magazines, hoping eventually to be able to present enough published credits to a book publisher to interest him in publishing a collection of their work.

Q. *I write religious material and would like to market my books on my own. What about agents in the religious publishing field?*
A. Unlike the secular book market, publishers in the religious field are generally willing to deal directly with authors. Agents aren't usually familiar with the religious markets and, as a result, can be of little help to the religious writer. The exceptions might be agents who have dealt with major trade publishers that have a special department for religious books. The writer who takes care to learn about the religious publishing business and marketing process can act as his own agent. For information on religious markets, refer to *Writing to Inspire* (Writer's Digest Books), and *Writer's Market*, which contains a listing of religious markets.

Q. *Are there agencies that handle crosswords, crostics and double crostics?*
A. Most agents are interested only in handling authors of books, television scripts, and other more profitable-length manuscripts. The financial return on items such as crosswords, filler material and poetry is so small, no agency can afford to handle just those. There are a great many magazines that use crossword puzzles other than crossword puzzle magazines themselves. They are listed throughout *Writer's Market*.

How Agents Work

Q. *Do agents offer client manuscripts to publishers on speculation and receive their money only after they make a sale?*
A. Yes. The only way agents can earn their money is by selling a writer's manuscript and deducting commissions from the sales. In essence, they are similar to writers who do magazine articles "on spec," in that when they accept a manuscript from a writer they don't know whether or not a publisher will buy it.

Q. *I've read in* Publishers Weekly *about agents establishing a "floor price" for a book they intend to auction, and getting "escalation clauses" if the book hits the* New York Times *best-seller list. Can I get my agent to make such deals for me and my book?*
A. It depends on the sales potential of your book. Auctions take place when an agent has what he thinks is a really "hot" property. He establishes a floor price — the minimum for which he will sell the book — and makes multiple submissions to prospective publishers, giving a deadline for responses. If one publisher's bid is topped by another, the first publisher is given the opportunity to top his competitor's offer. Escalation clauses provide that an author's royalty percentage will increase if the book sells particularly well; this provision is determined by various sales reports, including the number of weeks the book is on the *New York Times* or other best-seller lists.

Obviously, these contract provisions all hinge on one factor: The book must be one that everybody believed was going to be a big seller. That's why these deals can be obtained by established authors whose books the publishers *know* will be promotable and salable. "I must be sure that I have something everyone will want — because of the stature of the author, the brilliance of the manuscript, the timeliness of the subject, and the commercial value of the book—before I conduct an auction," says agent Diane Cleaver. "Nothing is more embarrassing than holding an auction that no one wants to participate in."

Q. *Can you tell me what the requirements are for becoming a literary agent or tell me where I may obtain such information?*
A. The main requirement for becoming a literary agent is knowing the publishing market so well that you can prove to prospective clients that you are able to successfully place the work of professional writers with magazine and book editors. Many literary agents came to their jobs after successfully marketing their own work or after being editors in the field and knowing what publishers want to buy.

Chapter 20

What Are Some Easy Ways to Get Started?

Unpublished writers have many opportunities to build their writing skills and confidence before tackling the full-length article or short story. Creating short filler material for consumer and trade magazines teaches economy of style and how to begin analyzing market needs. Working with local organizations on newsletters or publicity is good practice that later can be translated into paying markets. Even writing letters to the local newspaper editor – and getting them published – can provide assurance that people are interested in what you have to say. You'll find more information and potential writing projects in *The 30-Minute Writer: How to Write and Sell Short Pieces* by Connie Emerson (Writer's Digest Books).

Getting Started

Q. *I'm intrigued by the idea of being a writer, but having no experience, I'm afraid to get my feet wet. Can you give me ideas for basic, but challenging writing projects I could do to get some practice?*
A. As Peggy Teeters says in her guide, *How to Get Started in Writing,* "The only way to learn to write is to write." One often overlooked but excellent way to get practice is by writing letters to the editor. Everyone has ideas and opinions, but getting them down on paper in an organized and concise manner is the mark of good writing. Although you won't receive a response from the editor, you can compare what you wrote to what was printed to see how your copy was edited to exclude repetition, awkward sentences and excessive wording. Most clubs and various local organizations use volunteer writers to publish or contribute to newsletters and to handle publicity. Any such writing is excellent training and bolsters your confidence as well as giving you published work for your portfolio.

Q. *People with whom I've corresponded for years have told me I have a gift for writing. I'd like to make some money as a writer, but I don't know whether to try writing fiction or nonfiction. How can I determine which I would be better at?*
A. If you're solely interested in making money, you'd probably do better writing articles, as the magazine market needs them more than short stories. If you're

interested in finding your "niche" as a writer, consider the different features of writing fiction or nonfiction. The writer of nonfiction must be willing to do research and conduct interviews, always working to ferret out facts. Because their writing may cover a variety of topics, nonfiction writers rely on a variety of reading interests, an awareness of the world around them, and an ability to organize thoughts and ideas. Although many of these characteristics are also aids to writers of fiction, *these* writers also need an active imagination and an ability to tell stories. One important trait of a fiction writer is an interest in people: their emotions, personalities, and reactions to various situations. Take a good look at yourself, your interests, and your skills, and don't lock yourself into one form of writing too quickly.

Q. *Where do writers get their ideas? Every time I consider writing a piece of fiction, I find my mind empty of ideas. Do I really lack imagination or am I trying too hard?*
A. You may be expecting too much inspiration. Maxine Rock advises in the *Fiction Writer's Help Book* that "developing ideas can be a painful process. . . . Don't lock yourself into preset notions of how or when you should produce ideas. . . . Ideas usually don't flash before you like bursts of divine light. They ripen slowly. Be patient." You can't expect to sit down at a typewriter and always have a new idea. The only way to get ideas is to actively seek them all the time. Look at your experiences, your family, your workplace, your home, your reading, the newspaper, the television, and the places you've been. Things you're familiar with can provide a gold mine of ideas and make more viable stories than things you know little about. For instance, suppose a responsible woman in your office just didn't show up for work for an entire week. Would you wonder during that week what had happened to her? Where did she go? Would she come back? Many different plot lines can come from this very simple start. Constantly ask yourself questions. If an idea comes to you, write it down immediately. It may never pass through your mind again. Most ideas need to gestate for a while before developing. Get in the habit of keeping a journal, writing every day about *anything*. Go through it periodically to pull out and organize the good ideas; set aside those you see as less valuable.

Anecdotes, Newsbreaks and Other Fillers

Q. *I would like to write for the Christian markets, but I have no experience. Where is a good place for me to start?*
A. Good advice from Sue Nichols Spencer in the book *Writing to Inspire* is to write for your own church, where you won't be competing with scores of professionals. You could be a reporter or columnist for your church if it has a regularly published newsletter. If it doesn't, you could volunteer to develop one and be its first editor. You could write poems, prayers and meditations for Bible study groups. You could write a history of the church and bring it up to date with current church projects. Most of this will be volunteer work without pay, but you will develop your writing skills and confidence to submit short articles to national magazines.

Q. *Some magazine editors say they buy anecdotes. What is an anecdote?*
A. An anecdote is a short narrative "slice of life," a description of a particular incident, usually biographical, autobiographical, or stemming from something the author has observed. Anecdotes may employ humor, dialogue, plays on words or unexpected endings to make an insightful comment or illustrate a point. Successful anecdotes will evoke laughter, surprise, sympathy, or some other emotional reaction on the part of the reader. Due to their brevity, they work quite well as fillers. Here is one of many good examples that can be found in *Reader's Digest:*

A woman who works for the state of Louisiana got a call from a man who paused when she told him the name of her agency. He then asked her to repeat it again. 'It's the Governor's Office for Elderly Affairs,' she told him again. There was another pause. 'For gosh sakes, sign me up,' he said. 'I didn't do too well when I was young.'

Smiley Anders in the Baton Rouge *Morning Advocate*

When writing an anecdote, make sure that your narration is uncomplicated and free from extraneous detail. Since description has to be short, every word used should be essential to the picture. The impact of the anecdote comes with a good punchy ending.

Q. *What is a newsbreak?*
A. A newsbreak is a newsworthy event or item. For example, an opening of a new retail shoe store in a town might be a newsbreak for a shoe trade journal that publishes news items of new openings. Some publications (such as *The New Yorker*) use newsbreaks in a different sense—that is, to indicate a typo or an error in reporting that appears in a printed news story. Such newsbreaks—followed by tongue-in-cheek editorial commentary (known as a "tag line")—are bought from contributors and used in *The New Yorker* and other publications as filler items. Newsbreaks solicited by editors usually appear under "Fillers" in the editorial listings in *Writer's Market.*

Q. *What is meant by "filler material"? What is it used for?*
A. A filler is any of a variety of short pieces of writing, such as jokes, anecdotes, short humor, recipes, proverbs, household hints, unusual trivia, brain teasers, puzzles, insightful quotes and news clippings. Although editors originally used them to fill empty spaces at the ends of columns, fillers are now often used as regular magazine features. Because they are short and focus on one point, fillers are good practice for beginning writers and give novices a greater chance of being published. The trick to writing a filler lies in grabbing the reader, causing him to laugh or nod in agreement or sparking his interest to learn more. One can find ideas for fillers anywhere from strange road signs or bumper stickers to old books of poetry that might contain sage sayings. Everyday experiences often provide humor—but you may have to look hard at what's going on around you to see it, then develop it into a humorous anecdote. If you think you might like to write fillers, study the

fillers in several magazines to get an idea of what editors are looking for . . . and go to it!

Q. *Is it okay to submit identical 150 to 200-word fillers to markets that pay $2 to $3 per filler?*
A. As long as the markets are noncompetitive in subject matter or geography, you can submit fillers to more than one market at a time.

Q. *I recently bought some bound volumes of old magazines dating from 1897 through 1908 in which there are many perfectly delightful human interest fillers. How can I use them, if I can use them at all? Can I rewrite and bring them up to date to fit our more "modern" humor?*
A. Since these fillers are old enough to now be in the public domain, you may indeed use them however you wish. You can modernize them and try to sell them individually or as part of a collective article. They are also a possible source for unusual human interest anecdotes to incorporate into your own articles.

Q. *I have written several anecdotes and other fillers taken from my own personal experience. How can I find magazines that might be interested in buying these fillers?*
A. Successful marketing is a combination of writing what you want to write and what magazine editors want to print. Read *Writer's Market* to find magazines that publish what you'd like to sell (anecdotes, for example) and then look at copies of those magazines to help you get a feeling for the style, content, and audience they cater to. Knowing what an editor is looking for before you send in your work will save you from quick rejection you'd get if, for example, you sent your personal anecdotes to a political magazine that only publishes bureaucratic bloopers as fillers. Your chances of making a sale will be greatly enhanced if you are careful about deciding where to send your work.

Q. *Can I send the same filler items to more than one publication at a time?*
A. There's no reason why you can't, as long as you don't submit identical fillers to markets with common audiences. Editors of magazines with similar readerships don't want to see a filler they just bought from you published in a competitive magazine. You may want to type in the upper right corner of a manuscript that is going to more than one publication at the same time: "Simultaneous submission to publications not in your readership area."

Q. *How much money can I hope to get for my published fillers?*
A. Depending on the magazine, the filler, and how it is used, the average payment is anywhere from two to one hundred dollars. *Saturday Evening Post* pays fifteen dollars for jokes, gags, anecdotes, cartoons, and short humor of 300 words. *Home Magazine* buys anecdotes, facts and short humor of 20-100 words; and pays five cents per published word up to ten dollars maximum. Magazines that place a lot of emphasis on filler items, such as *Reader's Digest,* pay as much as three hundred

dollars for a published item. See *Writer's Market* for payment rates of other magazines.

Q. *Several months ago I sent a few jokes and a puzzle to a magazine. I have heard nothing from the editor so far. What kind of reply can I expect from the editor and how long should I have to wait before inquiring?*
A. Although some editors may hold a filler for six months before using it, if you have not received any sort of acknowledgment within two months, you should not inquire, but rather retype your piece and send it elsewhere. Due to the large volume of fillers that many editors receive, reply to individual contributors is often impossible. If you do receive a rejection slip, it may be very dry and to the point, or it may encourage you to keep trying. Look closely at the reasons given for rejection and consider them seriously before submitting other items to that magazine.

Greeting Cards

Q. *I understand that greeting card companies purchase "ideas" as well as original verse. Would a suggestion that they use a poem by a well-known author come under the classification of an "idea"? The poem I have in mind was written in the sixteenth century so there would be no copyright problem.*
A. Yes, your suggestion could be considered an "idea." Check *Writer's Market*, since various greeting card publishers have different requirements for submissions. Some will not accept ideas, preferring instead to see a mock-up or rough sketch of the complete card. Payment ranges from ten dollars to seventy-five dollars for greeting cards.

Q. *I'd like to write for the greeting card market. Other than going to greeting card shops and stores with greeting card display racks, how can I learn what cards are being marketed today?*
A. See *How to Write and Sell Greeting Cards, Bumper Stickers, T-Shirts and Other Fun Stuff*, by Molly Wigand (Writer's Digest Books), which contains how-to information on writing every kind of greeting card. Greeting card market information is updated annually through market listings that can be found in *Writer's Market*. Another helpful publication is *Greetings Magazine*, the business magazine for retailers and manufacturers of greeting cards, stationery, gifts and allied products. Write *Greetings Magazine*, 309 Fifth Avenue, New York NY 10016, for additional information.

An artist's and writer's market list is also available for a No. 10 SASE from the Greeting Card Association, 1350 New York Ave. NW, Suite 615, Washington DC 20005.

Q. *What qualifications do I need to write greeting card verse?*
A. Nothing more than the ability to study existing greeting card material and to provide appropriate copy to those editors. Greeting card verse sells best if your

ideas are original and they imply a "me-to-you" message in a conversational tone. Enthusiasm is important, since writing verse for greeting card publishers is not as easy as it might seem. Companies that publish greeting cards are listed in *Writer's Market*.

Q. *What is the proper format for submitting manuscripts to greeting card publishers?*
A. There are three basic formats. You can type the idea or verse on a 3″ × 5″ or 4″ × 6″ card, including your name and address on the back. Another method is to type the card's message on a folded sheet of paper, putting the material intended for the front and inside of the card in their proper locations. This format is especially good for humorous cards, since the punch line is hidden from view as it would be on the finished card. However, some editors insist on 3″ × 5″ cards for all ideas. Check individual companies writers' guidelines and follow their preferences. The third and most elaborate form of submission is to make a complete "dummy" that is close to what the finished product should look like. Mainly used for humorous, "studio," and juvenile cards, this format includes every element of the finished card, such as color, rough sketches, and any mechanical action.

Q. *What is meant by "identifying marks" on poems sent to greeting card firms?*
A. Since such poems often do not have titles, it's a good idea to number them (one poem to a page), and keep carbon copies with the corresponding numbers for your own records. When the editor sends payment for one poem from a group, he can refer to it by number.

Clippings

Q. *In the* Writer's Market *listings under "Fillers" some editors say they buy clippings. What do they mean?*
A. Clippings are short news items, clipped from newspapers and other publications, that can be submitted as interesting, humorous or odd material for filler space or as material pertinent to a particular trade magazine. For example, a trade journal might use clippings that relate to the business or industry of that particular magazine. Or it might buy a clipping as a source for a more developed piece in the magazine. *Writer's Market* lists magazines that buy clippings, and includes an indication of the kinds of clippings an editor will be interested in. The average filler length is 300 to 500 words, but some magazines will accept clippings as long as 1,000 words. While you can earn small payments for clippings (usually from two dollars to ten dollars), don't expect this to be a sizable monthly income, unless you have access to a great many different newspapers and magazines from which you can obtain clippings at no cost to you. It is important to remember that you should only send to an editor the specific kinds of clippings he requests. General mass mailings of clippings to editors will be a waste of your time and postage.

Submit clippings on an 8½″ × 11″ sheet of white paper, one to a page, with your name, address and telephone number in the upper left corner. The source and date of the item should be acknowledged underneath it. Don't include a SASE, as most editors receive too many clippings to be able to acknowledge or return them.

Q. *How can I send clippings to editors in such a way that they know I'm not sending them gratis, but to receive payment?*
A. Policies are established; either editors pay for clippings they use or they don't. Only submit to those publications which indicate in *Writer's Market* that they buy clippings. If you like, you can type "at your usual rates" in the upper right corner of each clipping you submit.

Q. *Do I need to get permission from the original publisher to submit clippings to another magazine?*
A. You do not need permission to submit clippings. However, you should always acknowledge the original source of the items so that the editor to whom you submit can decide whether or not permission is needed to publish them. If so, he will make the necessary inquiries.

Q. *I am in the process of starting a magazine for the elderly. If I use clippings as fillers, do I need to get permission to publish them?*
A. If a particular clipping is simply a news item, you won't need to get permission, since news cannot be copyrighted. However, if copy is of some length and comes from a copyrighted magazine or syndicated newspaper column, you will need to secure permission to use it. Write to the original publication. In the case of a syndicated newspaper column, the editor will inform you where further correspondence should be sent to get permission from the syndicate.

Q. *What is a tag line? Is it necessary to include one every time I submit a clipping?*
A. Author Connie Emerson says in *How to Make Money Writing Fillers,* "The tag or twist, when it's added to a news clip, is actually a kind of quip—a phrase that reverses what has been said or makes a humorous comment on it." Here is an example from *The New Yorker,* one of the best known users of tag lines:
>Ptarmigan Mountain Properties, one of the largest condominium rental/management firms in Mt. Crested Butte, may be sold in the present future—
>*Gunnison (Colo.) Country Times.*
>*Somebody's in an awful hurry.*

Some magazines require tag lines; others don't use them at all. However, payment for a clipping with a tag line often will be better than that without one. See *Writer's Market* for information on any particular magazine's requirements.

More Easy Sales

Q. *I would like to write book reviews, but I'm only a beginning writer. What chances do I have?*

A. If you live in a small town or in the suburban area surrounding a city, you may be able to interest the local paper in publishing your book reviews. About half the publications that accept reviews will look at unsolicited manuscripts. Call to get the name of the editor who should receive your review. To start, you may have to buy or borrow new books and review them to show the editor what you can do. If you have selected books she thinks will interest her readers and she likes your writing style, she may make you her regular book review editor. You can then write (on the newspaper's letterhead) to book publishers, requesting review copies of their latest books. Pay ranges from free books and tearsheets (which small publications and local newspapers might offer) to as much as six hundred dollars (if you land a major review in the *New York Times*). Even if you just get a byline, the experience could help you go on later to write book reviews for national magazines.

Q. *I am interested in writing gags for cartoonists. How do I submit these?*
A. Find a cartoonist who seems best to suit the style and mood of the gags you write. Then type individual gags single-spaced on 3″ × 5″ cards. Assign a number to the corner of each card and include your name and address in the opposite corner. You can send packets of ten to twenty gags at the same time to the cartoonist in care of the magazine in which his work regularly appears. If the cartoonist buys the gag, the writer usually receives between 25 percent and 40 percent of the sale price of the finished cartoon.

Q. *I want to sell information by mail and plan to start with something simple like recipes. Are recipes copyrighted? How do writers go about getting recipes?*
A. Recipes that appear in copyrighted magazines are covered by that copyright. Writers of cookbooks either create their own recipes or read about others in newspapers, magazines, and books, then alter the recipes, test them, and create their own versions for their cookbooks. Simple lists of ingredients cannot be copyrighted, but the directions for how to make something from those ingredients can be copyrighted.

Writers who like to cook are naturals for developing new, popular recipes that will sell. Look for recipes in newspapers and on food containers that you might adapt and promote. Be alert to comments at restaurants and pot-luck dinners and listen to your guests and family members. Once you have developed an easy, delicious recipe, write the directions and have friends test it to see if it works as well for them.

Q. *A friend of mine says hobby magazines are a good place to start. What do you suggest?*
A. If you have ever designed a pattern for an embroidery project, made your own Christmas tree ornaments, or built a home darkroom, there are craft, hobby and handyman magazines waiting to hear how you did it, step-by-step. Since these how-to articles are relatively simple to write (and you probably already subscribe to the magazines that will buy such pieces), many beginners find them an easy way to

get started writing. Then you can move on to articles that require more research, organization and writing skills. Another area open to beginners is that described in Marjorie Holmes's book, *Writing from the Heart: How to Write & Sell Your Life Experiences* (Writer's Digest Books).

Q. *I'm interested in writing for a newspaper, but I have no idea how to get started. What advice do you have for an aspiring journalist?*
A. If you are young and interested in a career in newspapers, you should secure a good liberal arts college education or go to journalism school. If you are older, submit feature articles to the editor of your local newspaper. Good articles will show that you know what a feature is and how to write one well, and may be a plus for you if there is a staff opening. If you want to be a stringer, find and submit news items not well covered in that newspaper's circulation area. Study the newspaper you are interested in working for and try to submit articles similar in style and subject to what they publish. For more information on newspaper writing, see chapter twenty-one in this book or a journalism textbook, such as *News Reporting and Writing* by Melvin Mencher (Wm. C. Brown Co.).

Q. *I have created several crossword puzzles. Where can I sell them?*
A. Magazines buying puzzles are listed in *Writer's Market*. Magazines usually want puzzles aimed toward their specific audience, so it's a matter of creating a puzzle to fit a specific magazine rather than creating some puzzles, then trying to sell them. There are crossword puzzle magazines also listed in *Writer's Market*. To find out which syndicates are currently marketing puzzles to newspapers, check *Editor & Publisher Syndicate Directory,* available in most libraries.

Other Concerns

Q. *If a filler writer publishes a one- or two-line quip, is it okay for another writer to copy it verbatim, change only one word, and pass it off as being his own?*
A. No. He should indicate the original source when resubmitting elsewhere. Jokes, however, cannot be copyrighted, so they're in the public domain.

Q. *I have written several hundred original epigrams and poetical proverbs which I believe are good. Would it be more profitable for me to submit them in manuscript form for book publication or in small lots to magazines?*
A. Since it is usually easier for a beginner to sell to a magazine rather than to a book publisher, it might be to your advantage to send these fillers to magazine markets. If possible, try to retain book rights so that eventually you can publish them as a collection in book form.

Q. *Some authors rewrite unusual news stories to submit to other markets. Are there laws against using and reusing ideas culled from newspapers? Does this apply to bylined features as well?*

A. News items are facts open to anyone's interpretation, but feature articles usually have a specific angle or slant, involve the research, selectivity and interpretations of the individual writer. The expression of these elements is protected by the overall copyright on the paper, if there is one; or by the syndicate if it is a syndicated feature. You may write a new article using the *facts* of the story or use the original item to suggest a new slant and new research—in short, a new article.

Q. *I am just getting started as a writer and have submitted some children's sayings and anecdotes to bring in a little extra income. Some of the material in them would fit well in a couple of larger pieces I am working on. Is it okay for me to incorporate these fillers into my other work?*

A. Whether or not you may continue to use your filler material as originally written will depend on what rights you sell to magazines publishing it. Under the 1978 copyright law, sale of first rights only is understood unless otherwise indicated in writing. This means that the magazine has claim only to the first publishing of your work and you are free to reuse it at any time. If they buy all rights, you would have to request the editor's permission to reuse the material. An alternative is to rewrite the material so it is different from the version originally published.

Chapter 21

Do Newspapers Use Freelancers?

Newspaper readers, often the first audience for many freelance writers, want news and human interest material directly related to their local community and they want it accurate and easy to read. Filling those needs are first lessons in writing for the market. Writers who have developed the techniques for newspaper reporting and writing have laid important groundwork toward future work in any type of writing. A host of journalism textbooks are available to help you learn more about writing in this field. You might also consult *A Guide for Newspaper Stringers* by Margaret Davidson (Lawrence Erlbaum Associates, Publishers).

Q. *I understand that a stringer is one who relates local news to a newspaper — a correspondent of sorts. Is obtaining a job like this a good way to break into newspaper writing? How does one become a stringer?*
A. Yes, if you are interested in obtaining a staff reporter's job, it could be a plus for you to be a stringer because you will get practice in being on top of the news, digging for facts and writing as a journalist, and your editor will know your abilities. If your town does not already have a stringer corresponding with a particular newspaper, you may be able to get the job by noting eight or ten local news stories that the paper missed over the last month; writing up three of them and submitting them with a cover letter to the editor of the local paper or to the state editor of the nearest large city daily. If an editor needs stringers, he will be most impressed by those who show the enterprise to approach him. Freelance writers pursuing other writing interests will also find that being a stringer keeps them out in the real world, in touch with ideas and up-to-date on information of value to the creative mind. Stringers are usually paid by the column inch, though some earn a flat monthly fee.

Q. *Are there any freelance opportunities as a stringer with the wire services like AP and UPI?*
A. Most of the wire service stringers are full-time news reporters with daily papers, but occasionally the state bureau chiefs for wire services will contract for certain columns or features from freelancers. To find out the name, address and phone

number of the bureau chief in your state, contact the Associated Press, 50 Rockefeller Plaza, New York NY 10020 and United Press International, 1400 I Street NW, Washington DC 20005.

Q. *I am interested in writing editorials. Is there a market for them?*
A. Unfortunately, there isn't much of a market for editorials, since most newspapers have their own staff writers who prepare the editorial page. You could send a few sample editorials to newspaper editors in your immediate area.

Most newspapers, however, welcome "op-ed" pieces. ("Op-ed" is short for "opposite editorial," which is the page where such pieces generally appear.) And many magazines will accept personal opinion essays. Check *Writer's Market* for length requirements and other specifics.

Newspaper Opportunities

Q. *I've submitted several factual articles to my local newspaper, but all of them have been rejected. Having read the paper for years, I know the kinds of things they publish. Could it be my writing? If so, what kinds of things should I consider when writing features for a newspaper?*
A. It's possible that the newspaper doesn't accept freelance material, or perhaps your stories were badly timed. The paper might have already covered the story or assigned it to a staff reporter. Or, it just might be that the editor wants more than just the facts in the features he prints. As I.E. Clark says in the *Writer's Digest Handbook of Article Writing,* "Newspapers use features to intersperse life and emotion among factual news; to interpret the news; to inform readers on subjects that are not 'news' in the sense they do not rise out of current climactic events." Feature writing style is not a slave to the strict formula required for straight news articles and can be as varied as styles of fiction are. A good basic structure for the feature article starts with an attention-getting lead that sets the mood and theme of the article, a narrative body sprinkled with anecdotes and direct quotes, and a quick conclusion. Features are human interest stories, so a good article will cover something or someone unusual or worthy of note. Often, it's the slant in the article that *makes* something unusual. For instance, a dry listing of facts about the opening of a museum of Indian artifacts will hold readers' interest a lot more easily if it is slanted toward the crazy adventure one of the curators had while he was searching for artifacts for one of the displays. Your editor may be looking for articles that are short, to the point and lively.

Q. *Are tabloids a lucrative market? How do I break in?*
A. Like any other freelance work, writing for a tabloid involves careful examination of particular newspapers to determine the writing style and subject matter they prefer. Stories found in tabloids include those on celebrities, strange phenomena, consumer issues, unusual human interest, self-help, and developments in medicine. Access to the kinds of facts you need to create a sensational article is a help in

breaking into the market. The money you make will depend on the size of the publication — payment may be less than fifty dollars or more than a thousand dollars. Editorial requirements for tabloids that buy freelance material are given in *Writer's Market.*

Q. *I've heard that newspaper stories written by staff reporters have their headlines written by another person, such as a copyeditor. Is this true also for material written by stringers, or are stringers expected to create and submit headlines with their work?*
A. Whether news articles are written by a staff reporter or sent in by a stringer, the headlines are always written at the time of publication by one of the copyeditors at the paper. The importance placed on the story at the time it goes to press and the column width allowed for it are factors in determining the wording of headlines written by an experienced newspaper staffer.

Q. *How is newspaper writing different from other kinds of writing?*
A. Since newspaper writing has to fit specific space on a page, writers will often find their stories have been cut. The most important parts of a newspaper story are in the first few paragraphs, so the ending is what is deleted if space is limited. Newspaper editors also tend to cut adjectives, images and other "nonessential" additions to a sentence, when space restrictions force tighter editing. Magazine article writers and book authors have more freedom to write more imaginatively and still include all the facts.

Practical Concerns

Q. *Is it ethical for me to submit a freelance feature article to more than one newspaper at a time?*
A. Yes, as long as they are in non-competing circulation areas. Some writers, when making multiple submissions of this kind, type in the upper right corner, "Exclusive in your circulation area."

Q. *What rights are usually bought by a copyrighted newspaper?*
A. Under the new copyright law of 1978, a newspaper or magazine buys only one-time publishing rights unless otherwise indicated in writing to the author. Thus, if a copyrighted newspaper prints an article of yours, you are free to use it again.

If the newspaper is not copyrighted, you should include your own copyright notice (for example, © 1994 by John Doe) on your manuscript's first page. Ask the editor in your cover letter to publish your copyright notice if he is interested in publishing your article. Most editors will honor that request if they publish your piece. If the notice is not used, anyone may use your article, since it would then be in the public domain.

Q. *If another newspaper lifts my article and prints it, are they obligated to pay me for it?*

A. If the newspaper in which your original article appeared was not copyrighted (and some newspapers aren't) then your article became public property as soon as it was published and any reprinting paper was not obligated to pay you. If the original newspaper in which your article appeared was a member of a wire service, the service may be permitted to pick up local news stories and offer them to member papers without permission or payment. If your article was a copyrighted feature, then yes, a reprinter would be obligated to pay you.

Q. *I am interested in syndicating my own newspaper column. Will it be necessary for me to copyright the column in my name in order to send it to several different markets? If I must copyright the column in my name, how do I go about doing this?*
A. Yes, it will be necessary for you to copyright the columns in your own name to protect your rights. A practice that has been followed by many national syndicates and persons syndicating their own columns has been to copyright a collection of columns. The author then puts the copyright symbol, year and name in the column "reprints" sent to newspapers. This is less expensive than taking out an individual copyright on each column, since there is a twenty dollar fee per column, or collection. Applications for either can be obtained by writing to the Register of Copyrights, Library of Congress, Washington DC 20559.

Q. *Is there any way I can protect the title of my column and the symbol I plan to use both as a business letterhead and at the top of my column?*
A. Titles are not copyrightable, but you may be able to get your title and symbol registered as a trademark. For information, write the Commissioner of Patents and Trademarks, Patent and Trademark Office, Washington DC 20231. To obtain a trademark, of course, you would have to personally search or hire a patent attorney to search the Trademark Office records to make sure the symbol you want to use isn't already in use.

Syndicating Your Work

Q. *I think I have enough experience under my belt to be able to write a humorous column that many might enjoy. I'd like to try selling my column to a newspaper—or even to several. How do I know if my style is one that will sell? How do I go about marketing my column?*
A. About the only way to find out whether or not your column will sell is to try selling it. Writer Kay Cassill suggests some questions an editor might ask himself as he looks over your work: Will it make complete strangers laugh? How diverse is the age group to which this would appeal? Is it easy to read? Does the writer know what she's talking about? Is my paper lacking something because it doesn't carry this column? If you've shown him something lively and original, you just might be able to make a sale. In marketing your column, be sure you know your markets well enough so that you don't send them something they already have—and don't try to sell the same column to papers with competing circulation areas. Personal

contact with each editor is a step in the right direction. Send a sincere, concise letter explaining what you feel are the merits of your column and enclose a SASE. Start out looking for local markets from which to build a base. If your column catches on, you may want to try to increase your sales. If so, be prepared to work hard as a businessperson and as a salesperson. You might be surprised at how well it can pay off.

Q. *I want to syndicate a column. How much material will I need to present to newspaper editors? The idea only? A sample? A month's or year's worth?*
A. It depends on whether you're suggesting a daily or weekly column. If a daily, then it would be best to have a month's columns ready to show; for a weekly column, have two months' supply written. In both cases, have ideas written for another three to six months' columns.

Q. *Can you give me a basic definition of a syndicate? Exactly what is the difference between self-syndication and national syndication? What are the advantages of each?*
A. A syndicate is a business that will simultaneously sell a piece of writing to many different publications. A writer can sell his column or feature to one hundred or more daily or weekly newspapers through a syndicate. Self-syndication involves a writer himself marketing his work to many newspapers. The major advantage of self-syndication is that the writer can collect full payment directly from the publications to which he sells his work, whereas he only gets 40 to 60 percent of the gross receipts when operating through a syndicate. However, the self-syndicator must do all of his own promoting and selling, which costs time and money. Syndicates, on the other hand, provide this service for the writer.

Q. *Where can I find a list of newspaper markets for my column?*
A. The worldwide *Editor & Publisher Yearbook* lists daily, weekly and minority papers along with feature agencies. It's published by *Editor & Publisher,* 11 W. 19th St., New York NY 10011. *Gale Directory of Publications* lists newspapers; magazines; and business, trade and professional journals. These directories, both set up geographically by state, then by city, are available at most large public library reference departments. *Writer's Market* includes some newspapers and weekly magazine sections in its "Regional" category, giving editorial requirements for active newspaper markets for freelance material.

Q. *How much can I expect to be paid for my self-syndicated weekly column? Is payment something that I should specify or do newspapers have a standard?*
A. Pay rate is for the most part what the paper is willing to pay and what your column is worth to the editors. You may only get five dollars from a small paper, but larger circulation dailies may pay as much as fifty dollars per column. Of course, well-known columnists will make much more than that for their columns—but they started small too. In the beginning, offer your column to newspapers "at your usual rate." If they haven't bought any of your material before and ask *you* to name your

price, you could ask for five dollars or more depending on the circulation of the paper. In some cases, especially if you're trying to break into suburban and small-town papers, you might want to offer the column on a trial basis, free of charge. If the column receives good reader response, then you can ask for payment after a few columns have been printed.

Q. *How do I market my column to a national syndicate?*
A. To find out what competition might already exist for your idea, check the *Syndicate Directory* published by the trade magazine *Editor & Publisher.* (If a copy of this isn't in your local library, write for information on the current price to *Editor & Publisher,* 11 W. 19th St., New York NY 10011.) This *Syndicate Directory* lists by title, author, and subject matter, all of the syndicated columns, features, and cartoon strips currently published. It also tells which syndicate currently distributes them and gives the name and address of the editorial director of the syndicate. If your syndicated column idea, for example, was a "Tips for Consumers" idea, you could see which syndicates already have similar continuing features. After you find a syndicate that best suits your needs, query the editorial director. Enclose at least six sample columns and, as always, a SASE. Sample columns should only be sent to one syndicate at a time. You should hear from the editor in one week to three months.

Q. *When a syndicate is said to pay $25, what does this cover?*
A. Such a flat rate usually refers to the payment for a single feature—a one-shot item rather than a continuing column.

Q. *When I submit a feature to a syndicate, how soon can I expect a decision? How can I make sure I get my percentage of sales?*
A. Most of the syndicates report on submissions in one week to three months. Unless the sum is large enough to warrant sending an auditor to check the accounts, most writers accept the syndicate's statements in good faith, since publishers and syndicates couldn't stay in business long if they weren't honest with their writers.

Chapter 22

How Do I Write and Sell a Magazine Article?

Webster's Dictionary reminds us that the original definition of the word magazine was that of a storehouse, and today's magazines literally are storehouses of information and entertainment. To fill this storehouse, most publications' editors depend heavily on freelance contributions. The magazine article writer's primary source for locating markets is *Writer's Market* (Writer's Digest Books), a directory of publications that buy manuscripts from freelancers. *Writer's Yearbook*, an annual published by *Writer's Digest* magazine, each year lists the one hundred top-paying magazine markets.

For more information on types of articles and the techniques of writing them, see *The Writer's Digest Handbook of Magazine Article Writing*.

Types of Articles

Q. *How many different kinds of articles are there?*
A. Articles most commonly published today include how-to, personal experience, interview, inspirational, humorous, exposé, historical, personal opinion, success story, travel, technical and new product articles. Article format depends on the magazine it's written for and the writer's individual style.

Q. *In college we wrote what teachers referred to as essays, but I don't see many markets for essays in* Writer's Market. *What's the difference between an essay and a magazine article?*
A. An article is usually based on fact uncovered in research and/or interviews and manifests itself in forms like the personality sketch, the exposé, or the how-to. It will have a particular slant, but any opinion will be backed up with quotes, anecdotes and statistics. While they are often entertaining, articles are usually meant to educate and inform.

In its original sense, the essay was meant to express opinion, to be persuasive, or to be interpretive. It is marked by a more personal treatment of the subject matter, which may or may not interest a wide audience. Although an essay may require research, the information is used along with subjective ideas in an essay, whereas an article remains fairly objective. More recently, newspapers have printed interpretive essays. These pieces are really extensions of the news story, analyzing the background of a political event. Editorials, humor pieces and inspirational articles could all be considered essays.

Q. *What is a feature?*
A. The term "feature" usually refers to those articles appearing in a magazine that are not columns or part of a regularly appearing department. Feature articles are usually longer than columns and department pieces, are most often the stories featured on the cover, and are grouped together in the "editorial well," which is most often at the magazine's center.

Q. *What is "new journalism"?*
A. "New journalism" is a school of article writing that is most evident by the employing of fiction techniques to relate an event or other story that is factual; it's a form of journalism that also involves the writer's own feelings about his subject, as opposed to "objective journalism."

Q. *What is a "think piece"? Does it mean a controversial article? Or does it mean all kinds of nonfiction? For example, even historical pieces, noncontroversial, will cause me to think—and doubtless most other readers.*
A. A "think piece" is usually any article that has an intellectual, philosophical, provocative approach to its subject.

Q. *I have known some very ordinary people who have done some very unusual things in their lives. Is there a market for articles about these people? It seems I only read stories about* famous *people.*
A. Your stories may not interest editors of major magazines, but they may very well sell to local newspapers and possibly to a specialized consumer magazine or trade publication. The only way to find out is to look through *Writer's Market* until you find some magazines interested in buying the human interest nonfiction you want to write. Make sure you study a magazine thoroughly before you decide to query or send a manuscript to its editor.

Q. *An editor said that he thought part of my article would work better as a sidebar. What does he mean?*
A. Sidebars are short articles that accompany longer features. They're boxed off and titled separately from the rest of the article and may even be set in different typeface. Sidebars are used to add information to or to take an in-depth look at a topic that is related to the main article, but is too tangential to be included in it. For example, included with a *Time* magazine article on a papal visit to the United States might be a sidebar recounting the city-by-city heavy security precautions. Other kinds of sidebars include historical notes, tables of statistics and how-to's.

Matching Article to Market

Q. *Is it better to have a specific market in mind when writing an article, or to write the article first, then look for a market for it?*
A. It is usually better to write with a specific market in mind so that your writing will match the publication's style and tone, and be directed toward its particular readership. Writers trying to earn a living as freelancers study potential markets before starting to write; this increases potential sales. However, you can write an article and then look for a suitable market. Make sure you carefully research the market before you submit anything. Editors do not appreciate writers who bombard them with material that is obviously not aimed toward their audience.

Q. *I would like to obtain sample copies of a number of magazines not sold locally. To whom do I address such a request and is payment expected?*
A. Send your request to each magazine's Sample Copy Dept., along with a SASE, and offer to pay for the sample copy and mailing costs if necessary. Some magazines charge; others don't.

Q. *What is meant by the "slant" of a magazine article? How does one go about putting slant in an article?*
A. A writer *slants* his article when he specifically gears it to a particular magazine's audience. Finding the proper slant demands in-depth market study to determine the subject matter and style an editor is interested in, and the kind of audience his magazine is intended for. Carefully read several issues of a magazine you wish to write for, analyzing the articles. Are there mostly opinion pieces? Factual features? Personality profiles? What's the tone of the articles? How about the average length? Close observation of the advertisements will give you an idea of the average age and socioeconomic status of the readers, as well as some of their hobbies and interests. By studying the market, you will be able to present an editor the kind of article she wants, thereby greatly increasing your chances of making a sale.

Q. *I have an idea for an article that would be perfect for* Better Homes and Gardens. *However, I found that the magazine published a similar article several years ago. Does this mean they won't be interested? Should I try other magazines instead?*
A. You can query *Better Homes and Gardens,* but emphasize your piece as an update of their previous article and suggest new ideas and angles. If you are rejected, query other home-oriented magazines.

Q. *Where can I find a listing of secondary markets where a neophyte can break in?*
A. Secondary markets are magazines with smaller circulations and lower payment rates, but their editors are quite demanding about the kind and quality of material they accept from freelancers. Hundreds of secondary markets are listed in *Writer's Market.*

Q. *What are "quality" magazines and "little" magazines?*

A. Quality magazines such as *The New Yorker, Harper's* and *The Atlantic Monthly* aim toward the educated, intellectual sectors of the population, concentrating on articles that analyze current events or trends and present informed opinions, thereby encouraging thoughtful analysis on the part of the reader. Humor found in these magazines is sophisticated and often satirical. Although payment for articles published in quality magazines may be less than from larger general interest magazines, writers whose work appears in a quality magazine have the respect and attention of other editors—an advantage when looking for further freelance work.

Little magazines are small circulation publications that print political, literary, often unorthodox material that might not otherwise be published. They represent creative writers interested in fine literary quality and are read by writers, editors and students of literature. Since these publications make little or no profit, payment for published work is usually no more than a contributor's copy or a subscription to the magazine. Writers should be warned that many little magazines are usually uncopyrighted, and if an article appears without a copyright byline, it becomes part of the public domain.

Techniques of Article Writing

Q. *I've done very little writing, but I'd like to write an article about working mothers—especially those with small children. I know several in my neighborhood and am impressed by what they manage to accomplish in a day's time. But whenever I begin to write, I quickly run out of things to say—after only a page or two. What's my problem?*

A. It seems that you have a fairly solid interest in your subject, so your problem might be a lack of ample research. Have you really *talked* to these women about their trials, the advantages and disadvantages of their two-career situation? Another problem may be that you do not have a clearly developed angle for your article. Instead of merely making random comments on how working mothers cope, you could perhaps better interest your readers by including specific tips on how they could manage their *own* time better, secure cooperation of other family members, etc. A writer who knows enough about her subject will never be at a loss for words: ideas, anecdotes, facts and angles will come easily. Begin by formulating a solid outline and strive for smooth transition between ideas. Take plenty of time to plan, research and write your piece; rushing things will result in disorganized and unclear writing. And it's a good idea to write such a piece with a particular publication in mind. That way, you can tailor your story to a magazine's style, tone and readership.

Q. *An editor rejected my article, saying he uses a more anecdotal style in his magazine. What does that mean?*

A. Used in article writing, an anecdote is a brief human interest story illustrating a point. Although each anecdote is complete in itself, it should be relevant to the purpose of the article. Anecdotes can serve to hold reader interest by breaking up a lot of factual material. They can be used to add insight to the personality of someone discussed or featured in an article, to act as a transition from one topic to another, or to provide a "grabber" of a lead in a news or feature article.

A good interview will easily yield anecdotes. Ask your subject open-ended questions like "What person influenced you most in life and how?" or "What was your greatest opportunity?" or "What do you consider the most important decision in your life?" Through such inquiries, you will learn much about the forces that guide and shape the person. If you are writing about someone not available for interview, talk to people who know him and get them to relate incidents and personal characteristics of your subject. Often writers use anecdotes stemming from personal experience, so be alert to what's going on around you. Using anecdotes in your writing, without overdoing it, will add the spice your article may need for you to make the sale.

Q. *Do the anecdotes I use in my articles have to be true? Is it ethical to make up anecdotes to suit the needs of my article?*
A. If you're going to mention people's names, then you'd better stick to real-life facts; but if you want to make up an anecdote to illustrate a point, then you might preface it with something like: "It's the sort of town where something like the following could easily happen: — " or "There's a rumor going around that — " or "I wouldn't be surprised if — ." The point can be made, but without giving the erroneous idea that the incident actually did take place. A true-life story may be fictionalized or could use a little "fixing" to give it the right charm, and small changes in time span and dialogue are acceptable. But as Connie Emerson says in *How to Make Money Writing Fillers,* "However much you alter what really happened, you must succeed in making the story 'read true.'" The secret of good anecdote-telling is the ability to spot a small true-life happening and describe it in such a way that your interpretation gives it new dimension and significance.

Q. *I sent an article to a magazine and got back a rejection with the comment, "Too general — no peg." What does that mean?*
A. It means that you did not concentrate on one specific aspect of your topic, rendering the article too general for the audience of that magazine. Most article ideas lend themselves to several pegs, each one of which could be developed into a separate article. For instance, an article on buying a computer could be geared toward the needs of a college student, a household, a self-employed businessperson, a teacher, or a corporation . . . five different article possibilities (or "pegs") that could end up in five different magazines, each with a different audience.

Dealing With Editors

Q. *If a magazine's masthead lists an editor and a managing editor but no articles editor, who should get my unsolicited manuscript?*
A. Since it is the editor's job in most cases to determine what stories are assigned and to whom, and what will be printed in a particular issue, you should send your

manuscript to him. At most magazines, the managing editor is concerned more with the actual production of the magazine.

Q. *Are there any rules concerning which editor or department should receive requests for writer's guidelines?*
A. Type on the outside envelope, in the lower left corner, "Request for Writer's Guidelines," and address the envelope and the letter to the editor of the publication. If you don't know the editor's name, just address the request to "The Editor." Your request will be routed quicker and get faster response with the corner notation.

Q. *Do magazine editors prefer queries rather than unsolicited manuscripts?*
A. It depends on the editor, who will usually reveal his preference in *Writer's Market* or the magazine's writers guidelines. When in doubt it's usually a good idea to query, especially when you're planning to invest a lot of time and effort in researching and writing a major article. Unless he knows your writing, an editor is not likely to give you a firm assignment after reading your query. But if he likes your idea and you are told to go ahead and write the article on speculation, your chances of making a sale are much greater than those of most of your competitors. Certain types of articles, such as humor, opinion and commentary, and book reviews, cannot be adequately described in a query, so are best submitted as a finished manuscript.

Q. *When a magazine published my article it was completely changed from my version although they used my facts. Does this mean they didn't like my writing and only wanted to use my research? I know they needed to shorten it, but I was surprised to see it changed so much from the way I submitted it.*
A. An editor will often change syntax, clean up grammar and rearrange ideas to make an article clearer and more easily read. If the article is longer than the specified number of words, it will be cut. Editorial space is limited. The editor may be forced to do a lot of rewriting, even though the article may contain valuable information, because he knows that it does not conform to reader expectations or the personality of the magazine. As former *Writer's Digest* editor William Brohaugh says, "Editors edit to make you sound better *relative to the rest of the magazine.*" You can avoid severe editing of your work by studying and knowing the slant and style of the magazine to which you are submitting. Look closely at the printed version of your article and analyze the reasons for changes. And it wouldn't hurt to drop the editor a note and ask *him* why the changes were made. He will probably be frank with you, and you may learn something from the experience.

Q. *A trade publication bought and published seven articles I submitted to the magazine over the last several months. Each check was accompanied by a letter encouraging me to submit more of my work. Should I continue to enclose a SASE? Would it be out of line to ask to write a regular column for the magazine?*
A. Continue to enclose a SASE unless the editor specifically tells you it's no longer

necessary. However, you needn't enclose a SASE if you are sending an article that you have written *on assignment,* after having queried the editor. Asking to write a regular column for the magazine would not be out of line, since you obviously write according to the magazine's style and are providing subjects of interest to the readers.

Q. *What exactly does a magazine correspondent do? How can I get a job as a correspondent?*

A. Magazine correspondents usually work on assignment, conducting interviews, making phone calls, and doing all sorts of other research for articles that are sometimes initiated by the magazine and written by staff writers. The results of this "legwork" are usually submitted as a research report and are incorporated into articles of larger scope. The correspondent may also be able to initiate, research and write articles of his own for the magazine. He's in a better position than the regular freelancer here, because his editors know the quality of his work and are more willing to consider it for publication.

To get a job as a correspondent, you usually must have a substantial track record as a writer and be able to demonstrate a wide knowledge and interest in the subjects you write about. These jobs are normally obtained with a particular magazine after the writer has had several pieces published in that magazine.

Q. *To what does the title of "contributing editor" entitle a writer?*

A. Contributing editors are writers who have written and sold several articles or items to a magazine, which then lists the writer as "contributing editor." It usually gains the writer no additional money or special favors, but it is prestigious in that it indicates that the writer knows how to successfully (and repeatedly) write for, and sell to, that magazine. It also gives him more visibility in that his queries and suggestions and manuscripts are given red-carpet treatment (they are read sooner and acted on more quickly than unsolicited mail). It also gives the writer more clout when arranging interviews for articles for the magazine to which he contributes. It may also give the writer more credibility when he wants to break into other markets.

Q. *Do editors accept* free *contributions from an author? I have written a moralistic essay that carries a message and do not feel that I should accept money to have it reach the public. What do you think?*

A. Some magazines do not offer payment for contributions. If it is a magazine's policy to pay for material it uses, you should not offer your contribution free. Don't be misled into thinking that just because it's free, an editor will use it. If, in the editor's estimation, it's worthy of being printed, he will automatically pay for it (and you can send the check to your favorite charity). If it doesn't seem publishable to him, then the fact that it's free will not persuade him to use it.

Selling Your Articles

Q. *Is it okay for me to submit more than one idea at a time to the same magazine?*
A. Submitting one idea at a time is preferred. Due to space limitations in a good query letter, it is difficult to fully develop more than one idea at a time. Since ideas may be considered by several editors at a particular magazine, it is easier for them to contend with only one idea per letter. They can get back to you sooner. However, you might develop each of your ideas into a separate query and send them all in the same envelope to an editor. It would show him that you spent some time analyzing the magazine's readership and could lead to more than one "go ahead on spec." (See chapter five about this term.) Magazines like *National Geographic* request that writers send a letter containing several one-paragraph ideas. If the editors find any idea promising, they request a more detailed two-page outline. However, you should look in *Writer's Market* or send for a magazine's writers guidelines to find out what a particular editor prefers.

Q. *When an editor requests samples of my writing, is it sufficient to send a copy of the first page of a six-page published article, or must I send the complete article?*
A. A photocopy of the complete published article is preferable so the editor can see how you handle examples, transitions and the conclusion as well as the opening. The same applies to a story so the editor can see how you handle character development, plot progression, and climax. If you have a very long article or story, you might mention its length and send only the first few pages, indicating the complete copy is available on request.

Q. *I want to do an article that will involve some travel expense to a nearby state. Will an editor reimburse me for these expenses in addition to payment for the article?*
A. If you are fairly new to the business of freelancing and have not built up many writing credits, you will probably be expected to cover extra expenses yourself—but it never hurts to ask! Expenses may include travel, extensive research, photography, photocopying, and the like, and should be negotiated prior to accepting the assignment. An established writer can often get an advance from the editor to cover expenses, and when writing on assignment may even get a flat-out expense-paid trip to wherever he needs to go. If you *do* have to cover your own travel expenses, keep receipts, and remember that travel expenses can be written off with your other business expenses as a tax deduction. Take full advantage of every trip by making notes, being observant, taking photographs, and following leads that will open and enhance other writing projects, too.

Q. *I've written a magazine article for which I've taken some photographs as possible illustration. How do I submit a manuscript-photo package?*
A. Choose a couple of your best shots and send 8" × 10" enlargements to the editor with your manuscript. Let her know in your letter that you have other pictures available. Mail the manuscript and photos flat, with some sort of cardboard rein-

forcement so the photos don't get bent in the mail. Identify your photos with your name and address, since they may be separated from the manuscript temporarily at the publisher's. Don't write on the back of the photo—use address labels or a rubber stamp with your name and address, and attach your typed caption with tape to the back of the photos.

Q. *Will including photographs with my article help sell it? What size photographs should be submitted with a manuscript?*
A. It depends on the magazine. Some prefer to assign the photography to professionals they know; others request or require photographs to come with the manuscript. (Consult the magazine's writer's guidelines or *Writer's Market.*) If you must submit photos, and you're not confident in your abilities as a photographer, you may need to hire someone to take the pictures for you. However, it will save you time, energy and money if you learn to do the photography yourself. Photographs submitted should be sharp and clear and should give the editors a good variety to choose from. Study the publications to which you want to submit your package to get an idea of the kinds of photographs they like to print with their articles. When submitting black-and-white photographs, 8″ × 10″ glossy prints are preferred. For color, don't send color prints—send transparencies. Mark each print or slide with your name and address and include caption material if it is appropriate. Don't overlook the possible free sources of photographs available to you from government agencies, professional organizations, corporations and others listed in directories such as the *Writer's Resource Guide.* (For more information on illustrating your work, see chapter twenty-three.)

Q. *What's the going rate for a magazine column?*
A. What a magazine will pay a columnist varies greatly with the size of its circulation and the eminence and expertise of the writer. A popular magazine with a large audience, like *McCall's,* might pay anywhere from $750 to $1,500 and up per column, depending on how well-known the author is. Smaller secondary publications pay up to $200 per column. The pay is much less enticing in this case, but chances of securing a regular columnist's position are much greater with these smaller magazines than with the larger ones. Although payment is usually on a per-column basis rather than per word, the editor will usually specify desired column length. If you have an idea for a column for a small magazine, send a query along with half a dozen sample columns to the editor, telling why you think the column would benefit his readers.

Q. *Is there any danger a writer might get too many articles going at the same time?*
A. Planning your production time—whether you are a part-time or full-time freelance writer—is important. If deadlines are too close together, you may be inclined to rush through an article without sufficient research, eliminate some important interviews, or turn out a draft that really needs better organizing and rewriting.

You will be judged by your readers and editors on what appears under your byline, so give only your best effort to each assignment.

Q. *Unsolicited manuscripts should always be sent with a SASE, but what about solicited manuscripts? To SASE or not to SASE?*
A. Editors should pay the freight for their own solicitations — that is, for an article *on assignment.* But if you query and an editor says, "OK, let me see it on spec," better include a SASE. That's not a solicited manuscript.

Selling . . . and Reselling

Q. *What is the difference between selling "one-time rights" and "first North American rights"?*
A. If you sell first North American rights to a magazine, you are guaranteeing that they will be the first publisher of your article in the United States and Canada, without restricting yourself from selling it to other North American publishers after that initial publication (or to publishers on other continents before publication). One-time rights can be sold to any publication, regardless of whether it's the first to print the story, but that publication can't run the story more than once. For more on selling rights and copyrights, see chapters seventeen and eighteen.

Q. *How do I indicate on my manuscript that my article submission has been previously published?*
A. In the upper right corner of your first page, indicate "Reprint Rights" and the name and date of the publication in which the material first appeared.

Q. *In such magazines as* Reader's Digest, *do the editors select the articles from perusal of various magazines or do authors submit printed articles they believe are suitable for reprint?*
A. Editors usually select the articles for reprinting, but an author may submit tearsheets to bring his material to their attention. *Reader's Digest* buys original articles as well as reprints. For their editorial requirements, see *Writer's Market.*

The Finer Points of Marketing Articles

Q. *I have written a human interest article that I think would be perfect in the Sunday supplement magazine in our local newspaper. How many weeks in advance should I make my submission since I have a particular Sunday in mind?*
A. It would be wise to submit your piece three to four months before the date you would like to see it published. This gives the editor plenty of time to make a decision concerning your article, and, if it is accepted, to decide upon the format and prepare accompanying artwork.

Writers should consider lead time (or the time between submission and publication) when writing articles that are time-sensitive. For a monthly magazine, you should submit your work no later than five months in advance of the issue date. A magazine's lead time for seasonal articles is usually listed in *Writer's Market.*

Q. *I have written some articles that I would like to see in more than one magazine. I take several religious magazines and would like to send the articles to each of them. Would this be legal? If these were paid for, would it be legal then to send to another editor?*
A. On future submissions, you might want to type in the upper right corner of page one of your manuscript: "Submitted on a nonexclusive basis at your regular rates." This tells the editor that he or she is not the only editor offered the manuscript. Many editors of religious magazines know that their readers are not likely to see the same article in another denomination's publication and are willing to accept these "simultaneous submissions."

Q. *When sending a query letter, can jokes and fillers that carry my byline be used as credits along with other published material?*
A. Jokes and fillers, if published in national magazines under your byline, can be used as examples of your published works. You should mention these credits only if the article you are querying about is somehow related to this short, humorous material.

Travel Writing

Q. *I just discovered the travel-writing field and am very excited about it. How can I get started in this field? How much money can I expect to earn, and would the money used for traveling be paid by my publisher or out of my own pocket? I have a fairly good paying job; would you advise me to leave it to become a travel writer?*
A. One way to get started in travel writing is to do some short travel features aimed at local newspaper and regional magazine markets. It helps if you have a general knowledge of newspaper and magazine article writing and some experience in free-lance writing. If you're new to the writing field, you can prepare yourself by reading many books on writing and taking a writing course at a local university or community college, or through a correspondence school. You can begin by reading Louise Purwin Zobel's *The Travel Writer's Handbook* (Surrey Books).

At the beginning of your career, you will have to finance your trips out of your own funds. Later, when your name becomes known in this specialty, the publications you write for will often pay your travel expenses. Payment depends on the newspaper, books or magazines you write for and the degree to which you sell reprints of your articles.

It wouldn't be advisable for you to quit your job to become a travel writer. You should work as a freelancer in that field until you have established enough credit with magazine and book editors to enable you to support yourself entirely from your writing income.

Q. *I'm planning a trip to the Middle East next fall and am interested in doing some magazine article writing while I'm there. Is there any way I could get some assignments before I leave?*
A. Unless you've written many articles in the past and editors know your name and your abilities, you probably won't be able to get any definite assignments. However, if you are able to suggest *in detail* some of your ideas in a query letter, you may find a couple of interested editors who will consider your work on speculation. Make sure your ideas have sharply focused angles; more general suggestions — for example, "I'd like to do an article about life in modern Arabia," — will only label you as a novice and yield few interested editors.

Q. *I am planning to take an extensive trip through the British Isles this fall and will be writing several articles for some newspapers that I have served for years as a correspondent and feature writer. I also plan to write some freelance travel features, which I hope to sell to one or more magazines or wire services. How does a traveling freelance writer handle work like this from abroad?*
A. It is customary for freelance writers submitting to markets from abroad to send a self-addressed envelope addressed to them at the point they next expect to be. Usually they enclose an International Reply Coupon, which can be bought in European Post Offices to cover return postage from anywhere in the world. If you'll be dealing only with American markets, of course, you can take U.S. postage with you to affix to your self-addressed envelope. You might want to consider submitting queries on your features rather than complete manuscripts since the publications may want a different slant than what you have in mind.

Chapter 23

Do I Need to Provide My Own Illustrations?

For freelance writers, "Double your talents, double your checks" might be an appropriate parody of a popular advertising jingle. Article writers find the investment in a camera will easily pay for itself in increased sales, since many editors want a manuscript/photo package and some may even require it. The same theory doesn't hold true for writer/artist collaborators since editors have their own preferences and contacts for artwork.

Providing Illustrations

Q. *I would like to offer photos with my future submissions. Where and how can I get training in photography?*
A. Courses, seminars and workshops offered through universities and other organizations can teach you the skill of taking photographs. *Photographer's Market* lists various workshops, and *A Survey of Motion Picture, Still Photography, and Graphic Arts Instruction* lists courses and degree programs in the three fields noted in its title. Both directories present listings from the U.S. and Canada. (Also see chapter two.)

Q. *In writing articles I often need pictures for illustrations and do not know where to get them. (I am not a photographer.) Of course, I would like them at a reasonable price, or better still, free.*
A. There is a wealth of stock photos to be had, and many of them for free. See the subject sections of *Stock Photography: A Complete Guide*. For a comprehensive list of picture sources, see also *World Photography Sources,* edited by David N. Bradshaw and Catherine Hahn. In addition to listing general stock photo agencies and freelance photographers, it lists sources located all over the world in areas such as agriculture, geography and history, industry, military, visual and performing arts, plants and animals, science and the social sciences and sports. Each listing gives names and addresses of contact people, procedure for obtaining photos, and what fees, if any, will be charged. You should be able to find the book in the reference section of your public library. Pictures from any of these sources can be used by

themselves or to supplement pictures shot specifically for your article, either by a professional photographer you engaged for the purpose, or by a photographer who has agreed to work with you on speculation for an agreed-upon fee if and when you sell your article.

Q. *Who covers the fees involved in securing photographs for magazine articles — writer or editor?*
A. It depends on individual magazine policy. At most magazines, it is usually the writer's responsibility to either supply the photographs or make arrangements to work with a local freelance photographer. The procedure at some magazines is to pay the writer a flat fee for an article/picture "package." If this is the case, the writer must arrange a fair split of the proceeds with his photographer. Check *Writer's Market* for the policies of individual magazines.

Q. *I submitted an article and fifteen photographs to a magazine and the article was printed with three of the pictures. However, I was not paid anything extra for the photographs. Is this common practice, or was it an oversight on the part of the editor?*
A. Your situation is most likely one in which the magazine buys article and photographs as a package, implying one payment for the two items. Some editors buy pictures separately. Make sure you understand a particular editor's policy before you agree to sell him your work.

Q. *I might have the chance to interview some celebrities this summer. I cannot take the pictures, but there is a good professional photographer in this city who can. He is a complete stranger to me. Should I contact him before I query an editor or should I get the writing assignment first? If the editor does not purchase the story and pictures separately, what percentage does the photographer usually get?*
A. Before you query the editor, explain your project to the photographer and ask if he would be willing and available to furnish his services this summer. Reach an agreement with him regarding payment. (Being a professional, he will let *you* know his usual fees.) Then in your query to the editor, you can have the added advantage of informing him that you will be able to furnish professional photos of the interviewees. It is up to you to make sure you are paid enough to cover your expenses as well as your photographer's.

Q. *I'm confused by the term "transparencies," which most editors use when discussing their requirements for color photos. Does it mean one thing to all editors, or does it mean slides to one editor and negatives to another?*
A. "Slides" and "transparencies" are terms used synonymously by most editors when referring to positive color film. "Negatives" usually refers to black-and-white (b&w) film only. Most editors will not work with color prints, developed from color negatives. They prefer the reproduction quality of color slides.

Marketing Your Artwork

Q. *What is the best way to send photographs with a manuscript so that they aren't mangled by the postal system?*
A. Black-and-white prints should be placed between pieces of stiff cardboard and secured with a rubber band. Paper clips can mar photos, so don't use them. Mark your mailing envelope "PHOTOGRAPHS – DO NOT BEND." This will alert postal workers and your pictures should make it through without being damaged. Color photos should be submitted as slides, not prints. They are best submitted in the page-size plastic sleeves that hold twenty 35mm slides. If you number them, the caption material can be typed on a separate sheet of paper with numbers to match.

Q. *How do I arrange to get an illustrator for my children's book?*
A. You don't need an illustrator, as most editors prefer manuscripts without illustrations. Publishers have their own preferences in illustrators, sometimes on staff. An editor is usually good at visualizing artwork to accompany a story, and if his ideas are radically different from yours, you run the risk of losing a sale. The final decision as to who will do the illustration lies with the editor, who has a group of reliable illustrators for the books his company publishes. If you have ideas that you feel are necessary to the success of your story, you might submit a dummy copy along with a copy of the straight text. Include sketches only though – don't bother with finished artwork until the editor has agreed that you will illustrate the book. (For more on collaboration with an artist, see chapter eleven.)

Q. *Can I expect to have photos returned to me that are not used with an article? How can I indicate that I would like to have the unused ones returned?*
A. The unused photos belong to you and you are justified in requesting their return. Enclose a SASE with your submission and ask in your cover letter that unused photos be returned.

Q. *I have written a nonfiction travel book. Should I send photographs with my manuscript when I submit it?*
A. First of all, editors rarely want to see unsolicited manuscripts for book-length work. Query your editor first and include several representative photos to show him what your illustration ideas are. Let him know that you can provide all photos needed for the book. After an editor has agreed to consider your manuscript for publication, send it to him with photos included.

Although some travel books, cookbooks, and books on photography are printed with color photographs, many other nonfiction books aren't. Using color illustrations greatly increases the cost of production, automatically leading to a higher cost for the consumer. So unless color photos are indispensable to your book idea, your chances of finding an interested editor are greater if you propose black-and-white photos, or don't use photos if they aren't absolutely necessary. And the editor may decide on his own that your manuscript should be illustrated with art rather than photos.

Q. *How many photos should I send with my article query?*
A. You are trying to sell your *idea* in a query, and photos aren't usually included (but if a couple of good photos buttress that sales effort, include them). When it gets down to submitting a completed manuscript with photos included, some writers send contact sheets of their black-and-white photographs along with a couple of their best choices as 8″ × 10″ glossies. Rohn Engh, author of *Sell & Re-Sell Your Photos*, doesn't recommend this – "don't display your less-than-perfect pictures by sending contact sheets," he says – and suggests rather that you submit only those 8″ × 10″s that you think best illustrate your article. If you have color shots, make sure they're transparencies, not color prints, and include up to twenty in one of the 8½″ × 11″ plastic sheets designed for submitting color transparencies to editors.

Q. *I am preparing a travel article for which I will need maps as part of the illustrations. I don't know what kind of maps to submit. Do I need permission to reproduce maps?*
A. Maps are copyrightable, so permission would be necessary to reproduce previously published, copyrighted ones. Submit the maps you think best for your article along with the copyright owner's address so that the editor can write for reprint permission if he decides to use them.

Q. *As a poet and artist could I submit illustrations to accompany my poems?*
A. Some little magazines and small presses that have limited budgets for hiring illustrators might welcome illustrated manuscripts. Check the individual listings in *Writer's Market* to see if the editors mention any such preferences, or include an illustration with your poetry submission and get the editor's reaction. Most smaller publications use black-and-white sketches only.

Q. *As an artist and writer, I think I would do well as an illustrator for children's books or magazines, but how should I market my work?*
A. Check the "Book Publishers" and "Magazines" sections of *Artist's Market* for publishers of children's literature. Then find copies of some of the works for children published by these companies, either in your local library or bookstore, or by writing to the magazine publishers for sample copies. As you study them to learn their styles and audiences, isolate two or three that you think might be interested in your work. Most magazine editors prefer that artists mail in a few samples, and book publishers usually request that artists mail them a portfolio or arrange an interview in which he can present it himself. Editorial preferences are listed in *Artist's Market*. Also included in that guide are articles describing good market technique, portfolio preparation, tips on business practices, and your rights as an artist.

Releases and Permissions

Q. *I want to submit some photographs with my fishing article, but my two partners are in most of the shots. Do I need model releases from them? When is a model release necessary?*
A. A signed model release is necessary if the photograph in question, whether it be of a person, someone's pet, or a recognizable building or piece of property, is to be used for any commercial purpose: advertising, endorsement, or promotion. Normally, you do not need to obtain releases for pictures used in the editorial sections of newspapers, magazines and books. It's important, however, that even photos used for editorial purposes not reflect unfavorably on their subjects, especially if those subjects are juveniles. If they do, you could face legal problems. And if you think that the photograph might be used on the cover and be construed by some as "advertising," it might be a good idea to have your two fishing partners sign forms permitting you to sell their photographs for editorial or commercial use. That way you will have the forms on file if your editor decides he needs them, or if you ever want to sell the photographs as advertising material. You can easily obtain release forms at most photography stores, or you can get your own printed. A sample form appears in *Photographer's Market*.

Basically, the model release is a signed and witnessed statement from the subject of a photograph (the model) giving the photographer the right to use the photograph for sale or reproduction, in consideration for value received. The "value received" is usually a copy print of the photograph.

For more information on model releases, see *Stock Photography: A Complete Guide* by Carl and Ann Purcell (Writer's Digest Books).

Q. *I have been asked to put together for publication a scrapbook on a world champion track star who has a collection of photos that tells his story quite well. Some of the photos are snapshots, but most are excellent, some having been published before, and many, published and unpublished, of nationally known personalities. Do I need the permission of the numerous photographers or individuals appearing in the photos? What about previously published photos?*
A. Since the photographs are all of "public figures" and you don't plan to use the photographs in any kind of advertising, you probably don't need any model releases signed by the subjects in the pictures. However, your publisher may want you to obtain releases anyway, in case some of these photos appear in advertising or promotion materials for the book. Unpublished photographs belong to the photographer, so you will have to obtain permission to use them. In the case of previously published photographs, who gives the permission depends on the rights the photographer sold to the original publisher. You'd have to write him to find out, then obtain permission where necessary.

Q. *If I used a Miami Seaquarium photo in a magazine article and it was given the appropriate credit line, could another author lift the photo and use it in his article as*

long as he transfers the credit line, giving the source proper recognition?
A. Since the photograph is the property of the Miami Seaquarium, each individual author must write for permission to use it. A credit line in one article does not imply permission is given to anyone else who wants to use it.

Q. *I hope to write a book on teaching high school art (I've had thirty-three years of experience in the field). Such a book would include the works of famous artists and sculptors, past and present. How do authors go about using reproductions of these works? Can I just cut pictures from books and magazines and include a byline of the creator, or would that be illegal?*
A. You may use the clippings only to indicate your ideas in the manuscript you send to an editor. If the book is accepted, you will have to request permission and photographs of the works from the museums where they're housed. In addition to owning the pieces of art, museums also usually own the reproduction rights.

Q. *I bought two oil paintings done by an Arizona Indian a number of years ago and think they would make good illustrations for a children's book I'm doing. Since I own the paintings, would a credit line be sufficient?*
A. No. Even though you own the paintings, reproduction rights still belong to the artist. You would have to contact the artist (or his heirs if he is dead) to obtain permission to reproduce the paintings as illustrations in your book.

Q. *A nonfiction book I am writing would be greatly improved if I could use the charts and drawings from another book I found on the same subject. How can I do this? Who do I contact and how would the artwork be reproduced?*
A. The usual procedure would be for the publisher to decide whether to write the original publisher for loan of the camera-ready art and reprint permission charges; or to write for permission and have his own art department redo the art. It's best for an author to only include photocopies of the art he wishes to obtain reprint permission on when trying to find a publisher who is interested in the book.

Copyright Concerns

Q. *What rights should I sell with photographs when they are submitted with a manuscript?*
A. Photographs are often bought in a "package" with the manuscript they accompany. Thus, editors will usually buy the same rights to the pictures that they buy to the manuscript. If they buy photographs independently, they will normally buy the same rights they buy for articles and stories printed in their publications. Ideally, you should only sell one-time rights to photographs, the same as you would to an article, story or poem.

Q. *When an editor says that "rights remain with the photographer," what does she mean?*

A. In the case of a copyrighted magazine, this means that the editor is buying one-time rights only. In the case of an uncopyrighted magazine, the photographer would have to secure copyright protection for the photograph by requiring the editor to carry the copyright notice, year, and the photographer's name under the published picture.

Q. *A magazine is using a photo of mine (along with an article) which I would like to copyright separately. Never before have I used a photo which I thought I wanted to protect, so I'm not sure how to go about this.*
A. If you wanted to copyright a photograph of yours, you would have to advise the editor in advance so she could publish the copyright symbol alongside the photo with your name as the copyright owner. You would also have to write for the necessary copyright forms from the Register of Copyrights, Library of Congress, Washington DC 20559, fill them out and return them with the $20 copyright fee and two copies of the published photo.

Chapter 24

How Do I Sell My Nonfiction Book?

What types of books are most popular among bookbuyers? Careful—the answer may surprise you. While a few blockbuster novels may grab the headlines, the overwhelming majority of books published each year are nonfiction books. How-to's, guidebooks, histories, biographies, self-help, exposeps—these are the books that remain popular year after year. Often, a nonfiction book begins with a writer's personal interest, or even as a magazine article that is carefully nurtured into a book-length package. What books are in your background? For more information, see *Twelve Keys to Writing Books That Sell* by Kathleen Krull and *How to Write a Book Proposal* by Michael Larsen (both from Writer's Digest Books).

Getting Started

Q. *I've written a lot of articles but I don't know if I have what it takes to write a book. Do you have to be an expert on something to get a nonfiction book published?*
A. A lot of what it takes to write magazine articles also applies to writing nonfiction books. In both cases, expertise is usually necessary to produce a successful how-to book or a work for a specialized or decidedly academic audience. However, other types of nonfiction, such as exposés, informational or historical pieces can be written by anyone who has good research skills plus organizational and writing abilities. For instance, author Harry Neal has published thirty-two books on subjects as diverse as *Chicken, The Secret Service in Action Saga,* and *The Story of Offshore Oil.* The ideas for articles and books all come from the same cache; that is, from what the writer sees, hears, thinks, reads and knows. The book author must consider broad topic coverage and a diverse audience.

Q. *I'm almost sure I have enough material gathered to be able to write travel books about England and Norway, but I don't know where to begin. I don't want to produce guidebooks, but would rather write descriptive books that could include some of my personal experiences. Ultimately, I'd hope that my memories would interest others in seeing these places. Can you help with my first step? Do I write a query letter?*
A. As a first step, you must search for possible markets for your idea. Look (in the

book publishers subject index section) of *Writer's Market* for publishers of travel books. Then go to your library, look up books of the type you'd like to sell, and match their publishers with your list from *Writer's Market*. Then send a query letter to the nonfiction editor at one of the publishing houses. In the letter, enclose an outline of your book and ask if the editor would like to see a sample chapter. If your idea is rejected, send the query to other publishers until you get an acceptance. If you can't find an interested publisher, it is possibly because the execution of your idea just isn't what the publishers think will sell. They may feel a guidebook for travelers is more practical, therefore more salable.

Your alternative would be to try to sell individual articles to travel magazines and other markets, although the preference here is largely for the practical rather than personal experience type of information.

Q. *I'd like to write a book on vegetable gardening. I've had a lot of experience and have many resources at my disposal. I understand that to market my idea, I should come up with a book proposal. What is a book proposal?*
A. A book proposal consists of a hard-sell cover letter, a sample of your writing — two or three finished chapters to allow the publisher to see your writing style — and an outline of the rest of the book, so the publisher can see where you plan to take your idea.

Your letter should convince the editor that there is a big market for your book and that you are most capable of writing it. Your outline can be a lettered and numbered topical breakdown, or it can be, as writers Barbara Toohey and June Bierman recommend, "small descriptive paragraphs that not only tell what will be covered in each chapter, but give the flavor of how it will be covered." They also suggest sending your proposal to several likely markets at the same time because editors are often slow about replying. Writing a book proposal will make you think your book all the way through, ultimately helping when it comes time to do the actual writing.

Q. *I've taught high school English for almost twenty-five years, and in that time have come across some common major weaknesses in the grammar texts I have had to use. I'd like to write a text of my own, but I don't know how to approach a publisher with my idea. Can you help?*
A. Look in *Writer's Market* for publishers specializing in the subject and level of your proposed text. Unless a publisher's listing states a letter of inquiry is necessary, you should send a prospectus that includes your experience and qualifications, a brief statement of title, contents and purpose of your text, a description of your competition (and a statement of why your approach is better), and samples of material you've written and tested in the classroom. Thus, short of sending a complete manuscript, you will be presenting as comprehensive a picture of your proposal as possible. A publisher should respond with either a polite rejection, a request for more material, suggestions for reworking your idea, or, in the rarest of cases, a contract.

Q. *I have a book-length manuscript on wit and humor, which is in the form of quips, jokes, doggerel, etc. What first step do you advise me to take?*
A. In your local library or bookshop, find some humor books and then query those publishers. Also consult the subject index list of book publishers in *Writer's Market*. If you cannot sell this material in book form, you may want to sell small batches to magazines as fillers, or to cartoonists who buy gags. Write the cartoonist in care of the magazine that publishes his work.

Q. *Is there any market for cookbooks from unknowns, on such subjects as menu planning and preparing easy meals or full-fledged dinner parties? How does a writer go about breaking into this field?*
A. It all depends on how appealing your ideas and writing style are, and your ability to find the right editor at the right time. Cookbooks have been bought from previously unknown writers. Send a query and brief outline to book publishers listed in *Writer's Market* who are interested in cookbooks.

Marketing Concerns

Q. *I have copyrighted some pieces that I am trying to sell as columns to newspapers. If they are published in the papers, would I have any copyright problems putting the same material into book form?*
A. As long as you are selling only simultaneous serial rights to the newspaper columns you have copyrighted, book rights belong to you. The best thing to do when submitting the printed column to the newspapers is to print in the upper right corner of the column, "simultaneous serial rights only." Be sure to request that newspaper editors print the copyright symbol, the year and your name, because if your column appears in an uncopyrighted newspaper without this notice, the column falls into the public domain. Your book must acknowledge the original copyright date of the columns.

Q. *In writing a nonfiction book, is it advisable to try to first publish single chapters as magazine articles?*
A. It isn't necessary to publish individual chapters because if your book idea is a good one, and your query convincing, you should be able to interest an editor. However, previously published articles can certainly be used to sell a book idea. They show the editor your abilities and that your idea is a marketable one. If you do sell your book chapters as articles first, make sure you don't sell all rights to the material. Some book manuscripts are rejected because they are simply a collection of articles. A successful nonfiction book has a definite focus and thread of continuity that runs from beginning to end. After the book is published, you might want to write related articles — or sell excerpts — to help promote it.

Q. *What advice do you have for a writer submitting his first finished book to a publisher?*
A. Keep a copy. If your manuscript is lost, the publisher will not pay for retyping.

Do *not* bind or staple the pages. Many writers use empty stationery boxes to ship book-length manuscripts to publishers. Manuscript box suppliers advertise in *Writer's Digest.* The post office also sells mailing cartons. You might also send your manuscripts in padded envelopes, although you'll need to prevent the page corners from bending by sandwiching the manuscript between cardboard cut a bit larger than your 8½" × 11" manuscript. Check your local postmaster for sizes and prices. The least expensive mailing cost would be the Special Fourth Class – Manuscript rate. Be sure to mark "Return Postage Guaranteed" under your name and return address on the package. Enclose a self-addressed label with correct return postage. Type your name and address on the title page and your name and page number on each succeeding page in the upper left corner. Information in your cover letter should be specifically important. In a cover letter, list your previously published works only if of some importance and issued by a respected publisher, as well as information regarding documentary evidence to support any facts in the book that might be questioned.

Q. *How do I prepare a manuscript for a how-to book? About half of the published page will be pictures and diagrams.*
A. The manuscript should be typed in the same way as other book manuscripts, with appropriate illustration references such as (See Figure 1) or (See photo, page 12). All diagrams and photographs should be numbered so that they correlate with both the text and a separate sheet listing captions. Standard photos are 8" × 10" black-and-white glossy prints and 35mm color transparencies. Diagrams are usually drawn on 8" × 10" sheets. Individual preferences will vary, so check with your publisher on this.

Q. *Is it okay to include snapshots with my how-to book manuscript?*
A. No. Most publishers want 8" × 10" black-and-white glossy photos or 35mm color transparencies (slides). Check *Photographer's Market* to see what individual publishers prefer. It's a good idea, when sending photos with your manuscript, to send a mixture of horizontal and vertical shots, so the editor has a better idea of how he might arrange the material on the pages of the book.

Q. *My nonfiction book was rejected by a publisher who said it wasn't "authoritative" enough. What does that mean, and how can I solve the problem?*
A. Saying the book wasn't authoritative enough could mean one of several things. The editor might mean that you have not researched the topic adequately, or that you have not used your research wisely. Or he might be saying that you are not adequately qualified to write about the subject, and that you have not included enough quotes from experts and other authorities on this topic to give your work credibility among readers. (Even if you are an accomplished person in the field, talking to other authorities makes for a better-rounded book.)

To find experts in a specific field, look in *The Directory of Directories,* found in the reference section of most libraries. This book lists guides to specialized directories in many subject areas that can lead you to the authorities you need. (For more information on finding experts, see chapter seven.)

Q. *I have an idea for a paperback pocket reference book, but I'm getting nothing but rejections from paperback publishers. Should I give up and try a hardcover publisher?*
A. Mass-market paperback publishers can only afford to produce books that will appeal to *millions* of readers. If your nonfiction book idea is specialized, appealing only to a limited market, no paperback publisher is likely to be interested. Study the book publishers' listings in *Writer's Market,* plus the appropriate subject bookshelves in the library and bookstores in your town, then make up your list of hardcover publisher prospects.

Q. *Please let us know what you think of sending book-length manuscripts in "jiffy bags," and enclosing correct return postage.*
A. They're all right as long as you protect your manuscript by sandwiching it between cardboard cut to just above the 8½″ × 11″ manuscript size. This will prevent page corners from bending.

The Story on Biographies

Q. *What is the difference between an authorized and an unauthorized biography?*
A. An authorized biography is written with the cooperation of the person it's about—or his estate, if he's deceased. This means the writer has access to in-depth interviews with the subject and his family and friends, and to private records and correspondence. In some cases the writer shares byline, advance, and royalties with the subject. Authorized biographies are sometimes rejected by the critics for their lack of objectivity. An unauthorized biography, on the other hand, is written without the cooperation of the subject or his estate. Publication of these works is strongly based in current public interest and they cover such people as television personalities, rock stars, sports heroes and political figures. Although there have been claims that a celebrity has the right to write and/or authorize his own biography, the courts have not upheld them.

Q. *In writing a biography about a deceased person, do you have to be careful about what you tell, or can you tell the truth?*
A. Most state laws prevent the heirs of a person from suing for either libel or invasion of privacy. Usually these suits can only be brought by a living person who feels he has been defamed or his privacy invaded. In writing about a deceased person, if you also discuss others who are living, be sure of your facts, since the truth (if you can prove it) is the best defense against libel. Truth is not a defense, however, against invasion of privacy, so if you have any qualms about possible suits from living persons on that score, you had best either get releases or eliminate those references.

Q. *Through my experience as a freelancer, I have had contact with someone who would make a good biography subject. If I write the book, I think it will have national appeal. Any suggestions on how I can get started?*
A. Depending on the situation, it might be wise to discuss the possibility of a biography with your subject before you approach any publishers. Whatever you decide, look in *Writer's Market* and find publishers interested in biographies, and query one of them, indicating your contact with the proposed subject and why he or she would make a salable biography. If you fail to find an interested publisher, it may be because the publishers don't think your idea would sell well. You will have to rethink it and either change the emphasis or abandon the idea. Once you *do* receive a positive response, your research is cut out for you. If you've already interviewed and written an article on your subject, you've got a head start. However, you should read all other material written about the person as well. Then approach the subject (if you want it to be an authorized biography), family members, and close acquaintances for interviews. In planning the book, you will need to know about outstanding events and conflicts that your subject has encountered so that you can show how he became the person he is now. Earlier biographies were usually done in strict chronological order, but now they often open with some dramatic episode attesting to the subject's character and/or fame, and later recapitulate the formative years. A sound knowledge of your subject and of the other people strongly influencing him is necessary to write a strong and viable biography. But avoid tedious detail and references to relatively unimportant people. Focus on highlights and the impact such events had on the subject's life.

For a list of comprehensive guides to writing biography, check *Subject Guide to Books in Print* under "Biography as a Literary Form." Reading plenty of contemporary biography will give you a good idea of what publishers are interested in these days. Titles of single and collective biographies currently in print can be found under the heading "Biography" in *Subject Guide to Books in Print*.

Technical Matters

Q. *I am writing a book which, though not an authoritative document, uses material from about twenty references. In all except one or two instances, I have taken no quotations from these sources. I don't wish to clutter up the book with a lot of reference symbols to indicate where I have drawn from sources. I would like to acknowledge all such unquoted references in an appendix. Can you advise me?*
A. Why not simply prepare a bibliography to accompany your manuscript and precede it with a statement such as, "The author acknowledges the following references used in preparation of this text: . . ." If your publisher prefers a different method, you can work that out between you. Where you have quoted directly, you should footnote within the text the appropriate books quoted.

Q. *I am writing a how-to book. Do I need permission to use names and addresses of sources of equipment and supplies necessary to execute the project I explain in the* *book? What about obtaining permission for titles, authors and publishers of books I recommend for supplementary reading?*

A. It is not necessary to request permission for use of book titles in your bibliography, but you should check with suppliers for permission to include their names and addresses in your reference list to make sure their equipment and supplies will be available as long as your book is in print. General suggestions, such as what heading to consult in the Yellow Pages or what type of store would carry the products, are very helpful to the reader.

Chapter 25

Why Don't My Short Stories Sell?

When queried by a reader about how he worked, Somerset Maugham replied, "Madame, all the words I use in my stories can be found in the dictionary—it's just a matter of arranging them into the right sentences." Of course, that arranging—challenging as it is—isn't the end of the process. Once a beginning writer learns the necessary ingredients for a short story he is challenged not only to write it effectively, but to get it to the right editor at the right time.

The Elements of a Short Story

Q. *I like to write short stories, but my teachers have said that the things I write are not exactly stories. How can I find out what a short story is?*
A. The basic elements of a short story include plot, setting, characters and theme. What is it that turns these items into an appealing manuscript and a salable story? A story involves a logical connection of incidents. A story needs a character who, while participating in these incidents, meets conflict, either within himself, with another character, or with some other force outside of himself. Encountering the conflict and finding a resolution should leave the character changed in a way that he might not have been otherwise. It is this change, for better or worse, that makes a story. Consider for example the idea of two young boys on a Saturday afternoon fishing trip. If the author tells us about the nice time they had looking for the right spot along the bank to cast their lines and the large number of fish they caught before they trotted happily home, would it be a story? Not unless one of the boys, who always thought of himself as a coward, had to muster up his courage to save the other boy who fell into the rushing river and couldn't swim. Here a character is in conflict with what he sees as his own limitations and learns that he can go beyond them—and a series of incidents has become a story.

Look closely at what you've written. Does it contain character conflict, change and growth, or are you just relating a series of events that involve one or more characters? That may be the difference between what you've written and what a story is. Two good reference books written for the beginning short story writer are

Writing in General and the Short Story in Particular by Rust Hills (Bantam Books) and the *Writer's Digest Handbook of Short Story Writing.*

Q. *What is the difference between crisis and climax in a short story?*
A. The crisis in a short story arises from conflict that leads to a turning point. After a series of obstacles, the major character experiences a dark moment in which he or she sees no way to solve the problem. Then there is a moment of revelation as the character figures out everything. The climax normally follows the crisis and represents the most intense point in the story line. Here the character finds the solution to his problem and often regains what he thought he lost. The story should end shortly thereafter.

Q. *What is a story theme? Is it any different than a story problem?*
A. A theme is the message an author imparts to his readers through the plot and characters in his story. The writer starts with an idea and as his story develops, it is influenced by his own philosophy or observation of the human condition. This is his theme. A story problem is the vehicle by which an author presents his theme. For instance, the problem facing Dorothy in *The Wizard of Oz* is getting home to Kansas from the Land of Oz. It is through her trials and adventures there that she learns of her folly in wanting to run away from home earlier in the film, finally deciding "there's no place like home," the overall theme of the story. Thomas Wolfe chose an opposing theme for his book, *You Can't Go Home Again.*

Q. *How does a writer get his point across in a story without repeating it?*
A. It is through the change occurring in the major character as a result of his experiences that a writer often makes his point. In the course of the story, the major character must experience a moment of revelation or make a decision and, just as in real life, he changes as a result of these experiences. He wouldn't have to change from all-bad to all-good, but he should gain insight into a negative aspect of his personality and either decide to change it or accept that it cannot be changed. It is through these revelations and decisions that the writer sends his message, not through overtly stating it.

Q. *Does my short story have to contain a message?*
A. If you want to call it a short story rather than a sketch, an incident, or an anecdote, it should contain a message or theme that can be summarized in a single sentence. This gives your writing added purpose. It is not always advisable to start writing with a specific theme in mind, as you may try to elaborate on it in such a way that the story becomes mechanical and the characters unnatural. If you have the emotional involvement and present your character with an obstacle, your theme will most likely generate itself from your characters, setting, situation and emotion. Some magazines, such as juvenile and confession publications, stress the importance of the theme being stated directly somewhere in the story. It might be incorporated into the narrative after the moment of revelation, for instance, or into the

main character's thoughts or speech as she reflects on what she has learned. Other magazines, such as science fiction and quality publications, prefer an implied theme, allowing the reader to relate to the theme in his own way.

Q. *What is the difference between a plant and a false plant in a story?*
A. A writer "plants" any information such as people, places, objects or facts to be used later in the story so as to eliminate any possibility of coincidence. For example, in a short story, if an adventurer whose horse has died, and who is sun-parched and dying of thirst himself, is traversing the desert of the American Southwest and suddenly comes to an old deserted homestead that has a spring close by, the reader will be bewildered. Where did that house and spring come from? A good writer will find a way to plant them earlier in his story, thus getting rid of contrived coincidence.

The "false plant" is deliberately placed by the author although it has no connection with the conclusion or resolution of conflict in a short story. Introducing innocent suspects with viable motives in a mystery story is a common use of this device. False plants differ from "dangling plants" in that they are always adequately explained somewhere in the story. If the writer of that short story mentioned an old homestead with a spring close by and didn't put it to some use later in the story, he would have placed a dangling plant. These can be annoying to editor and reader and should be avoided.

Q. *How can I effectively create a character in the limited space of a short story?*
A. Think of your character and examine him closely in your mind. Try to determine what is so unique about him that warrants a story. Try to find a single fact which sets him apart and gives him a recognizable trait. Then portray him in *one* sentence. Though difficult to write, one-line character descriptions can be extremely incisive and are definitely space-saving. For example, note this passage from Damon Knight's short story "Semper Fi": "Price came forward with his heron's gait, folded himself into a chair, twitched, knotted his thin fingers together." In one sentence we have a clue to Price's appearance and to his nervous emotional state. Character traits should not be thrown at the reader, but rather should be woven gradually into the story. Consider the difference between the above passage and "Price was a long, thin, nervous man." A writer should let words, actions and reactions be the defining features of a particular character.

Q. *I have often wondered whether a man can write effectively about a woman, or vice versa. If he is writing from the viewpoint of a woman or girl, could he possibly portray her problem and her various reactions to situations? Would he be better advised to choose a man as protagonist, or does it matter? What is the practice among successful writers?*
A. There is enough proof in literature of the world that a writer can successfully portray a member of the opposite sex. Look at what Flaubert did with Madame Bovary, what Margaret Mitchell did with Rhett Butler, and Tennessee Williams

did with Blanche Dubois, to name just a few. The ease with which a male writer can slip into the consciousness of a female character and vice versa depends ultimately on the individual writer and how much insight he has into the workings of human nature, regardless of sex.

Q. *How does a writer go about isolating a scene, in dissecting a short story? To me the scenes seem somewhat continuous. I fail to see any sharp dividing line in a taut story.*
A. Whenever the action moves to a different setting, that's automatically a new scene. If, for example, a story opens in a young couple's kitchen, then moves to an incident in the husband's office, these two different settings constitute two different scenes. But suppose the story is a taut short-short in which all the action takes place in the kitchen. Then we look for a division that is not geographical but a time change. This could develop if your first scene shows the husband and wife in the kitchen at breakfast time. Then after setting this stage, you may want to have a time break to five o'clock when the wife is preparing dinner. This is a device used often. For example, "Jim stomped out during breakfast without finishing his coffee. As Ellen prepared dinner, she thought of the silly argument they had had early that day."

Q. *When writing a short story, are you supposed to underline everything that is spoken or thought?*
A. As a general rule, use quotation marks for dialogue spoken by story characters. Magazine styles vary for punctuating a character's thoughts: Some use quotation marks, some put a character's thoughts in italics (meaning you should underline them in your manuscript), some merely set them off with a comma and capitalize the first letter, and some make no special designation at all if it's clear that the thoughts are the narrating viewpoint character's. Check out the magazine you're submitting your story to, so that you can match their form. If you are submitting to multiple markets, you most likely won't have the right style for every publication. If your story is purchased, it will undoubtedly be edited to conform to the magazine's style; but an effort to match the style shows your professional skill.

Deciphering Story Types

Q. *What is the difference between a formula story and a nonformula story?*
A. When editors speak of the formula story, they usually mean a familiar theme treated in a predictable or familiar plot structure, such as the formula plot of boy meets girl . . . etc. mentioned earlier. The editor who is looking for a nonformula story wants to get away from such plot situations and development. He wants an unusual central problem treated in an original manner. Very likely characterization or symbolism in the story will be more important than the situation, as can be seen in stories like Ernest Hemingway's "Big Two-Hearted River." You might find examples of other nonformula stories in magazines such as *The Atlantic* or *The New Yorker*, and in some women's magazines as well.

Q. *Fiction requirements of many magazines specify either "no contrived" or "no slick" stories. What doe they mean by these terms?*
A. By "contrived," editors usually mean plots whose action is constructed in an artificial, implausible way. For example, if a character purposely sets fire to a barn to kill the man inside, that's a credible, well-motivated act. But if a fire happens to break out in the barn for no reason other than the obvious one of helping the author dispose of the man inside, that's contrived. "Slick" *did* originally refer only the type of paper used in a magazine, but it has come to mean the familiar, formula-type story; for example, boy meets girl, loses girl, gets girl, which has a neat, pat (and usually happy) ending.

Q. *I've read that some publishers accept "gimmicks" for publication. What does this term mean?*
A. A gimmick is a short, mystery-type story giving clues to help the reader solve a puzzle or uncover a secret before checking the solution on another page. Gimmick stories are usually 500 to 1,000 words and appear in crossword puzzle and game books, such as Dell's various puzzle publications. They are written in short story form up to the point of the climax, when the reader is asked an all-important question, the answer to which is intrinsic in solving the puzzle or "mystery."

There are at least three types of gimmick stories. One kind, the fact gimmick, involves some verifiable common knowledge needed to unravel the story, such as knowing the legal meaning of *habeas corpus*. Seasonal gimmicks are based on a fact tying in with a holiday or special season; they should be submitted to editors six to eight months before the tie-in date. The detective story gimmick is based on skill-fully concealed clues that require no special knowledge to understand.

Successful gimmicks must be carefully constructed. Clues should not be unbe-lievable or contrived. Both content and "gimmick" must be believable if a writer wants to make a sale.

Q. *Many magazines' guidelines state, "No vignettes or slice-of-life pieces." What does that mean?*
A. A "slice of life" story or vignette is usually one that depends less on plot for its interest than on mood and atmosphere and the detail with which the setting and/or environment and their effects on the characters are described. *Writer's Encyclopedia* describes it as "a seemingly unselective presentation of life as it is; a brief, illuminat-ing look at a realistic rather than a constructed situation, revealed to the reader without comment or interpretation by the author." This form does have a plan, however, and the viewpoint character experiences at least a slight change. Since it is not strongly based in plot, this form is most often published in the literary and little magazines, rather than in the larger commercial magazines.

Q. *How long is a short-short story compared to a short story?*
A. The average short-short story is from 500 to 2,000 words and the short story runs 2,500 to 5,000 words. Individual publishers may have varying requirements

which would be listed in *Novel & Short Story Writer's Market*. For average word lengths on a variety of manuscripts—novel, play, juvenile book, etc.—see "How Long is a . . . ?" in the Appendix of *Beginning Writer's Answer Book*.

Q. *Besides the obvious one of length, are there any other differences between short stories and short-short stories?*
A. Plot in a short story is limited to a small chain of events. It is confined in a short-short, however, to a single power-packed incident that gives the story its thematic value. There is no room for extensive character development; rather, it is the change of attitude of the central character in the incident which gives the story its depth. The writer doesn't try to do more than focus intensely on one truth of life that may or may not be new to the reader. Good subjects for short-shorts include changes in parent/child or husband/wife relationships, a child's awakening to some facet of life, or an individual's reevaluation of his role in society.

Q. *It's hard to draw the line between short stories and novels, now that there are also novelettes and novellas. Just what are the differences in length, subject matter and form in all of these types of fiction?*
A. Although there are no set rules of length, the short story usually runs 2,000 to 5,000 words. The novelette and novella (editors use the terms interchangeably) can both be viewed as long short stories or short novels and will range anywhere from 7,000 to 40,000 words. Herman Melville's *Billy Budd* and Ernest Hemingway's *The Old Man and the Sea* are examples of this genre. Novels are the longest types of fiction. The structure is similar to that of a short story in that it presents a series of conflicts and temporary obstacles leading to a climax where the major conflict is resolved or accepted as unsolvable. The difference lies in the fact that the novelist has more time and word space to develop his plot and characters and can more easily change the viewpoint of the narrator.

I Have This Problem . . .

Q. *I have trouble translating thoughts to paper. I have stories in my head, but when I try to write them, it becomes difficult. Do you have any suggestions?*
A. Maybe you're worrying and concentrating too much in the beginning on *how* you put your thoughts on paper. Write in fragments, and don't be concerned about the style of writing or if the notes you are jotting make sense or are structured in any way. Or try dictating into a tape recorder—writers sometimes feel more comfortable "telling their stories" then transcribing them. Some writers write a synopsis of their story, which makes it easier to organize their notes into a unified whole. Once they have decided what's going to happen in the story, and to whom, the words begin to flow. Then they do the final editing and polishing of the story.

Q. *Must I outline my story? What are the advantages? Outlining takes so much time.*
A. Although it is not always necessary to construct a detailed outline before you

begin to write, you will end up saving yourself a lot of time if you do some planning. As author Damon Knight says in *Creating Short Fiction,* "It is inefficient, certainly, to leap into a story without any idea where you will end up." It is inefficient because the less you know about your characters, setting, situation, and emotions you wish to convey, the harder it will be to decide what can and will happen in a story. Every author has her own method of planning and writing stories, and only trial and error will tell you what you need to know before you start to write. It's a good idea to write your plan. Knight suggests that before you start writing you should at least know *who* the story is about, *why* they're doing what they're doing, *what* the story is about, *where* the story takes place, and *when* it takes place.

Q. *An editor told me I should strive to present a single viewpoint in my short story. Why should I? How do I decide whether third person or first person is better?*
A. In a short story, strong reader identification with one of the characters is very important and is easily lost when the author employs a multiple viewpoint. Suspense and continuity are often lost in the transition from one viewpoint to another. For these reasons, short stories told from more than one viewpoint are rarely successful. The choice between first and third person should be made with the plot, characters, and desired market in mind. Usually first person only can be subjective, lending itself well to strong emotion and fast reader identification. Third person, on the other hand, is useful if your plot and characters demand an objective treatment. Study your potential markets to determine what viewpoints are prevalent in the stories they publish.

Q. *One of the editors who rejected my story told me he liked the basic idea very much but the whole story was much too complicated. How can I simplify it?*
A. If you have too much going on in your story, it may be because you've tried to incorporate too many characters or incidents into it. You have to decide who the story is about and focus your narrative on that character and his problem. All other characters should be a part of the story you build around the major character. You may have to reduce arbitrarily the number of characters (to three or four at the most) and restructure your plot from there. The result should be greater simplicity and unity.

Q. *I submitted my story to an editor and he returned it saying it was "too slow-paced." What is he talking about?*
A. If your story is too slow-paced, you are giving too little attention to action and dialogue that moves the story toward the problem and its resolution. Editors often complain that stories written by beginners don't even start until page five of the manuscript. If the reader must watch the main character wake up, light a cigarette, make coffee and start breakfast before he learns what the problem in the story is, the story is too slow-paced. Since word space is so limited in short stories, the opening scene, as well as every other scene, should be short on exposition and

quick to provide action and dialogue that engages the reader and is pertinent to the story's end.

Q. *The transitions in my stories never seem to work. How can I handle them without being abrupt or taking too much time?*
A. Scene transitions involve changes in time, place, and emotion. As Louise Boggess says in *How to Write Short Stories that Sell,* the key to smooth transition is to "link the old with the new." Boggess suggests that in the last paragraph of a scene, preferably the last sentence, the writer should indicate the present place and time period, and if possible, imply the new ones. Then the first sentence in the new scene can establish the time lapse and change of place. Note these points in the following example:

Natalee halfway hoped the Crandalls wouldn't like her antiques, but that must wait until tomorrow, she reminded herself, and tried to get some sleep.

The next morning worry about the Crandalls completely left her mind when . . .

Q. *How do I detect rambling in my story? A teacher told me I was rambling at some places where I thought description was necessary.*
A. Examine the passages your teacher marked and evaluate them for their relevancy to the story. Be able to define the purpose of each episode and descriptive passage. If you can't determine a function for each part, either discard it or rewrite it. If you determine that the information really is necessary, your teacher's assessment that it rambles is a sign that it should be incorporated into the story more subtly. For instance, can your spelled-out characterization be compressed into the character's actions or his dialogue? In *Creating Short Fiction,* Damon Knight says that "every passage must perform three or four functions at the same time—advance the plot, add to the characterizations, introduce background information, and so on. . . ." Being able to write this concisely takes practice, but in the long run, your stories will be better and more salable.

Q. *When an editor says my story has loose ends, what does he mean?*
A. Your story needs tightening up—inconsistencies need to be resolved. This may mean adding or omitting incidents or merely adding a phrase that refers to an earlier part of the story. Your story needs to be unified in time and action and the course of events must be logical. For instance, don't introduce some line of plot action for which the reader expects some meaning in the story and then arbitrarily drop it. It only confuses and annoys editor and reader.

Q. *Looking at the short story I've written, I can see that the conclusion is weak and unconvincing. How can I fix it?*
A. There are a couple of possible reasons for your disappointment in the ending. For one, is it too obvious? Is the outcome exactly what a reader would expect from your characters and plot? Your problem may be that you failed to plan for your

ending before you started writing the story. If you were hoping something would come to you as the story progressed, and nothing did, your ending undoubtedly seems irrelevent or illogical. In either case, your solution will involve going back to the beginning of the story and doing some replotting. Make your major character's decision a difficult one rather than an obvious one. Or use the conflict structure to misdirect your reader, leading him to expect a different ending than what you finally give him. Changes like these must be incorporated into the whole story, for if you merely tack on an ending, it will remain inappropriate and weak because it is not justified by the rest of the story.

Q. *I'm taking a course in short story writing and my teacher keeps noting "overstatement" in my stories. But she's never given me a solid definition of the problem. Can you help?*
A. Your teacher may be referring to what others call "overwriting" or "purple prose." Redundancies, an excess of adjectives and adverbs in descriptive passages, or an overplay of emotion can all be considered overstatement. Passages that seem contrived or just don't fit the tenor of the story may be overwritten. While it's most easily spotted by someone other than the writer, you should develop the skill of recognizing and correcting this flaw that would obviously hinder sales.

When Truth Meets Fiction

Q. *Why aren't true-life experiences the best way of planning a story? How could I possibly improve on the way it really happened?*
A. True-life experiences often make a good skeleton for a short story, but they usually need to be dramatized before they will interest others. If the basic action of your story needs a lot of exposition, which it invariably does, you may need to invent action and dialogue to get it across more effectively. Readers will be bored by a straight narrative explanation. If your characters are based upon people you are acquainted with, chances are you don't know them as well as a writer of fiction must know his characters. In order to provide them with sufficient motivation, you may have to provide traits that make them unique and worthy of the reader's sympathies. Plot may need changes in time span and in order of events so that it effectively moves the story along.

Q. *For the past ten years I have been active in religious work in a rural county. I want to write these experiences in book form. Each chapter will represent a short story with a unifying overall story thread and quite a bit of local color. What effects can I use to heighten story interest?*
A. Use plenty of dialogue, including vivid human-interest details, build a mood (through weather, landscape, etc.), try to create suspense by suggesting your characters' emotional reactions to a situation and humorous observations about life in general as a result of some specific experience. Above all, keep your style lively and colorful so that readers will enjoy your narrator. Fictionalize the events and

make enough changes in the characters so that they become *your* literary creations, even though originally based on real people.

Q. *My short story embraces a true event in a nineteenth-century man's life that is recorded in newspapers and books. Can I properly call it fiction since two-thirds of the story contains my own dialogue and events?*
A. Yes, it is permissible to fictionalize a historical event. Since you are creating the dialogue and much of the dramatic action, it can properly be called fiction.

Q. *In a juvenile fiction story based on true historical incidents, may I use authentic names of teachers, mayors, ministers, businessmen, etc.?*
A. If the people you mention were part of that historical event and were public figures at that time, there should be no problem with your use of their names.

Q. *I would like to set my story in the city of Detroit. Do I have to use real names of streets and places, or can I mix fiction with fact?*
A. If you're going to use a real city as the setting of your story, you had better use names of real streets and places. It will give your story authenticity. Make sure all facts in your story are correct. Just because your story is fiction doesn't give you the right to present any factual inaccuracies. Fiction writers must spend time re-searching so that they can write with a sure knowledge of their subjects.

Q. *I know of no living relatives of the real-life character I am basing my short story on. Am I free to continue my short fiction without thought of his living heirs?*
A. Go ahead and write your story, since most state laws say heirs can't sue—only the live person who is libeled or has had his privacy invaded. Many writers feel safer changing names, dates and places in their stories.

Q. *Should a confession story be completely true, or can it be fictional? Should the byline be a pen name?*
A. The important thing about a confession story is that it *could* happen, not that it did. However, recently there has been a much greater emphasis on the reality of confession stories, or at least their basis in reality. Magazines are even requesting *readers* to send in their true-life experiences. Readers go to the confessions for answers to their own problems, and what better way to write about alcoholism, divorce and unemployment than to draw upon real life? Of course, the incidents may be altered to dramatize or condense them, but most stories are based on true happenings. Most confessions do not give bylines, so it is unnecessary to be con-cerned about pen names. Only the editors know who the authors are . . . and they don't tell the readersp For more information, see the *Confession Writer's Handbook,* by Florence K. Palmer.

Sales Stories

Q. *I have finally made a short story sale. Should I indicate this sale on the first page of future manuscripts to ensure more careful consideration?*
A. You should mention this as part of a brief biographical statement in future cover letters. It may not increase your story's chances of selling, but it will show that you've written at least one salable story, and it could wind up in a published "bio note" at the end of your story, if it's accepted.

Q. *There are very few magazines on the newsstands that contain stories. Magazines print mostly articles. Who buys stories today?*
A. While a few major magazines—*The New Yorker, Esquire, The Atlantic Monthly* and others—are still active fiction markets, the majority of markets for short stories are magazines that you won't find on the newsstand. Some religious, juvenile and specialized consumer magazines buy stories, as do literary magazines (also known as "little magazines" or "lit mags"), published by small and university presses. You'll find their requirements in *Novel & Short Story Writer's Market.*

Q. *Can you give me information about the lead time required for submitting stories to quarterly publications? At the moment I am interested in submitting a Christmas story to a quarterly religious magazine.*
A. A Christmas story for a quarterly publication should be submitted nine months to a year in advance. Lead times for monthly magazines vary from four months to a year, and for weekly publications, three to six months. Check with each editor for his preference. This information is often contained in the writers guidelines that are available to potential contributors of a publication. Some listings in *Writer's Market* offer such guidelines to writers on request with an accompanying SASE. (A business-size envelope will suffice unless otherwise specified.)

Q. *In submitting short fiction to general slick magazines, what is the best procedure to follow when a good title does not come to mind? Is it better to submit an untitled story or to submit a title that does not satisfy the author?*
A. Titles are often changed by the magazines, but a good title is more than a label; it's often an enticement to read the story. For purposes of identification, it *is* advisable for a manuscript to have a title, so choose the best one you can rather than none at all.

Q. *I have written a story about a woman's emotional disintegration as various pressures upon her reach the point where she can no longer cope with them. It does not end happily. A recent rejection comment was, "It's a little too grim to be entirely satisfactory to us." I believe this attitude toward an unhappy ending is shared by all women's magazines. I am discouraged by the apparent lack of markets for this kind of story. Do you have any suggestions?*
A. If the caliber of your writing is high, you could try the quality markets, such as

The Atlantic, Harper's or some of the university literary magazines. Bear in mind, though, that your story must have something to say to readers above and beyond the mere chronicling of one woman's misfortunes. It must in some way deepen readers' insight through its larger view of life.

Q. *If I sell my short story to a magazine, can I retain the rights to expand it into a novel?*
A. If you sell only first serial rights to your story, it is yours to use as you wish. Often, if you have sold all rights to your story, you will be able to get them back on request. Some publishers, however, may insist on purchasing all rights to a story. If you aren't sure about a publisher's policy, send a polite letter of inquiry.

Q. *Does a male writer, writing as a female, have a chance in the confession markets? Is it true that some of these publications require an affidavit attesting to the truth of the story?*
A. Since confessions often don't carry bylines, men have just as good a chance as women in this field, provided they can write convincingly. Most confession publications today require the writer to sign a release form that is not notarized, but attests to the originality of the story and the fact that it is based on true happenings you've experienced, heard about or know about.

Q. *Do book publishers put out collections of short novels and stories that haven't previously been published?*
A. Yes, but rarely. More often in the case of established writers, they prefer collections to be a combination of both published and new stories. In the case of an unknown writer, however, the publisher is usually reluctant to bring out a collection of work that has not stood the test of print. It is easier for the beginning writer to establish his reputation through periodicals, then try to get a book publisher interested in a collection.

Q. *Maugham and Hemingway were considered great writers, but most of their short stories did not have plots or conflict. If either writer were alive today, would his stories sell?*
A. These writers' stories *did* have conflict: the conflict of man's relation to humanity or to himself. They continue to sell today because of their authors' inherent skill in bringing characters to life and making their problems interesting.

Q. *The library in the small town I live in has a very limited supply of magazines and I can't afford to send away and pay for a lot of sample copies. How can I find out the kinds of stories magazine editors consider good so I can read and learn from them?*
A. There are several anthologies published annually that will give you a good overview of the stories that various magazine editors consider among the best they've published. *Prize Stories: the O. Henry Awards* and *The Best American Short Stories* reprint stories that have appeared in magazines like *The New Yorker, Redbook,* and

leading literary magazines. *The Pushcart Prize: The Best of the Little Presses* reprints stories from some of the smaller magazines that you wouldn't find in most libraries. Each anthology prints a list of the magazines from which they selected stories. You could then refer to the listings for such publications in either *Writer's Market* or *Novel & Short Story Writer's Market* and write for sample copies of those magazines that interest you most. Where editorial guidelines are available, be sure to ask for those too.

Chapter 26

Can a New Writer Sell a Novel?

Susan Scarnecchia, then an editorial assistant at G.P. Putnam's, had just finished reading a host of novel manuscripts, and wrote: "What makes a good novelist is not total recall, nor the ability to articulate 'the way it really happened.' It is the author's own peculiar vision—the world view that he has distilled from experience that makes what he writes worth reading." That challenge to separate reportage from representation, "to recollect experience, sift it down, spread it out in a new light and restructure it—not all of it, but select parts, not the whole truth as it happened to one man, but that element of his personal truth that may have meaning for many men,"—that's what drives the writer to the novel form, again and again. For more tips, see *How to Write and Sell Your First Novel* by Oscar Collier with Frances Spatz Leighton.

Types of Novels

Q. *Explain what is meant by "genre" fiction. An editor said that's the kind of fiction he buys, but I've never seen any reference to it before now.*
A. Genre fiction, sometimes called category fiction, includes stories that can be easily labeled, such as science fiction, fantasy, mystery, suspense, Gothic, western and erotica.

Q. *What are "experimental" and "mainstream" fiction and the differences between them?*
A. Mainstream—the type of fiction that most often becomes a bestseller—employs conventional techniques to tell the story, while experimental fiction is unconventional. Experimental novelists such as John Barth and William Burroughs share a common interest in form—style, structure, symbol, narrative technique—over and above the development of the "story." Beginning writers usually are urged to follow the traditional route for their first attempts, since markets for experimental fiction are limited.

Q. *I've got a couple of good ideas for mystery stories, but I'm not quite sure how to go*

about getting them into the form of a novel. What are some of the basics one should be aware of before attempting to write a mystery?
A. One of the problems facing mystery writers today is a need for new ideas to revitalize the genre. Be careful of imitating other popular writers too closely, although it's important to notice the format, style and techniques of the genre itself. Mystery writers often get so wrapped up in the intricacies of the puzzle that must be presented to the reader that the novel ends up lacking any strong theme or well-rounded characters. Try to step back from your writing enough to be able to add some human elements to it. You can be sure you'll have a better chance of selling your manuscript. Some basic elements of mystery stories are described in Lawrence Treat's preface to the *Mystery Writer's Handbook.* He says that necessary components include a crime dastardly enough that the readers care about it (which usually means murder), a criminal that appears early in the story, though the reader doesn't have to know he's the bad guy, an honest author who, subtly or obviously, presents all of the clues to his reader, and a detective who *tries* to solve the mystery, meaning coincidences aren't allowed. For some other good novel-writing basics, see Lawrence Block's *Writing the Novel: From Plot to Print.*

Q. *What does the word "faction" mean?*
A. A work of faction is one that is written and sold as fiction, even though it's about real people and events. One form of faction, called the *roman à clef,* or "novel with a key," thinly disguises the famous people and events it portrays. An example is Robert Penn Warren's *All the King's Men,* whose central character most readers took to be the politician Huey Long. Some publishers use the word faction to describe novels in which a great deal of fact about a particular industry is woven into the story. Arthur Hailey's *Hotel* and *Wheels* are typical of this form of faction, because Hailey did extensive research into the factual operations of the industries he wrote about in his novels.

Q. *What is an epistolary novel?*
A. An epistolary novel is written completely in the form of letters, usually letters to and from the protagonist. Both plot and characterization are achieved through the letters. Because it is a very demanding form for a writer, epistolary novels are not very prevalent today. However, it is an old form: the nineteenth-century thriller *Dracula,* written by Bram Stoker, is in the form of letters and diary entries. Two more recent examples include Alice Walker's *The Color Purple* and Elizabeth F. Hailey's *A Woman of Independent Means.*

Technical Concerns

Q. *How important is research in the novel?*
A. Many beginning writers know a novel is a work of imagination, but seem unaware that the factual material in a novel must be as accurate as that in a nonfiction work. The fiction writer uses the same research tools as the nonfiction writer—

sources on the period he is writing about, whether it's a Regency romance or a novel set in 1930s New York. And the research must be carefully woven into the story, not dropped in awkwardly to interrupt the flow of the story. Study good novels to see how professional authors handle research.

Q. *I'm writing a novel about two central characters. How do I decide which to use as my viewpoint character? What are the various advantages for writing in first and third person?*
A. In using third person omniscient viewpoint, where both of your characters as well as other minor characters can become viewpoint characters, you can more easily develop subplots, develop suspense by allowing the reader to know more than the characters, and be freer to delve into the personalities of more than one character. Care must be taken to switch viewpoints only at scene changes — never within a scene. In the case of third person limited viewpoint, the author portrays only those events that involve one particular character. By showing the way the hero perceives and reacts to events throughout an entire novel, the author is able to make him very well-rounded and demanding of reader sympathy. First person viewpoint, which must also involve only one character, allows closer reader identification. However, all other characters must be developed only through their actions and dialogue as observed by the hero, which is difficult and limiting. To choose the best point of view for your story, you might try writing several different passages, each with a different point of view and central character. Play around with it a bit to see which you (and your characters) are most comfortable with. And once you've decided on a particular viewpoint, stick with it throughout the *entire novel.* Inconsistencies in viewpoint destroy the reality in your novel and will render it unsalable.

Q. *I keep reading warnings not to switch viewpoints in the middle of a scene, but I can't seem to find out how to detect accidental shifts. What's wrong with switching viewpoints, anyway?*
A. The reader needs time to shift gears as the viewpoint of the story changes. Switching viewpoint also destroys the reality of a scene. Through how many viewpoints do *you* see the world? Only one, of course. You cannot see into any mind other than your own, ·so you cannot perceive things any other way. You can only know as much about other people as is indicated by their actions and what they tell you. You can detect an accidental shift in viewpoint in a scene by noticing how many characters' minds you have entered as the writer. It should only be one.

The effectiveness of a single viewpoint per scene is apparent in Colleen McCullough's novel, *An Indecent Obsession.* In an early scene, Honour Langtry encounters Michael Wilson, and we learn of her growing love for him. But all we know about Michael is that Honour thinks he is aloof and therefore must not have similar feelings. His *true* feelings are not revealed. It is later, in a scene written from Michael's point of view that we learn of his deep love for Honour, even at that early encounter. The result? The reader can identify with and become more deeply involved with each character individually and the scenes can develop with more intensity.

Q. *I am writing a novel about a fourteen-year-old ballerina. She is telling the story. I am concerned about reader identification. Will adult readers "identify" with a leading character of this age?*
A. It's rare, but adult readers *have* been known to identify with younger heroes and heroines. Shakespeare's Juliet was only about fourteen. Since there is presently a strong need for books geared to teenage interests, you might be wise to develop your story as juvenile fiction. With teenage girls making up most of your readers, you should have no worries about their identification with your young ballerina. Some editors report that young readers identify best with a central character who is a little older — not younger than themselves — so perhaps you'll want to make your ballerina fifteen or sixteen.

Q. *Editors tell me my dialogue passages are too long, but I'm only telling it the way it is in real life. What's wrong?*
A. You're probably doing too much in the way of "telling it the way it is in real life." You need to refine your dialogue so that you present the reader with only the *essence* of that reality. Conversation in real life is never as pointed as writers present it in fictional dialogue. Readers will be bored by dialogue that merely recounts the polite rituals and trite conversations that are a part of everyday life. Compress and focus your dialogue so that your characters get right to the point when they talk. All dialogue should either advance the plot, characterize the people or both. If it doesn't do these things, it's not effective or necessary.

Q. *My writing teacher says dialogue has to do more than just let characters talk. What does she mean?*
A. Besides the fact that good dialogue makes a novel easier to read by relieving the reader from long descriptive passages, it also effectively characterizes and adds to the reality of the speakers. It can take the place of long, tedious character descriptions. What and how a character speaks about herself, other characters and events should give messages as to her personality, emotions, attitudes, opinions and desires. Good dialogue is also structured to convey a character's meaning, since voice inflection is not easily reproduced in print. Good dialogue must also advance the plot.

Q. *An editor wants me to revise parts of my novel. One of his complaints is that the exposition in the first chapter is too long. Can you tell me how much exposition I should have?*
A. Everything in your exposition should have a purpose, whether it is to give tone or mood, describe the setting and time, for characterization, or to provide necessary background. One thing beginning writers often forget is that background information doesn't have to come in the first paragraphs of the novel. The reader doesn't

need to know what you're telling him, and you're likely to lose him quickly if you start with a long, uninteresting, history. However, if you start off with an interesting situation that grabs the reader's attention, he will *demand* explanation. Then breaking into the flow of the plot is more easily justified. Author Nancy Ann Dibble puts it this way: "Make everybody fall out of the plane first, and *then* explain who they were and why they were in the plane to begin with."

Q. *I've heard editors say how important it is for a character to be well-rounded. What makes a character well-rounded?*
A. Well-rounded characters are distinctly individual because the writer allows the reader to see not only the physical aspects of a character but also the character's motivation, flaws, emotional traits, and other distinctive qualities. These can be related through a character's actions, his reactions to situations and other characters, dialogue, and also through narrative. A flat character, in contrast, usually carries only one distinguishing trait. With the limitation of space, short story protagonists and minor characters in novels are often flat, whereas the protagonist in a good novel is invariably well-rounded.

Writing Problems

Q. *What kind of planning should I do before I start to write a novel? How detailed should my plan be?*
A. Planning methods vary greatly among writers and writers will modify their systems as they gain experience and maturity. Some are satisfied with a general outline summary of the plot, the characters' problems and the resolution. Others may put together as much as fifty pages of detailed charts of action, character, and environment sketches. You might want to start by thinking the novel through and writing a skeleton plot. Novelist Tom Cook advocates exploring and outlining characters before doing any other writing, because if you know your characters well enough, a logical plot will be much easier to produce. However you do your planning, be sure to ask yourself plenty of exploratory questions and be flexible enough to anticipate needed changes in the plot. Most likely, as a beginning writer, the more detailed your plan the better. It will save you from encountering dead ends and having to do endless writing.

Q. *What makes up a chapter in a novel? How do I separate scenes within a chapter?*
A. Exactly what and how much goes into a chapter is up to the individual author. Chapter divisions are an author's means of organizing the major events and developments in his novel. In planning the novel, a writer should have a general idea of the length of the chapters and what will go into each one so that he will be able to keep them balanced. Chapter breaks can provide easy transitions in time, place, or point of view. Changing scenes within a chapter can be accomplished by a simple paragraph change, starting the new one with a transitional phrase like, "The next morning, she promptly. . . ." Or it can be accomplished by leaving several blank

lines between paragraphs, especially when the scene change also involves a change in viewpoint.

Q. *I have had a novel in mind for almost ten years. My insurmountable problem is one of skillfully covering too many years without confusing the reader. Please advise whether to 1) cut down on the number of years covered in the novel; 2) cut down on the detail during those years; 3) cut down on both of the above; 4) lengthen the novel to include both, then return later with a more skillful knife.*
A. First you'll have to decide exactly how many years the story needs. If the same basic story can be told in either five or fifteen years, by all means choose the shorter period. Remember that for dramatic purposes, you can telescope events that might, in real life, be spread over several years. Regardless of how much time the story spans, you must be discriminating in your choice of detail. Don't include anything that does not keep the action moving forward toward the climax. Avoid all irrelevancies and descriptions for description's sake. Important incidents will be developed in full scenes. But information of minor significance can sometimes be handled by brief transitional summaries that link the highlights together. Flashback can help a story make a time leap, but this technique should be used sparingly because too much hopping back and forth between the past and the present can create havoc with readers' time sense.

Q. *Must a novel include sex in order to sell to a publisher these days?*
A. No. Many novels are published each year that have little or no sexual activity in the plot. A glance at the bookshelves and any of the major bestseller lists reveals many books which rely on plotting, characterization and style rather than sex. The novels of Michael Crichton, for example, are diverse in setting and style; they contain little, if any, sex. If you don't feel comfortable putting sex into your novel and if you don't feel it advances the plot or deepens the characters, there's no reason to include it.

Marketing the First Novel

Q. *I am interested in having my novel published. However, I've had no experience in getting a novel accepted. Where do I start?*
A. Check the Book Publisher's section of *Writer's Market* for companies likely to be interested in your book. Then check the library or bookstores to see first-hand the kinds of novels the companies on your prospect list publish. The listings in *Novel & Short Story Writer's Market* will tell you whether to send a query letter or several sample chapters and an outline/synopsis, to send the completed manuscript, or whether to submit through an agent. Send a SASE with every submission.

Q. *How can I find out which publishers are most likely to be interested in a new novelist?*
A. The American Library Association publishes *Booklist Magazine,* which periodi-

cally lists profiles of first novelists and information about their books. This is a handy indicator of these publishers that consistently produce first novels, and a guide to their subject matter.

Q. *Do all large publishers read unsolicited manuscripts?*
A. No. Publishers who accept unsolicited manuscripts usually indicate that in their listings in *Writer's Market* or *Novel & Short Story Writer's Market.* Others only accept manuscripts submitted by agents. Some publishers, however, will read queries only, then ask to see those manuscripts they want to consider.

Q. *When a novel publisher wants a query first, what should go in the query letter?*
A. As novelist Jean Hager says, "Query letters should be brief, but complete and persuasive. If at all possible, try to keep the letter to one page." Address the letter to a specific editor at the publishing house, as listed in *Writer's Market* or *Novel & Short Story Writer's Market.* The first paragraph should state what kind of novel it is (for example, historical or contemporary romance), the approximate number of words in the manuscript and its title. In the second paragraph, describe in fifty to one-hundred words the general story line of the book. Try to write this as though it were the selling "blurb" that might appear on the jacket. In the third paragraph, give quick sketches of your hero and heroine. In the next paragraph, include details about books you've previously published or any specialized expertise that qualifies you for writing this book. In a final paragraph, ask if the editor would like to see a synopsis and sample chapters, or the complete manuscript. In any case, ask for a copy of the publisher's editorial guidelines.

Q. *I've read that many book publishers want a synopsis along with an outline for a fiction book proposal. How do I go about writing a synopsis? How is it different from an outline?*
A. By synopsis most editors mean a comprehensive description of the basic plot of your novel. An outline, on the other hand, is a chapter-by-chapter summary of your plot. In it you should introduce all of the characters, include subplots as well as the major plot, and you should reveal the ending. Your outline may be as long as twenty or thirty pages, depending on the length and complexity of your novel.

Q. *Is it a good procedure to send the first few chapters of a novel to a publisher, with a synopsis of the rest of the novel?*
A. Many publishers suggest a synopsis, sample chapters and cover letter rather than the complete novel manuscript. But if a publisher lists in *Novel & Short Story Writer's Market* that he prefers to receive the entire manuscript, then that's what you should send.

Q. *In preparing the outline or synopsis, is it permissible to write one scene in your usual style of writing? It seems difficult to write in a straight narrative and give it the color of your own style.*

A. Writers usually let editors see their writing style by submitting two or three sample chapters along with the novel outline and synopsis. This way, the synopsis can be as brief and pointed as possible, allowing the editor to see just what the story is about, and the outline can be a chapter-by-chapter summary of what occurs in the novel.

Q. *In writing a novel concerning the life of a professional person, such as a laboratory technician, would the author need official verification of the accuracy of technical matter in it before a book publisher would publish it?*
A. In a cover letter, it might be helpful to state the sources on which the technical information is based. If the publisher is interested and requires further substantiation, he will let you know.

Q. *I've written a novel strongly based in football, and I know it would sell best if it came out during the fall season. What is the lead time required when submitting novels for seasonal publication?*
A. There is at least a one-year—sometimes two-year—delay between the arrival of the finished manuscript at a book publishing company and the date the book appears in bookstores. And since you may have to allow a number of months for your query to find an interested publisher you can take that time into consideration as well. An established and reputable book publisher will time the release according to guidance from experts in the marketing department, so the seasonal aspect of publication date will probably be their responsibility rather than yours.

Q. *A close friend insists an editor will not accept a mystery novel if it exceeds 50,000 words. My novel will exceed this amount by 10,000 to 20,000 words. Will an editor insist I cut my words to reach his required length?*
A. Publishers generally look for quality, not specific length. If any publisher were producing a series of mysteries with word limits, those requirements would be listed in *Writer's Market.*

Q. *What kind of advance and royalties can I expect on my novel?*
A. It depends on the publisher. Some companies produce only books sold to libraries, pay only a few hundred dollars advance and have a limited press run. Others will pay a larger advance and royalties based on the terms listed in *Novel & Short Story Writer's Market.* In general, hardcover books will pay 10 percent of either the retail price or the net moneys received by the publisher on the first five thousand copies and a sliding scale upward on subsequent sales. Mass-market paperback publishers of original novels will usually pay an advance and royalties of 4 percent to 8 percent of the cover price on the first 150,000 copies sold. For more information on book contracts, see chapter thirty-eight on book publishing.

Q. *Is it proper to indicate in a cover letter that my novel is the first of a series? Also, may the publisher who accepted a portion of a series turn down any succeeding books* *in that series? Would it be ethical to submit these to another publisher?*

A. Indicate the proposed series, but do it in an initial query, rather than in a cover letter sent with your manuscript. Don't send the complete manuscript unless the publisher asks for it. Check *Novel & Short Story Writer's Market* for submission requirements. It is possible that a publisher could accept one or two books in a series, then turn down succeeding books in a series. It is doubtful that the series could be divided among different publishers, but if you change the characters' names and make no references to events in previous books, there's no reason why these books couldn't be marketed on a separate basis without any tie-in with the series.

Chapter 27

Does Anyone Buy Poetry?

Robert Graves once remarked, "There's no money in poetry, but then there's no poetry in money either," and writers continue their pursuit of the perfect poem even though the rewards often are only psychological. For the beginner, the ability to write about intense personal experiences is eagerly sought but often denied. "The poet still has to find the verbal and technical means," says James Dickey. "You have to rely on form—the right words in the right order." Then the poem can be the Emersonian ideal: "as new as foam and as old as the rock." Two good books to refer to are Judson Jerome's *The Poet's Handbook* (Writer's Digest Books) and William Packard's *The Art of Poetry Writing* (St. Martin's Press).

Poetic Forms

Q. *I find myself with many thoughts and emotions that I'd like to be able to express as poems. I've kept a journal for many years, but I can't seem to get from the prose to poetry. Any suggestions?*
A. If you've never really studied the techniques of writing poetry, you should read some books on the subject to get an idea of where to start. Poetry differs from prose in that it utilizes metaphors, similes, allusion, imagery and sound patterns such as rhyme and alliteration. As is stated in *Writer's Encyclopedia,* "The emphasis in poetry is on economy of language—as the poet compresses as much meaning as possible into the fewest possible words, the language is elevated to a unique artistic expression." This may be something you should think about as you learn more about converting your journal into poetry.

Q. *What is the difference between free verse and blank verse? Is rhyming in either necessary or optional?*
A. Blank verse is unrhymed five foot iambic verse. Free verse does not follow any of the patterns of alternating accents and unaccents of metric verse. It sets up a music all its own that is neither a measured beat nor haphazard prose. As a general rule, lines that are not metric verse, accent verse or prose are probably free verse. Free verse can be rhymed (as in some of Ogden Nash's work), but most frequently

it isn't. Blank verse is not rhymed. For additional help with versification, consult *The Poet's Manual and Rhyming Dictionary* by Stillman and Whitfield.

Q. *When editorial listings in* Poet's Market *say they'll accept "traditional forms" of poetry, what do they mean?*
A. The editors want to make it clear that they will accept forms other than contemporary free verse. They will accept poetry that rhymes and has a definite and consistent meter. There are some fixed forms of poetry that are considered traditional, like the Japanese haiku (sometimes mentioned specifically by editors in *Poet's Market*) and the five-line cinquain. The sonnet, which originated in the thirteenth century is almost always fourteen lines of iambic pentameter and follows one of several rhyme schemes. Much of what is considered traditional poetry (in terms of form rather than subject matter or theme) can be found in the works of many pre-twentieth-century poets. "Traditional" may mean different things to different editors, so it's always best to study a particular publication before submitting any work to them.

Q. *I write a poetry column for a local journal. Some of my recent poetry is unrhymed and has no regular rhythm. Readers constantly hound me with the comments, "That's a poem?" or "It doesn't rhyme!" or "It has no set rhythm!" The truth of the matter is, I have sold more so-called "offbeat" poetry than "perfect" poems. What can I say to my readers?*
A. Tell them you are writing free verse. Point out to those readers that this is an accepted literary tradition followed by Walt Whitman and T.S. Eliot, to name just two.

Q. *What is light verse? What are some markets for it?*
A. Light verse is a form of poetry (usually less than ten lines) intended only to amuse and entertain the reader, rather than to impart any deep literary message. It is marked by its wit and subtlety and conventional rhyme and meter schemes. Subject matter is varied, and light verse often deals with ordinary topics common to the experience of many, such as nature and personal and family relationships. Markets include many magazines, since light verse is universally appealing. In addition to listing markets for light verse, *Poet's Market* includes editorial requirements and pay rates for the individual magazines.

Q. *I write some poetry that I think would make good song lyrics, but I can't write music. How can I get some of my poems put to music?*
A. Your best route is to collaborate with a musician. If you don't have contact with anyone who can write publishable music, you may have to seek musicians in your area and approach one of them about collaborating. Make sure that you are aware of a particular person's talent with melody before you approach him. Beware of "song sharks" that advertise in certain publications that, for a fee, will set your lyrics to music. Many are interested only in profit for themselves and will accept

lyrics that have no chance of ever earning any money for the writer. Don't pay anyone for setting your words to music. It is better to collaborate with a song writer/musician and have a reputable publisher decide whether or not your work is good. (Also see chapter thirty.)

Techniques of the Poet

Q. *I don't understand most modern poetry. Is there some book that has taken these kinds of poems apart, analyzed them and discussed what the poet is saying?*
A. Yes. *The Poet and the Poem* and *The Poet's Handbook,* both by Judson Jerome, have chapters on this subject along with discussions of other matters of interest to writers attempting to become professional poets.

Q. *Please explain* unimagistic *and* imagistic *in relation to poetry.*
A. Words that describe with some clarity the physical appearance of something are referred to as *images.* Thus, a poem that is *imagistic* is one that creates sensory impressions or sense-pictures of the events or objects in the poem. Most images are visual, creating a focused photographic mental picture. But a good many images touch the other senses and permit us to participate in the aroma, spice and heft of the poem's subject. *Unimagistic* words are words that have no physical presence. Ideas, philosophical abstractions (for example, eternity, soul) are unimagistic words. Most dictionaries of literary terms give a more thorough definition (see *Imagery*) and one that is especially useful for poets is *Princeton Encyclopedia of Poetry and Poetics.*

Q. *I have written and sold a poem based on an idea that I do not believe was original. Is such borrowing considered unethical?*
A. Set your mind at ease. Ideas cannot be copyrighted, so you have done nothing unethical.

Marketing Poetry

Q. *Where can I find a list of current and new magazines that use poetry?*
A. In *Poet's Market* (Writer's Digest Books) and the "Markets" section of *Writer's Digest* magazine. While not all of the publications pay for poetry, they are excellent markets for beginning poets.

Q. *I have yet to sell one poem. What are some of the reasons poetry doesn't sell today?*
A. It isn't original enough. Poets want to write about the everyday human emotions that stir us all—the birth of a baby, impending death, the strange quality that we call charisma—but unless the poet brings imaginative insight or language to the reader on the subject, editors won't buy it. In some cases, poetry has faulty construction or uneven meter. You've probably read many books on the principles of poetry, but it doesn't hurt to review them again and read the poetry in the magazines you

want to sell to, to analyze what it is about those poems that made the editor buy them. Are there any magazines that print the kinds of poetry you like to read? If so, aim for these magazines.

Q. *I study the markets and I'm sure the poetry I submit is appropriate, but I haven't had an acceptance yet. What could be wrong with my poetry?*
A. Your problem may lie in the technical form of your poetry. The diction, meter, line and stanza divisions, and sound patterns should all be an integral part of what you want your poem to say. Editors tend to reject poems in which the sound patterns (such as rhyme and alliteration) seem forced or overdone. Imagery that is trite and overused, such as "the golden dawn" and "twinkling stars" is also a problem for many beginning poets. Make sure the rhythm, or meter, in your poetry is smooth and fits in with the other elements. Look for original word arrangements and relationships. Your poetry should involve the reader, showing, rather than telling him how you feel. There really is no definite answer to your question, since "good poetry" is such a relative term. Spend some time studying the various techniques that go into writing poetry—and do a lot of practicing and revising. Study and analyze existing poetry, both traditional and contemporary. Study especially the poetry appearing in magazines you have submitted to. You might learn from seeing how the published work is different from your own. Above all, don't give up—keep submitting your poetry to editors.

Q. *Is it wise to let a "little magazine" use my poetry to get it into print or should I hold out for better markets?*
A. "Holding out" can be a frustrating game. There is prestige and satisfaction in being published by the "little magazines," so don't be afraid to try them—if they are copyrighted. "Little magazines" are the publishers of poetry, even for the best-known poets. If an uncopyrighted magazine accepts your poetry, make sure the editor runs your own copyright notice with the published poem.

Q. *How should I prepare my manuscript when I'm submitting a poem? Should the byline be just beneath the title or in the upper right corner?*
A. Type your name and address in the upper left corner of a plain white sheet of 8½" × 11" bond paper. The title of your poem should be centered above the body of the poem. Center the poem on the page, with equal distances above and below, and approximately the same margins to the left and right. You should double-space short poems, but you can use double- or single-spacing on long poems. If your poem is longer than one page, be sure to put your last name and the page number on all succeeding pages. As a last line, your byline should be typed off to the right so that it ends about where your average line ends. Type only one poem per page. Include a SASE with each submission.

Q. *Must poetry always be double-spaced? Length requirements are given in numbers of lines. Does the number of lines, then, replace the usual word count? Or should both*

be given? How should I arrange the manuscript for a book of verse? One poem to a page? If illustrations are offered, how should the page for which they are intended be indicated? What are the established minimum or maximum length requirements for a book of verse? Is it wise to combine humorous and inspirational verse in a single volume?
A. Preferably all manuscripts should be double-spaced. It is not necessary to include a word count—only a line count. Prepare the manuscript with one poem to a page, in the order you prefer, and insert the illustrations, also one to a page, where you would like them in the printed version. In view of your two different themes, it might be helpful to divide the volume into two sections, with appropriate headings for the inspirational and humorous segments. There are no strict rules about length, but have at least twenty poems.

Q. *Why do some poetry markets ask that batches of ten to fifteen poems be submitted at one time? Surely, any one poem speaks for itself.*
A. A single poem certainly does speak for itself, but a batch of poems gives the editor an idea of the style, versatility and scope of your work, and a selection from which to choose.

Q. *Do I need a cover letter when submitting poems?*
A. No.

Q. *I'm sending my poetry to several magazines listed in* Poet's Market. *Some magazines specify that the writer should send "4-6" or "3-5" poems. Since I will sell one, at the most, to each publication, I don't want to have the others tied up for a couple of months while an editor makes his decision. Couldn't I just send one poem and save time for everyone concerned?*
A. It would probably be all right to send only one poem, but it might be to your advantage to send three or four. Most poetry publishers specify the minimum limit because they want to see a fair representation of your work. If they like one of your poems, they'll probably like others just because they like your style. Go ahead and send in a group of poems. It can't hurt, and may improve your chances of publication.

Q. *Is it okay to submit my poetry to more than one magazine or journal at the same time?*
A. Major magazines usually expect to get an exclusive look at manuscripts they receive. But many of the small poetry magazines and journals are used to receiving multiple submissions, so sending your poetry to several of those publications is quite acceptable. Some, however, specify that they will *not* look at simultaneous submissions, so first check the listings in *Poet's Market.*

Q. *May a poem be offered for sale to a magazine if it was entered in a prize contest and read over the radio, or if it received a prize, or if it was circulated in a mimeographed brochure that carried notice that the author retains all rights?*

A. Yes, such a poem may be submitted to professional markets, but some indication of its previous exposure should be included in a cover letter.

Q. *Does being published in a poetry anthology count as a published credit in the same way publication in a magazine does?*
A. If your poems appear in a published anthology, they can be listed as credits. On the other hand, if the anthology was the type requiring you to pay a fee or buy a copy to have your poems included, editors and your peers would not hold this in as high regard as publication in a magazine that paid *you* for the privilege.

Q. *I keep getting form rejection notes. Does that mean my poetry's no good?*
A. Although editors usually don't have the time to write comments on the rejection slips they send, rejection doesn't automatically mean your poetry is bad. It may mean that you're submitting your work to markets that don't publish the kind of poetry you write or that the editors' files are overstocked. Always explore your markets carefully. You might also have better luck with some of the small literary magazines where poets can get a start. And if you keep reading and analyzing published contemporary poetry in the magazines you want to appear in, you will better prepare yourself to write salable poems.

What Are My Rights?

Q. *Our weekly newspaper recently started a poetry corner and invited contributions. I've contributed several and enjoyed seeing them in print. A friend tells me I've lost all rights to the poems I've sent in to the newspaper. Would I be able to sell them to a magazine? I hate to lose the poems, as someday I might want to put them in a book.*
A. If the newspaper in which your poems appeared is not copyrighted (and some of them aren't), then your poems are now in the public domain and can be used by anyone, including you — if you want to submit them to other markets. You might be able to sell them to a magazine, but the copyright of the magazine would not cover your particular poems since they are still in the public domain. And you must notify the magazine that your poems are in the public domain. If you assembled them later into a book, those particular poems are not covered by the copyright on the book. The only way this material can be copyrighted in the future is if you revise it, and submit it as original poetry.

Q. *A few years ago, I had a volume of poetry published at my own expense. Fortunately, the books sold well. Now I would like to submit some of these poems to magazines, but have hesitated to do so as I'm not sure if this is permissible.*
A. As long as the volume of poetry you had published at your own expense was copyrighted, then all rights to the poems still belong to you. It would be advisable to let the magazine editors know that your submissions originally appeared in book form.

Q. *If my poems have been sold to a magazine that buys all rights, how do I go about getting permission to publish them in a book? What if I only sold first North American serial rights? Is there any fee involved for getting permission to use my already published poems?*

A. Write the original publishers to see if you can get all but first serial rights released to you for the purpose you mention. They may not release the rights to you, but they may grant permission to a book publisher to use them as long as the magazine's original copyright line appears on the acknowledgment page. If you only sold first North American serial rights, then all other rights belong to you and you need not get permission from the first publisher. Some magazine publishers who bought all rights may expect you or the book publisher to pay a permission fee. Those who bought only first rights should not expect a permissions fee.

Q. *I have some poems scheduled to be published in a book I've already signed a contract for, and I'd like to give free public readings of them. Would such reading in any way endanger my future copyright? Is there any good, practical reason to first copyright such poetry as a lecture, then later change its category to book?*

A. Under the copyright law, your readings of poetry would not jeopardize your statutory copyright on your book — as long as you make sure no recordings are being made of your readings. If copies of such recordings were distributed with your authorization, these could jeopardize your future book copyright.

Q. *If my poem wins a contest prize, will I retain the right to sell the poem to magazines?*

A. Check carefully the contest rules for each contest you wish to enter. Some contests permit you to retain rights to your work; others do not.

Q. *When my poetry is adapted to other forms — such as greeting cards and plaques — is my work being placed in the public domain, or do I retain my copyright?*

A. Most companies that manufacture plaques, posters and greeting cards purchase all rights to the copy they use. Copyright notices printed on the products are usually there to protect the company or, in the case of a syndicated cartoon feature, to protect the syndicate. Thus, in having your poetry adapted to these other forms, you don't necessarily put them in the public domain, but you do give up all of your rights to the material.

Q. *Does having a poem published in an uncopyrighted magazine entitle it to be reprinted without the author's knowledge or consent?*

A. Unfortuntely, once the material appears without copyright notice, it falls into the public domain and anyone may make whatever use of it he wishes. This would include reprinting it without notifying the author.

Q. *My great-grandfather was a poet and published a book of poems. He had only three hundred books printed and distributed them to friends. The book went out of copyright years ago. There are some wonderful poems in this book and I would like to see them* reprinted. *Would it be legal to take these poems and have them reprinted in magazines? If this would be legal, would I still use his name on them or my own?*

A. You could try to bring these poems to the attention of current magazines, but under no condition would it be ethical to sign your name to them. They are the original work of your great-grandfather and should remain so. If magazines decided to publish some of them, they would make payment to you, since you would, in effect, be acting as his agent. In such a case, assuming his other heirs were agreeable to your attempt to market the poems, the profits would be yours or yours and theirs as you agreed.

Collectible Poems

Q. *I don't see much in the way of poetry collections on the best-seller lists. Is there a demand for it at all? I would like to see mine published, but how do I decide where to send it?*

A. The market for books of poetry is very small today, because only poets and a few readers with a serious interest are willing buyers of poetry. Most poets cannot make a living on the monetary returns, and a serious poet usually writes for his own pleasure, concentrating on the quality rather than the mass distribution of his work. Your best chance for publication is through the magazine markets. Read poetry published in the literary and quality magazines and find those magazines that publish poetry similar to yours in taste, skill and values. If you think the editor would be interested, follow her submission guidelines (often listed on the same page as the magazine's masthead) and send her some of your work to consider.

If you don't feel your poems would suit this type of publication, you might want to explore the popular women's magazines, religious and inspirational magazines as well as general interest publications as possible markets. You can find many poetry markets listed in *Poet's Market* and in the *International Directory of Little Magazines and Small Presses.*

Q. *I have what I consider a worthwhile manuscript of poetry. Are there any publishers who would consider publishing it on a straight royalty basis?*

A. Yes, there are publishers who have a regular royalty contract for poetry books (see *Poet's Market*). However, most of them hesitate to gamble on an unknown poet and would prefer to publish poets with established reputations. To lay the groundwork for the possible future publication of your book, it would be helpful for you to get your poems published in magazines first, while retaining book publishing rights.

Q. *I have a collection of favorite poems by other writers. I've clipped the poems from newspapers and magazines over the years. Can I publish them in book form? How do I go about it?*

A. Yes, you could try to get your collection published as an anthology. However, in order to find an interested editor, you will have to be able to suggest to him something more than just a book of poems. Try to find a central theme that could unify them into a book. This may mean dropping some of them from your collection and searching for others. Query one or two publishers that you think might be interested. In your letter you'll have to argue your case to the editor — explaining why you think your book would be worth his risk, and include half a dozen or so of the poems you'd like to see in the book. If you find an interested publisher, you'll have to secure permission from the original publishers or authors for reprint.

Q. *I am writing a small book of poems, and I wish to include a few poems given to me by a friend. She told me the lady who wrote the poems never published them. Both my friend and the writer are dead. I tried to contact the writer's sister but the postmaster did not know her. Probably she is dead also. Should I use these poems in my book?*
A. It is not advisable to use the poems given to you by a friend, since their publication with the author's byline might turn up some heirs who would frown on the use of this work. You seem to have made an effort to locate the author's sister, but you might open yourself to a legal problem here if you include these few poems.

Q. *Some of the poems I would like to include in my anthology come from uncopyrighted publications. Does this in any way affect my copyrighting the anthology as a whole?*
A. If your anthology contains original and/or other copyrighted poems, you could copyright the collection. The acknowledgments page, however, would have to indicate those poems in the book that were previously copyrighted. You will have to get permission to use copyrighted material from either the poets or the magazines in which the poems were printed.

Chapter 28

Is It Easier to Write for Children Than Adults?

In his National Book Award speech, Isaac Bashevis Singer gave a number of reasons why he began to write for children, and one of them was, "Children read books, not reviews. They don't give a hoot about critics." If a book is boring, children won't read it just because an adult says they "ought to." If a book is interesting and enjoyable, they can't wait to tell their friends to read it. Beginners who want to write for young readers must know what children are like today—not write only from their own remembrances. But when they successfully capture those emotions, dreams, and curiosities of childhood and adolescence, they'll find young readers eager for their stories, articles and books.

There are many excellent sources of additional information on writing for children. Three good ones are: *How to Write a Children's Book and Get It Published* by Barbara Seuling (Charles Scribner's Sons), *Writing for Children and Teenagers* by Lee Wyndham and Arnold Madison (Writer's Digest Books), and *Writing and Publishing Books for Children in the 1990s* by Olga Litowinsky (Walker and Co.).

Basic Guidelines

Q. *I've written stories for adults for many years and would like to try writing for children. Can you give me some general advice concerning the differences between writing for children and writing for adults?*
A. When it comes to the basics of producing a good story, there isn't much difference between writing for children and adults. As Lee Wyndham points out in *Writing for Children and Teenagers,* "The truly appealing [central] character is not wholly good or wholly bad, but possesses a balance of positive (good) and negative (bad) qualities." For instance, you must work in the same way to create believable characters with plausible motivations; strong plot is still important in stories for all age groups. Conflict and emotion must be integrated into the story. The difference is that all of these things must be accomplished with the simplicity and subject matter geared to young readers. Remember that a story that pleases an eight-year-old, such as Beverly Cleary's *Ramona the Pest,* will not be very entertaining to a

twelve-year-old who would be more interested in books by Paul Zindel and M. E. Kerr, so you must gear your stories accordingly.

You must be well aware of the problems and attitudes of children so that you can incorporate them realistically into your stories. Extent of characterization increases with the age of the reader, to the point that stories written for young people twelve to fifteen years old are different from stories written for adults only in the kinds of situations the characters face. Try to put yourself on the level of your reader so that you don't inadvertently "talk down to" or patronize him. The best way to get a feeling for how stories for children are written is to read lots and lots of them.

Q. *What are the most common age-level groups for which juvenile publishers produce books?*
A. Publishers differ, but Lee Wyndham, author of *Writing for Children and Teenagers,* describes five common groups: 1) Picture books for children ages two to five. 2) Picture story books to be read by adults to children ages six to nine. 3) Easy-to-read books for children ages six to nine to read themselves with their first- to third-grade skills. 4) Fiction and nonfiction for children ages eight to twelve. 5) Fiction and nonfiction for teenagers, ten to fifteen. Study each publisher's requirements in *Children's Writer's & Illustrator's Market* and write for editorial guidelines if available.

Q. *I've been hearing about "high interest, low level" readers and the market for books catering to this group. What age reader does this concern? Do you have any tips for writing these kinds of books?*
A. Short stories and books for "high interest, low level" readers are written for high school students who read at about a third-grade level, either because they are reluctant or slow readers, or they haven't yet learned to speak fluent English. These stories combine a high-interest subject with a lower-level vocabulary. The writing must be direct and involve plenty of action, through dialogue rather than exposition. The plot must move quickly into the action so that the reluctant reader is immediately hooked. Subject matter should concern the problems of contemporary teens, such as drugs, dating, prejudice, family relations, etc.

If you plan to write for this group, you might investigate the readability formulas, such as those by Frye and Dale-Chall, that some publishers use when choosing and editing easy-reading manuscripts. Write the publishers for their individual guidelines.

It is best to write your story first, then check its readability. If readability is a concern as you write, a stiffness in your story could arise that might actually make it more difficult to read. If, after it's written, you determine the readability to be too high, you can lower it by simplifying the words and breaking up sentences.

For publishers of "high/lo" books, check *Children's Writer's & Illustrator's Market.*

Q. *I'm trying to write books for children. I've been all through the library and bookstore in my town to see what's on the market right now. However, my town is very small, so I don't get the full picture. Are there any other resources available that would give me a good idea of the popular children's books presently in print?*

A. The Children's Book Council (CBC), Suite 404, 568 Broadway, New York NY 10012, offers several annotated bibliographies, free with a 6½" × 9½" SASE with first-class postage for one ounce. The CBC also offers two helpful lists: "Outstanding Science Trade Books for Children" (write "Attn: NTSA" on the outside of the envelope) and "Notable Children's Trade Books in the Field of Social Studies" ("Attn: NCSS"). If you request both, include $.75 in postage. The CBC is an association of children's book publishers that works with groups in other fields through joint committees to create children's book programs.

Another valuable resource is "Children's Choices," a list of schoolchildren's favorite books. It is compiled annually by the International Reading Association. For a copy, send a 6" × 9" or 9" × 12" self-addressed envelope with stamps to cover two ounces to P.O. Box 8139, Newark DE 19714-8139.

Q. *At what age do children start to enjoy juvenile novels? What kinds of subject matter are most popular?*

A. Children eight to twelve years old enjoy books of 20,000 to 40,000 words, and their interests are limitless. Detective stories are especially popular as first novel reading, but trends in subject matter for children's books often reflect trends in public interest. Realistic treatment of current themes, such as dealing with divorce and other problems of growing up in today's society, interest readers ages eight to twelve, as well as ages twelve to fifteen. Books written for children in these groups are usually geared either for boys or girls, and the protagonist is always older by a year or two than the reader. Also, it is best to keep adult involvement in these stories to a minimum.

Q. *Could you give me information on the Newbery and Caldecott awards? How do you get a book nominated?*

A. These awards are given annually through the American Library Association by a member committee of children's and school librarians. Usually in November, members of the Association for Library Service to Children receive blanks for nominating their choices of published books for the awards. The Newbery Medal is awarded for fine writing, while the Caldecott Medal is awarded for excellence in illustration.

Manuscripts Suitable for Children

Q. *I am interested in writing children's stories for elementary school-aged children. Where can I obtain a suitable word list for these stories?*

A. Publishers of trade books for leisure reading by children do not use formal vocabulary lists, but publishers of textbook readers for the primary grades often have formal restrictions on vocabulary (based on studies made in elementary schools). Consult individual publishers, enclosing a SASE, for vocabulary requirements. You might also refer to dictionaries written for specific age groups, and check your local library for books on readability that contain word lists.

Q. *I have written a book about children in Mexico that I think could be the beginning of a great series for children about youngsters in foreign cultures. So far, publishers have rejected it, some saying that they like the idea, but that it isn't geared closely enough to any particular age group. I thought it would reach a larger audience that way. Any suggestions?*

A. Two or three years' age difference in children can mean a vast difference in reading ability and topics of interest. For this reason, children's books, both fiction and nonfiction, must be geared to a specific age group. Your best bet is probably the eight- to twelve-year-old group, since these children are interested in a wide variety of topics. A good way for you to gear your book to a certain age group would be to make your central characters one or two children in Mexico in that age group, rather than presenting it in straight narrative form. In this way, readers have someone they can identify with and the reading is made all the more enjoyable. Remember to make your characters one or two years older than the age group for which your book is intended.

To see what other kinds of books about children in foreign cultures have been successful, see *Best Books for Children,* in your public library. It categorizes recommended books selected by librarians and other critics, both by subject matter and age level.

For a specific example of a novel set in Mexico for eight- to twelve-year-olds, Elizabeth Borton De Trevino would be a good author to study.

Q. *I've tried to write biographical pieces for children's magazines, but I can't seem to get the total picture of the subject's life into a short article that children would understand. Any suggestions?*

A. One of the hardest things about writing biographies for juveniles is deciding what to leave out. This is especially true when the writer is confined to the length of a magazine article. When researching your subject, pick out one important event and focus the entire article on it. You might concentrate on some childhood experience, if you are lucky enough to find information on it. (Read juvenile biographies by Jean Fritz to see how this author uses period detail to bring the *setting* of a subject's childhood to life in lieu of bona fide historical detail.) Then your ending can state what this child grew up to do that made him famous. Lacking any good information on your subject's childhood, it's still a good idea to open the article with a reference to his early years in order to let young readers know that these famous people were children once, too. Then focus the article on an incident important in your subject's adulthood—probably the one that made him famous—but keep it simple. Force yourself to delete anything extraneous, remembering that children don't have the conceptual framework to remember historical details. Keep your story to the editor's prescribed length. Most children's magazines will send editorial guidelines for a SASE.

The subject of a biography for juvenile magazines can be anyone with courage and determination, whether it's the Revolution's Paul Revere or twentieth-century poet Gwendolyn Brooks.

Q. *In the writing of biographies for children, is it possible to make the reading more interesting through use of fictional dialogue and setting? If so, to what extent can liberties be taken in order to assure a relatively accurate account of the nonfictional material while providing "readability" for youngsters?*
A. Working with the basic facts, you may create conversations and incidents that will best dramatize them, but don't devise anything that would not be in keeping with the character of the subject or times.

Q. *I've been trying to sell a children's fantasy with no luck at all. What could be wrong with my book?*
A. Fantasy is difficult to write well because it demands from the writer the ability to make real the unreal, believable the unbelievable. If you are just starting out as a children's writer, you may need practice writing here-and-now stories before you attempt to write fantasy. A solid understanding of the techniques of plot, character, scene-building and viewpoint are necessary because a fantasy story must be as logical as any other story. It must give the illusion of reality.

You don't say what kind of fantasy your story is, and it may be the kind that just isn't selling right now. The market for stories like the classical fairy tales of Andersen and the Brothers Grimm is nearly nonexistent. Editors are looking for stories that are totally different from anything published in the past or present. Popular fantasy books are those in which animals are personified — either as having human traits and participating in human activities, or merely as talking animals in a human world. Joseph Slate's *How Little Porcupine Played Christmas,* published in 1982, is an example of an animal fantasy. Dr. Seuss-type imaginary animals are much harder to sell. Few fantasies today feature inanimate objects, like the old favorite, *The Little Engine That Could.* Also popular with children of all ages are trips taken through time and/or space such as *The Tunnel to Yesterday* by Jerome Beatty. Study the market carefully and strive for originality in your stories. Then you may find yourself making sales.

Q. *It seems like a lot of what makes up adult mystery novels, such as the severe crime, violence, and fearful suspense, just doesn't belong in juvenile mysteries. But what can be put into juvenile stories?*
A. You are right in assuming juvenile mystery editors shy away from descriptive violence — especially murder. Most juvenile mysteries contain elements of humor along with hair-raising suspense that make the story effective. One key to success is knowing children well. Anything of interest to children in the age bracket you want to write for can be used as the subject of a mystery. Tight plotting and a

fantastic climax are important, as is a main character who is actively involved in solving the problem of the story. To learn of current subject matter and techniques used in writing juvenile mysteries, spend some time reading and analyzing books from that section of your public library. To further study this genre, you might want to read books by Richard Peck, Jean Lowery Nixon and Mary Blount Christian.

Getting Your Stories Published

Q. *I'm interested in writing children's books, but I don't know how to prepare the manuscripts. What form is preferred?*
A. Children's books are typed in the same standard manuscript format that applies to short stories and novels.

Q. *I've written a few short stories for children and would like to get them published. The problem is, I don't know how or where to sell them. What would you advise?*
A. Markets for your work are listed in *Children's Writer's & Illustrator's Market*. Children's magazines are carefully geared to specific age levels of readers, so you should get some sample copies of magazines you think might be prospects for your stories and read them before you submit your manuscripts to the editors.

Q. *Should I include illustrations with my children's story?*
A. It's usually best not to submit illustrations with the manuscript. An editor may like the story, but not the illustrations. He may think you're offering the text and illustrations as a package and would be unwilling to sell the text without illustrations. If you feel picture ideas are essential to the story, prepare a "dummy" book with pictures or picture ideas included. Make a two-column text with illustration ideas facing the text of the story or cut up a copy of the manuscript and paste it into place with your rough sketches. Don't send this with your initial story manuscript, but mention in your covering letter that you have artwork ideas available if the editor would like to see them. Most editors of children's books have their own preferences for artists they like to work with, whose styles they like and who can work according to the firm's production specifications.

Q. *I've written some stories aimed to help physically disabled children deal with their problems. Do you think I could get them published?*
A. You could look through the *Children's Writer's & Illustrator's Market* for magazines that might be interested in your stories. Since the market for which your stories are written is very limited, you could try rewriting them to help the healthy child understand the disabled person. You might want to write for sample copies of the juvenile magazines that you think would be interested in your subject matter and study their styles to see how to prepare your manuscript.

Q. *Is there a special time of year that material is read and accepted by publishers of children's books? If not, how far ahead should seasonal material be sent?*

A. Most publishers read manuscripts year-round. Seasonal material should be submitted at least one year in advance, but book publishers work so far in advance that you probably will not see the finished product until the second season. One might expect a Christmas book submitted after Christmas and accepted in July to go into Christmas advertising the following summer.

Q. *A friend sold all rights to her children's book to a small publisher and only received a flat fee for the book. Is that common practice?*
A. No, but whether a publisher pays an advance and royalties or buys outright varies with each company. Terms are presented in a contract that a writer can accept or decline.

Q. *My partner and I have collaborated on a children's book. She is writing the text and I am illustrating. Can you tell us approximately what the going rate is on a book of this type? What can the writer and illustrator expect to receive?*
A. Royalties on heavily illustrated children's books range from 6 to 10 percent with splits between author and illustrator depending on the amount of work by each. You could each expect an advance of between $2,000 and $5,000.

Q. *I have an idea for a series of children's books. How would I sell this series to a publisher? What are my rights? What are the usual rates?*
A. Query the publisher with an outline of the proposed series and sample chapters. The question of rights (such as book club, reprints, etc.) and rates, including the advance, would usually be negotiated by the writer or his agent with the publisher upon acceptance of the work and receipt of his contract terms. The usual royalties on a juvenile book are 5 percent to 15 percent, often split fifty/fifty with the illustrator. In some cases, where there are only a few illustrations, the illustrator is paid a flat fee and the author receives full royalty, which could vary from 5 to 10 percent, depending on the type of book, publisher and author.

Q. *Since so many schools these days have "media centers" instead of libraries and teachers use films and filmstrips as teaching aids, how can I break into this audiovisual market?*
A. Few film producers will accept scripts from any source other than a recognized agent, and few agents will accept work from a writer who isn't established, so you may have to break into the business through the back door, so to speak. Often adaptation of a successful book or story for use as a film or filmstrip will bring an author into the realm of audiovisual writing. Author Jane Fitz-Randolph suggests you set two goals for yourself: to get your work published in the print media and to learn as much as you can about film writing and production. Once you have achieved these goals, you will have a good grip on the techniques of writing a good story, and you will be ready to take on the additional, very exacting demands of the audiovisual media. Courses in television and film production offer practical help, as well as a possible route to contacts in various production companies. Pro-

ducers listed in *Children's Writer's & Illustrator's Market* under "Audiovisual Markets" will indicate their preferences for queries, unsolicited scripts, or scripts submitted through an agent, as well as their specific needs in terms of films, filmstrips, and cable and regular television programs for adults and/or children.

Q. *I am a professional storyteller via radio. I write children's stories and songs. My animal stories would lend themselves to film cartoons. Will you please advise me if there is an open market for this?*
A. Most film companies work through agents or on the basis of assignment. Write to a West Coast agent (send $1 to the Writers' Guild of America, West, 8955 Beverly Blvd., Los Angeles CA 90048 for a copy of their list of agents). Tell him about your radio credits, asking for his representation for your stories with an animated film company.

Q. *I think my eleven-year-old niece has the potential to become a very good fiction writer. Her imagination seems boundless and she has a knack for developing good stories. Is there any way she could get some of her stories published?*
A. Some children's publications have sections for stories, poems, articles and drawings by children. *Stone Soup* is a magazine written entirely by children. Other magazines, such as *Seventeen* and *Straight*, sometimes accept material written by teenagers. You'll find details on these, and many others, in *Market Guide for Young Writers* by Kathy Henderson (Writer's Digest Books). You (and your niece) should also look through *Children's Writer's & Illustrator's Market* and *Writer's Market*. Of course, each of these publications has its own editorial needs and submission formats, so your niece should study sample copies before submitting. In some cases, she may have to include a letter from her teacher or a parent confirming the originality of the work.

Chapter 29

How Do I Market My Script?

Some of the pitfalls of scriptwriting were pinpointed by Herbert Selby, Jr. in a *New York Times* article. "A couple of years ago a network was going to do a series on the Ten Commandments," he recalled, "and I wrote one of the two-hour segments. The entire project was ultimately cancelled, probably because it was too radical. But the thing that really amused me was the fact that the network only took five of the Commandments with an option on the other five. That, my friend, is television."

While most other manuscripts can be successfully marketed directly by the writer, scripts usually require the intermediary of an agent to make it to the producer. This chapter details this and other concerns of the playwright, TV or screenwriter. For more information on playwriting, see *The Playwright's Handbook* by Frank Pike and Thomas G. Dunn (New American Library) and *The Elements of Playwriting* by Louis E. Catron (Macmillan). For advice on writing scripts for television and motion pictures, see *Making a Good Script Great* by Linda Seger (Samuel French Trade books) and *Screenplay: The Foundations of Screenwriting* by Syd Field (Dell Books).

Script Mechanics

Q. *I'm trying to break into movie and television writing. What's the proper way to type a script?*
A. The basic difference between writing straight prose and writing scripts is that scripts also contain instructions regarding action, sound, light and camera usage. These directions are typed single-spaced on a full-width line of type at the points in the script where they occur. Dialogue and scene descriptions are typed single-spaced in a column in the page's center, indented ten spaces from the margin both left and right. Characters' names are typed in caps and centered over their dialogue. Acts and scenes are numbered. Double-space between scene directions and dialogue. The manuscript should be submitted in a softcover binder, which can be purchased in a stationery store.

Q. *I'm writing plays for local productions. How do I type the dramatic form?*

A. Character names are typed in all caps, followed by a colon, two spaces and the dialogue, which is double-spaced. All stage directions are enclosed in parentheses within the lines of dialogue. Dialogue and stage directions are typed in caps and lowercase. You might want to get some published plays from the library to help you get the usual pattern established in your mind. Like film scripts, plays should be submitted in a flexible binder; the exceptions are short one-act plays, which can be paper-clipped.

Q. *I am writing a screenplay for the movie industry and need to learn more about the camera shots. I want someone familiar with movie writing to take parts of my screenplay and set them to the proper shots.*
A. Your best bet would be to study some actual movie scripts to get a feel for how this is done. Several publishers have produced books that contain the complete scripts of both classic and contemporary movies. These include Ballantine Books, Viking Compass Books, and The University of Wisconsin Press. Also, companies that sell television and movie scripts advertise in the classified pages of *Writer's Digest.*

Usually, however, it's not necessary to include a great deal of production technicalities (such as camera angles) in a script you're trying to sell on speculation. Those details will be added by the production staff after the script is purchased.

Q. *In writing for industrial film production companies, are scripts prepared like TV scripts?*
A. Industrial scripts are prepared like TV scripts. These film production companies are not preparing films for exhibition in regular movie theaters as you probably know. Their films are "nontheatrical" and specifically designed for industrial public relations use, for free loan to schools, libraries, community groups and others.

Q. *When writing a screenplay format, what is the difference between "fadeout" and "dissolve," or are they synonymous?*
A. The term "fade-out" is used only once, at the very end of the script, signaling its conclusion. "Dissolve" is used as a transition between scenes or to indicate a short lapse of time within a scene. It is accomplished by having the first scene gradually disappear as the second scene appears.

Q. *What is the difference between "synopsis" and "treatment"?*
A. A synopsis is a short, concise summary of the story. A "treatment" is a scene-by-scene explanation, indicating the specific action, motivation, possible special effects, etc. It provides a fuller interpretation of the script's potential. Established writers can sell a script on the basis of a treatment, but beginners must have a complete script if they wish to make that important first sale.

Q. *What is a "documentary" and to what extent may a writer fictionalize and still maintain a "factual" format?*

A. A documentary is a dramatically structured account of an actual event. A movie or television documentary may include real people "playing" themselves and real people or actors recreating based on research and factual information about the subject. You can be flexible in fictionalizing these creations, but don't stray from the actual facts, or you'll lose the credibility of the work.

Q. *I am writing a play on a historical character. How would I incorporate exact quotations of his and other characters into my own dialogue? For example, in a papal brief I think I would have to use the exact words of the Pope and also the exact words of the reply, of personal letters, etc., that are in the public record. How would I do this and also use dialogue of my own creation?*
A. Steep yourself in the life and speech of that historical period to the point where there would not be any noticeable difference between the verbatim quotes and the dialogue you invent, as Arthur Miller has done in *The Crucible.* Or, impose your own style of speech on the period, paraphrasing the sources to make them sound compatible with your characters' dialogue, as in Robert Bolt's *A Man for All Seasons.*

Q. *I'm planning to write a play based on a song. Is it necessary for me to get permission from the songwriter before publication of the play? What about songs that are used as incidental music in the play?*
A. Yes, in either case, you must secure permission in advance from the copyright holders of a published song or record.

Q. *When writing a screenplay musical, is it necessary to collaborate with a composer or songwriter, or should the writer simply make insertions in the play where a song should enter?*
A. Since motion picture producers have their own ideas about who should write the songs for musicals, your best bet would be to simply make insertions in the play where the song should enter, describing the type of song you have in mind, comparing it, perhaps, to a currently popular one. Remember — most motion picture producers will only look at scripts submitted through script agents.

Q. *What is the copyright status of radio broadcast material — helpful hints, short features, poetry, recipes, etc.? Can this material be reused verbatim or are there restrictions?*
A. Radio scripts *can* be copyrighted, so your use of brief items should be governed by fair use guidelines. In considering fair use, decide: 1) whether use is for profit or nonprofit; 2) the nature of the copyrighted works; 3) how much you're using; 4) how it could affect the market value of the work you're quoting.

Q. *What is the actual performing time per page of dialogue?*
A. Since actors are not constantly in dialogue in a play (each manuscript page has a mix of dialogue and action in which dialogue is not present), the following figures are given for performing time per manuscript page rather than page of dialogue.

The average playing time of a 20- to 30-minute one-act play is 20 to 30 typewritten double-spaced pages. A 90-minute to 2-hour full-length play usually runs 90 to 120 double-spaced typewritten pages.

Q. *Could you please tell me how many typewritten pages are in an average half-hour TV script and an hour-long teleplay?*
A. There are about twenty-six pages in a half-hour teleplay and twice that in an hour-long script.

Q. *How many words will make an average radio story of sixty minutes?*
A. Radio feature copy usually runs fifteen full-width double-spaced lines to equal one minute, so a sixty-minute radio story would run about thirty-six typed, double-spaced pages, twenty-five lines to the page, or nine thousand words.

Breaking Into Scriptwriting

Q. *Can a beginner break into scriptwriting for TV or movies?*
A. Yes. Articles about beginners breaking into scriptwriting have appeared in *Writer's Digest.* These writers were not overnight successes. They studied existing TV series, for example, and prepared complete scripts based on the characters in the series, whose personalities they're familiar with. They obtained names of agents from the Writers Guild of America West (for $1, 8955 Beverly Blvd., Los Angeles CA 90048). They queried a few agents to see if they worked with previously unproduced writers and included a description of the complete script they had to offer. Since writers for movies also need agents to represent them with producers, the same system would apply: a query to an agent with a description of the script available.

Q. *With the growth of the cable industry, it appears that there are a lot more opportunities for writers in broadcasting today. Is this true?*
A. Yes. The increase in cable services has meant an increase in locally and minority-oriented programming. The opportunities for beginning telescript writers are excellent, for these new stations provide an outlet and a place to gain experience for those who haven't had enough credits to sell to the big networks. Pay-cable channels and other national commercial channels, which started out sending viewers a wide selection of movies and variety specials, are beginning to see a need for more original programming in the form of soap operas, miniseries, weekly series, documentaries and the like. Thus, these cable channels also open up many new avenues for the telescript writer.

Q. *How does a writer go about submitting his book or short story to a production studio for possible televising as a series?*
A. Although you may occasionally see credits on the television screen such as "From a story by . . . ," if you are an unknown writer, you would probably first

have to rewrite your short story into an actual script. Producers won't look at ideas from unproduced writers. Most TV producers work through agents who know the markets for various story themes. You can obtain a list of TV agents by writing the Writers Guild of America West, 8955 Beverly Blvd., Los Angeles CA 90048. The price is $1.

Submitting Scripts

Q. *I have been writing one- and two-act plays for little theaters. Is there a writer's guild? Is it necessary to submit play manuscripts through an agent?*
A. Yes, the Writers Guild of America, East and West (East: 555 W. 57th St., New York NY 10019; West: 8955 Beverly Blvd., W. Hollywood CA 90048) serves radio, TV and film writers. The Dramatists Guild (234 W. 44th St., New York NY 10036) serves playwrights. Not all producers require that plays be submitted through agents; check the "Scriptwriting" section of *Writer's Market* for names of those who do and don't. For lists of dramatic agents, see *Guide to Literary Agents Art/Photo Reps* and *Literary Market Place*, available in most libraries.

Q. *I have a great idea for a television series. Can you sell ideas like this to other writers or to television networks or producers?*
A. You can't sell ideas for either existing television programs or for a new series. Your idea must be presented in the form of a television script. And, since television producers usually will not look at scripts from writers directly, you'd best present your pilot script to a television agent. You can obtain a list of accredited agents for $1 from the Writers Guild, 8955 Beverly Blvd., Los Angeles CA 90048.

Q. *On completion of an hour-long TV script adapted for a program that is filmed in California, would it be wiser to contact an agent in New York or California, or would it make any difference?*
A. If the film producer is located in California, it would be better to work with an agent who is in that area.

Q. *Are there any conditions under which television producers will look at a script submitted directly by the writer rather than through an agent?*
A. If you submit your script with a signed release form, you *may* be able to get a producer to look at it. Among other things, the release form makes it clear that you understand your idea may not be new to the producer, and the company is under no obligation to you if, although your script is rejected, a similar idea appears later on television. To avoid having the script returned unopened, be sure to type "Release Form Enclosed" on the outside of the envelope.

Q. *I need information concerning requirements for play submissions — whether sales are made on a cash or royalty basis, information about rights, and a list of reputable agents. I also need information on the Dramatists Guild contract that says the author*

can demand his living expenses while participating in a touring production. Does this pertain to previously unproduced authors or just members of the Guild?
A. Plays for the legitimate theater are handled through a dramatic agent. A list of dramatic agents appears in *The Literary Market Place*, available in most libraries. Payments are made on a royalty basis usually with an advance payment to the author before the play opens. For complete details on the Dramatists Guild contracts, write Dramatists Guild, 234 W. 44th St., New York NY 10036. Plays are copyrighted by sending a filled-out copyright application form PA (Performing Arts), two copies of the play and $20 to the Register of Copyrights, Library of Congress, Washington DC 20559.

Q. *I am writing a story about myself and my early life. I believe my story would make an interesting movie. How can I get it into the hands of the right producer? I am writing it in play form. Is this acceptable and where would I send it upon completion?*
A. The play form is acceptable, but motion picture producers and studios will look at original scripts only if they are submitted through recognized agents. A list of these can be obtained (for $1) from the Writers Guild of America, West, 8955 Beverly Blvd., Los Angeles CA 90048.

Q. *Is it necessary to have copyrights on all scripts before they are used for production purposes?*
A. Although "production" does not imply "publication," your play will be protected if it is copyrighted before it is used for production purposes. Show your copyright notice on all copies of the script. To register your scripts, write to the Register of Copyrights, Library of Congress, Washington DC 20559. Request application forms PA (Performing Arts). Then mail the filled-out form, two copies of the script and $10 to the copyright office.

Q. *How can a writer protect a TV script he has submitted to an agent?*
A. Nonmembers of the Writers Guild of America can mail their scripts to that Guild with a check for $10 and have the script's completion date registered. Registering simply verifies that you were the author of that particular script on that particular date should a similar story be subsequently produced and you wished to challenge the other author, the producer or the agent. The address of the Writers Guild of America, West is 8955 Beverly Bld., Los Angeles CA 90048. The price for registration is subject to change, so you might want to verify it before you send your script.

The Art of Adaptation

Q. *Several years ago I read a story that I felt would make a good TV play. If I adapt the story, whose permission do I have to get? Do I write the play first or ask permission to adapt the story first?*
A. You'd have to get permission from the original author to do a TV adaptation

of the story. Write the author, in care of the magazine in which you saw the story, before writing the adaptation, since there is the possibility permission may not be granted.

Q. *My problem concerns a children's play I have written in which some of the characters are dolls or cartoon characters that have been made into dolls. Do I have to obtain permission from these doll manufacturers and the cartoon originators before I can use them? I would also appreciate any information you might give me concerning markets for children's plays.*
A. Yes, you'll need to obtain permission. Write the doll manufacturers (any large shop can provide their names and addresses) and the cartoon originators in care of the movie studios or newspapers that present their work. Explain your project and request permission to use the characters' names in the way you have described. Be sure to enclose a SASE. Some markets for children's plays are listed in *Writer's Market* under the playwriting, juvenile magazine and education trade journals sections.

Q. *I have written a short religious play that has already been successfully produced. I think it would also work as a film. How do I find an interested producer? Who is responsible for adapting the play to a film script? How is my copyright affected by this adaption?*
A. As creator of your play, you hold all rights to it, including the right to adapt it to film production. For a possible producer, check the "Scriptwriting" chapter in *Writer's Market*. If you find an interested film producer, he may want to assign another writer to do the adaptation. In that case, you and the producer can negotiate for film rights to your play.

Q. *Do all plays — one-act or full-length plays — have to be bound before they are submitted to a play publisher, producer or little theater? Some contest rules state they consider only "bound" plays.*
A. Very short plays can be submitted as loose pages held only by a paper clip. The request for "bound" plays means only that they should be submitted in a flexible binder, available in a stationery store.

Chapter 30

How Can I Sell My Songs?

Unless a lyricist is also a musician, he must collaborate with a composer who can help him put his ideas and words into acceptable format; then find a music publisher or record company or recording artist, or advertising jingle buyer. The specialized field of songwriting has specific requirements that must be followed for success. Here are some guidelines.

Songwriting

Q. *How can I learn to write songs? Is it easy to break into that area of writing?*
A. Just as with any other type of writing, songwriting success comes with concentrated study of the existing market, practice, trial and error. There are several ways you can get information and training. Many songwriters organizations will send information on memberships, workshops and other services they offer to both beginning and established songwriters. Helpful organizations include the American Guild of Authors and Composers/The Songwriter's Guild, 276 Fifth Ave., New York NY 10001, and National Academy of Songwriters (formerly Songwriter's Resources and Services), 6381 Hollywood Blvd., Hollywood CA 90028, and Nashville Songwriter's Association, International, 1025 16th Ave. S., Suite 200, Nashville TN 37212.

There are also many helpful publications available: *If They Ask You, You Can Write a Song,* a book by Al Kasha & Joel Hirschorn, and *Songwriter's Market* (containing how-to articles on songwriting and listings of song buyers). Available workshops and classes listed in *Songwriter's Market* would also be beneficial. And be sure to check local colleges and universities for their course offerings in this area.

Q. *I can write lyrics and a sketchy melody for a song, but I need a co-writer to write the music. How much will I have to pay that person if a particular song makes it?*
A. If you use a co-writer's melody, the situation is always open to negotiation, but usually royalties and rights are split 50-50.

Q. *I would like to be a songwriter, but I haven't made any sales yet. Is there any other* *way I can make money with my abilities?*

A. As you continue to practice and refine your songwriting talent, you might consider writing advertising jingles. You can try to get assignments from an advertising agency or sell directly to local businesses that don't employ advertising agencies. Advertising agencies don't look for a finished product in the demo tapes they listen to, they look for versatility and an ability to create a mood. Agencies listed in *Songwriter's Market* specify what types of clients they sell to and how they want samples to be submitted. Demo tapes submitted directly to businesses should cater to the needs of that particular company. Writer James Dearing has some advice for would-be jingle writers:

Before you begin recording, spend some time watching and listening to commercials. What do they say? How do the lyrics sell the product? Is the appeal "hard" or "soft" in its approach? Your jingles should closely approximate the ads now running. This isn't to say that originality isn't important. Advertisers are always looking for that special "twist" that will make consumers notice and remember their advertisement. The twist can be your song—the way you meld lyrics and music into an identifiable, repetitive, even haunting, theme. A good jingle is really very much like a top-forty song: It has to be catchy and have a strong hook that listeners will walk about humming or singing.

Q. *I have a talent for songwriting and have composed many songs in my spare time, just for the fun of it. Now I would like to get serious about it. How can I inexpensively protect my material until I find out if it's any good?*

A. Protect your songs by registering them for copyright. The price is $20 per song or "collection" of songs by the same writer(s). Write the Register of Copyrights (Library of Congress, Washington DC 20559) for application forms and more information.

Q. *I have several proposed titles and lyrics for songs, but I fear if they are sent to songwriting people, I'll have no protection. If I get a song copyrighted, can the title be stolen?*

A. Titles are not subject to copyright, but you can copyright your lyrics. If you established prior use of the title, you might be able to prevent reuse of it by others through the challenge of unfair competition, rather than copyright infringement.

Song Selling

Q. *How do I go about getting my song published? I have music and lyrics.*

A. There are two ways you can try to get your songs published. Song publishing companies look for new songs and peddle them to the artist and recording directors of record companies, or directly to artists who are looking for songs to record. These companies also handle the business end of music publishing, for example, demo-making, lead sheet preparation, and royalty payment agreements. Read carefully the listings of song publishers in *Songwriter's Market* to determine what type of music they publish, what songs they've had recorded and by whom. Individual listings will specify whether to send a query first, or to send a demo tape and lyric sheet.

Although record companies usually depend on the publishing companies for songs to record, many will accept demo tapes directly from songwriters. Record companies listen to new songs with specific artists and projects in mind, so study their listings, too. Some indicate that first contact should be made through a publishing company. Whatever direction you take, it won't be easy, but if you stick with it and listen to any advice a knowledgeable person might give, you may be able to sell your songs.

Q. *I just finished writing a song I know would be perfect for one of my favorite popular singers. How do I go about bringing my song to her attention?*
A. Approach the person who produces your artist's albums, since he has the most say in the artist's choice of material. Locating him may take some detective work. Start by finding out all you can in the way of names and addresses of your artist's record company, publishing company, producer and manager. Names can be found on album covers and record labels. Check *Songwriter's Market* for addresses and phone numbers. You may have to do further digging through phone directories. If you can't find an address or phone number for the producer, try calling the recording or publishing company that appeared on the album cover. They may be able to direct you to him so that you can call or write about submitting your work.

Q. *I've written a couple of songs that I'm sure would be acceptable to a couple of the radio stations around here. How can I get my songs played on the air by a disc jockey?*
A. As a rule, disc jockeys play songs that are chosen by the program director of the radio station. These songs are almost always songs by major artists, recorded on major labels and promoted heavily. The exception to this might be very small local stations or a public broadcasting station, if your material merits air time. Submit your record to the station's program director, and keep in mind that songs will usually only be aired if the records are available for sale.

Chapter 31

What Other Writing- Related Skills Can I Sell?

Freelance writers who think only in terms of articles, stories, poems or books often overlook hundreds of other opportunities awaiting the use of their writing skills, many of them in their own backyard. If you've been walking too narrow a path as a writer, broaden your horizons with some of the other ideas suggested in this chapter. The range of writing opportunities open to you is limited only by your imagination. For a few ideas, you might consult the *Writer's Digest* special publication, *The Basics of Turning Your Words Into Cash*.

Jobs and More Jobs

Q. *I'm not making as much money as I had hoped I would as a freelance writer. Can you suggest other sources of extra income that might utilize my skills as a writer?*
A. There are many part-time, seasonal or "one-shot" opportunities that will help you during the lean periods of your writing career. For example, there might be a local advertising agency that needs someone to write an annual report or do other types of staff-related work for clients. Do you know of a national, regional or local association that might need a newsletter, public relations help, or any other kind of writing help? You might also contact manufacturers about their need for technical writers. Local politicians and others of authority may be able to use your abilities as a speech writer. If your town is large enough to attract a convention, you might find out if any groups need someone to man the press office and act as a liaison with the local media. Are there any local printers in need of competent writing, copyediting or proofreading for themselves or their customers? If you've had enough experience, you might consider teaching journalism at the high school or community college level. Use your Yellow Pages as a job finder and put on your sales hat.

Q. *How does a writer get started in theater and movie criticism?*
A. One way beginners get started in theater and movie criticism or review is by writing sample reviews and sending them to local newspapers that don't have a

staff critic. The newspapers sometimes can be persuaded to take the beginner on as a stringer—a part-time correspondent.

Q. *Do I need special training to write book reviews?*
A. You don't need special training, but you should know how to write interesting, brief reviews that editors will want to publish. Most local newspapers don't pay for reviews—although the reviewer gets to keep the book. See *Writer's Market* for magazines that pay for reviews. When contacting book review editors to see if they can use your work, enclose a sample review you've written of a relatively new book.

Q. *Do the publishers of comic books buy freelance material? Is the story sent in standard manuscript form or is there a special form? Are there any books on the subject?*
A. Comic book publishers have different policies concerning the purchase of freelance material. Usually the editorial staff determines current needs, then assigns a story to a writer and designates its length. There are no how-to books on the subject, but beginners in the field often start by writing for fanzines—small, often amateur productions devoted to study of the field. A "Fanzine Index" of such publications with their addresses appears in *The Fandom Directory* published at 7761 Asterella Ct., Springfield VA 22152. When you're ready to submit ideas, most publishers prefer *brief* plot sypnoses of two pages maximum; since comics are a visual medium, only essentials are necessary to judge a story.

Q. *How can I get my comic strip published? Can I get it copyrighted?*
A. You can submit to newspaper markets yourself, or you can market your work to various national syndicates. (For more on syndication, see chapter twenty-one.) It would probably be best to try to sell your strip to noncompeting local markets first. When submitting to a newspaper or syndicate, you should have finished art samples to submit and a backlog of perhaps six months of ideas to carry on the strip.

You can copyright your strip, but it is expensive to copyright each one individually. Many national syndicates and persons syndicating their own material have a collection of strips copyrighted. For more information, contact the Register of Copyrights, Library of Congress, Washington DC 20559. Ask for Circular R44 on cartoons and comic strips.

Q. *Is there a market for freelancers interested in researching and writing other people's family histories? I'd like to try that kind of writing, but where do I find potential customers? How much will I get paid?*
A. Most of the market for writing family histories comes from the elderly, so you could try placing ads in local newsletters to senior citizens, or on bulletin boards in places you know they gather. Direct mailing is often effective. You can get names and addresses of elderly in your area through senior citizen centers, church newsletters, and sometimes company pension rosters and labor union lists of retired

personnel. If you make yourself known to area museums, librarians and historians, they can refer inquiries to you.

Payment will vary according to the extent of research involved. One writer received $100 for editing research data that a family had already gathered, and $1,000 for a project that involved extensive research on his own. Depending on the client and the writer, research fees could range from $5 to $30 per hour plus expenses. Your fee for writing would be added to this.

Comedy Today

Q. *Can cartoonists be trusted not to steal my ideas if I send them batches of gag ideas for cartoons?*
A. Cartoonists who are good illustrators, but who lack the original gag lines (cartoon captions) and ideas to create salable cartoons, are eager for good writers to work with them. Your concern that someone might steal your ideas is shared by other writers as well. But it happens so rarely that it should in no way prevent you from sending work out for consideration.

Q. *Where can I find markets for jokes?*
A. Markets for jokes include magazines, disc jockeys on radio stations and comedians who work in nightclubs and on television. The magazine joke markets are listed in *Writer's Market.* Gags for disc jockeys can be submitted to them directly with a SASE for return. Jokes submitted to nightclub comics are usually submitted to them in care of the club where they are performing. Contact TV comedians through the shows they've appeared on; big-name comedians depend almost entirely on staff writers, however, so there is not much of a freelance market for jokes for them.

Q. *I've written several short comedy skits. Where and how can I submit them?*
A. Much would depend on the subject matter and the level of humor that is employed. There are various possible markets such as TV, school productions, etc. If your skits could be used on TV, for example, you would have to submit them through an agent to specific TV entertainers. If the skits are one-act plays suitable for school productions, send them to play publishers who specialize in this area. Check *Writer's Market's* scriptwriting chapter.

Q. *Where can I find names and addresses of entertainers needing comedy routines?*
A. Several avenues are open to you. Since it's helpful to know a comedian's style of delivery, watch for rising young entertainers on TV comedy shows and contact these newcomers in care of those programs. You might also subscribe to *Variety,* the show business newspaper that mentions the names and places where lesser-

known comedians appear. In fact, you might get this information from city newspapers. Write the performers in care of the clubs where they appear.

Business and Advertising Writing

Q. *How can a freelancer get work writing brochures and other copy for businesses?*
A. Many large corporations have full-time staffs to produce speeches, new-product literature, annual reports, articles, catalogs, brochures and the like. However, a lot of this copy is purchased from advertising agencies, public relations firms and freelance writers. The market is quite lucrative for the writer who has the patience and persistence to know and understand the market. Locate potential buyers in your area by studying *Million Dollar Directory*, published by Dun & Bradstreet and probably available in your local library. This directory lists, alphabetically and by location, companies that claim a certain amount in yearly sales. Talk to a local printer, who might have contact with both the local companies and the freelancers, to find out which companies might need your work. Selling yourself to those companies is more difficult. Business writer Robert E. Heinemann recommends in-person queries. Having a referral always helps, too. Sometimes when dealing with small companies, you may have to ferret out the right person to approach for an interview. It may be the advertising manager, the public relations director, the vice-president of marketing, or a number of other people. When you do get in to talk to someone, don't suggest assignments. Rather, explain what you do and offer your services. If you've had no previous experience as a business writer, suggest that you'll work on speculation. Remember that this is not a hard-sell business. Buyers take their time when hiring for this kind of work, and the best thing you can do to get yourself some of those big assignments is to do a quality job on the little ones that come along first. The opportunities in business writing are discussed in a *Writer's Digest* special publication, *The Basics of Making Big Bucks in Business Writing*.

Q. *A computer company is willing to hire me to write a book on the uses of personal computers, with promotion of their products emphasized, of course. How much should I charge for my services?*
A. Payments for this kind of work are usually in the form of a flat fee and will vary with the size and importance of the company, your reputation as a writer, your evaluation of the extent and difficulty of the work involved, and what you think your time is worth. A booklet of twelve to sixteen pages might bring $750 to $3,000, while a hard-cover book of two hundred pages might bring $15,000 to $30,000 or more.

Q. *I think I would do well as a technical writer. What steps should I take to break into the field?*
A. If there are no nearby large manufacturing or industrial plants where you can apply directly, your best bet would be to go through a "body shop" — an agency that provides technical writers and other services to manufacturers and research

firms that need them. Look in the Yellow Pages under "Employment Contracts—Temporary Help" for the names of some of these organizations. This work is usually secured on a per-job basis. You might also look under "Technical Manual Preparation Service and Engineers—Consulting" for potential tech-writing jobs. If prospects in your area don't look good, you can find out about possibilities in nearby communities by writing C.E. Publications, P.O. Box 97000, Kirkland, WA 98083 for the current price of their *Directory of Contract Service Firms,* which lists 750 technical service firms throughout the world.

Q. *How do I locate speakers who need a ghostwriter—that is, someone to write material for them?*
A. Politicians, business executives, educators and community leaders often lack the time and skill to write a speech they've been asked to deliver. Chambers of commerce, large corporations, and community service and nonprofit organizations can sometimes let you know who needs a speechwriter; you can find the names of town leaders and local businessmen in the newspapers. Also advertise your services in the Yellow Pages under "Writers."

Once you've found a likely customer, submit a query, including samples of your writing and evidence of your knowledge and interest in the subject; deliver it in person whenever possible. Establish a price for the assignment, including a cash advance, and a first-draft deadline, at which time you and the speaker will smooth out any rough spots in the speech. The final draft is delivered to the speaker in some prearranged form, such as a typed manuscript accompanied by an outline on three-by-five index cards. The speech then becomes the permanent property of the speaker, who may use it as frequently as he wishes.

Fees for ghostwriting a speech could range from $100 for writing a six-minute talk for a local businessman, to $1,000 or more if you write for a national political figure.

Q. *How do you measure the length of a speech, that is, how many words equal how many minutes?*
A. Usually a speech can be measured in this way: two hundred fifty words equal about two minutes; or twelve to fifteen manuscript pages (typed, double-spaced) equal a one-half-hour speech.

Q. *What qualifications does a person need to write advertising copy? How do I reach businesses that need copy?*
A. To land freelance assignments with an advertising agency, you must have hard experience writing advertising copy. However, a willingness to study what's already been produced and for whom, and to hit the streets asking for business, could get you copywriting jobs in a number of different areas. Small businesses, nonprofit groups and industries that don't have advertising agencies usually rely on outside help for their advertising, and although they pay less than the big ad agencies, they are more willing to work with an inexperienced person. Retail department stores

put out volumes of advertising copy in the media and in their direct mail catalogs. Newspapers, radio and television stations often need people to write copy for their smaller advertisers who have no agency. Check *Standard Directory of Advertisers* in your local library. In a geographical supplement you should be able to find out which companies in your community use advertising agencies to write their copy. Companies that aren't listed either write their own advertising copy or hire freelancers to do it.

Q. *Can you offer suggestions for selling original mottoes and slogans for advertising?*
A. Selling original mottoes and slogans for advertising is difficult since many national advertisers automatically reject any idea submissions of this type from individuals because they are afraid of plagiarism suits. A few freelancers have been successful in placing advertising slogans with local advertising agencies handling local clients' work. For your slogan ideas for nationally distributed products, consult *Standard Directory of Advertisers.* Companies are grouped in this book by products. Select a company, then find from the listing which advertising agency is currently handling their account. Then write the advertising agency to find out whether they would be willing to look at your ideas and, if usable, pay you for them.

Q. *Where can I find advertising agencies and companies that might use material I'm writing for commericals?*
A. Very few advertising agencies will buy freelance material for commercials. You might try breaking into the business by approaching advertisers in your area. Ask for an appointment with the creative director. If you want to contact national companies, see *Standard Directory of Advertising Agencies* (available at large libraries), which lists names and addresses of manufacturers and their advertising agencies.

Assignments From Publishers

Q. *Do publishers use freelancers to index the books they put out? Do you have to be an expert in a subject before you can index a book on it? How can I get started in work like this?*
A. Ideally, a book should be indexed by an expert, preferably the author himself, but many authors are not interested in learning this specific and tedious skill. A professional indexer must be prepared to do some research while putting together an index. Basic sources such as biographical, geographical and historical dictionaries; a good set of encyclopedias; an almanac, an atlas and a thesaurus are usually adequate, though specialized sources would be needed for work of any technical nature.

You must have experience to get indexing assignments. To have been an editor or librarian helps. You might also look for an index you consider inadequate, work up a sample of how you would handle it, and submit it to a publisher along with your request for work.

Contact the American Society of Indexers at 1700 18th St. NW, Washington DC 20009 for information on how to get started in indexing. They will also be able to direct you to some of their workshops and seminars.

Q. *What's the difference between copyediting and proofreading? Does anyone hire free-lancers to do this type of work?*
A. A copyeditor deals with a manuscript before it goes to the typesetter. He checks for proper syntax and spelling and makes sure the manuscript makes sense and reads well. Names and facts are verified, which means that a copyeditor must have some background in the subject his editing assignment covers. He looks for consistency in spelling, abbreviations and numbers, making sure they comply with the publishing house standards.

A proofreader compares typeset galley proofs with the original manuscript to make sure that nothing is omitted, added or changed. He also makes sure that the typesetter has followed specifications for typeface, style and margins. The proof-reader must be on the lookout for mistakes in the original manuscript. This is very good training for copyediting. Some colleges offer courses in copyediting and proofreading. To locate firms that often need copyeditors and proofreaders on short notice and are willing to work with beginners, look under "Typesetting" in the Yellow Pages. If you live in a rural area, there may be no listings under this heading, so look under "Printing" for firms that advertise typesetting services. Whenever you apply for this type of work, specify the fields in which you have enough background to be able to edit someone else's writing. As you build up credits and experience, you can approach some of the larger publishing houses.

Q. *Are there book publishers who hire freelancers to do copyediting and proofreading work?*
A. Larger publishers have more of this kind of freelance work available, but small publishers may not have enough full-time work for regular employees, so they'd be prospects, too. Check listings in *Writer's Market* or *Literary Market Place* to locate publishers who produce one hundred or more books per year. These houses are probably your best prospects for work.

Q. *I have been thrust into the position of "agent" and I need help! The book I've been asked to market is a good one (it's an exposé) and I have confidence in its salability. I know that since it is nonfiction, I need only send to prospective publishers two or three chapters, a table of contents, and the author's credentials. What I don't know is how to present myself as an agent. I am not familiar with book contracts or with agents' shop talk. Just what do I say in my cover letter?*
A. Simply write a cover letter to the prospective publisher, indicating what you're enclosing on behalf of your client and why you think it's a good prospect for that firm, its market potential, and so on. If you're eligible to join the Authors Guild—because you've published a book or written for national magazines—do so, so that you can get and study their sample book contract. The Association of Author's

Representatives, 10 Astor Place, New York NY 10003 publishes a pamphlet entitled *The Literary Agent,* which may be helpful. When requesting a copy, enclose a SASE. Keep in mind that contracts will vary from publisher to publisher. The amount of advance and terms of subsidiary rights will also vary depending on whether the book author is a first-time writer or a well-established professional with a "name." Read *Publishers Weekly* to see what books are being published by whom and what kind of sales can be expected.

Q. *I once saw a request for someone to do research for other writers. How can I locate and obtain such a job?*
A. Writers who need researchers advertise in writers magazines and book review supplements, so watch the classified ads there.

Translation, Please

Q. *Is there a listing of translators with details on which languages they're proficient in? I'd like to find out if my qualifications are acceptable to be included in such a listing.*
A. There is a listing of translators in the directory, *Literary Market Place.* Send your qualifications to the editor of that directory, published by R.R. Bowker Co., 249 W. 17th St., New York NY 10011. If you qualify, there is no charge for your editorial listing.

Q. *How can I get a job as a translator? I speak German and English equally well and am also an aspiring writer. Could I start by translating technical articles or books? If so, how?*
A. Translation jobs are available primarily with companies that have technical reports and correspondence to translate, although a few book publishers might be prospects. A professional association of translators can supply additional information. Contact the American Translators Association, 109 Croton Ave., Ossining NY 10562. If there are companies in your city with foreign subsidiaries or foreign export markets, they also might be prospects.

Q. *What are the markets for translations of foreign stories, articles and books?*
A. Few magazines are interested in translation material, but you can contact any magazine whose subject matter is similar to what you propose. A few book publishers have published translations of previously published foreign works. To find these publishers, see *Subject Guide to Books in Print* under the appropriate categories such as "French Fiction — Translations Into English." Other languages are similarly listed.

Q. *I speak and read French and found a marvelous short story in a foreign magazine. I'd like to translate and sell the story to an American magazine. How do I do it?*
A. If you have a facility with another language and would like to submit a translation of a foreign short story, you must write to the publication in which the foreign

story appeared and get permission from the author and the publisher to do your translation. Whether you would be required to share payment from the American publisher with the original author or publisher depends on what arrangements you make with them. It's always best to clarify this point before you approach any American editor so there is no delay if she is interested in your idea.

Chapter 32

How Do I Submit My Manuscript?

May manuscripts be sent folded? Should pages be loose or in a binder? To whom must manuscripts be sent? The publisher? The editor? Her assistant? When you're ready to submit manuscripts, you don't want great writing to be overshadowed by improper submission techniques. Check the procedures outlined in this chapter—and in writer's guidelines from the magazines you're submitting to—before you mail.

What Should I Say?

Q. *What is a cover letter and when should it be used?*
A. A cover letter accompanies a manuscript that an editor has asked to see. They usually are not used on unsolicited manuscripts where there has been no previous correspondence between writer and editor, especially when the work must be judged exclusively on the writing style, as with fiction or humor. But cover letters are useful when you are submitting finished material at an editor's request; they can serve to remind the editor, "You asked me to send this." A cover letter should be short and to the point, and should not mention rates or fees; no biographical information about the writer should be given unless such information would help demonstrate the writer's credentials to write a given work. If the material is timely, the writer may request that the editor reply within a certain time period.

Q. *How much information should I include with a manuscript? Also, what do editors think of short manuscripts sent folded in half in 6½" × 9½" envelopes?*
A. The only personal information necessary is your name and address in the upper left corner of your manuscript. A manuscript folded in half in a 6½" × 9½" envelope is satisfactory, but be sure to include a SASE for the editor's reply or for the return of your manuscript. Many freelancers find it cheaper to simply have an editor recycle a rejected manuscript and use the SASE for reply only. The writer can print another copy for less than the postage necessary to return the manuscript.

Q. *Most editors want to see "clips" or "tear sheets"—examples of my published work.*

How are these usually obtained?
A. Publishers frequently furnish free tear sheets or clips on request. If these aren't available, you may offer to buy copies of the issue your work appeared in from the publisher. If you have only one copy of your published piece, photocopies may be sent out with future submissions.

Q. *When editors ask to see my previously published work, should I send them photocopies of my tear sheets instead of the originals?*
A. Yes. Make sure your copy is clean and readable, however.

Q. *Can I mail my manuscript folded instead of flat?*
A. Yes. Short stories, articles, and poems of fewer than six pages may be folded in thirds and mailed in a regular No. 10 business envelope. However, any manuscripts *longer* than six pages should always be mailed flat. Never staple a manuscript. Use new (non-rusty) paper clips; and be sure to include a SASE of the proper size with any submission.

Q. *Is it an advantage to send along to an editor photocopies of one or two "friendly rejections" I've received on a project from previous editors?*
A. Since your idea has to be appealing to the new publisher you're submitting to, the idea is going to be the deciding factor, not whether you enclosed some "near misses" with other editors.

Working With Editors

Q. *I submitted a manuscript to a magazine's top editor. The assistant to the editor replied: "Although we can't use this piece, we'd like to see more of your work." Now I have an idea for that magazine. Do I now correspond with the assistant, or with the top editor?*
A. Direct all future ideas or manuscripts to the person from whom you received the last correspondence. Top editors rarely are the first to review incoming manuscripts. It's best to submit to an articles editor or associate editor.

Q. *Many publishing companies produce several magazines with similar editorial content. Will my manuscript automatically be considered for possible use in all the magazines, or should I submit to each one separately?*
A. Unless otherwise noted in *Writer's Market* or in a magazine's writers guidelines, it's to your advantage to query each magazine separately. This allows you to personalize your submission — addressing it to the proper editor, mentioning a previously published article you admired, etc.

Q. *I submitted a seasonal article too late and received a rejection slip. Should I resubmit to that same market in about four months?*
A. Seasonal material should be submitted at least six months ahead of schedule.

Some editors prefer material at least one year ahead of season. So, if you receive a rejection for seasonal material with a note stating "received too late," resubmit it again in plenty of time for the editor to consider it for next season. See *Writer's Market* for individual publishers' policies. Be sure to reevaluate the material before resubmitting. "Received too late" may also mean that it is not good enough to keep on file for the following season.

Mail Matters

Q. *Ordinarily, I send my manuscripts to publishers by first-class mail. Are there any other ways to deliver my work?*
A. Writers who are submitting heavy manuscripts such as article/photo packages or book-length works often use the Special Fourth-Class Rate — Manuscripts which is cheaper than first class. It's a little slower in delivery, but much less expensive. (Be sure to write "Return Postage Guaranteed" on the address side of your package because if for some reason it's incorrectly addressed, the post office is not obligated to return it to you unless you have guaranteed postage for its return.)

Another alternative to regular mail service is United Parcel Service, which sometimes can save a day over the postal service on coast-to-coast delivery. And since the recipient must sign a receipt, there is a record of a publisher receiving your manuscript. If you're delivering against a deadline, you have several choices for one-day delivery. But priority mail (air mail) is often adequate if you don't need guaranteed one- or two-day delivery.

Q. *Writers who mail a lot of manuscripts can save postage by using the fourth-class rate. But do I downgrade my material by using this rate? Most magazines seem to use first class when responding to my submissions.*
A. The fact that some of your manuscripts are returned by magazines first class instead of special fourth-class rate is to your advantage. The special fourth-class rate is an advantage for the writer who is making a great many submissions, especially of packages containing photos, and you do not downgrade your material by sending it at that rate. Editors understand the financial concerns of freelance writers and realize it is professional to mail material the least expensive way.

Q. *Can you explain the difference between "certified mail" and "registered mail"? And when is it necessary to use special types of mail when submitting manuscripts?*
A. Certified mail is used when you just want a record of receipt of mail at a certain address. It's handled like regular mail, but a signed receipt is mailed to you. Registered mail is used to send valuables such as stock certificates and jewelry, because the post office signs a receipt when *they* get it and they know where the package is at all times. Certified mail is the less expensive way to query a publisher, to follow up on a manuscript that's been held too long by an editor or to withdraw a manuscript. A receipt is mailed to you, so you have a record that the editor received your correspondence. That record should be kept in your files. For more informa-

tion, ask for the booklet, *A Consumer's Guide to Postal Services and Products* at your post office, or write for a copy to the Consumer Advocate, U.S. Postal Service, Washington DC 20260.

Q. *After sending my submission, I waited three months for a reply, then sent a letter asking about the status of my manuscript. The magazine had no record of it. Is there a way I can trace the manuscript?*
A. If your manuscript was sent at the special fourth-class rate and it did not carry the phrase "Return Postage Guaranteed" on the front of the mailing envelope, it can't be traced because the post office is not obligated to return it to the sender if for some reason it was misaddressed or undeliverable. If your manuscript was sent first class, you can ask the post office where you mailed it to put a tracer on it. Magazines are not responsible for unsolicited manuscripts. Keep a clean photocopy to save retyping time and cost in a situation like this.

Crossing Borders

Q. *How can I sell my work to foreign markets?*
A. Many factors affect the sale of foreign rights, but magazine articles and short stories can be sold in foreign countries, either as original manuscripts or in reprint sales. (Some American magazines that have foreign editions often buy worldwide periodical rights from the author, and in such a case would have the right to reprint articles from their American editions without further payment to the author.) Magazine markets abroad are scattered throughout *Writer's Market,* and *International Writers' & Artists' Yearbook* lists some English language foreign magazine and book publishers. For book reprints, the contract between author and publisher should specify which party has the authority to contract with foreign publishers. If the publisher handles foreign sales, the author will usually receive 75 percent of the royalties. An agent negotiating a foreign sale will usually work with a foreign counterpart, and each of them will receive a 10 percent commission. If the author owns and sells all foreign rights independently, she receives all royalties.

Q. *What are the mechanics of submitting manuscripts to foreign markets?*
A. They should be typed double-spaced on $8\frac{1}{2}'' \times 11''$ white paper, and in many other ways the submission techniques are the same as those for submitting to American publishers. The main difference is that the manuscript must be accompanied by International Postal Reply Coupons in sufficient number to cover the cost of return postage. One of these coupons can be exchanged in any other country for the number of stamps necessary to mail a single-rate, surface-mailed letter of the first unit of weight, which is usually $\frac{7}{10}$ oz. (For an airmail letter reply, postmasters would usually suggest two coupons be enclosed with your letter.) The number of coupons required for a manuscript is determined by the weight of the manuscript at the post office, which is where the coupons are purchased.
    If you will be dealing regularly with a particular foreign market, you may find

it easier and less expensive to arrange to purchase foreign postage stamps from the country's postal service. The specific nation's embassy office in Washington DC, whose address can be obtained from your local public library, can provide information about how to purchase postage.

Some foreign markets are interspersed throughout the various chapters of *Writer's Market*. For more information on foreign markets, consult *International Writers' & Artists' Yearbook* (A&C Black Publishers, 33 Bedford Rd., London WCIR 4JH). This annual reference gives information on book, magazine and newspaper publishers in English language countries abroad, as well as TV, radio and theatrical producers; agents; literary prizes; clubs; and music and art markets. There is also a section on copyright and tax information pertaining to foreign sales.

Q. *Do Canadian writers stand an equal chance in the American market with writers who live in the United States? How can a Canadian writer manage return postage?*
A. Yes, Canadians stand an equal chance in the American market. There are several ways Canadian writers can solve the stamp problem. You can order stamps from any U.S. post office—write to Postmaster, city, state, zip code. U.S. currency is required. You can also order U.S. stamps through Stamps by Phone (800) 782-6724. Charge your purchase to your Visa, MasterCard or Discover. You might also try a visit to a local stamp dealer, whose supply will almost certainly include U.S. stamps.

Q. *What procedure should I follow for submitting manuscripts to publishers abroad? The difficulty seems to be in getting them back again at a reasonable postage rate. Is there a cheaper method than the International Reply Coupon, which I understand is limited to first class?*
A. The International Reply Coupon is the most convenient method of handling the return postage, but some countries also have special rates for manuscripts. Inquire about specific countries' postal rates at their embassies in Washington. Your local library can give you addresses and phone numbers of the embassies.

Chapter 33

How Many Times Can I Sell the Same Idea or Manuscript?

Freelancers who discover the magic of multiple markets and reprint sales often discover the difference between being a working writer and a working, *selling* writer. In the chapter that follows, learn how to use one article's research as the base for more articles. It's the best way to achieve a maximum return on a minimum investment.

Can I Sell My Article Again?

Q. *Can I use the basic research for one article I sold to a magazine and rewrite it, reslant it, add additional interviews and quotes to it, and sell it as original material to another magazine? Is it true that the research a freelance writer does is always his property, even though he sells an article written from that original research?*
A. Yes, research always belongs to the writer, and you are free to rewrite, reslant and resell articles based on that research as many times as you can. In fact, you owe it to yourself to try for as many sales as possible. Look for different angles, different spins you can give your reseach to write an article for another publication. One caution: Don't send rewritten articles to publications with similar slants as the one you originally sold to, unless they accept reprints or material from competing markets.

Q. *Under what conditions may I* not *resell a work?*
A. You may not sell a published work to another publication if you sold all rights to the piece to the first publication. If the first-rights purchaser has not yet published your manuscript, then you can only sell second rights to a publisher if he agrees to hold off his publication until the holder of first rights has printed the work. You cannot sell a piece that was written as work made for hire. You can't blatantly resell a work if it belongs to somebody else. Some people find old pieces of writing and try to have them published under their own name. Even if the piece of writing in question is not covered by copyright and is in the public domain, this practice would be ethically wrong.

Q. *A public service newspaper column I write in connection with my job has the potential to become a regular syndicated feature. After it has been printed for the purpose of my job, can I sell it elsewhere?*
A. Companies generally feel that the writing produced as a part of a person's job falls under the category "work for hire" and belongs to the company rather than to the writer. However, it's possible that you might be able to work out an agreement with your employer allowing you to have outside use of the material. If that happens, you might have to rewrite columns that appeared in any uncopyrighted newspapers since they would be in the public domain if they ran without copyright notice.

Q. *A magazine article a publication rejected was slanted so specifically that I can't find another market. How can I make the article marketable elsewhere?*
A. Change the slant. Although your particular arrangement of the facts in your article isn't salable to other magazines, revision and rewriting could make it suit the slant of another publication. *Writer's Digest* columnist Art Spikol points out for example, that an article about stress tests could be sold to an airline magazine, with a slant toward executives; with the same research, another article could be written for a sports magazine, slanting the piece toward how stress tests can improve sports performance. In any rewritten article, open the piece with the specific tie-in to that magazine's readership. Amplify the point with some extra quotes and information you've gathered through additional research. (For more on writing and slanting magazine articles, see chapter twenty-two.)

Q. *Can I use my published story as the basis for writing another piece to sell elsewhere?*
A. Unless you sold your right to create derivative works when the publisher bought the story, you can. The author of a work owns the right to adapt his work to another form or create a derivative work. If you sold the first publisher all rights to the work, then you no longer have the right to use the piece. If you sold first rights only, then you can go ahead with your project.

Q. *Can I use characters from my short stories in other works, if different publishers buy them?*
A. Yes. The writer of an original story owns exclusive rights to his specifically created and named characters, so they may be used in future stories. The only characters that are uncopyrightable are historical characters or otherwise well-known types of individuals. You might run up against a different set of circumstances if you're working in genre fiction, however. Some action/adventure publishers, for instance, often want to own a particular character to capitalize on any fan following. Again, check your contract carefully.

Q. *Several times in the course of my writing career, newspapers have written me for permission to reprint my articles. I've always given my permission, but I've never been paid for this use of my material. Should I request pay when this happens, or should I*

just be content with the publicity?
A. If you've never brought up the subject of payment, then that's why the newspapers haven't paid you! As long as you give permission without asking for payment, the newspapers aren't going to volunteer to pay you. "I used to allow newspapers to reprint my work for nothing, thinking I was lucky to have additional readers and the publicity," says writer Hayes Jacobs. "Now, nobody prints or reprints any of my work without paying me . . . Sometimes it's only token sums, but one can have a lot of fun with token sums."

Q. *If I am unable to trace the copyright owner of my story, can I resell it?*
A. If you don't own the copyright and have made an honest and reasonable attempt to contact the original publisher—and you didn't sell all rights to the story—you can resell the story. Keep records of correspondence in your attempt to locate the copyright owner. It might be wise to put 25 percent of any reprint sales aside in case the current copyright owner is located, and remuneration is required.

Q. *A magazine that recently folded had accepted several of my poems and stories. The pieces were never published. Can I remarket them?*
A. If the material was not paid for, you are free to market it elsewhere. If, however, the magazine paid for the poetry and short story, the company that owned the magazine may choose to sell the rights to publish to another investor who may resurrect the magazine under its own or another name. The deciding factor, then, is whether or not the material was *purchased.* If it was, contact the magazine owner and request that the rights be reassigned, in writing, to you.

Q. *I submitted an article to a magazine that ceased publication with the issue in which that article appeared. I was never paid for the article. Can I submit it to other publications?*
A. Since the publication never paid for your article, although it was published, you would be legally free to use it elsewhere. Be sure to inform the editor who buys the article the circumstances under which it was originally published.

Q. *I have contributed a great deal of material, free, to our local natural history group's mimeographed magazine. Is it permissible to sell some of these articles? If so, is it necessary to tell the prospective buyer the details about how it has been used?*
A. Since the mimeographed magazine presumably is not copyrighted, all the material it contains is in the public domain, which leaves you (or anyone else) free to make whatever use of it you wish. It would be ethical to advise prospective buyers where and when the articles first appeared. You would have to significantly rewrite these articles to obtain copyright protection in magazines.

Q. *I wrote several articles for a semimonthly rural newspaper and received no payment. Must I get a release from the publisher to submit revised versions to national magazines?*
A. Since you weren't paid and there was no written statement by the publisher that

he wanted further rights to any of the material he obtained from you, you can submit the articles elsewhere. Keep in mind that if the newspaper was not copyrighted, the original articles are in the public domain. You'll have to substantially rewrite them to make them copyrightable for resubmission to national magazines.

Q. *As a publicist I write and send feature stories to newspapers, which frequently use the material verbatim. If I select one of these stories, delete the commercial overtones and send it to a magazine, where do I stand legally and ethically?*
A. Many companies and institutions feel that what you write as their employee belongs to them and it isn't ethical to resell it for your own gain. Discuss this with your employer and clarify his attitude. He may feel that what you're writing—while it doesn't mention the company specifically—does benefit it in general from the national coverage, and will give you permission.

Q. *I have sold some verses and articles to a British magazine and would like to sell them to American publications also. Can I still offer first North American rights? Should I mention that they have already been printed in Britain?*
A. Technically, yes. But check your British contract—there might be restrictions. Tell the American publications of the previous sale.

Q. *A short story of mine appeared in my high school's literary magazine. Since then, I have added to the story and changed the beginning, but some of what appeared in the magazine is still the same. I would like to know if this work is considered a published manuscript. I would like to try to sell it, but most magazines want short stories not previously published.*
A. Yes, your work has been "published"; but since the school magazine probably wasn't copyrighted, and since you have revised the story, thereby technically producing a new work, you are free to market the *new* version as an unpublished manuscript. ("Publication" in an uncopyrighted magazine places that version of your work in the public domain.)

Q. *For several years I have edited a monthly bulletin for a club (I am a member). I may want to gather all my bulletin material and publish it in a small book. Each issue of the bulletin is published with the notice, "Permission to reprint material from this bulletin is granted provided proper credit is given." May I legally gather and print my material without permission from the club? I intend to make it clear that the material came from the bulletin.*
A. Yes, you can. But in the interest of good relations, you'll probably want to mention it to the other members. Make sure you remember to give credit, too.

Q. *An original party plan that I recently sold to a leading children's magazine included a novel idea for a party invitation. Do the rights purchased by the magazine prohibit me from selling the invitation to a greeting card company?*
A. If the children's magazine lists in *Children's Writer's & Illustrator's Market* which

rights it buys, or if it indicated which rights it buys on the contract or check you received for the plan, you'll know if those rights prohibit your further use of the material. If you don't know what rights the magazine bought, drop them a note and clarify this point before you resubmit your idea to a greeting card company. If they only bought first, or one-time serial rights, you can resubmit. Although ideas themselves cannot be copyrighted, the particular presentation of the idea—in this case, a party invitation—might be covered by copyright.

Q. *After submitting a two-thousand-word article to a magazine, I received a letter of acceptance saying they were buying five hundred words of the article at five cents a word, with a check for twenty-five dollars enclosed. Is this a usual procedure, or should a publisher pay for the whole article even if he only wants five hundred words? And what about the remaining fifteen hundred words? Are they still my property to sell?*
A. A publisher who is not able to use a full article may offer to buy a part of it from the writer. If the writer accepts, then he agrees to the terms. The balance of the article can be sold by the writer to a *noncompeting* market since he still owns the rights to that material.

Can I Sell My Book Again?

Q. *A magazine published my children's story. I'd now like to offer the story to a book publisher. What's the procedure?*
A. You can do this only if you've retained the book rights to the story. Check the contract you signed with the magazine. (If the magazine bought all rights, you might negotiate for their return.) The story's previous publication will be a plus with the book publisher.

Q. *I wrote and sold a series of short biographical pieces several years ago. I now have the opportunity to expand them into full-length books on the subjects. Do I have to contact the original publisher and get permission?*
A. You should be able to expand the shorter pieces into more comprehensive biographies, since the facts and specifics of each person's life are not copyrightable. You won't have to contact the publisher for permission unless you intend to use verbatim a large portion of the earlier works, you sold more than first rights, or you wrote them as part of a work-for-hire contract.

Q. *My hardcover book exhausted its sales potential and the publisher is taking it off the market. The publisher has not made any plans to sell it to a paperback house. Can I sell it to a paperback publisher myself?*
A. If your hardcover book sales have run their course and you think the book has potential sale in paperback, write a query to a reprint publisher describing your book, providing details on the date and publisher of the original version, number of copies sold and asking if he'd like to see the book for possible reprinting.

Q. *Would it be possible for me to have my juvenile book, now out of print, published as a reprint edition? If so, which publishers could I contact?*
A. You might query publishers of reprints in the juvenile field. Check *Writer's Market* for possible publishers.

Q. *While my nonfiction book is circulating among publishers, may I sell parts of it as magazine articles? If so, what rights should I sell to the article? If I sell first rights, what happens if the book is published before the article is printed?*
A. You can sell parts of your book as magazine articles. Type in the upper right corner of the manuscript's first page, "First Serial Rights Only," while your book is circulating among publishers. If you do subsequently sell the book, and it is published before an article you have also sold, then you should write the magazine editor and explain the circumstances. Since he would, in effect, only be buying second serial rights at that point, he may ask that a portion of the payment be returned.

Q. *I'm arranging to publish a volume of my poems. What is the proper and simplest procedure for securing release of copyright from publishers of magazines where the poems first appeared? Must individual letters be written to each editor giving the titles and dates of publication of the various verses? What if a magazine has ceased publication and the original publisher or editor is deceased?*
A. The basic letter can be the same; all you have to do is change the poem titles and publication dates for each. Even though a magazine is no longer being published, or the publisher or editor is deceased, the copyright still continues to run the course of its term and would be owned either by the publisher or his heirs, so you will still need a release. You may have to write to the Chamber of Commerce or Postmasters in the cities where the magazines were published for the most recent address of the copyright owner.

Q. *I paid to have a collection of short pieces published by a subsidy publisher some time ago. Can I now submit them individually to magazine publishers? Can I submit the entire book to regular publishers?*
A. Since rights to a subsidy-published book remain with the author, the contents of your book are yours to use as you please.

Q. *An unscrupulous publisher accepted my novels, heavily edited them, changing both style and content drastically. Although the contract I signed promised payment, I was not paid. Can I resubmit my novels (as originally written) to another publisher?*
A. Since you were never paid, the manuscripts are yours, and you are free to use them.

Marketing Concerns

Q. *I'd like to offer reprint rights to several of my manuscripts to different publications. Should I send these markets original copies or the published versions?*

A. Sending a clean retype *and* a photocopy of the originally printed article is preferable. Include the issue date of original publication and the title of the magazine in which the article appeared. Typesetters prefer to set type from original typed manuscript copy, but editors also like to see the published form.

Q. *About 20 years ago, I had a book of poetry published. Can I now submit these poems to other markets? Should I mention the book?*
A. Again, it's a matter of what rights the publisher bought. If you own the rights, by all means, send those poems to market. Be sure to check a copy of the original contract—many publishers require that you give a credit line in any reprint publications.

Q. *When a magazine specifies "contributions cannot be acknowledged or returned," how long must a contributor wait before submitting the item to another magazine for consideration?*
A. Submit articles or items to other publications after a "reasonable" length of time—about eight to ten weeks.

Q. *I've submitted manuscripts to small publications that never returned them or notified me if the pieces were published. How can I find out if they were ever printed so I can sell them to larger markets without infringing on other publications' rights?*
A. First, try to get a response. An editor on staff should certainly be able to tell you if a particular piece appeared in the publication. But if all letters and phone calls go unanswered, send a final letter withdrawing your manuscripts from consideration and submit them elsewhere.

Rights and Other Conditions of Sale

Q. *What rights to my story should I sell to a magazine so that I also may sell it to a number of other magazines?*
A. Although most editors will specify the rights they want to purchase, you might be successful in negotiating the rights purchase. Try to sell one-time rights or first rights, which means the whole gamut of reprint and second rights will be an option for you.

Q. *Many publishers buy first and second rights. After a story has been sold once, does the term "second rights" apply to each consecutive sale? Much of my writing has been to small religious magazines. I have been told the possibilities of selling a story numerous times are good because of the nonconflicting audiences. If a story has already sold three times, should I signify this by printing "Reprint Rights" in the upper right corner, followed by names of the three publishing companies and the dates purchased, or is this unnecessary?*
A. When a publisher buys first and second rights it usually means he will consider material that has been sold before as well as original material. Some editors, how-

ever, mean that they're buying the rights to publish the manuscript first, and then reprint it either in another publication they own, in an anthology, or in the same magazine several years down the road (when the audience is new). If you're unsure, ask your editor.

Second rights mean simply that an editor buys (typically for a lower price than you originally received) the right to publish an article, story or poem that has already appeared in another publication. When you're submitting a previously published piece, write "Reprint rights offered" in the upper right corner of the manuscript, and then give the piece's history in your cover letter.

Q. *If I sell first rights to a magazine article, does a certain amount of time have to pass before I sell reprint rights to a second publication?*
A. Unless otherwise specified in your contract, the piece you sold may be resold immediately after the first publication publishes it. Actually, you can *sell* reprint rights any time after you sell first rights; but the second magazine may not publish the article until the owner of the first rights has done so.

Q. *I've had work published in an uncopyrighted magazine, so it's now in the public domain. But I'd like to get it copyrighted. How much do I need to change and revise to create a "new work" that I can copyright?*
A. The law doesn't say how much—it just says that the revisions would have to be substantial. Copyright of a new version, whether the original was copyrighted or in the public domain, only covers the additions or changes that appear for the first time in the new work. Unless you extensively rewrite your work and change it considerably from the way it appeared in the uncopyrighted magazine, it must remain in the public domain.

Q. *I sold a story to* Modern Romances. *There was no mention of serial rights, but the check I endorsed stated they were buying all serial rights. Can I sell second serial rights to another publication?*
A. Since the magazine bought all rights, the second serial rights are no longer yours to sell. You might try writing the editor to see if she will reassign the rights to you.

Q. *I plan to compile a book of poetry from my published work. Is it necessary to write for permission from each publication that has published my poems? Some indicated they bought first rights only. Does this automatically give me permission to sell or publish again? And if some poems were published under pen names, must they be republished under the same name or can they be published under my own name?*
A. If you sold only first rights, then you own book rights. If the poems were published before 1978, your book rights are held in trust for you by the original publisher and he must be contacted. If there are some instances where you're not sure what rights were purchased, you'd better check with the publisher. Though written originally under pen names, the poems may now be presented under your own

name. Your projected book should contain a list of acknowledgments, indicating where the poems first appeared.

Q. *Would you explain how "digest" magazines pay for articles they reprint from other magazines? What percentage does the original publisher get, and what percentage goes to the author? If the author has sold first serial rights only to the original publisher, does the author receive the entire reprint amount? Should he try to sell a reprint of his article to a digest magazine, or do digest editors read most publications and make their own selections?*
A. In the digest reprint market, payments vary. Some pay 50 percent to the original publisher and 50 percent to the author. Others pay the publisher or the author — depending on who owns reprint rights. Digest editors *do* make many of their own selections, but don't let that stop you from submitting. When you sell reprint rights to publications on articles you own, you are entitled to the entire reprint fee. But before 1978 when the new copyright law went into effect, the original publisher held other rights in trust for you, even if he bought first rights only. So you must write and ask that the rights be returned to you.

Q. *One of my stories was published in a non-paying magazine. Can I sell it to a paying magazine?*
A. Yes, but the fact that your first "sale" was to a non-paying magazine does not change the general rule. A publication can still acquire rights to your manuscript *without* paying you for them — your "compensation" was publication. First, if the magazine was not copyrighted, your material is now in the public domain and anyone could have reused it as is. To submit it now to a copyrighted magazine and get it copyrighted as part of the magazine, it would have to be revised sufficiently to be considered a new work by the Copyright Office. If the magazine in which it originally appeared *was* copyrighted, you'll have to clear with the editor whether they acquired only first rights or all rights to the material.

Q. *What will I get paid if my article is reprinted in another publication?*
A. Assuming you only sold first rights to the original publisher, the reprint publisher will either make an offer or ask the writer to suggest a fee. This payment will be a per-word rate or a flat fee, which could be, for example, 50 percent of what the publication would pay for an original article.

Chapter 34

How Do I Cope With Rejections and Writer's Block?

There is no easy way to face rejection, and there is no sure-fire system for beating back the "blank page blues." These are the tests of the writing life. When you encounter them—and, at some point all writers do (beginners more so than others, perhaps)—face them with courage. "Success begins," says one editor, "where most people quit."

Obstacles to Writing

Q. *What causes writer's block and how can I combat it?*
A. Ask twenty writers what causes writer's block, and you'll probably get twenty different answers. The causes of writer's block usually don't have anything to do with writing, but rather are connected to factors that serve to distract the writer, keeping him from concentrating on his craft. Overwork is one such factor. A writer who is fatigued from overwork should stop writing for a couple of days. Financial worries, personal problems and illnesses all could keep a writer from his work.

Look at your article and see if you're actually ready to begin writing; it may be that you haven't done all your preliminary work yet. If you haven't gathered enough information or haven't outlined the piece clearly enough, you might not have a firm idea of what you want to write. Step away from the work and try to look at it objectively. You may be trying to write it without having a clear understanding of how you want it to turn out. You may be writing it one way, when you know subconsciously that it would be better if it were treated some other way.

Freelancer Brian Vachon says that a writer should make sure he *wants* to write about his current subject; if you're trying to make yourself write about something you just don't like, your mind could be rebelling.

Anxiety about the quality of writing is a frequently cited cause of writer's block. Novelist Dean Koontz claims this is easily solved: "Read a novel by a really bad writer whose work you despise, and tell yourself, 'If this junk can get into print, publishers will fight one another for the rights to *my* book'."

The important thing to remember is that worrying too much about writer's block will only make it worse. If the block persists, take some time off from writing.

Read, or do some correspondence. Buy a new piece of equipment or a reference book. The best way to fight writer's block is to remember that the harder you push against it, the harder it struggles to remain.

Q. *I have never suffered from an extended period of writer's block, but I do find it difficult to put enough time together in one segment to get any writing accomplished. What can I do about this problem?*
A. Your problem seems to be one of time management rather than writer's block. In other words, the work seems to be so enormous that you don't know where to start. Here are a few suggestions. Get up at least forty-five minutes earlier than you normally would, and spend at least thirty minutes of that time on writing and related work; if you're not a "morning person," do this at the end of the day. "Brown bag" your lunch at least once a week and work during your lunch break. You can also do research reading or review your notes on the bus or other public transportation on the way to work. If you work at home during set hours, let friends know you prefer not to be called at those times. Plan your time for outside "leg work," such as interviewing, research, library visits, and other calls so you can do them all on one day. Save your home office time to write. Take writing-related work with you to the doctor's office; if you have a long wait you can get some work done. Above all, never say you don't have enough time to do the work. Even if you only have an hour on a given day, that can really add up over the course of a year.

Q. *I've been writing for a couple of years and have had some small success with magazine sales, but a writer who started about the same time I did has managed to sell a couple of novels, along with getting an advance for a third. I'm jealous. Why can't my career take off like his?*
A. Novelist Dean Koontz says, "Writers should be supportive of one another and should take pleasure in one another's successes. Don't waste time stewing in envy . . . just work harder than before and put in longer hours than ever, until you finally get your own huge advance." You are your only competitor; your only goal is to make each of your works better than your last.

Q. *Because magazines depend on advertising for revenue, would they reject articles because of controversial subject matter that might offend some advertisers?*
A. Magazines are businesses so they are sometimes forced to think long and hard about running controversial material. Any article that will likely offend a regular advertiser probably won't be accepted. Some editors have been courageous enough to run controversial material—for example, material leading the way to needed improvements in some industries—but most magazines choose carefully the controversies they start.

Q. *How many rejection slips do you consider the cutoff point—where you give up on that particular article?*
A. If the idea for the article was good enough at the onset for you to take time

and work to produce the finished manuscript, you should not abandon it too soon. Look at the rejection slips as bits of advice for improving the original manuscript. Glean whatever an editor jots as the reason for rejecting the article or story—and improve, revise, take from or add to, until the piece is sold. Rejections, if used properly, can be learning lessons to improve your writing. Be sure to send your work to the appropriate market. Sending an article to a market that is completely unsuitable is a mistake that many beginners make, but marketing—just as writing— is a skill that one learns from experience and study. Some ideas and manuscripts have to be set aside after a dozen or so submissions because either the market isn't ready for them—or they're not ready for today's market.

Life After Rejection

Q. *What should I do after an article is returned with a rejection slip?*
A. Freelancer Kay Cassill recommends sending a rejected query or manuscript to another appropriate publisher the day it is returned to you. "You'll have it off your desk and on its way to another possible sale," she says. "You won't sit around feeling dejected, and the current project won't have suffered from the interruption."

Q. *If I'm aiming at a specific type of market, should I continue to submit my manuscripts to publications that have rejected my past work? Do editors begin to recognize certain authors as "losers" and push their work aside because of past rejections?*
A. Just because a market has rejected your manuscripts in the past doesn't mean that will always be the case. Editors reject manuscripts for many reasons that have nothing to do with your manuscript's value. For example, the editor could have recently bought or assigned an article on a topic similar to yours. Don't assume that the sight of your name on a manuscript will cause an editor to automatically reach for a rejection slip. Assuming your manuscripts are neat, appealing, and suited to the publication, the next manuscript you send may be the happy combination of the right idea in the right place at the right time, while your earlier pieces weren't. On the other hand, tread carefully. If you've submitted six stories in the past six months, and they've all been rejected, you might want to back off that market for a while. Watch the publication closely and try to make your articles as good as the ones the magazine is publishing.

Q. *Is it advisable to submit a story more than once to a magazine that has rejected it?*
A. If the editor tells you he's rejecting it because he's overbought at the time, or he's recently bought something similar, it isn't at all impossible to sell that piece to the same market at a later date. If you wait one year before resubmitting, you may have a chance. Also watch the magazine's masthead. If an editor leaves, the new one might have different tastes, and you might be able to sell her your manuscript. But use your best judgment before resubmitting. Try to ascertain if the editor

was simply being polite, or if your manuscript may really stand a chance at a later date.

Q. *I am puzzled by writers who claim that after mailing a piece nineteen times and having it rejected, they mail it once more and sell it. Are they telling the truth? It seems that if a piece is slanted to a given magazine and it's rejected, there can't be nineteen other magazines with similar editorial needs.*
A. These writers *are* telling the truth, because they have carefully explored all possible allied market areas. For instance, a piece about Washington state fishing may not sell to other specialized sports magazines, but it might find a place in one of that state's Sunday supplements or in general men's magazines, fraternal order publications, etc. The number of markets a writer finds depends on her own resourcefulness and ability to revise, where necessary, to suit the new market.

Q. *After four years of freelance writing and not selling a word, I would like a personal remark from an editor about why my manuscript didn't qualify, instead of the usual cold-blooded rejection slip. Is there a special approach you can recommend?*
A. An editor's job is to find publishable material, not explain rejections. Most editors have too much work and too little time, so personal analysis of the thousands of manuscripts that cross their desks is impossible. For constructive criticism, take a writing course, join a writers club, or use a criticism service such as those advertised in writers magazines.

Q. *I've received manuscripts from reputable publishers that have had very encouraging remarks scrawled across the first page in red ink. Is this acceptable editorial practice?*
A. It is considered improper for an editor to mark on a rejected manuscript, but there are many writers who would be delighted to have such personal attention from an editor, even if it did mean typing the first page again.

What Does It Mean?

Q. *I receive letters from editors saying my manuscripts are interesting, but "not quite right for us." What does this mean? If it's so interesting, why isn't it right?*
A. These letters expressing interest are meant to encourage you and show you your work does have a degree of promise. The material's style or content, however, may not be in keeping with the magazine's editorial requirements, or something similar may have been published recently or bought for future use. Get to know the markets better by studying what these publishers are buying. Current magazine issues and book catalogs give writers valuable clues as to what kinds of work editors are looking for. *Writer's Market* and other market books also can help you determine editorial needs of publishers.

Q. *If an editor writes "Sorry. Try us again" on a rejection slip, what does that mean?*

A. When an editor indicates some interest in future submissions, it means he thinks enough of your work to offer the encouragement of a personal note. It means your writing style and approach are suitable for his readers, and he wants to see more ideas from you.

Q. *On recent rejection slips from greeting card companies were handwritten messages, "Terrific possibilities but more punch" and "Ideas good but lack sales appeal." I don't know what comprises "punch" and "sales appeal." Should I take these handwritten remarks to be encouraging?*
A. These handwritten criticisms certainly should be regarded as encouraging. By referring to "punch" and "sales appeal," these editors probably meant that your work lacked the impact necessary to make the prospective card buyer immediately react favorably to the cards. It would seem, then, that your underlying ideas are good, but you need to present them in a more colorful, entertaining, or dramatic way that will catch the customer's attention and make him buy. If, after studying published cards and revising your own work, you feel your ideas now have the right sales appeal, don't hesitate to resubmit them.

Q. *If an editor keeps my manuscript a long time, does that mean he likes it? Or am I setting myself up for disappointment?*
A. It takes most magazine editors anywhere from two weeks to two months to comment on a manuscript. Check *Writer's Market* for a publication's stated response time. If that time passes without any report, it's possible that your manuscript passed the sumbmission editor's approval and is now being read by the other editors. However, it could also mean that your manuscript is buried under a pile of submissions, or that the editor is out of the office, or even that your manuscript was lost in the mail. So it's best not to get your hopes up too high. If you still haven't received word two to four weeks beyond the stated response time, write the publication (include a SASE) and ask for an update. If that letter receives no response, call the publication.

Q. *A children's story of mine was recently rejected. Instead of the usual rejection slip in the return envelope with the manuscript, I received a letter saying my manuscript was sent under separate cover. When I received it, it was insured. Does this have any special meaning that my manuscript has any merit that would interest another publisher?*
A. Some publishers just have a company policy of returning manuscripts insured. If the original company had any special comments to make on the merits of your manuscript, they would have said so in their rejection letter. Do not hesitate, however, to send it to another publisher right away.

Q. *My first story was recently returned. It did not have the usual printed rejection slip attached. I received instead a short personal note telling me the publication was* *overstocked and I should not submit material until late August. Was my story rejected completely or should I feel it was adequate for that magazine?*

A. It is possible that your story wasn't read, but was automatically returned because the market is overstocked at present. You should resubmit the story in late August, as suggested, since the note seems noncommittal about rejecting or accepting it.

Chapter 35

What Do Editor and Writer Owe Each Other?

In his book, *Max Perkins: Editor of Genius,* A. Scott Berg comments, "Two qualities . . . distinguish the professional editor: the vision to see beyond the faults of a good book, no matter how dismaying; and the tenacity to keep working, through all discouragements, toward the book's potential." Magazine editors are equally eager to help the promising writers they deal with achieve their best efforts. If along the way there are occasional misunderstandings, the writer should not overlook the editor's essential goodwill toward his work. For more insights into the editing profession, see *Editors on Editing,* edited by Gerald Gross (Grove Press).

The Relationship in General

Q. *In December, I submitted an article to a new magazine. The following February, I received a rejection slip with the note: "We are quite taken with your style and would appreciate receiving material from you in the future." Then, this magazine's August issue appeared on the newsstand, bearing an article with the same title as mine. Though the printed article is admittedly better than my submission, longer and more thoroughly researched, it is similar. The title, style and content are almost identical. It is hard for me to accept this as coincidence. Do I have any right to question this similarity? Can I copyright my manuscripts in the future so editors can't steal my ideas?*
A. Many writers get the same idea at the same time and often use the same language in writing, so *your* idea may not have been "stolen." Someone else may get a similar idea to yours at the same time you do (as often happens in science) and execute the article better than you did so that the editor chooses to use their story. Ideas cannot be copyrighted; you can only copyright the *presentation* of an idea. Under the copyright law, a manuscript is copyrighted automatically at the moment of creation. The law says if you created it and can prove it's yours, you're protected. Protect your presentation by showing the copyright notice (the copyright symbol, the year, and your name) on the first page of your manuscript. Keep carbon copies and research that show you created the work. Put dates on these and on the manuscript.

Q. *If an editor addresses me by my first name, do I address her, for example, as "Clarissa" or "Ms. Jones"?*
A. Until the correspondence reaches a friendship stage in a long editorial procedure, the safest salutation is probably "Dear Clarissa Jones." A good guide is to follow the editor's lead. If she is using the familiar, feel free to do the same.

Q. *Is one editor liable for another editor's commitment? When an editor assigns something to a writer or offers payment for a manuscript, then leaves the magazine staff, is the replacement editor liable for that assignment or payment?*
A. There are no rules on this one. Often it depends on the terms of departure for the editor. If he is fired, chances are his replacement or his former manager wants to disregard his editorial thinking—perhaps that was the reason for his dismissal. If he was promoted, transferred, or if he departed on good terms, there is likely to be more transitional grace, and old projects and commitments may be honored. The writer should summarize the situation in a letter to the new editor, including copies of all correspondence. The new editor then will be in a position to judge whether he wants to keep the writer on assignment or kill the idea. Whether this is accompanied by a kill fee (usually a minimum of 20 percent of the anticipated payment for the piece) depends on whether a kill fee was part of the original agreement and how far the writer has gone with the idea. If an article has been written on assignment for a previous editor and a kill fee was agreed upon, this may have to be discussed with the magazine's publisher or owner. Most editors will be fair with the writer. But when a magazine staff changes, it is often because the publisher is unhappy with earlier staffers—and it can signal a new editorial direction for the publication.

Q. *Why do I have to revise according to an editor's suggestions? My story is written exactly how I want it. How do I know an editor's criticism is valid?*
A. Writers who are new to the business sometimes consider an editor's requests for revision a personal affront, when in reality the editor is only trying to get the best possible manuscript for his market. "I don't believe a writer exists today who can't occasionally profit from that editorial blue pencil," says author Kay Cassill. Editors know what works for their audience, and have the experience and expertise necessary to objectively criticize work. Author Stuart Woods says, "Sensible suggestions come from editors," and this is generally true. If you don't want to revise your work to the editor's style or suggestions—and you could be right—you can always withdraw it. But there's a good chance you will never get your work published if you don't learn to take constructive criticism from editors.

Submission Etiquette

Q. *What should I do if a magazine tells me they would like to keep my query letter for future consideration? I had planned several other slants to the story that might interest other publications.*

A. Write to the editor, acknowledging your interest in his future consideration but indicating your intentions to query elsewhere with different versions of the story in the meantime.

Q. *How long should I wait for an editor's decision on my manuscript? How do I follow up on an article that's being held by an editor an unusually long time?*
A. Depending on a magazine's staff and the amount of mail it receives, an editor may take from three weeks to two months to report on submissions. A book editor may require three months or longer. Check *Writer's Market* for specific reporting times. Remember that when an editor says she reports in six weeks, that means six weeks from the time she receives your manuscript. If you live on one coast and she's on the other, it may take a week to reach her. If you've had no report from an editor by the maximum reporting time, send a brief inquiry asking if your manuscript or query is still being considered. Include the story title, date of original submission and brief description of the piece as well as a SASE. In the rare case where a publisher fails to report even after your inquiry, send a certified letter to the editor, advising that you are withdrawing your manuscript from her consideration so you may submit it elsewhere. Be sure to notify *Writer's Market* editors of the problem.

Q. *Is a magazine publisher responsible for stories he received but apparently lost in his office? My story was lost by a major magazine. I have a letter from the editor stating he cannot find it. Should I ask him to pay for it, since I cannot send it elsewhere?*
A. You could try, but many magazines go on record as indicating they are not responsible for unsolicited manuscripts, so legally they cannot be charged. If you have kept for your file a clean photocopy of the story, make another copy and submit it.

Q. *Three months ago, I sent some of my best poems to a publisher who never acknowledged receiving them. Eager to put them back in circulation, I requested their return. My letter was not acknowledged, nor have the poems been returned. A SASE was enclosed with correspondence. May I legitimately write the editor stating that I withdraw my offer of the poems, then send them to other editors?*
A. The procedure is to send the editor a certified letter indicating that you are withdrawing the poems from his consideration. Be sure to list the titles of the poems and date of submission. Then resubmit this material elsewhere. Hold on file the return receipt and a copy of your certified letter. This is a perfect example of why writers should never send their original copies to publications. Always send photocopies or make sure you have another copy in your files.

Q. *After reading the outline of my proposed historical novel, a leading publisher asked me to mail a synopsis and four chapters. The manuscript was mailed with first-class postage enclosed for return. The publisher acknowledged receipt, but I did not hear from the publisher again. After three months I wrote a letter inquiring as to their decision.*

The editorial department replied that my manuscript had been misfiled; they did not know it had arrived until receipt of my letter. Within a few weeks the senior editor wrote a vague letter saying the chapters had not lived up to the outline; that the manuscript was being returned fourth *class. More than two and one-half months have passed and the manuscript has not arrived. The publisher says they have asked the post office to trace it. If the post office is unable to locate it, as now seems possible, do I have recourse against the publisher? There's something illogical about the publisher's explanation.*

A. Major publishing houses deal with thousands of manuscripts annually, and while yours is an unfortunate incident, you are probably unduly suspicious of the publisher. In this situation it's best to cut your losses and make a new copy of the proposal to send out again.

Q. *A Christmas poem I mailed in August to a top publication was returned the following February. Would sending seasonal material by registered mail help, or would this antagonize an editor?*

A. When sending seasonal or timely material, include in a cover letter a brief request that since the material is timely, you would appreciate a reply by a specific date. This won't help in every case, but it may reduce your frustrations with a few editors. By the way, August is cutting it close for a Christmas issue. For unsolicited work, it's best to submit six to nine months in advance.

Acceptance Etiquette

Q. *What happens when a story is accepted by a magazine? Does the writer get a check in the mail or are there preliminaries to go through, such as signing something regarding rights or originality?*

A. The writer is customarily notified of acceptance by mail. A contract or check may be included or may follow later, depending on the policy of the publisher. Check *Writer's Market* for information on what rights the magazine buys, or ask the editor. The editor assumes the writer is the story's originator, so there is rarely any paper to sign to this effect. While acceptance by mail is the usual policy, some small magazines use the story or article, assuming that the writer is selling whatever rights the magazine usually buys at whatever price the editor pays. Be sure you know what rights you're selling for what price by checking the *Writer's Market* listings before you submit.

Q. *Once in awhile I sell a story that the magazine pays for, yet I never see it in print — even though the editor says he will send copies of the issue containing it. Can you give me some advice explaining this situation?*

A. Sometimes magazine editors forget to send copies of stories they published to the original authors. Write a note to each of the editors asking for a copy of your story, if it has been published. In some cases, editors leave a magazine or editorial policies change, and although stories are bought, they are not used. Many magazines keep a large inventory of manuscripts, so your piece may not have run. Be patient. If you feel that you simply cannot wait the necessary amount of time, you might try buying the manuscript back from the editor.

Q. *I sold a piece to a magazine, and it took a year before it was published. When it was published they spelled my name right, but that was about all. The style was hacked apart until there was no style. What's more, facts were altered, so the reader was bound to get an impression different from what I had intended. How much can my story be edited or changed without my permission?*
A. Ethically, an editor should discuss any significant changes with you, especially if they affect the intent of your piece. Some editors will show galley proofs to authors; others will not. You might ask to see galleys at the time the piece is bought. If you see galleys and don't like what is there, you can ask to have your original meaning restored or the manuscript returned to you for submission elsewhere. But be sure you aren't mistaking tight editing for changes in meaning, as beginning writers sometimes do. Most of the editor's changes are to make the story more readable – not different.

Q. *Can a magazine change the title of my story?*
A. Just as the editor has the right to make editorial changes, so too does he have the right to change your title. Some editors might consult you first, but titles are changed routinely for a variety of reasons. If the editor should change your title in a way that distorts your meaning, you certainly have cause to complain.

Q. *I've queried an editor about an article that will require extensive research. The editor gave me the assignment, but the deadline he gave me is one that I find impossible to meet. What can I do that won't alienate the editor? I want to be honest.*
A. Write the editor a short but courteous note explaining that you will need more time than he has suggested for the deadline, and let him know the approximate date you will have the article to him. Most editors will understand this and appreciate the honesty.

Q. *A magazine editor assigned an article to me, based on a variation of an idea I queried him about. When I got into the actual research I found the article wasn't going to produce what the editor was looking for. There just wasn't enough solid information available to support the editor's thesis. What's the best way to handle this?*
A. Let the editor know right away what the problem is. The editor will either abandon the idea and pay you a kill fee based on the amount of work you put into the research or suggest some contact persons who may be able to supply you with what the editor is searching for. Editors, as well as writers, sometimes have to admit that a certain idea has to be temporarily abandoned.

Q. *When a manuscript is accepted for publication, should a writer acknowledge that acceptance? If so, should it be on acceptance, on receiving the check, or on publication?*
A. A response isn't necessary, but neither is it inappropriate.

Payment Etiquette

Q. *Can I set the price on my articles or must I accept what the magazines offer? Can I negotiate payment?*
A. Most magazines have a certain rate they pay writers and make an offer based on those standard rates. If you're a new writer and have never sold anything to the publication before, you can't expect to get more than that. Remember that sometimes, especially early in your career, a byline is more important than a check, since it bolsters your confidence, builds your reputation, and may lead to other sales. Your value increases as you prove yourself to an editor, so keep a file of all the work you've done for him to substantiate your future requests for a raise. If you're a well-established writer and think you might be able to negotiate a better rate because of your experience and the value to them of the particular article you're offering, go ahead and suggest a higher rate than their standard. All they can do is say no, or offer a compromise figure and in either case you've lost nothing.

Q. *My magazine article was published four months ago and I haven't received payment for it. What recourse do I have? How can I get the editor to pay me?*
A. If the magazine's policy is "pay on publication," you might expect to receive payment within thirty or sixty days after publication. You should *never* be expected to wait longer than ninety days. If you still haven't received a check, send a follow-up letter requesting the specific amount of payment. Give the editor all the details — whether the manuscript was submitted on speculation or assignment, date of original submission, date and title of the published piece.

If you get no satisfaction from the magazine's editorial department, try sending an invoice (include your name, your article's title, and a copy of the contract) to the magazine's accounting department.

If you are still unable to get a response, write the state's attorney general, the Better Business Bureau and the post office in the city where the magazine is located. Its Postal Inspection Service sometimes investigates such claims. Also send a letter with all the above mentioned information to *Writer's Digest*, which will notify its readers to be wary of dealings with this publication. You might also try The National Writers Union at (212) 254-0279. Other than that, there is no recourse but to sue — which can cause you financial loss because of legal fees, unless you can take your case to a nearby Small Claims Court.

Q. *The publishing contract I signed promised me a six hundred dollar advance when my book was published. I now have copies of the book, but no advance. The contract was signed two years ago. Do I have any chance of getting the advance? I've written to the publisher several times, but have received no answer.*
A. If you have sent a registered letter to the publisher and still received no reply, it might be advisable to take the publisher to Small Claims Court. If the six hundred dollars is promised in the contract, you should receive that money. You would be wise to contact a lawyer and let him look over the contract and suggest a course of

action you might take. You may also want to tell the U.S. Postmaster in the publisher's city about your grievance and notify *Writer's Market* as well. They operate a complaint service which solves 50 percent of the conflicts writers have with listed publishers. The Authors Guild, which you are eligible to join once you have signed a book contract, can give you advice as well. The guild's address is 330 W. 42nd St., New York NY 10036.

Q. *When a magazine lists in* Writer's Market *payment of a set sum per word, shouldn't they be expected to pay it? It was only a six-line verse filler, but they used it. I received no letter of acceptance or rejection. To add insult to injury, they didn't even give me a byline. How can I be sure this won't happen again with a longer, more important piece?*
A. You should write to that editor, asking why you received neither byline nor the payment listed in *Writer's Market.* Don't submit future material to this publication. Before you submit to other magazines, you might ask about filler payment if there's no rate given in *Writer's Market.*

Chapter 36

How Can I Avoid Legal Problems?

"Ignorance of the law excuses no man" is an often quoted adage of English jurist and scholar John Selden, and one that writers especially should keep in mind. While in recent years a few book publishers have offered libel insurance to their authors, the burden of legal awareness still lies with the writer on any work of his that appears in newspapers, magazines and books. Truth is a defense against libel, but not against invasion of privacy. Writers must know not only their own rights, but the rights of the persons they write about and quote in their manuscripts. Here are some basic reminders for beginning writers. For more tips, see one of several books available on law and writing, such as *The Law (in Plain English) for Writers* by Leonard D. DuBoff (John Wiley & Sons, Inc.)

I Need Help

Q. *Where can I get legal assistance?*
A. Volunteer Lawyers for the Arts is a national organization of lawyers offering free legal services to creative artists, including writers. Eligibility for the service is based on the writer's income, with the writer sometimes paying court costs even if representation is free. Contact VLA at 6th Floor, 1 E. 53rd St., New York NY 10022, (212) 319-2910. Also helpful is the National Writers Union at Suite 203, 873 Broadway, New York NY 10003, (212) 254-0279. You could also contact the Lawyer's Referral Service of your local Bar Association. This service is not free, but you could obtain an initial consultation for a nominal fee ($10 and up).

Q. *My brother and I worked together on his manuscripts. He asked me to help rewrite, edit, and type his work. When he passed away, all the manuscripts he had were packed into a box and given to me. I have found some I am sure will sell with some rewriting and corrections. I would like to submit these for publication using both our names. What are my legal rights? Will it be necessary to ask permission from his other heirs, and would I have to share any profits with them?*
A. If these manuscripts were transferred to you by your brother's written will or some other valid form of transfer, then they are your possession and you may get

them published without asking permission of the other heirs. If there is any doubt about the legality of ownership, it would be best to consult an attorney.

Q. *I sold an original story and screenplay almost a year ago. Since the time the contract was signed and my work was taken, the producer has not been in touch with me. He hasn't paid me. According to the contract, he has to pay only when they start the principal photography or when the production money is banked. Since there is no time limit in the contract, I wonder if there is any law that protects me? What can I do if the producer is unable to raise sufficient money for the production?*
A. Unless you had a time limit written into the contract you signed (which is always advisable), you do not have much choice except to wait for him to obtain production money. On the other hand, if he has abandoned the project, he may be obligated to return the material to you depending on the terms of your contract. It is up to you to contact him to see what can be worked out.

Q. *I'm having trouble getting paid by a magazine. Can I sue a publisher in another state?*
A. Many states have adopted a "long arm law" which provides that business transactions are subject to the jurisdiction of courts in the state where some part of the transaction occurred. Check with a lawyer to see if you can use this law to sue an out-of-state publisher. If you're unable to sue from your location, you will have to file suit in the district where the magazine is—usually a greater expense than it's worth.

Q. *I work for a trade publication that owns a consumer magazine. I recently found my work for the trade magazine appearing in the consumer publication. I was not notified or paid extra. My fellow employees and I want to know if this practice is legal.*
A. Work produced by salaried and work-for-hire employees is usually the property of the employer. Therefore, the magazine probably has every right to reprint your work in its sister publication. You might wish to take the matter up with your employer, however, if you and your fellow employees feel that you deserve some compensation. Work-for-hire writing belongs to the company, but publishers have been known to make concessions when workers present a reasonable argument.

Can I Be Sued?

Q. *If I write the introduction to a book and later there is legal trouble involving the book's contents, am I liable?*
A. If the plaintiff felt that your introduction lent credence to the book's contents, then you could possibly be named in the lawsuit. Before writing an introduction, become familiar with the book's contents and be sure you are in agreement with the author's viewpoint, since anyone who sues the author may also sue you.

Q. *A neighbor of mine is a disfigured recluse. I have built a story around such a woman.*

I slander her in no way, yet my husband feels I will have a lawsuit on my hands if the story gets published. I would appreciate any advice.
A. It would be best to change as many of the obvious true-to-life facts as possible to avoid an invasion of privacy suit. Give your heroine a different age, size, hair coloring, nationality, etc. Add new mannerisms, idiosyncrasies and other aspects of personality. Use a totally different setting if you can. After all, the only basic idea you need is that of a disfigured recluse. It is not necessary to make the type of disfigurement identical to that of your neighbor. Use your creative imagination to produce a completely new character based on the general idea but not the exact details of your neighbor's life. In fact, you might even experiment with the idea of making the leading character a man instead of a woman.

Q. *How careful must a fiction writer be with names he contrives, but which could turn out to be names of living persons? For example, if I name the villain in a story Jack Bowlton, could a real Jack Bowlton sue me for defamation of character for characterizing him as a villain? Also, what became of the old disclaimer, "Any similarity to persons, etc., is strictly coincidental"?*
A. Unless the real Jack Bowlton happened to be circumstantially similar in personality and actions to the fictional character you gave that name, there probably wouldn't be any cause for legal recourse. The old disclaimer probably doesn't appear anymore because a person who can prove that a real person was used in a fictional account and can also prove defamation or invasion of privacy may still have legal recourse in spite of the disclaimer.

Q. *Could a person actually named William Faulkner, or Ray Bradbury, or Ann Landers publish work under that famous name?*
A. No. Ann Landers, William Faulkner and Ray Bradbury have already established the reputation of those names; anyone who tried to publish his work using the names would be guilty of infringing on the reputation those writers have already built. This holds true even if the writer's real name is the same as that of an already-published author. The second writer would have to take a pen name. Remember, actor Stewart Granger had to adopt a stage name at the beginning of his career, because somebody else was already using his real name: Jimmy Stewart! (For more information on pen names, see chapter sixteen.)

Q. *Will a magazine's libel insurance protect me from libel suits for articles I write?*
A. It depends on the publisher. Many major magazine publishers have libel insurance that *can* be applied to a freelancer at the discretion of the publisher, and in most cases the publisher will extend coverage to protect the writer. But if the publisher feels the writer has been negligent in preparing the material, he may decide to let the writer get himself out of the situation. Many publishers have no coverage for freelance writers.

If an article involves investigative reporting and/or a potential lawsuit, a freelancer should consider asking the magazine about freelance insurance when negotiations are underway for such an assignment. The writer should ask the publisher the circumstances under which he would be covered if his article caused any libel action. But don't count on publishers' insurance bailing you out of hot water if you haven't properly researched and written your article. Accuracy is still the best insurance against libel.

Do I Need Permission?

Q. *Do I need the permission of a corporation to publish an article or book about it?*
A. No, and if the company has been treated fairly, you should have no legal problems. However, if the company takes exceptions to any part of your work, you may have a lawsuit for libel on your hands. Even if what you write is true, the company might sue simply as a way of denying what you have written. Books about corporations written without their consent include: *CBS: Reflections in a Bloodshot Eye* by Robert Metz, *Big Mac: the Unauthorized Story of McDonald's* by Max Boas and Steve Chain, and *The Condensed World of The Reader's Digest* by Samuel A. Schreiner Jr. Writers should exercise extreme caution when writing such material and make sure that all facts are verified.

Q. *I am writing the life story of a remarkable woman I knew a couple of years ago who has since died. I'm sure she would have given permission, but I'm not sure her husband would be so willing. Do I need permission to write about someone who isn't in the public eye?*
A. The husband may interpret your work as invading his privacy and institute a lawsuit. It is possible to use the woman's story as the basis for fiction, but you'd have to substantially change the names and situations so that there were no obvious, direct connections between your story and the real people or happenings.

Q. *I want to write a memoir of my World War II experiences. Do I have rights to photos I took while on Air Force assignment?*
A. In situations where you produced photos or other work in connection with your regular duties, you'd have to contact the Air Force to see what their regulations are regarding this. You may need permission from them before you can use the photos.

Q. *If a writer buys a plot from an advertised source, or if a writer pays for extensive help in plotting his story or novel, is the finished product legally and ethically his own?*
A. In both cases, the finished product belongs to the purchaser who has actually produced the written manuscript, even though he has used the help of others and paid them for it. When you've received extensive help on your novel, you could include an acknowledgment in the foreword.

Q. *I recently wrote a short story as an assignment for a correspondence course. When the assignment was returned, a number of specific word changes were suggested. When*

I sell the story, can I legally use the wording suggested by the instructor?
A. It is okay to appropriate revisions of correspondence course instructors. They lay no claim to any word changes made as part of the teaching process.

Q. *I am writing a cookbook in which I am going to use old family recipes adapted to present-day materials. Do I need a release form from people from whom I secured recipes? There will be no payment made, other than a copy of the cookbook.*
A. Yes, you need a release from the people from whom you are assembling recipes for your cookbook. Ask them to sign a form similar to the following: "For value received, I assign the rights to my recipe for _____ to _____ for use in her cookbook, _____." The "value received" is the copy of the cookbook you're going to give each of the contributors.

Q. *If I want to include in an article a remark about a magazine or article I have read, or comment on something I saw on TV, am I free to, or do I have to obtain permission from the writer? I'm not going to quote directly, but will mention actual names.*
A. You may make the comments you wish concerning actual names and places without getting permission from the people involved, but be sure your statements are accurate and not libelous.

Q. *I have written a song based on another writer's poem. Some words are different, but others are words of the original author. Is this legal? If not, how can I get permission from the original author? Could I use the music from another original song or do I need the consent of the composer? I have written "answers" to several hit songs. The words are different, but they fit the original music.*
A. You cannot use music or a number of words from another writer's song if the copyright is still in effect on that song. If you want to use older songs, check the directory, *Variety Music Cavalcade,* to determine if the copyright is still in effect on the songs in question. This book lists songs by title and tells when the copyright was originally issued. It also gives the name of the publishing company to whom you should write to inquire about permission to use parts of the song. Check *Billboard's International Buyer's Guide* for publishers of current songs.

Source Worries

Q. *Is it unethical to print information that a source has labeled off-the-record or not-for-attribution?*
A. If you have taken information off-the-record or not-for-attribution, then you are obligated to keep it that way. Failure to do so can damage your reputation as a trustworthy writer and harm your chances of getting information from that source in the future. Some writers have the practice of telling sources who want to speak off-the-record that they don't want such information. These writers reason that they may already have the information from another source, or that the present source might be convinced to reveal the facts on-the-record later.

Q. *Can a person I interview for an article be sued by a third party he mentions in the interview? Can the writer be sued for what the interviewee said?*
A. The interviewee can be sued for libel or defamation by the third person. The writer and publisher of the interviewee's statements can also be sued. A writer, therefore, should not include such possibly libelous statements unless he can prove their truth if challenged.

When Fact Becomes Fiction

Q. *If I write a true story, but change the names, is it fiction or nonfiction?*
A. If the story is a factual account, with only the names changed, then it would be nonfiction. One example of this type of writing is *Cold Storage* by Wendall Rawls Jr. The book is an exposé of the horrible conditions at a hospital for the criminally insane. Most of the patients' names were changed, as were the names of hospital personnel.

Q. *Can I use the names of famous people in my fiction?*
A. Using the famous as characters in your fiction causes no problems as long as they are depicted in a favorable light. However, if your work makes negative allegations about the people involved, you could be asking for a lawsuit. Famous authors have used celebrities in their stories, but beginners should play it safe and use fictitious characters.

Q. *Can I base my fictional characters on real people, only change their names?*
A. Even if you change their names, real people might think readers would recognize them and consider your work an invasion of their privacy. If these people believe they are shown in an unfavorable light, they might sue for libel. It's safer to make a composite character with traits and characteristics culled from several people. It's more creative to alter the events and characters of real life, since they are rarely suitable for use in fiction without some authorial control.

Q. *I've used a man I knew as the central character of a personal account that I plan to use to start my article. I refer to him as "Bill S." and I'm using made-up quotes and other details to illustrate the situation. Can I do this?*
A. What you might do instead is use a composite character—the creation of a fictitious person who symbolizes several people by combining their experiences, attitudes and/or quotes. This technique is useful when the writer needs to protect individual identities or to avoid having numerous people make similar comments. The writer using this technique should always advise the editor of the fact, so the editor can in turn inform the readers. Newspaper writer Janet Cooke lost a Pulitzer Prize because she didn't let her *Washington Post* editor know that her young drug user "Jimmy" was a composite.

Q. *In a book of personal experiences, is it permissible to use real names and to relate* *real episodes without obtaining written permission from the persons mentioned? Or should characters and events be fictionalized?*

A. It's advisable to change the names of real persons and the locale of real episodes to avoid suits for invasion of privacy by the parties concerned. Even if your reference is complimentary, the individual sometimes resents being placed in the public spotlight and goes to court to prove his point.

Q. *What rules pertain to fictionalizing an actual event? The event was a semiscientific experiment that was unique and widely publicized, so the event and all its participants would be easily recognized. Because military security is still in effect about the experiment, I am sure there is no possibility of doing a factual piece on the subject. Where and how is the line drawn between fact and fiction in such a case? To what degree would the event and characters have to be changed to make them fictitious?*

A. You may use a similar idea in a fiction plot, but you would be wise to surround it with a new, invented set of characters (e.g., one character could be made considerably younger than the real-life one and given different personal traits and appearance), and sufficiently altered circumstances (perhaps in a different locale) so that the resultant story will be the product of your own creativity rather than straight reporting.

Q. *I am doing research for a proposed biographical novel. The famous people on whom I am basing my novel lived in the early 1800s. I am not always able to get to an original letter or document written by the subject, so I am taking material from factual books by other authors in which they quote from these originals. Can you tell me the rules about biographical novels? Must I get permission from all the authors I have read in order to provide character dialogue? Must I get permission from the people who have the original letters, manuscripts or documents, if I can find them? And how about a book that was written in this 1800 period by the famed person himself? May I use his material to build my character? Could living descendents of these famed people object?*

A. In a novel of this type, you could acknowledge, in an introduction or preface, the sources on which the factual material is based. Write to the book publishers, describing your project and asking their permission to use information in the letters they published. To be on the safe side, you might also write to the publisher of the book written by the famous character himself, requesting permission to make use of that material. As for the descendants, there is the delicate question of the "right of privacy." Since each state has its own laws about this right, consult a lawyer who could advise you how much latitude you have under law. Incidentally, a fact worth remembering is that playwright-producer Dore Schary paid $18,615 to Franklin D. Roosevelt, Jr. to compensate for "loss of privacy" brought about by *Sunrise at Campobello.*

Q. *Can a writer legally use the name of a business firm in fiction if the story doesn't reflect uncomplimentarily on the business?*

A. Well-known companies do not look unfavorably on a little free advertising inbedded in a nationally distributed piece of fiction, provided such usage is strictly for purposes of atmosphere and realism. Nothing even remotely illegal or distasteful should be connected with the company name. For example, if your story deals with a criminal who dupes a department store, you'd be on safer ground if you used a fictitious company name, to avoid the possible impression that the real store is not smart enough to escape being duped. As a rule, when in doubt, fictionalize.

Copyright Concerns

Q. *A recently published book of cartoons around a single theme has given me the idea for a similar book based on a related concept. Can I use this idea?*
A. You are probably in the clear. After all, it's impossible to copyright an idea. The only possible problem would be if the publisher felt you were taking advantage of the book's success and trying to cash in on it by modifying their idea. In that case, they might be able to challenge you on the basis of unfair competition and try to get an injunction preventing you from selling your book. Your best plan of action would be to submit the idea, along with a couple of sample cartoons, to a potential publisher and see what its reaction would be. This would be your best guideline on what is legally permissible in this situation.

Q. *I have been writing a vocabulary column that I would like to sell to small newspapers. Without realizing it, my column is much like a column printed in* Reader's Digest. *Is there a copyright on the column? If I sold my newspaper column, would I have to get permission from the author? I am not using the same words, but my test methods resemble his.*
A. Although the column title, "It Pays To Enrich Your Word Power," is a registered trademark, the column's actual test method is a simple multiple choice format: the word, followed by the possible definitions a, b, c, and d from which the person chooses the correct answer. The individual words and choices of definition could be copyrighted, but the test format itself could not; many textbooks and universities use the multiple-choice format.

Q. *I haven't written nonfiction articles because I don't know where "research" ends and plagiarism begins. Where do you draw the line?*
A. If long passages are lifted verbatim, the writer must get permission from the copyright owner. Ideas can't be copyrighted, so after you've researched the facts, simply relate them in your own words. Make certain you use only *facts* from a work, rather than the author's conclusions or observations. Facts belong to everybody, but an author's conclusions and opinions are his alone.

Q. *I recently found a pre-1850 magazine that has a piece I would like to publish. The magazine's so old it's in the public domain. Can I retype the piece and submit it to a magazine?*
A. Not under your name. While such use is possible without copyright infringe-

ment, it violates all standards of ethics for a writer. Such an act is called plagiarism. You would in essence be a thief, having stolen someone else's work and passed it off as your own. If you plagiarize another's work and people find out about it, you will have ruined your reputation as a writer.

Q. *I read a story in which the main character had many suppositions as to how his adventure would end. None was right. I want to write a short story using one of these suppositions for my ending, but my story would have to be very close to the original. Is this plagiarism?*
A. It's not exactly plagiarism, but if you use the original author's character in a replay of his story, it would probably be considered copyright infringement. You wouldn't want another writer using *your* situations and characters, would you? Originality is your best bet.

Q. *I'm working on a photo essay that necessitates my taking photos from the television screen. Is there any legal problem involved in my doing this?*
A. You may be guilty of copyright infringement since most TV shows are copyrighted. Check with the individual producers of the shows.

Chapter 37

Are There Any Business Tips I Need to Know?

As new writers quickly discover, the actual writing of a manuscript is only part of the battle. You still must market your work, negotiate with editors, and keep track of the finances. When you're rich and famous, you can afford to hire bookkeepers and accountants to do this for you. Until such happy times, you must keep accurate and complete records of all your expenses. After all, you never know when the IRS might come to call. For more information on the topics presented here, see Gregg Levoy's *This Business of Writing* (Writer's Digest Books).

Taxing Matters

Q. *I'm just starting out as a freelancer. How do I handle my bookkeeping?*
A. First, set up a separate checking account for your writing business; this will make it easy for you to keep track of income and expenses related to writing, and keep them separate from your other income and expenses. For the beginner, a single-entry account book is adequate. This method has one column each for you to record expenses and income. Each entry should be verified at the end of the month with your canceled checks. Avoid paying cash for writing expenses; if you must, establish a petty cash fund, putting money in the fund each month and keeping receipts for cash outlays.

You'll need to keep a filing system for all your receipts so you can verify expenses at the end of the month. A budget sheet for each month can help you keep track of any problems arising in your writing business—what expenses are exceeding expectations, which markets aren't buying as much as you had planned, etc. A file for submissions helps you keep tabs on your marketing track record, what you submitted where, how long ago, what you were paid, etc.

These simple procedures will get you started. As your writing business gets more successful, you'll probably want to consider a more detailed system. Many computer software companies make programs that help keep track of finances. Contact a local computer store for recommendations.

Q. *I've been writing for years, but I don't make a lot of sales. Can I still take business* *deductions for writing-related expenses?*

A. If you've been pursuing a writing career for years without much success, the IRS may challenge your deductions on the basis that you did not have any profit motive in writing, and therefore you were writing only as a hobby, not as a business. In that case, you would only be able to deduct expenses up to the amount of income you made from writing, whereas if the IRS regarded your writing as a business, you could deduct any business expenses, even if they exceeded any profit from writing. One guideline used by the IRS is that you must make a profit in three out of five consecutive years, or you cannot deduct losses as a "business." You'd be considered a hobbyist.

Federal regulation lists these nine criteria that the IRS considers to determine if a writer is writing for profit: 1) the manner in which the taxpayer conducts the activity; 2) expertise of the taxpayer; 3) time and effort the taxpayer spends on the activity; 4) expectations that assets used in the activity may appreciate; 5) taxpayer success in similar activities; 6) taxpayer's history of income or losses in the activity; 7) the amount of the occasional profits, if any, that are earned; 8) taxpayer's finances; and 9) element of personal pleasure or recreation. Remember, too, that tax laws change every year, and these changes might affect your status. So keep informed.

Q. *When can I begin taking my writing expenses as deductions on my income tax return? What kinds of things can I deduct?*

A. If you have made any amount of profit from your writing—in other words, if your earnings are greater than your writing-related expenses—you must pay income tax. However, you cannot claim deductions unless you make a profit in three of five consecutive years. If you don't meet this test, the government considers your writing as a hobby, not as a business. Keeping detailed records is important when claiming deductions. Writing supplies, including paper, carbons, pens, ribbons, and mailing and copying costs are deductible. Typewriters, word processors and other equipment can be depreciated. Courses and conferences can also be deducted, as long as they were to enhance or refresh writing skills; you can also deduct transportation, lodging and meal expenses when traveling for business purposes. Be sure to keep accurate records when traveling for business purposes. Write down the mileage before starting out and when arriving home or at new point of outset and indicate the writing job covered by those miles. Dues to writers organizations are also deductible.

Q. *I don't have an office outside my home, but I write in my home and have sold a few freelance articles. Is there any way I can deduct my home work space on my tax return?*

A. A home office can be deducted, but only up to the amount of your writing income, and only if it is a room or distinct portion of a room set aside for writing alone, and is used on a regular basis. For example, if you rent a five-room apartment, and use one room only for research and writing, you can deduct one-fifth of your rent, heat and electric bills. If you own a seven-room house, and have a writing room that represents one-seventh of the total space, your deductions can include one-seventh of your total interest on your mortgage, real estate taxes, repairs to the house, utilities, home insurance premiums, and depreciation on the room. In either case, any long-distance phone calls and similar home expenses directly related to your writing are deductible. If you have a second phone in your home office used just for your business, then, of course, the entire cost of that phone is deductible.

In the late 1980s and early 1990s the government severely tightened the restrictions on home-office deductions. It's crucial that you check the appropriate IRS publications or consult a tax expert annually for new regulations.

Q. *If I take a vacation and pick up information on that trip that I later use in my writing, can I deduct the trip as a business expenditure?*
A. If the trip is a mixture of business and pleasure, then the author must keep accurate records of how much time he spent on business during the trip and only deduct that percentage of the costs. For example, if you took a trip to California for three weeks, and spent a week of the time researching an article about the movie business, while the remaining two weeks were spent visiting relatives, you could only deduct one-third of your expenses for travel and lodging. If the entire trip were spent on business, then all such expenses could be deducted if you can produce receipts and records to that effect. (Only 80 percent of meals and entertainment costs are now deductible, not 100 percent as before 1986.) You must also be able to prove to the IRS that you're a business, not a hobby writer.

Q. *I write for outdoor, travel, recreation, and other such magazines. Can I deduct any costs related to my recreational vehicle or boat as business expenses?*
A. Much like the stipulations for travel expenses, the amount you can deduct on these vehicles would depend on what percentage of their use is related to your writing. If you spend one-fourth of your time on each in the pursuit of freelancing, then that amount of the maintenance and repair costs for each could be deducted. However, the IRS would probably assume that you use the vehicles for your own pleasure and recreation too, so it's doubtful you could deduct these expenses in full. Keep a "ship's log" of your travels with these vehicles, along with receipts and documentation that they were being used for business.

Q. *The magazines for which I've worked have paid me the fee and expense money in one check. Since business expenses aren't real earnings, how do I treat this on my tax forms?*
A. Since publishers don't have a convenient method for separating business expenses from payment for manuscripts, they usually send one check to cover both. You can, however, deduct your expenses on your IRS tax form. Even though reimbursed expenses are shown as gross income on your tax form, they would be deducted before figuring the net income on which your tax is paid.

Finding Professional Help

Q. *How can I find a freelance editor to help me with my manuscripts?*
A. Check the "Editorial Services" listings in *Literary Market Place.* You'll find many editorial services, freelance editors, and book doctors who might help you with your work. There's also a cross-reference listing each by field of activity. Write to several and compare their fees.

Q. *I am going to tape record the second draft of a novel. What is the fastest talking pace for a good typist to get everything down on paper and the exact wording to indicate punctuation, parentheses, italics, spacing, etc.*
A. Record at your own pace. The typist will adjust her speed accordingly. A good typist should be able to punctuate correctly from the way in which the lines are spoken. Indicate parentheses by saying, "Open parentheses" and "Close parentheses." Say "Underline" when you want italics, and say "Paragraph" when you want to start a new paragraph. Before you begin, you can explain that you want double-spacing except where you indicate otherwise, and indicate margin width, etc. Remember that all instructions throughout the tape should precede the dictation. Have your typist try a sample chapter to see if your recorded instructions are easy to follow.

Q. *What should I look for in a lawyer?*
A. To find a lawyer versed in publishing and copyright law, contact the local lawyers referral service of your state or city bar association. Be sure the lawyer knows something about laws that pertain to publishing. "Publishing law is not particularly arcane," says publishing veteran Carol Meyer, "but is based on accepted ways of doing business, and a lawyer inexperienced with these customs and procedures can create a lot of confusion and unnecessary fuss."

Q. *How can a full-time freelancer provide for retirement?*
A. Since the full-time freelance writer has no employer to provide a pension plan, if he wishes to have retirement benefits, he must set aside funds himself. The federal government has provided two ways for the freelancer to do this. In 1962, Congress passed the Keogh Act, which allows a self-employed individual to establish a retirement fund—contributions to which are deductible and the income of which is tax-free—until he begins to make withdrawals when he retires and his tax bracket is lower. The law allows the person to deposit up to 15 percent of his net annual income, subject to a certain maximum per year, in an Internal Revenue Service approved account. He may then deduct this payment on his income tax for that year. He may not make withdrawals until he is 59½ years old; he must have begun withdrawals by the time he reaches 70½ years. The owner of the account isn't required to deposit money every year. If he makes a withdrawal prior to reaching age 59½ he will be subject to a 10 percent penalty on the amount withdrawn.
    Another way for a writer to provide for retirement is to start an Individual

Retirement Account (IRA). The maximum amount per year you can invest in an IRA varies depending on your status. Consult IRS Publication 560 on Keogh Plans and IRS Publication 590 on IRAs.

Information about Keogh and IRA accounts is available from banks, savings and loan associations, and your local Internal Revenue Service office.

Q. *Are there any special provisions an author should make when drawing up a will?*
A. When a writer dies, his literary works remain for someone to look after. In the will, the writer may specify who is to inherit the copyrights to his works and who is to receive any royalties after his death. He may also appoint a person to make artistic decisions about his work after his death, such as whether and under what circumstances unpublished works may be published posthumously.

Building a Reputation

Q. *How can I promote my work and myself?*
A. For a freelancer, one of the best techniques to help boost sales is to keep his name in front of the public and editors. There are a number of ways to do this. Lecture dates can help keep interested parties aware of what you're writing, and get them to buy your book or the magazine in which your series of articles appears. The small response of a lecture audience can grow by word of mouth, leading to successful sales. Send published material to editors you've known who might be interested in a particular work; doing this can lead to reprint rights sales or assignments on related topics. Sending "For Your Information" clips of your work to editors and former interview subjects can keep your name fresh in their minds. You can send out news releases to appropriate newspapers and magazines for any of your writing-related activities, whether lecture appearances, a new book, or a series of magazine articles on a given topic that might be of interest. TV and radio stations can receive this information too; a media interview can let readers know about your work. If you've published a book, work with your publisher's publicity department to suggest any avenues of promotion related to your special expertise.

Q. *When I visited a corporation's library to research a project, I was denied entry by officials who said I needed "credentials proving I'm a writer." A press pass would have helped. Are there any organizations that provide writers with the backing, credentials and benefits of say, an industry union?*
A. There are many freelance writers organizations designed to meet the needs of specific groups of writers—The National Writers Union, American Society of Journalists and Authors, and The Authors Guild, among others. There are also many groups for writers in specific genres—The Romance Writers of America, The Mystery Writers of America, among others. You can find addresses and phone numbers in *Literary Market Place* and the *Encyclopedia of Associations* in your library. If you're not already a member of such groups you might consider it. Otherwise try to get letters from individual publishers while you're working on a project

to present as your credentials. Perhaps your approach needs polishing. Many writers never show press cards and are welcomed courteously.

Q. *I did some ghostwriting for a friend who wanted to self-publish a book. I'm breaking into other fields of writing now, but have few published credits except for this book. Can I use this as a sample of my writing to show an editor?*
A. The nature of ghostwriting is exactly what the name implies: work by an unseen hand. Ghostwriters receive money for their work, but the "author" receives all credit. Therefore, you must receive permission from your friend before revealing to anyone that his book is your work.

Me, the Publisher

Q. *I'd like information about how to start a literary magazine. Where can I learn more about this project?*
A. Direct your questions to the Committee of Small Magazine Editors and Publishers (COSMEP) at P.O. Box 420703, San Francisco CA 94142-0703, (415) 922-9490.

Q. *I am trying to start a small magazine and I need advice. Do I have to register with any state office? How do I handle having it printed? What about advertising? Can I have it distributed on newsstands or would I have to sell subscriptions? As owner and publisher, could I be sued for what is printed?*
A. The first thing to do when starting a new magazine is to determine if an audience exists for your idea. Are there lists available of potential subscribers? Are potential advertisers a likely source of revenue?

Make up an editorial "dummy" — a facsimile of the finished magazine — and get bids from printers, based on the number of copies you want to print. Then you'll have to decide whether your costs will be covered by income from subscriptions and newsstand sales or from circulation *and* advertising revenues. Your local post office can give you information on obtaining a second-class mailing permit.

If you elect to use advertising, check the *Standard Directory of Advertisers* to find out which agencies handle ads for companies you would like to advertise in your magazine. Figure out an advertising page rate based on your planned circulation. Develop a list of prospective subscribers and work with an advertising letter shop on how to find subscribers through direct mail. You'll have to notify the department of taxation in your state of your decision to start publication; if you'll have a number of employees, you'll also have to pay workmen's compensation and work out any other legal requirements. Your city may also require you to obtain a vendor's license or file notice of your venture.

As owner and publisher, you could be involved in any lawsuits for libel, invasion of privacy, or copyright infringement that might arise from an article you publish. You could also be sued for nonpayment of debts, should you neglect to pay any bills. A magazine requires much hard work and investment, so you should examine your plan carefully before starting to work.

Q. *I'm starting a magazine and have decided on a title. How do I check to make sure the title isn't already in use?*

A. Titles cannot be copyrighted, so you should have no trouble using the title of your choice. However, some magazines have had their titles registered as trademarks by their owners who have well-established use of the title. Obviously, you should avoid such imitative use of currently successful magazine titles. You can research in-use titles in *Oxbridge Communications's Standard Periodical Directory*, available in most libraries, or phone (212) 741-0231. Libraries also have directories of trademarks. Another option is to hire an attorney to conduct a title search, a job which could run from as little as a few hundred dollars to $1,500 or more.

Chapter 38

What Do I Need to Know About Book Publishing?

The majority of freelance writers don't have agents, so when they have a book project and want to approach a publisher, they're pretty much on their own. They read reports in the *New York Times* or *Publishers Weekly* about million-dollar advances and escalator clauses in best-selling authors contracts, and try to equate that with the modest terms of their own first book contract. They want the best deal possible without jeopardizing the sale. Here are some basics about book publishing to help beginners. For an insider's look at the book business, see *Beyond the Bestseller* by literary agent Richard Curtis (NAL Books).

Inside a Publishing House

Q. *How does a book publisher handle an unsolicited manuscript? If the first person to read the manuscript doesn't like it, does it go any further or is it rejected then and there? If he thinks it has possibilities, does it then go to a second and third reader? Also, does a standard rejection slip without any comment usually indicate that the manuscript did not arouse any interest at all with that particular publishing house?*
A. The first reader is as eager to find a bestseller as you are to write one. Through his experience and training he is able to spot those unsolicited manuscripts that show promise and those that do not. If he feels the manuscript has no market potential, he will reject it then and there. If it has possibilities, it may be given to another reader or to an editor. By a process of consultation and elimination the marketable manuscripts are decided upon. A standard rejection slip can mean several different things: They may have just bought a similar novel, they've already asked one of their other authors to do a similar book, or they don't think they could make money with that particular book, even though some member of the staff may have found some degree of merit in the work.

Q. *Once a writer submits his final manuscript to the publisher and it is accepted, what part does he play in the production process?*
A. First of all, you'll have to read the copyedited manuscript and respond to any challenges of fact or clarify any vague statements. Then you'll have to read either

galley proofs (the typeset copy prior to actual page makeup) or page proofs, if the publisher works with word processors and does not use galley proofs. These must be checked for errors on the part of the typesetter, or last-minute corrections you may have previously overlooked. In special cases, such as illustrated books, the publisher may wish you to review a photocopy of the pasteup to proofread the captions for illustrations. If your book is nonfiction, you may be responsible for providing an index. Usually the publisher will hire the indexer at the author's expense (this could cost $500) and this appears as a deduction on the first royalty statement. You'll have to proofread the contents page, the glossary, and the bibliography if there are any, plus the acknowledgments page where any copyright permissions appear, along with any thanks for research help or access to special documents, etc. You'll be asked to review the jacket copy and your biographical information, along with the photograph if you provided one.

Q. *Why are some books published in hardback and others in paperback?*
A. Originally, most paperbacks were reprints of hardcover books. But today, many publishers of paperbacks buy original fiction and nonfiction — especially of the types that can be sold to large numbers of buyers. Hundreds of thousands of people will pay $3.95 for a romance novel, but won't pay $15.95 for a hardcover book. Other kinds of book buyers will buy the latest nonfiction book or mainstream novel by a best-selling author and pay the hardcover price.

Q. *What is a book packager?*
A. A book packager is a middleman supplying books to publishers. He may supply the books in any form, from raw manuscript to mechanicals (pasted-up, camera-ready type), films for platemaking or bound copies. The packager usually signs a contract with a publisher, then signs a different one with the writer based on what he thinks he can get the writer to do the work for, and what the writer thinks he's worth for that particular job. Some packagers pay the writer a flat fee, others split the advance and royalty with the author on a basis that may be fifty/fifty or some other terms. In either case, the author may not make as much money as he could if he sold his own book idea directly to a publisher. On the other hand, if the book packager has sold a set number of books to the publisher, the packager will be paid upon publication. This means that the author usually gets paid right away; whereas in the case of a regularly published book, the author has to wait another nine months or so for that first royalty statement and check. Also, depending on the packager's contract with the publisher, if the packager sells fifteen thousand copies, the author gets paid for fifteen thousand, not fifteen thousand minus, say, six thousand books that eventually are returned.

Submitting Books

Q. *What's the best book I could write to make sure I'd be published?*
A. Former *Writer's Digest* editor Bill Brohaugh says it best: "The best book you can

write to be published is *your* best book." In other words, your best shot at selling a book to a publisher is to write about what you want to write about, and write it as well as you can. It doesn't necessarily matter what's currently selling; the book business is full of unknowns and unexpecteds. Who would have ever thought that a philosophical novel about a bird, or the story of a Mafia family could have become best-sellers? It happened with Richard Bach's *Jonathan Livingston Seagull* and Mario Puzo's *The Godfather*. If anybody doubted the observations of a harried housewife, the life story of a Yorkshire veterinarian, or an eccentric English lady's tips on dog training would be successful, Erma Bombeck, James Herriot, and Barbara Woodhouse proved them wrong.

If you're writing a genre book such as a romance novel, you will have to follow some rather specific guidelines. Beyond that, however, choose whatever interests *you* and query a publisher with a good letter and a solid proposal, including sample chapters, to convince her that others will be informed, inspired or entertained by what you've written.

Q. *What are the steps to getting my book published?*
A. First, read the listings for book publishers in *Writer's Market* to find which companies would be most likely to have an interest in your manuscript. Check libraries and bookstores to see which publishers have published books that are compatible with your interests. Make a list of several suitable publishers. Settle on your most likely publisher and send him a query letter outlining a proposal for your book with at least a few sentences on each chapter's contents and an offer of a sample chapter. If your book is nonfiction, it would also be helpful to explain why you think the book you're proposing is different from, and better than, any others that have been published in the same field. The editor also wants to know the market for your book and how many prospective buyers there are.

Be sure to enclose a SASE for reply so the publisher can let you know whether he would be interested in seeing more. After that, it's up to the publisher to decide whether he is interested in your book. If the publisher says "No," go on to the next publisher on your list. Sometimes finding the right company to publish your book can take a while.

Q. *I published my own book. I'd like to query commercial publishers about a second edition, but how can I approach them about this idea?*
A. Submit a copy of your book to several publishers along with a concise description of it, and indicate what you consider the market potential for the book, details on the sales record you achieved on your own, and any other pertinent information likely to convince them to invest in your project. Include copies of notable reviews and special promotional contacts you may have. You should mention that you are making a simultaneous submission of this book to a number of publishers and would appreciate a response from them as to whether or not they would be interested in publishing a second edition.

Q. *When submitting a proposal to a book publisher, should a synopsis be an overall or abbreviated chapter-by-chapter content? How extensive should an outline be?*
A. A synopsis should provide a comprehensive summary of the contents in about two typewritten pages. An outline could cover chapter-by-chapter highlights.

Q. *When submitting a book manuscript to a publisher, what data concerning rights should be attached?*
A. It's not necessary to discuss the matter of rights when submitting a book manuscript to a publisher. If they decide to publish the book, the contract they draw up and present to you will have all the rights provisions spelled out. If you agree with them, you can sign the contract; if you don't, you can discuss it further with them before coming to terms.

Q. *I can write a good introduction for my book, but wouldn't it be better if a specialist in the field wrote the introduction?*
A. An introduction by a specialist lends more authority to a book. This is usually handled by the publisher. In your cover letter, indicate that you know of several prominent persons in the field who might be willing to write an introduction if the publisher is interested in the book.

Q. *Are book forewords paid for or are most of them complimentary? A well-known author knew the subject of a biography I am about to publish and I'd like to ask him to write the foreword for my book. Will he expect payment, and if so, how much should I offer him?*
A. Most are complimentary, but people who write forewords are sometimes offered an honorarium. If offered, rate depends on several things: length required, the "name" of the person who is asked to write the foreword, the complexity of the material to be written. Rates range from one hundred to five hundred dollars and up. It depends on how much work is involved — if the author knows the subject of a biography you are about to publish and if that author is a good friend of the subject, he may be willing to write the foreword as a compliment and may not require payment for it. Suggest to your publisher that this person do the foreword, giving details about why you think he might be the best one to provide a meaningful foreword. In some cases, the publisher will pay the person who writes the foreword, or costs may be split between publisher and author.

Q. *Is it acceptable to submit copies of my book manuscript simultaneously? A playwright I know says that if two editors make offers, then you can take the best offer or even bargain. Is it all right to do this without telling editors it is a simultaneous submission?*
A. Many writers who have tired of the long wait for replies from publishers have adopted this technique. Some writers advise the editor it's a multiple submission. Others say no, they'll worry about that if they get more than one acceptance.

Q. *My partner and I have sent several query letters to different publishers to see if they were interested in our children's book. We received a letter from a publisher who said he would like to see the material immediately, so we sent it to him. In the meantime, we have received answers to all our letters, all saying they are interested and would like to see the material.´ Can you tell us the best way to answer these letters?*

A. You have two choices. You can write to the other publishers saying that your book is currently being considered by another company and enclose a copy of the manuscript. This might either heighten their interest or turn them off completely, depending on the editor. The other possibility is to write the other publishers saying you had decided to revise your manuscript before submitting it to them and that as soon as you have done that you'll send it to them. This will buy you a little time while waiting for the first publisher's decision.

Q. *Some authors have more than one publisher, others seem to stay with the same one. Why is this?*

A. Some authors produce books that are not handled by their original publisher — for example, science fiction novels and specialized books on golf. Other authors have publishers that produce a wide range of fiction and nonfiction in both hardcover and paperback. They are satisfied with the way their books are published and promoted, so they stay with one company.

Contractual Matters

Q. *Is an author required to furnish a large sum of money before his book is published? If photos are in the book, will these cost extra?*

A. Only if his book is published by a subsidy publisher will the author have to pay. Trade publishers assume all regular production costs and usually pay the author an advance against potential royalty earnings. Photos increase the cost of publishing a book, and the author's contract with the publisher will determine who absorbs this extra expense. Black-and-white photographs are less expensive than color photographs.

Q. *What are the elements of a standard book contract and what terms should the author agree to?*

A. There is no standard book contract — terms vary depending on the type of book, how it is sold, the track record of the author and other factors. The Authors Guild recommends that authors negotiate for royalty percentages on trade hardcover books of 10 percent of the retail price on the first five thousand copies, 12½ percent on the next five thousand and 15 percent thereafter. Publishers of textbooks and other specialized nonfiction books, however, often base their royalty percentages not on the retail price but on the publisher's net receipts — that is, the retail price less the bookstore discount, and often it is a flat percentage, not a sliding scale. Royalty contracts offered on paperbacks vary widely, but some common ones on trade paperbacks are: 6 percent on the first twenty thousand copies and 7½ percent thereafter. Mass-market original paperback royalties are often 6 percent on net copies sold—the number of copies distributed minus the number of returns. And, of course, since paperback reprint rights are usually split 50 percent between author and original hardcover publisher, that means the author's royalty would only be 3 percent on a paperback reprint. Heavily illustrated children's books may split a 10 percent royalty (based on either retail price or net receipts) between author and artist.

Copyright should be in the author's name and the author may or may not grant "all rights" exclusively to the publisher or may share the rights to foreign editions, recordings or movie contracts on a non-exclusive basis.

A summary of other contract terms appears in the appendix to the *Writer's Encyclopedia* and recommends ideals the established author should negotiate. Obviously the beginner with no previous publishing credits will probably have to settle for less.

Q. *If a publisher sends me a contract and I don't agree with certain parts of it but I do want that publisher to handle the book, what is the proper procedure? Should I cross out the questionable sections, sign it and return it? Or should I return the contract unsigned, with explanatory notes on the parts I don't like in the hope that the publisher will make the changes I want and send it back?*
A. Handling the problem clauses by phone or mail is the usual practice. Contact the editor who issued the contract by phone and discuss the changes you want. If you handle negotiation by mail, you don't have to return the contract, since the publisher knows the contents. Just send a letter outlining your objections and the publisher will look it over and make his decision. Crossing out objectionable portions and signing the contract can be a good, aggressive way to get your point across, but this practice usually doesn't work for a beginner with no published books. If you've already had three or four books published, this tactic might work. But make sure you have a little clout before trying it.

Q. *What is an advance, and when does the author receive it? If it is indeed an advance on royalties, what happens if the book doesn't sell well? Does the author have to give the advance back?*
A. An advance is an amount of money a publisher pays a writer before the book is published, in partial consideration for the time and effort the writer expends in producing the work. Often, the advance is a gauge of how well the publisher thinks the book will sell; advances are usually computed as a percentage of a book's estimated first-year sales. When sales begin, the amount of the advance is deducted from the author's royalties before any payment is made to the author.

Ideally, the author's contract with the publisher should state that the advance is nonreturnable in the event that it exceeds the amount of royalties actually collected. A contract would also ideally provide that the publisher may not make any attempt to recoup the advance if he decides not to issue the book or that the advance will be repaid only after the book is placed with another publisher.

Advances are usually paid in installments; for example, one-half of the advance might be paid when the author signs the contract and one-half when he delivers a complete manuscript. The amount of advance will vary with the type of book, the author's writing ability and reputation, the type of publisher, and the specific book idea. There may be no advance at all in some cases, and the beginner can receive as little as $500. But as he writes book after book, and his audience and sales increase, he will usually receive increasingly larger advances.

Q. *Do textbook publishers have a standard royalty schedule? Does the same royalty apply to textbooks as well as books in the trade division?*
A. Textbook publishers do not have a standard royalty or the same royalty schedule as trade book publishers. College textbooks may vary from 8 percent to 19 percent of the *net* price the publisher receives, while elementary and secondary texts may be only 3 percent to 5 percent, depending on illustration costs and the amount of staff work that must be done by the publisher.

Q. *What are subsidiary rights and how should they be handled in my contracts?*
A. "Subsidiary" is the classification for all rights to a book other than actual book publication. These rights include paperback reprint, book club, dramatic, radio, television, movie, foreign reprint, foreign language translation, audiovisual production, novelty and serial rights. The author and publisher divide profits from subsidiary rights, with the terms of percentages and who has the right to make subsidiary sales specified in the contract. Authors Guild guidelines suggest that the established author negotiate for at least 80 percent of the earnings on British editions of a book, 75 percent on other foreign reprints, 50 percent on paperback and book club sales, and 90 percent on sales to movie and television production companies. These terms should be discussed and agreed upon by author and publisher and included in any book contract. Actual earnings will, of course, depend on the success of the publisher or author's agent in selling the rights to the book.

Q. *How does an author keep movie and TV rights when a book is published?*
A. Read carefully the clause in your book contract that pertains to those rights. A first-time book author usually can't keep *all* such rights. The Authors Guild recommends that book contracts should give the author 90 percent and the publisher 10 percent of movie and TV sales. Read the contract carefully before signing it and ask questions by phone of the editor who sent it to you about anything you don't understand.

Q. *I sold a novel about fifteen years ago and the contract gave the publisher a sixty-day option on each of my next two novels. He has rejected my second novel since that time, and I'm almost finished with my third. Do I still have to submit it to him first, after all this time? What if he puts the same clause into the new contract?*
A. Although fifteen years have passed, you are still required to submit the third

book to the publisher to satisfy the terms of the contract. You may want to check with a lawyer about the wording of your option clause.

In answer to your second question, *don't sign* a contract with such a clause in it. Option clauses bind the author, not the publisher; this is why the Authors Guild recommends deletion of the clause from a book contract. Also, some option clauses state that the publisher can buy your book at the same price he bought the first; obviously, if the first book is a surprise best-seller, the writer would be able to sell the second book for a lot more money; so would come up the loser in a deal like this.

Until a publisher makes a decision on their option, you cannot submit the book to other publishers. If you must agree to some sort of option clause, novelist Dean Koontz advises limiting it to thirty days. That's long enough for a publisher to make up his mind. And the option clause should indicate that the terms are negotiable at that time.

Some other option items to remember: The option clause time period should not be keyed to publication of the first book, since this may hold up the author for a year on his next book. The author should be free to submit a new proposal anytime after the first book has been accepted by the publisher. Also, the author should not have to submit a complete work under the option clause, but merely an outline and sample chapters.

Q. *My friend says his book contract has a clause that states the manuscript "must be acceptable to the publisher in form and content," and that if it isn't, he must return the advance he was paid. Do most contracts have this clause?*
A. Yes, although there are variations in the wording. Some clauses require the return of the advance only if the manuscript is sold to another publisher; others require it whether the manuscript resells or not. In attempting to avoid the burden to the author when his manuscript is subjectively pronounced unacceptable by his publisher, the Authors Guild recommends a rewording of the clause: "The Author shall deliver a manuscript which in style and content is professional, competent, and fit for publication." Publishers may find manuscripts unacceptable for several reasons. The author didn't deliver what his outline promised, and despite editorial suggestions refuses to revise. The market may have changed and the publisher is dissatisfied more with the terms of the bargain than the manuscript itself. The publisher's lawyers may have concluded that publishing a controversial book would put the house in danger of many lawsuits. All of these reasons help courts decide the good faith of the author or publisher when the unacceptable clause is invoked.

Q. *Will I have any input on the cover design for my novel?*
A. When a publisher accepts a book, he reserves the right to decide on such selling points as title and cover design, but you can make suggestions after the book is accepted. Most publishers usually prefer to work with their own graphic designers.

Q. *After a contract has been signed and the publication date set for my book, what do*

I do if the book isn't released on that date?
A. Whether publication postponements occur due to factors outside of or within a publisher's control, they *do* happen. Production schedules are often juggled when unexpected manuscripts and potential best-sellers bump from the publisher's list other, lower-priority books or "problem manuscripts" that need much work. There should be a specific time of publication inserted in your contract (usually a certain number of months after receipt of an acceptable manuscript). After you've delivered your manuscript, keep in touch with your editor by correspondence. Don't hestitate to ask, "What is the schedule for my book? When should I expect to receive the copyedited manuscript?" If the answers are vague and the time of publication as stated in the contract passes without production of your book, remind the editor with a prodding letter. Follow with a phone call, if necessary. If you still receive no word on when your book will be published, contact your editor's superior, the president of the company. When the delay reaches the point where you feel it's unreasonable, you can legally reclaim the rights to your book and try to sell it to another publisher.

Self- and Subsidy Publishing

Q. *What is "self-publishing" a book?*
A. If an author submits his book and it is published by Random House, Doubleday, or another commercial publisher, the sales, promotion, production, and other facets of publishing are handled by them. If you self-publish your book, you in essence become your own Random House or Doubleday, and all the steps in publishing and marketing a book become your responsibility. You pay for the manufacturing, production, and marketing of your book, but you also keep all the profits. The basic steps in self-publishing are: having the manuscript typewritten or typeset in camera-ready form, planning or hiring the artwork, getting it printed and bound, advertising and distributing the book on consignment to bookstores or selling by direct mail order, keeping records and overseeing the entire publishing process. Each step involves considerable effort and some expense. Before self-publishing, you must decide whether sales of the book will earn enough money to pay back your investment. For more information on how to self-publish, see *The Publish-It-Yourself Handbook* and *How to Get Happily Published.*

Q. *How can I get a Library of Congress catalog card number for my book?*
A. Your publisher's production or editorial department will usually do this for you. If you've self-published your book, apply for the number by contacting the Cataloging in Publication Program, Library of Congress, Washington DC 20540. They'll send you an application to complete. When your book is published, you must then send the Library of Congress a complimentary copy, and they'll determine whether or not to keep the book for their collections and prepare suitable catalog cards.

Q. *My book is now out of print, with all rights reassigned to me. I have the opportunity to self-publish it. Can I use the old plates purchased from the original publisher for this purpose?*
A. As long as you have purchased the plates and have the rights from the original publisher, you can self-publish a reprint of your book using the original plates. You will need to find a printer who is able to use the plates on his press.

Q. *I have recently self-published my book. Where can I find book sellers and distributors to handle it?*
A. *The American Book Trade Directory* (published by R.R. Bowker Co. and available in most libraries) contains a list of names and addresses of major paperback distributors and book wholesalers, as well as bookstores. The work is divided into states and cities for easier reference.

Q. *I am in the process of publishing my own book. How can I notify libraries and advertise at an inexpensive rate?*
A. To call your book to the attention of librarians, send a publicity release or similar newsworthy article to the various library magazines. Ask your librarian to show you some of these publications, such as *Library Journal,* the *ALA Booklist,* etc. Write advertising managers of these publications to learn their less expensive classified advertising rates. Another way to bring your book to the attention of librarians would be to send a mailing to the list of libraries in the *American Library Directory.*

Q. *I have a collection of short pieces, many of which have been purchased and published by periodicals. I plan to offer these for publication in book form and have received letters of release from the periodicals. If I self-publish, will I own the copyright? If I sell the collection to a standard publisher, will he own the copyright?*
A. All books published by standard royalty book publishers are copyrighted in the name of the author. Even if the author pays to have the book published by a subsidy publisher, he should require that the book be copyrighted in his name.

Q. *If I have a book published, have it copyrighted, and advertise and sell a few copies, will I later be able to offer it to a larger publisher, or do you think this would ruin my chances of selling it to a larger firm?*
A. Before printing this book on your own, first see if any "larger publisher" would be interested in it. If you couldn't interest a larger publisher in it before self-publishing, you might still find a buyer later, depending on your own success with the book.

Mimeographed Book?

Q. *I am writing my first book manuscript and I plan to publish my own book. It will be eighty to one hundred pages. I will use letter-size paper folded, making pages about*

$5\frac{1}{2}'' \times 8\frac{1}{2}''$. *Has anyone ever produced a mimeographed paperback book? Can I copyright the mimeographed book? If, after offering it as a mimeographed work, I later wish to have it done by the printer I might choose, would there have to be another copyright?*
A. Mimeographed paperback books have been produced, usually for local sales only. As far as the Copyright Office is concerned, a mimeographed manuscript is a "published work" and can be copyrighted. If you wish to have the mimeographed version redone later by a printer, you would simply show on your copyright page, after your original copyright notice, "Second Printing" and the year.

Q. *I paid for the printing of a small how-to booklet (thirty-four pages), but don't know how to promote it. Could I send it to a publisher and expect it to be accepted, or because I printed it myself, would he refuse it?*
A. A publisher would not necessarily refuse your booklet just because you printed it yourself, but rather because book publishers don't buy such short books. You could sell copies of it to a how-to-do-it magazine that might use it for a subscription premium or for resale to their readers. Or, you might sell copies of it to some manufacturer of how-to tools or materials that might resell it or give it away to customers. An author has to be constantly searching for promotional ideas when promoting a book he's published himself. Paid classified ads in newspapers and magazines bring results, but you must be prepared to mail the books and keep accurate records, including state sales tax, if applicable.

Q. *I have written a book and am considering having it printed, taking out my own copyright, and distributing the book myself until it realizes a market or dies. What kind of license, if any, will I need to sell and distribute my book?*
A. If you are going to sell copies of your book to consumers in your state, you will need a vendor's license and must collect sales tax. Contact the tax department of your state. If there are any local licenses required, you had best clarify this with local city officials. A list of book manufacturers appears in the directory, *Literary Market Place*, R.R. Bowker, 249 W. 17th St., New York NY 10011 (also available at most main branch public library reference departments). You may also wish to contact companies listed under "Printers" in the Yellow Pages.

Q. *Two kinds of ads in writers magazines confuse me. One is for "book printers"; the other is for a company that you pay to publish your book and that calls itself a "publisher" or "press." What's the difference?*
A. The companies calling themselves "publishers" are usually subsidy presses, which produce your book for a fee. They do some advertising and send out review copies. They are discussed elsewhere in this chapter. Book printers print and bind a writer's book, leaving marketing and promotion to him. Local printers are often used by a writer who self-publishes his book; they are listed in the Yellow Pages.

Q. *Is it okay to pay a publisher to handle my book?*
A. Subsidy publishers will issue your book only if you pay for the printing. That's

the difference between subsidy and commercial publishers. Commercial publishers are willing to take a chance on the books they publish, but subsidy publishers make all their profits on the actual printing of books. Subsidy publishers provide minimal promotional effort. They usually agree to distribute copies of the book to reviewers and reprint rights buyers at other publishing companies, but these people usually ignore subsidy publishers' books. Consequently, publicity and sales prospects are not very encouraging. Since there is not a promising market for subsidy-published books, the publisher usually will not bind many copies of the first printing. When the contract expires, the author usually is offered all remaining stock of his title for purchase if he wishes—and that stock is usually in unbound sheets.

True, subsidy publishing *does* permit you to see your work in print, and some 10 percent of those writers who use subsidy presses recoup their losses. But a writer shouldn't subsidy publish unless he has tried without success to sell his book to commercial publishers and is willing to make the investment for an unsure return.

For more information on subsidy publishing, send a SASE to *Writer's Digest,* 1507 Dana Ave., Cincinnati OH 45207. Ask for the free reprint, "Does it pay to have it published?"

Anthologizing

Q. *I want to compile an anthology of essays. Should I secure copyright releases before submitting it? Can I copyright the anthology?*
A. You shouldn't get copyright releases before submitting to a publisher since a publisher may not want some selections and may want others not included in the original manuscript. After the manuscript is accepted, you should write the requests for permission, citing chapter and page, and preferably, also including a copy of the passage. Any reprint fees are usually paid for by the publisher, but deducted from the anthologist's royalties before he gets paid.

Anthologies may be copyrighted in the name of the author/editor or the publisher, depending on the type of book and the terms of the contract. The use of essays in your anthology does not inhibit their future use in some other anthology.

Q. *Over the years I've collected many articles on a particular topic that interests me. If they were compiled into an anthology, they would make very interesting reading. Putting together an anthology doesn't sound too difficult, but I don't know where to start. Any suggestions?*
A. Rather than jumping into the preparation of a full manuscript, send some queries first to find an interested publisher. With your query, include photocopies of the first pages of a few selections to be included. You may have trouble selling your idea because many editors feel that a book written by a single author stands a better chance for big sales. In your query, establish your authority in the subject area to be covered. You should know your subject well, or you'll have trouble compiling enough material for a book in a reasonable amount of time. You will have to work hard to convince an editor that your topic is important and warrants his risk in publication.

Chapter 39

Where Can I Find Writers Groups, Conferences and Colonies?

Writing can be a lonely art. If you don't know other writers, it can be difficult to get critiques and suggestions for improving manuscripts. Often writers feel isolated from others involved in the trade. But a multitude of local and national writers organizations, writers conferences and writing workshops can ease this sense of isolation. Such opportunities allow us to network, learn new skills and techniques — and socialize with kindred spirits.

Groups for Writers

Q. *Should I join a local writers club? How can I find one in my area?*
A. There are many different opinions on the value of writers clubs, basically because there are many different types of clubs. A good club can provide the opportunity for you to establish friendships and contacts while gaining valuable tips from professionals who are currently writing and selling. Clubs that criticize manuscripts honestly, discuss only writing-related topics and invite prominent local writers to speak, instill motivation and zest in their members and are an essential lifeline to what's going on in the publishing world today. If you find a club in your area with these qualities, it would be a good idea to join. Writers need camaraderie.

Writers dislike some groups because they have a nonprofessional atmosphere where the emphasis is more on socializing than criticizing manuscripts or studying the markets and learning from each others' experiences. Others don't like clubs that allow their members to read their own work in a self-glorifying manner. Avoid clubs that have these amateurish characteristics, as well as those which seem to do nothing other than sit around and gripe about lack of sales.

Your local librarian or newspaper book critic may have names and addresses of clubs in your area. Or if there is no local club in your area and you'd like to start one, send fifty cents and a business-size SASE for a copy of "How to Start/Run a Writers Club" to Writer's Digest Books, 1507 Dana Ave., Cincinnati OH 45207.

Q. *Should I join a national writers organization? Are there specific organizations for different types of writers?*

A. Membership in a national professional writing group can help you establish a professional image, as it increases your visibility and may help you land assignments. Some of these organizations can also help you by acting as your representative in certain legal cases or disputes, as well as giving you access to specialized information and publications. Most national organizations require that you qualify for membership as a "professional," which may mean having sold to various reputable publications or publishers.

There are organizations for just about every type of writer, from the Mystery Writers of America to the Poetry Society of America. You can find addresses and phone numbers in the *Encyclopedia of Associations* and *Literary Market Place*, available at your library. You should join the organization that is aimed at your field of writing. Membership fees are usually under fifty to one hundred dollars. A helpful organization for beginners is the National Writers Club, 1450 S. Havana, Suite 620, Aurora CO 80012.

Q. *Is there a professional organization for magazine writers?*
A. Yes, the American Society of Journalists and Authors. It is located at 1501 Broadway, Suite 302, New York NY 10036, (212) 997-0947.

Q. *What's the difference between the Authors Guild and the Writers Guild of America?*
A. The Authors Guild is a national professional organization of book and magazine writers. The membership of the Writers Guild consists of movie, TV, and radio script writers. Prospective Authors Guild members are required to have published a book at an established American publishing house within seven years prior to application for membership, or three fiction or nonfiction pieces in a general circulation magazine within the previous eighteen months. The Guild is involved in such issues as free speech, copyright, and taxes, and has represented the interests of writers both in Congress and in the courts. The organization also provides writers with information on contract provisions. If you are eligible for membership, contact the Authors Guild, 330 W. 42nd St., New York NY 10036-6902, (212) 563-5904.

The Writers Guild of America (WGA) has two branches, East and West (divided by the Mississippi River for administrative purposes), each of which publishes its own monthly newsletter and operates a manuscript registration service for the purposes of verifying the date of script authorship. You must have sold to or been employed to write a TV, radio or movie script within two years prior to your application. Initiation fees are $1,500 for WGA, West and $1,000 for WGA, East. Basic dues are $25 per quarter for WGA, West and $12.50 per quarter for WGA, East. In addition, there are quarterly dues based on a percentage of a writer's earnings in certain writing areas. WGA, West: 8955 Beverly Blvd., Hollywood CA 90048, (310) 550-1000. WGA, East: Room 1230, 555 W. 57th St., New York NY 10019 (212) 767-7800.

Q. *I have heard there are some organizations that provide services for writers in prison. How can I get in touch with these groups?*

A. PEN American Center, a writer's organization, operates a Prison Writing Program. See details in chapter one.

Gatherings for Writers

Q. *I have heard about writers workshops and conferences. Do I have to be a published author to attend one? What will I gain by going to a workshop?*
A. Writers workshops and conferences are considered a great source of information and inspiration for all writers, beginning or experienced. They allow you to establish friendships with other writers and editors and escape the loneliness of writing. They offer not only encouragement but practical advice and information on market trends and needs, and writing techniques. At a conference, you may hear lectures from published authors, get to talk with an editor or publisher, or even acquire an agent — it all depends on the type of conference you attend. Conferences are varied — some have a focused theme while others are very general; some last one day or a weekend while others may run for two weeks. Writers conferences are held throughout the year, but mostly in the summer months. Locations vary. Many are held on college campuses or in large hotels, but some meet at state parks or libraries.

You don't have to be a published author to attend; in fact, beginners have the chance to gain the most by meeting other writers and establishing contacts with editors — fueling their enthusiasm for writing. You can get more information on conferences and workshops by consulting the May issue of *Writer's Digest* for a state-by-state listing of conferences and when and where they are held. Then write to individual conference directors for information.

Q. *I'm about to attend my first writers conference and want to be sure to get the most out of it I possibly can. What should I do to ensure I get my money's worth? What should I bring with me?*
A. Take advantage of *everything* the conference has to offer. Come on time to each session. Attend all the informal events as well as the structured ones. You may learn as much at lunch as you do in a lecture room, because the best "shop talk" always occurs at luncheons or banquets. Even if you don't get to talk to a staff member, you'll learn a lot just by staying in the circle and listening. Always ask good questions, but don't overstep your bounds by stopping speakers on their way to the lecture hall or monopolizing the question period. And if you find yourself in a group more concerned with casual chitchat than "writing" talk, move to another group. You'll get more out of your time that way.

The most important thing you can bring with you to a writers conference is an open and alert mind, ready and willing to listen and learn. You will probably want to take along a specific manuscript to work on as new ideas are presented to you, as well as copies of some work you submitted for criticism, if that service will be available. And before going, inquire as to what clothes you'll need, as it may be totally casual or there may be one or two formal affairs. A typewriter, alarm clock, notepads, business cards (if you have them), and a bag to hold handouts can be beneficial.

Q. *How do I select the right workshop for me?*
A. The key word to remember when selecting a workshop or conference is *research*. First, decide which type of conference will be most helpful to you—make sure the focus of the conference matches your writing interests and goals. Next, write for details about the conference's staff, location, accommodations, fees, length and dates. Study the conference program: Will there be a chance for personal consultations with members of the staff? Are there opportunities for manuscript criticism? Research the staff carefully—check *Contemporary Authors* and *Books in Print* to see what they've written and, preferably, read some of the staff's works. That way you'll know what they are qualified to speak about, and you'll be able to ask pertinent questions. You might also ask the conference director for the name and address of someone who has attended the conference in the past who might be willing to give you his opinion of it. If you take the time to do this basic research, you should feel confident that the conference you select is one that is well-tailored to suit your needs and will give you your money's worth.

Q. *Is it worth going to the same writer's conference you may have attended a year or two before?*
A. Since the writers who are brought in to act as workshop leaders, panelists, and luncheon speakers are usually different each year, yes, most writers find it worthwhile to attend a conference more than once. Some writers who live within commuting distance of more than one conference, however, like to try new conferences from time to time, especially when a particular writer or editor they want to meet will be featured.

Q. *I have heard of special places where writers go to write on a daily schedule and where meals and facilities are included. Is this what one can expect at a writers colony?*
A. If you are looking for a peaceful place away from the hustle and bustle of the everyday world, where you can write, uninterrupted, for hours each day, a writers colony is the place for you. Though each colony is slightly different from the others (some accept beginners, others do not, for example), all provide a comfortable and private atmosphere, which seems to encourage writing, and the opportunity for interaction and discussion with other writers, if you desire it. The cost of a stay at a writers colony varies greatly—some are free, while others offer scholarships or charge a weekly or seasonal rate. The cost may or may not include meals, again depending upon the colony. Some require you to submit an application, which may ask for writing samples and recommendations from former residents or other notable people. Information about writers colonies is sometimes available from Poets & Writers, Inc., 72 Spring St., New York NY 10012 and from The Center for Arts Information, 1285 Ave. of the Americas, New York NY 10019. An article in *Writer's Yearbook '93* described twenty-eight writers colonies. Issues are $5.25 (postpaid) from Writer's Digest Books, 1507 Dana Ave., Cincinnati OH 45207.

Chapter 40

What Full-Time Jobs Are Available to a Writer?

People who seek full-time writing or editing jobs usually traverse one of two routes. They attend journalism school or they acquire a good general liberal arts background. There are exceptions, of course; some start out in science and wind up in scientific or technical publishing; others turn from teaching to corporate communications. Being a full-time freelance writer is a challenging goal and many writers opt to use their writing skill to bring home a regular salary.

Opportunities in Publishing

Q. *What can a beginning writer do to get a job on a small newspaper staff?*
A. Try to place some freelance features with the newspaper you'd like to work for, so the editor can see that 1) you know what a good feature is, and 2) you write well. Also supply them with news items from a section of their newspaper circulation area that is not well covered. Show them samples of your work that are similar to what they publish. For information on newspaper writing, see *Into the Newsroom* by Leonard Teel and Ron Taylor (Globe Pequot Press).

Q. *What are the advantages of working for a magazine versus working for a newspaper?*
A. One of the major differences is that newspapers work against much shorter deadlines than magazines, often a matter of hours for a newspaper as opposed to weeks or months for a magazine. A writer who doesn't like or doesn't work well under this kind of pressure is better off working for a magazine. Another difference is that due to the longer deadlines, magazine writers have a chance to develop their ideas into more in-depth articles, and newspaper writers must be concerned with quick, up-to-the-minute reporting.

Starting minimum salaries for newspapers range from $9,000 on small papers to $18,000 on the larger dailies or weeklies. Magazine editorial trainees average $12,000-$14,000. Salaries for experienced writers vary depending on the circulation of the publication, whether a union is involved, and the qualifications of the individual.

Q. *How can I find out about internships in journalism?*
A. Peterson's Guides, Inc. (Box 2123, Princeton, NJ 08543-2123) publishes *Internships*, an annual directory of available intern positions, including information on how to apply. Besides the thousands of listings, it offers articles about creating your own internship opportunities.

Q. *What kinds of writing jobs are available in the book publishing industry?*
A. Although duties vary with the size and scope of each publishing house, here are some of the jobs that might be available: copyediting and proofreading, if the work is not usually sent out to freelancers; editorial assistants who screen unsolicited manuscripts; publicity writers for the promotion department, who do a variety of writing, including advertising copy, brochures, letters of policy and product introduction, press releases, and dust jacket copy.

A good direction for the novice to take when looking for work in a publishing house is to read the classified ads in *Publishers Weekly,* which list job openings in publishing companies, as well as the names of employment agencies that specialize in hiring for publishers. Another thing to consider is the Radcliffe (College) course in publishing procedures, which is offered each year and whose graduates usually go on to jobs in the industry. A helpful book listing the Radcliffe and other specialized courses is *Peterson's Guide to Book Publishing Courses/Academic and Professional Programs.* This book is updated quarterly by the Association of American Publishers, 220 East 23rd St., New York NY 10010, in the *Publishing Education Newsletter.*

Q. *Where can I look for a writing job in the publishing field? Are there any magazines with classified sections I can refer to?*
A. You might wish to consult the trade magazine, *Publishers Weekly,* which has a large classified ad section that lists job openings with book publishers. *Folio,* a trade magazine for the magazine field, has a smaller classified section. *Editor & Publisher,* a trade magazine for the newspaper industry, has a large classified section that separates newspapers by region. Advertising in the "Positions Wanted" column of these publications may bring you results. These magazines are available at public libraries. Finally, consult the Yellow Pages for private commercial employment agencies that may also help you find newspaper, magazine or book publishing positions.

Other Writing-Related Professions

Q. *How can I get into the advertising field and put my skill to work writing copy for ads?*
A. You have several options. Try to get freelance assignments from a local advertising agency. Send a letter of introduction to the creative director, possibly offering to write an ad on speculation for one of their clients. "Be honest about your inexperience," says writer Jean M. Stone. (For more on freelance ad copywriting, see chapter thirty-one.) If you want to work for an advertising agency as a staff copy-

writer, you might have to start out learning the trade in journeyman fashion. Small agencies occasionally have openings for new writers. These positions are usually low-paying and often involve mechanical, routine chores. However, they provide an excellent opportunity to learn the business, and to work up to a copywriting job. Also, some large corporations offer formal training programs for employees in their creative departments.

Q. *Where can I find out more about writing-related jobs in the broadcasting industry?*
A. For books describing the different kinds of jobs available, check the *Subject Guide to Books in Print* under the categories of "Broadcasting" and "Broadcasting as a Profession." Read trade magazines for the field such as *Broadcasting,* available in most libraries, and contact professional organizations such as the National Association of Broadcasters, 1771 N St., NW, Washington DC 20036. A wide variety of internships available at both radio and television stations are listed in Petersen's *Internships.*

Q. *I'd like to own my own public relations agency someday, but before I can do that, I have to break into the field. How can I go about this?*
A. To start, it's a good idea to obtain training in the theory and techniques of public relations, whether through courses taken in college or, if you aren't attending college, through workshops presented by professional groups such as the Public Relations Society or Women in Communications. However, the best training comes when theory and experience are combined in an internship. You don't need experience to get one of these entry-level (but usually short-term) jobs, and they are available with public relations firms, advertising agencies, business firms, newspapers, and television and radio stations. From this kind of work, you can gain valuable knowledge of the mechanics and operations involved in public relations. Furthermore, you will have a decided advantage over others with little or no experience when you apply for a job. If you don't want to deal with work as an apprentice, you could begin by applying directly to public relations firms or departments for a beginner's job. When making personal calls upon prospective business employers, ask to see the director of public relations, the personnel manager, or the office manager. At a newspaper or broadcasting station, ask to see the Advertising and Promotion Manager. It may take a lot of calls and letters to land a job, but the stronger your efforts, the better your chances are of breaking into the field of public relations. For more information on the subject check *Subject Guide to Books in Print* under "Public Relations" and "Public Relations — Vocational Guidance." Then see if any of the listed books are in your local, public or college library or bookstore.

Q. *What is a clipping service and how profitable is it to work for one?*
A. Clipping services hire people to read thousands of newspapers and magazines and clip out items on various subjects that writers or publishers request. Authors often engage clipping services to collect information on a subject they are researching that is currently in the news, and publishers generally employ them to clip

reviews of books they've published. Costs for a clipping service vary, but usually cover a set monthly fee and an additional amount for each clip provided. These firms are sometimes listed in the Yellow Pages under "Clipping Bureaus." Most services require their employees to work out of the company office, so it's not something you could do as a freelancer. Some people try to set up at-home clipping services, submitting newspaper articles to magazines. Few magazines accept such clippings.

Q. *I'd like to work on a newspaper but am having trouble finding any openings. What other similiar career choices do I have?*
A. There is a wealth of related careers that you can pursue if you're having no luck finding a job on a newspaper. Businesses and industries are always looking for people to edit and write their company publications, just as unions need people to perform the same tasks for their newsletters and various labor press items. Charitable and health organizations also need freelancers and provide excellent contacts for future job opportunities. Trade magazines of industries where scientific or engineering work is reported need writers and editors. If none of these interests you, consider writing or editing for a city or town. These need people to work on their Chamber of Commerce magazines, write historical booklets on the city, or write tourist brochures. Doing this kind of work entails becoming as closely involved with the goings-on of a city as you would if you were a reporter with a certain local beat. If you want a job almost identical to that of a newspaper staffer, you could work as a wire service reporter or write columns and articles for the syndicated news feature services. Don't rule out writing for TV or radio even if your primary interest isn't on-air broadcasting; the reporters who work behind the scenes for these media do the same work newspapermen do. Finally, you can consider contacting the Office of Personnel Management about possible openings the U.S. government may have in one of the several thousand media-related jobs it has from time to time. In a government writing job you may find yourself doing work for the press, TV or other public information media, or creating pamphlets that describe public services and government projects. Any one of the above-mentioned careers may pay close to or more than a newspaper job pays, and if you land a job in an area that really interests you, you may find it even more rewarding than a newspaper career could have been for you.

Chapter 41

How Much Can I Expect to Earn?

How much a writer can earn working as a staff person with a newspaper, magazine, book publishing, or broadcasting company is pretty well determined by already established rates in the industry and the writer's experience. How much he can earn as a freelancer depends on his ideas, energy, research and writing skills, and the marketplace. Before he can realize a profit, a freelancer needs to cover his overhead plus an additional 25 percent to cover the fringe benefits of insurance and hospitalization normally provided by an employer. But that doesn't stop a dedicated freelancer who is working to fulfill the dream of full-time self employment as a writer. For tips on profitable freelancing, see *Secrets of a Freelance Writer: How to Make $85,000 a Year* by Robert W. Bly (Henry Holt).

Pay Day

Q. *What is the best market for freelance writers? What sells most easily?*
A. There is no such thing as one best market since so much depends on the type of writing each individual writer does. A market is good for a particular writer if he writes the kind of material that market needs. In general there are many more markets for articles than short stories.

Q. *Does fiction or nonfiction writing pay better?*
A. It depends. There are many more markets for articles than short stories, so at this level, nonfiction probably pays the energetic writer more. In the area of books, a novel that has the potential for subsidiary paperback, book club, movie and TV sales probably offers a greater return than the average nonfiction book. On the other hand, a how-to book that sells well year after year or a textbook that obtains wide adoption among schools or colleges can be very lucrative nonfiction book projects.

Q. *Every so often I read something about the average salary of writers in America. The income mentioned is so low that I cannot see how the supposedly high-priced TV and movie writers can be included in this average. Is the average writer someone like me*

who works full-time at another job and has never sold anything for more than $15?
A. The "average salary" is arrived at by a study of the incomes of all types of writers. Since there are so many more part-time and low-earning writers (like yourself) than there are top TV and screenwriters, it is not hard to see why the resultant average income is not very high.

Q. *I will soon graduate from an accredited school of journalism. Can you give me any information on the starting salaries for entry-level positions at newspapers and/or broadcasting stations?*
A. The *Journalist's Road to Success*, formerly the *Journalism Career and Scholarship Guide,* prepared by the Dow Jones Newspaper Fund, Inc., reported in 1991 that the beginning weekly salary at daily newspapers averages $350. Weekly newspapers average $289 for starters, and television stations average $269 to $278.

Q. *How much should I earn as a writer before I can feel secure enough to quit my job and become a full-time freelancer? Can writers really make a living freelancing?*
A. It's safe to start thinking about becoming a full-time freelance writer when your freelancing income over a period of several months equals or is greater than the salary earned on your regular job in that same time period. Plenty of writers have succeeded after breaking away from regular full-time employment, but the road to success isn't easy. You'll be better off if you enter into the venture with your eyes wide open to the disadvantages that you'll face. If you quit your job, you'll lose your steady income and all fringe benefits, like health and life insurance, retirement security, and paid vacations. You must also be prepared to discipline yourself to eight or more hours at the keyboard every day. As Clair Rees, author of *Profitable Full-time/Part-time Freelancing* says, "It's not poor writing skills that defeat so many full-time freelancers, but a lack of economic preparedness." It's best to start planning your switch to self-employment about a year in advance. Begin to cut down on your spending, try to accrue about six months' income for your savings account, and, several months before the break, begin to step up your editorial contacts and magazine sales. A clear view of the difficulties to be encountered in the first months, some penny-pinching and a lot of hard work are the keys to succeeding in the field of full-time freelance writing. *Writer's Digest* magazine periodically carries articles on making the break to full-time freelancing. For the most recent advice, check the editorial index in the December issue each year.

Collecting from Publications

Q. *Should I set a price for my feature article, or does the newspaper editor set the rate of pay? How do I determine my own pay scale?*
A. If you are just getting started as a freelance writer, don't try to do too much bargaining with an editor. Take what he offers and give him the best piece of writing you can. If he wants you to rewrite, do it. It is important that you get quality work published. When you feel you have made enough sales to warrant it, you might

begin to set your own rates. Before you quote a price to an editor, do some thorough researching of the going rate in your area and have a general idea how much work is involved and how long it will take you to complete the assignment. What payment you finally receive will depend on your previous record, the locale, and your ability to negotiate.

Q. *How much money can I expect to earn from a typical magazine article sale?*
A. What magazines pay freelancers depends largely on what they *can* pay (in terms of circulation and advertising revenue), the length of the article in question, and the reputation of the writer. So paychecks can vary from a few dollars to a few thousand dollars. With some publications, the fee paid is standard, and with others it is negotiable. Check the market listings in *Writer's Market* for the specific rates various magazines will pay for freelance material.

Q. *When a story is accepted with "payment on publication," is payment to the writer assured?*
A. Payment on publication is risky, though it is sometimes necessary to the beginning writer trying to get established. No, there is never a guarantee that an article will be published or paid for when it's accepted by the "pays on publication" market. Sometimes an article is accepted, with payment promised on publication, but editors change their minds and the piece is eventually returned to the author neither used nor paid for. Most publications, though they may take a long time to actually publish the piece, will pay after publication. It doesn't happen too often that you don't get paid, so it's worth the risk, if you want to get published. In the case of new markets that pay on publication, you have the risk that they may fold (discontinue publication) after one or two issues are published, and you'll never be paid. If a magazine folds, you will not be paid, but you are free to submit that material to other markets.

Q. *I want to submit a how-to article to a magazine listed in* Writer's Market *that pays by the word. The problem is that I spend much more time on the charts and diagrams that accompany the article than I spend on the actual writing. In fact, my articles often contain very little copy. What should I do?*
A. The magazine will most likely consider payment for graphics separately from that for the article itself depending on its quality. Often an editor must have his staff redo the artwork. You might write and ask this particular editor for an answer to your question.

Q. *What is the average rate charged by ghostwriters for articles and books?*
A. Fees for general magazine article ghostwriting range from two dollars per word to $300 to $3,000 per article. In books, if you're writing with an "as told to" credit, you can expect a full fifty-percent royalty. If your subject is self-publishing, ask for twenty-five to fifty dollars per hour. If you're not getting an "as told to" credit and your subject is self-publishing, ask for one hundred dollars per page or anywhere

from $5,000-$35,000. You'll want to negotiate a pay schedule, as well.

Q. *What is a fair price for writing historical articles to be published in a commemorative book marking the hundredth anniversary of a village?*
A. Remuneration will have to be based on two factors: what you think the job is worth and what the customer will pay. You will have to calculate approximately how much time and effort will be spent on researching and writing these articles, try to find out the budget of your client, then charge accordingly.

Royalty Arrangements

Q. *A book I've written has been accepted for publication. How soon will it be before I can expect to receive any of my royalties?*
A. For starters, it probably will be at least a year before your book is published. After your book goes on sale, your first royalty statement will probably arrive six to eight months later. Publishers usually send royalty statements every six months.

Q. *Is there an agency whose service might be to investigate the actual number of books sold by a publisher? My royalties to date have been very low and I'd like to know just how many copies of my book have been sold.*
A. Your royalty statement should show the actual number of copies sold. The only way to verify the actual number of books sold by a publisher would be to have access to the publisher's accounting records. Some book contracts have a clause that says the author has the right to bring his Certified Public Accountant to the publisher's office to check the sales records and accounting procedures. Even if your contract does not have such a clause, you still have the legal right to request such a review, provided you are willing to go to the expense of hiring a CPA. Royalty examinations can cost several thousand dollars, so only an author with sales sufficient to warrant such an audit should engage a CPA.

Collecting From Other Writing Jobs

Q. *I have an opportunity to sell some of my work to a well-known humorist for one of his books of collected jokes. He asked me to send my material and quote a price per joke. What is a reasonable price?*
A. This answer depends on the comedian's income. Try to estimate how well his books are selling. Basically, you can expect to earn anywhere from $2 to 25 per individual gag. You can cover yourself by stating a willingness to negotiate.

Q. *An entertainer asked me to show him a few of my skits, which run from five to fifteen minutes. How much should I charge for permitting him to use the material?*
A. What you should charge for your material depends largely on how much you can get. Minor entertainers obviously cannot afford large fees, while big-name entertainers can afford more. Skits and routines typically fetch $100-$1,000 per

minute. Some comedians will offer $150 for a five-minute skit. Others will pay $1,500. Again, know the status of the comedian you're pitching, and state your willingness to negotiate.

Q. *I am trying to get started in the typesetting business. How do I decide what to charge for final page, camera-ready copy?*
A. First, decide what your fixed costs are and the profit margin you need to successfully operate your business. Then make some phone calls around town as though you were a prospective customer, to find out what the going rate is among your competitors. Base your final price on a balance between what you think the current traffic will bear and the profit you need for successful operation of your business.

Q. *I have a friend who wants me to help him write a book. My job would include manuscript rewriting, research work and editing. What should I charge for these services?*
A. In the section entitled "How Much Should I Charge" in *Writer's Market,* fees for book rewriting are listed at $18 to $50 per hour, sometimes $5 per page. Doing research for another writer can bring $15 to $40 an hour and up. Book copyediting runs $10 to $30 per hour and up; sometimes it's one dollar per page. To find out what the going rate is in your area, seek out other writers or friends in related businesses or agencies that hire freelancers and find out what has been paid for these specific jobs in the past. You might also try to get your friend to quote you his budget before you name your price.

Bibliography

This list includes all the reference books and books on writing mentioned in *Beginning Writer's Answer Book*, with the exception of library references such as the *Encyclopedia Britannica, Subject Guide to Books in Print* and the various periodical indexes.

Unless otherwise noted, the books mentioned in this bibliography are in print and available as of this revision. However, this status can change. You may be able to locate out-of-print books in your library (or through interlibrary loan) or through book search services (which advertise in many book reviews and other magazines).

American Library Directory. New York: R.R. Bowker Company, 1983.

Art of Poetry Writing: A Guide for Poets, Students and Readers, William Packard. New York: St. Martin's Press. 1992.

Artist's Market (Annual). Cincinnati: Writer's Digest.

At a Journal Workshop: The Basic Text & Guide for Using the Intensive Journal, Ira Progoff. New York: Dialogue House, 1977.

Bantam Medical Dictionary, edited by Lawrence Ordang. New York: Bantam Books, 1982.

Bartlett's Familiar Quotations. Boston: Little, Brown & Co., 1980.

Best Books for Children, 2nd edition, edited by John T. Gillespie and Christine B. Gilbert. New York: R.R. Bowker Co., 1981.

Beyond the Bestseller: A Literary Agent Takes You Inside the Book Business, Richard Curtis. New York: NAL-Dutton Books, 1990.

Billboard's International Buyer's Guide. New York: BPI Communications.

Books That Changed the World, 2nd edition, edited by Robert B. Downs. Chicago: American Library Association, 1978.

The Chicago Manual of Style, thirteenth edition. Chicago: U. of Chicago Press, 1982.

Children's Writers & Illustrators Market (Annual). Cincinnati: Writer's Digest.

The Complete Handbook for Freelance Writers, Kay Cassill. Cincinnati: Writer's Digest Books, 1981, out of print.

Concise Columbia Encyclopedia. New York: Columbia University Press, Avon Books, 1983.

Confession Writer's Handbook, Florence K. Palmer. Cincinnati: Writer's Digest Books, 1980, out of print.

Contemporary Authors, vol. 106, edited by Frances Locher. Detroit: Gale Research Company, 1982.

The Copyright Book: A Practical Guide, Wm. S. Strong. Cambridge: MIT Press, 1981.

The Craft of Interviewing, John Brady. Cincinnati: Writer's Digest Books, 1975.

Creating Short Fiction, Damon Knight. Cincinnati: Writer's Digest Books, 1981.

Cumulative Subject Index to the Monthly Catalog of U.S. Government Publications, 1900-1971, 15 vols. Woodbridge, Conn.: Resource Publications, Inc., 1975.

The Directory of Directories. Detroit: Gale Research Company.

Editor & Publisher Syndicate Directory. New York.

Editor & Publisher Yearbook. New York.

Editors on Editing, Gerald Gross. New York: Grove Press, 1993.

Elements of Playwrighting, Louis E. Catron. New York: Macmillan, 1993.

The Elements of Style: With Index, William Strunk, Jr., and E.B. White. New York: Macmillan, 1979.

Encyclopedia of Associations, Detroit: Gale Research Company, 1981. *Also E of A: Geographic & Executive Index 1984. E of A: New Associations & Projects 1983.*

Every Writer's Guide to Copyright and Publishing Law, Ellen M. Kozak. New York: Henry Holt & Co., 1990.

Fiction Writer's Help Book, Maxine Rock. Cincinnati: Writer's Digest Books, 1982, out of print.

Find it Fast (revised and enlarged edition), Robert Berkman. New York: Harper-Collins, 1990.

Gale Directory of Publications. Detroit: Gale Research Company.

Good Reading: Guide for the Serious Reader, edited by J. Sherwood Weber. New York: New American Library, 1980.

Guide for Newspaper Stringers, Margaret G. Davidson. Hillsdale, NJ: Lawrence Erlbaum Associates, 1990.

Guide to Literary Agents and Art/Photo Reps (Annual). Cincinnati: Writer's Digest.

Guinness Book of World Records. New York: Sterling Publishing Co., Inc.

The Handbook of Nonsexist Writing for Writers, Editors and Speakers, Casey Miller and Kate Swift. New York: Harper & Row, 1981.

Harbrace College Handbook, edited by John C. Hodges and Mary E. Whitten. New York: Harcourt Brace Jovanovich, Inc., 1982.

Harper Dictionary of Contemporary Usage, 2nd edition, William and Mary Morris. New York: HarperCollins, 1992.

Harvard Brief Dictionary of Music, edited by Willi Apel and Ralph Daniel. New York: Pocket Books, Washington Square Press, 1968, out of print.

The Holy Bible: New International Version. New York: New York International Bible Society, 1984.

How to Be Your Own Lirterary Agent: The Business of Getting Your Book Published, Richard Curtis. Boston: Houghton Mifflin, 1984.

How to Get Happily Published: A Complete & Candid Guide, Judith Applebaum and Nancy Evans. New York: New American Library, 1982.

How to Get Started in Writing, Peggy Teeters. Cincinnati: Writer's Digest Books, 1980, out of print.

How to Make Money Writing Little Articles, Anecdotes, Hints, Recipes, Light Verse and other Fillers, Connie Emerson. Cincinnati: Writer's Digest Books, 1983, out of print.

How to Write a Book Proposal, Michael Larsen. Cincinnati: Writer's Digest, 1990.

How to Write a Children's Book and Get It Published, revised and expanded edtition, Barbara Seuling. New York: Macmillan, 1991.

How to Write and Sell Greeting Cards, Bumper Stickers, T-shirts and Other Fun Stuff, Molly Wigand. Cincinnati: Wrirter's Digest, 1992.

How to Write and Sell Your First Nonfiction Book, Oscar Collier and Frances Spatz Leighton. New York: St. Martin's Press, 1990.

How to Write Irresistible Query Letters, Lisa Collier Cool. Cincinnati: Writer's Digest, 1990.

How to Write Short Stories That Sell, Louise Boggess. Cincinnati: Writer's Digest Books, 1980, out of print.

If They Ask You, You Can Write a Song, Al Kasha and Joel Hirschhorn. New York: Simon & Schuster, 1979.

Information Please Almanac. New York: Simon & Schuster, 1979.

Information U.S.A., Matthew Lesko. New York: Penguin Books, 1983.

Inside Publishing, Bill Adler. Indianapolis: Bobbs-Merrill, 1982, out of print.

Insider's Guide to Book Editors, Publishers and Literary Agents: Who They Are, What They Want, And How to Win Them Over, 1993-1994 edition, Jeff Herman. Rocklin, CA: Prima Publishing, 1992.

International Directory of Little Magazines and Small Presses, edited by Len Fulton and Ellen Ferber. Paradise, Calif.: Dustbooks, 1983.

International Writers' and Artists' Yearbook (distributed by Writer's Digest Books). Pub. by A & C Black, England, 1983, out of print.

Internships (Annual). Cincinnati: Writer's Digest Books, out of print.

Internships: The Guide to On-the-Job Training Opportunities for Students and Adults, 12th edition. Princeton, NY: Peterson's Guides, 1991.

Into the Newsroom: An Introduction to Journalism, Leonard K. Teel and Ron Taylor. Old Saybrook, CT: Globe Pequot, 1988.

Jerusalem Bible, edited by Alexander Jones. New York: Doubleday, 1975, out of print.

Journalists's Road to Success (formerly *Journalism Career and Scholarship Guide* (Annual). Princeton: Dow Jones Newspaper Fund, Inc.

The Law (in Plain English) for Writers, Leonard D. DuBoff. New York: John Wiley & Sons, 1992.

Literary Agents: A Writer's Guide. New York: Poets and Writers, Inc., 1983.

Literary Market Place. New York: R.R. Bowker Company.

The Living Bible: A Topical Approach to the Jewish Scriptures, by Sylvan D. Schwartzman and Jack D. Spiro. New York: Union of American Hebrew Congregations, 1962, out of print.

Magazine Writing: The Inside Angle, Art Spikol. Cincinnati: Writer's Digest Books, 1979, out of print.

Make Every Word Count, Gary Provost. Cincinnati: Writer's Digest Books, 1980, out of print.

Making a Good Script Great, Linda Seger. Hollywood: Samuel French Trade Books, 1989.

Market Guide for Young Writers, 3rd edition, Kathy Henderson. Crozet, VA: Betterway Books, 1990.

Max Perkins: Editor of Genius, A. Scott Berg. New York: Pocket Books, 1979, out of print.

Mystery Writer's Handbook, edited by Lawrence Treat. Cincinnati: Writer's Digest Books, 1982.

The New Diary: How to Use a Journal for Self-Guidance and Expanded Creativity, Tristine Rainer. Los Angeles: J.P. Tarcher, Inc., 1979.

News Reporting and Writing, 5th edition, Melvin Mencher. Madison: Brown and Benchmark, 1991.

Novel & Story Story Writer's Market (Annual). Cincinnati: Writer's Digest.

Occupational Outlook Handbook. Washington, DC: U.S. Government Printing Office.

On Writing Well: An Informal Guide to Writing Nonfiction, William Zinsser. New York: Harper & Row, 1980.

One to One: Self Understanding Through Journal Writing, Christina Baldwin. New York: M. Evans & Company, Inc., 1977.

Outline of History: A Plain History of Life and Mankind, H.G. Wells. New York: Doubleday, 1971.

The People's Almanac Two, David Wallechinsky and Irving Wallace. New York: Bantam Books, 1978, out of print.

Peter's Quotations: Ideas for Our Times, Laurence Peter. New York: Bantam Books, 1979.

Peterson's Guide to Book Publishing Courses/Academic and Professional Programs. Princeton: Peterson's Guides, 1991.

Photographer's Market (Annual). Cincinnati: Writer's Digest Books.

Playwright's Handbook, Frank Pike and Thomas G. Dunn. New York: NAL-Dutton, 1985.

The Poet and the Poem, Judson Jerome. Cincinnati: Writer's Digest Books, 1979, out of print.

The Poet's Handbook, Judson Jerome. Cincinnati: Writer's Digest Books, 1980.

The Poet's Manual and Rhyming Dictionary, Frances Stillman and Jane S. Whitfield. New York: T.Y. Crowell, 1965, out of print.

Poet's Market (Annual). Cincinnati: Writer's Digest.

Princeton Encyclopedia of Poetry and Poetics, revised edition, edited by Alex Preminger et al. Princeton, NJ: Princeton University Press, 1974.

Profitable Part-Time/Full-Time Freelancing, Clair F. Rees. Cincinnati: Writer's Digest Books, 1980, out of print.

The Publish It Yourself Handbook: Literary Tradition and How to, edited by Bill Henderson. Wainscott, N.Y.: Pushcart Press, 1979.

Punctuate It Right, Harry Shaw. New York: Barnes and Noble, 1963.

The Quotable Woman, 2 vols. New York: Pinnacle Books, 1980, out of print.

Random House Handbook, edited by Frederick Crews. New York: Random House, 1983.

The Reader's Digest Bible. Pleasantville, N.Y.: Reader's Digest.

The Reader's Encyclopedia, edited by William R. Benet. New York: T.Y. Crowell, 1965, out of print.

A Reader's Guide to the Holy Bible: Revised Standard Edition, Nashville, TN: Thomas Nelson, Inc., 1978, out of print.

Reference Books: a Brief Guide, edited by Marion V. Bell and Eleanor A. Swidan. Baltimore: Enoch Pratt Free Library, 1978, out of print.

Roget's International Thesaurus. New York: T.Y. Crowell Company, 1977.

Screenplay: The Foundations of Screenwriting, revised edition, edited by Syd Field. New York: Dell Books, 1984.

Secrets of a Freelance Writer: How to Make 85,000 Dollars a Year, Robert W. Bly. New York: Henry Holt and Co., 1990.

Sell and Resell Your Photos, Rohn Engh. Cincinnati: Writer's Digest Books, 1981.

Songwriter's Market (Annual). Cincinnati: Writer's Digest Books.

Standard Directory of Advertisers. Skokie, IL: National Register Publishing Company, 1983.

Standard Directory of Advertising Agencies. Skokie, IL: National Register Publishing Company, 1983.

Standard Periodical Directory, 15th edition. New York: Oxbridge Communications, 1992.

State-of-the-Art Fact-Finding, Trudi Jacobson and Gary McLain. New York: Dell Books, 1993.

Stock Photography: A Complete Guide, Carl and Ann Purcell. Cincinnati: Writer's Digest Books, 1993.

A Survey of Motion Picture, Still Photography, and Graphic Arts Instruction. Rochester: Eastman Kodak Company, 1981, out of print.

Teach Yourself to Write, Evelyn A. Stenbock. Cincinnati: Writer's Digest Books, 1982, out of print.

The 30-Minute Writer: How to Write and Sell Short Pieces, Connie Emerson. Cincinnati: Writer's Digest Books, 1993.

This Business of Writing, Gregg Levoy. Cincinnati: Writer's Digest, 1992.

Toward Matching Personal and Job Characteristics. Washington, DC: U.S. Government Printing Office.

The Travel Writer's Handbook, Louise P. Zobel. Cincinnati: Writer's Digest Books, 1980.

Twelve Keys to Writing Books That Sell, Kathleeen Krull. Cincinnati: Writer's Digest, 1989.

Ulrich's International Periodicals Directory. New York: R.R. Bowker Company.

United States Government Manual. Washington, DC: U.S. Government Printing Office.

Variety Music Cavalcade. Englewood Cliffs, NJ: Prentice-Hall, out of print.

Webster's Dictionary of English Usage. Springfield, MA: Merriam Webster, Inc., 1989.

Who's Who in American Art. New York: R.R. Bowker Company.

Working Press of the Nation, 5 vols. Chicago: Automated Marketing Systems, Inc., 1982.

World Almanac and Book of Facts. New York: World Almanac.

World Photography Sources, edited by David N. Bradshaw and Catherine Hahn. New York: Directories Publishing.

The Writer's Complete Guide to Conducting Interviews (formerly *Creative Conversations*), Michael Schumacher. Cincinnati: Writer's Digest Books, 1993.

The Writer's Digest Guide to Manuscript Formats, Dian Dincin Buchman and Seli Groves. Cincinnati: Writer's Digest Books, 1987.

The Writer's Guide to Conquering the Magazine Market, Connie Emerson. Cincinnati: Writer's Digest Books, 1991.

Writer's Digest Handbook of Article Writing, edited by Frank A. Dickson. New York: Holt, Rinehart and Winston, 1968.

Writer's Digest Handbook of Short Story Writing, edited by Frank Dickson/Sandra Smythe. Cincinnati: Writer's Digest Books, 1981, out of print.

Writer's Encyclopedia, edited by Kirk Polking. Cincinnati: Writer's Digest Books, 1983, out of print.

Writer's Handbook, edited by Sylvia K. Burack. Boston: The Writer, Inc., 1983.

Writer's Market (Annual). Cincinnati: Writer's Digest Books.

Writer's Resource Guide, edited by Bernadine Clark. Cincinnati: Writer's Digest Books, 1983, out of print.

Writing and Publishing Books for Children in the 1990s: The Inside Story from the Editor's Desk, Olga Litowinsky. New York: Walker and Co., 1992.

Writing and Selling Nonfiction, Hayes B. Jacobs. Cincinnati: Writer's Digest Books, 1975, out of print.

Writing in General and the Short Story in Particular. Rust Hills, NY: Bantam Books, 1979.

Writing for Children and Teenagers, Lee Wyndham, edited by Arnold Madison. Cincinnati: Writer's Digest Books, 1980.

Writing From the Heart: How to Write and Sell Your Life Experiences. Cincinnati: Writer's Digest Books, 1993.

Writing Romance Fiction for Love & Money, Helene S. Barnhart. Cincinnati: Writer's Digest Books, 1983, out of print.

Writing the Novel: From Plot to Print, Lawrence Block. Cincinnati: Writer's Digest Books, 1979.

Appendix

Note: Notice how the author makes the idea of a ranch vacation seem appealing no matter what your age, budget or preferred location. Although Mrs. Jones queried *Modern Maturity Magazine* (and her fourth paragraph showed the perspective she would bring to its readers), the editor chose to run the article in its sister publication for the National Association of Retired Teachers. Her original letter, of course, included both a date and her home address.

Ian Ledgewood, Editor-in-Chief
Modern Maturity Magazine
3200 East Carson
Lakewood, CA 90712

Dear Mr. Ledgewood:

Few people are aware of the advantages of some very special fun and relaxation places, where all ages can enjoy being together, yet each doing his or her own thing. Our dude and guest ranches stretch from the Everglades to the Pacific, from Canada to one in Arizona where we rode along a fence that separates the USA from Old Mexico.

Singles, families and groups are looking for a special place where guests of all ages may individually join or watch activities or just soak in tranquility. Newcomers to areas as well as natives are totally unaware of the ranches within a few miles.

Ranches have expanded their activities beyond horses, food and hospitality. Some include all types of resort activities. Others specialize in unusual or educational interests.

My husband and I are 72 and 68 and began going to ranches 10 years ago. We have been to more than 60 ranches in 13 states and found a variety to fit every pocketbook. Some have excellent camping or house-keeping facilities. We have had our meals with the family and we have been assigned a table with a uniformed waiter. Guests were singles, teen-agers, retirees, several 3, and one 4, generation family reunions—all pursuing their own interests and enjoying the activities and each other.

Ranches attract interesting people. Age, social status and financial prestige are forgotten in the fun together, blue jeans (yes, even great-grandma) atmosphere. Participation in the action is the label by which a guest is known.

Would you be interested in an article enlightening your readers about delightful experiences that combine comfort, indoor and outdoor activities from which to choose or relax in away-from-it-all surroundings?

I am a freelance writer and have credits in the *Dude Rancher* magazine, organization publications and newspapers.

Sincerely yours,

Mrs. E. Aliene Jones

How to Submit Mss.

Short articles, poems, stories of fewer than five pages may be folded in thirds and submitted in a #10 envelope to most magazines: everything should be typed double-spaced on 8½ × 11 white paper. Type poems one to a page. Always enclose a self-addressed envelope and return postage.

Longer articles, stories of more than five pages should be submitted flat in a 9 × 12 or 10 × 13 envelope with a self-addressed envelope enclosed, and return postage.

Book length manuscripts should be submitted loose in a manuscript paper box. Although a few book publishers prefer to receive manuscripts held together in a binder of some sort, most editors feel it is too heavy to hold to read comfortably. Always enclose sufficient postage for the manuscript's return.

Photographs and other illustrative materials should always be submitted flat, of course, with cardboard protectors and sufficient return postage. In the case of small filler items, a few trade journals and hobby books will accept (although they do not prefer) Polaroid shots of the item in question.

Play manuscripts should be submitted bound in a flexible binder of some sort, along with sufficient return postage. A few publishers of one-act plays have indicated that for the very *short* lengths they have no objection to the materials submitted flat, held only by a paper clip.

Television and motion picture scripts should be submitted in a softcover binder with sufficient return postage. Unagented scripts are rarely accepted.

Greeting card ideas and gag ideas for cartoonists should be submitted on 3 × 5 white slips of paper, flat, with sufficient return postage. The writer's name and address should appear in the upper left corner and the gag idea or verse centered

Manuscript Preparation Guidelines

Jones—2

Title of Manuscript (optional)

Begin the second page, and all following pages, in this manner—
with a page-number line (as above) that includes your name, in case
loose manuscript pages get shuffled by mistake. You may include the
title of your manuscript or a shortened version of the title to identify
the Jones manuscript this page 2 belongs to.

Chris Jones
1234 My Street
Anytown, State, Zip
Tel. 123/456-7890
Social Security Number

About 3,000 words
First Serial Rights
© 1989 Chris Jones

YOUR STORY OR ARTICLE TITLE HERE

by

Chris Jones

The manuscript begins here—about halfway down the first page. It
should be cleanly typed, double-spaced, using either elite or pica type.
Use one side of the paper only, and leave a margin of about 1 1/4 inches
on all four sides.

To begin a new paragraph, drop down one double-space and indent.
Don't put extra white space between paragraphs.

**If the author uses a pseudonym, it should be placed on the title page only in the
byline position; the author's real name must always appear in the top left corner
of the title page—for manuscript mailing and payment purposes.**

on the page. A code number, for convenience in identifying the gag idea or verse in correspondence, should appear in the upper right corner. Studio and humorous card ideas may also be accompanied by a rough drawing on a separate folded sheet of paper similar to the published card. Always enclose a stamped, self-addressed envelope.

Manuscript Length, Average

The following table provides average word counts for each of the basic forms of writing; it gives the beginning writer the usual expected length of most manuscripts. When submitting work to magazines, though, the writer should adhere to the editor's requirements, which may be more specific than the average word count. *Writer's Market* lists individual editors' preferences as to word length. (Note: The average full double-spaced typewritten page contains 250 words of pica typewriter type.)

How Long Is a . . . ?

	Average Words
Short-short story	500-2,000
Short story	2,500-5,000
Novella	7,500-40,000
Novelette	7,000-25,000
Novel-hardcover	25,000-150,000
Novel-paperback	35,000-80,000
Children's picture book	500-2,500
Juvenile book	15,000-80,000
Nonfiction book	20,000-200,000
TV script: ½-hour	25-40 double-spaced typewritten pages
TV script: 1-hour	55-70 double-spaced typewritten pages
Play: one-act	20-30 minutes playing time
	20-30 double-spaced typewritten pages
Play: three-act	1½-2 hours playing time
	90-120 double-spaced typewritten pages
Movie scenario	1½-2 hours playing time
	120-250 double-spaced typewritten pages
Radio feature copy	1 minute = 15 double-spaced lines
	3 minutes = 2 pages
Poem	2-100 lines (most mags. prefer 4-16 lines)
Query letter	1 full-page, single-spaced
Speech	250 words = 2 minutes
	12-15 pages = ½ hour

Index